THE READER'S
COMPANION TO
ALASKA

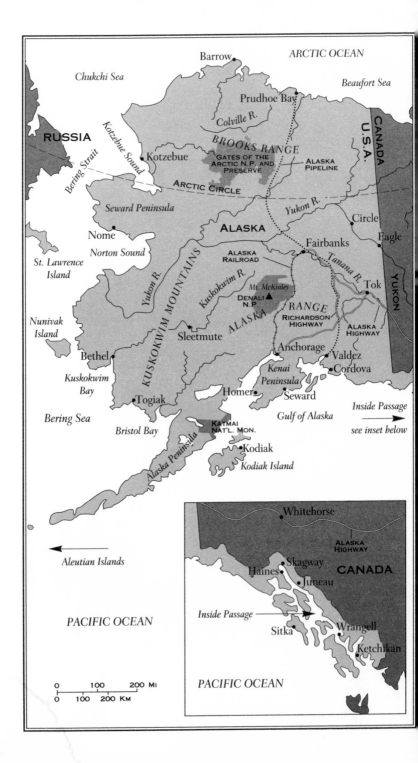

THE READER'S
COMPANION TO
ALASKA

EDITED BY **ALAN RYAN**

A Harvest Original
Harcourt Brace & Company
SAN DIEGO   NEW YORK   LONDON

Library of Congress Cataloging-in-Publication Data
The reader's companion to Alaska/edited by Alan Ryan.—1st ed.
        p.   cm.
  "A Harvest original."
ISBN 0-15-600368-6
1. Alaska — Description and travel — Anecdotes.   2. Frontier and
pioneer life — Alaska — Anecdotes. 3. Alaska — Biography — Anecdotes.
I. Ryan, Alan.
F910.5.R43   1997
978.8'051'092—dc21   96-47184

Text set in Fairfield Medium
Designed by Ivan Holmes

Printed in the United States of America
First Edition

O N M L K J I

MY PRAYER IS THAT ALASKA WILL NOT LOSE THE HEART-
NOURISHING FRIENDLINESS OF HER YOUTH—THAT HER PEOPLE
WILL ALWAYS CARE FOR ONE ANOTHER, HER TOWNS REMAIN
FRIENDLY AND NOT COMPLETELY RULED BY THE DOLLAR—AND
THAT HER GREAT WILD PLACES WILL REMAIN GREAT, AND WILD,
AND FREE, WHERE WOLF AND CARIBOU, WOLVERINE AND GRIZZLY
BEAR, AND ALL THE ARCTIC BLOSSOMS MAY LIVE ON IN THE
DELICATE BALANCE WHICH SUPPORTED THEM LONG BEFORE
IMPETUOUS MAN APPEARED IN THE NORTH.

—MARGARET E. MURIE

CONTENTS

"Sunshine streamed through the luminous fringes of the clouds and fell on the green waters of the fiord, the glittering bergs, the crystal bluffs of the vast glacier, the intensely white, far-spreading fields of ice, and the ineffably chaste and spiritual heights of the Fairweather Range, which were now hidden, now partly revealed, the whole making a picture of icy wildness unspeakably pure and sublime."

"Our vessel tooted itself hoarse outside the harbor to get a pilot over the bar, but none was to be had till late in the day, when a pilot came out to us showing plainly by his condition that he knew every bar in and about Victoria."

INTRODUCTION

THE ARTIST ROCKWELL KENT SPENT THE winter of 1918–19 with his young son on a small island off the coast of Alaska near Seward. His account of that winter was published as *Wilderness: A Journal of Quiet Adventure in Alaska* in 1920.

In that book, Kent writes: "I wonder if you can imagine what fun pioneering is. To be in a country where the fairest spot is yours for the wanting it, to cut and build your own home out of the land you stand upon, to plan and create clearings, parks, vistas, and make out of a wilderness an ordered place!"

And there, in a single, thoughtless paragraph, are all the questions that stir arguments about Alaska.

In fact, Kent wasn't exactly "pioneering." He found a cabin on Fox Island, built and ready to receive him. And within sight of his cabin was another, where an old-timer named Olson lived, ready and willing to offer help and advice. And, when the weather permitted, Kent could cross by boat to Seward and easily restock his supplies.

We certainly do understand his pleasure in "the fairest spot" and his expression of the very basic human satisfaction of building one's own dwelling place. Such pleasures are universal.

But he becomes much more troubling when he huffs with equal energy about "clearings, parks, vistas," and making the wilderness into "an ordered place." How much of a stretch is it to imagine him approving a plan to pull down the trees and put up a parking lot?

These ideas, voiced but unexamined by Rockwell Kent, shape much of the daily life and conversation of Alaskans.

Should the wilderness be left untouched? Or should it be made accessible? Should Alaska's natural resources be exploited? Should a pipeline be stretched eight hundred miles across virgin territory? How can the wilderness be safeguarded and used at the same time? What if there were a huge oil spill? Who is responsible for cleaning up ten million gallons of crude oil spilled into Prince William Sound? And how best to protect the interests of the Native Americans, both Indian tribes and Eskimos, who have long lived off the land's resources . . . many of whom now reap substantial profits, through the Native corporations, from the oil beneath their traditional lands?

Nothing about Alaska is simple. Everything about Alaska is dramatic.

Alaska is bigger than Texas. It has national parks that dwarf in size some European countries. It has the richest oil deposits in the United States. It has the tallest mountain in North America, a mountain that, in fact, measured from base to peak, has the highest rise of any mountain on earth. With a few more than 550,000 people, Alaska has twice the population of Iceland but ranks forty-ninth of the fifty states. Some of its towns that would be considered tiny elsewhere have runways for jet aircraft. Two Alaskan islands were occupied by the Japanese in World War II. As Tom Bodett has pointed out, Alaska is as far as you can go without a passport. Residents really do refer to the rest of the United States as "the lower forty-eight" and the rest of the world as "outside." And bears are a common hazard.

Where is the real Alaska? In the wild and trackless wastes of the Brooks Range in Gates of the Arctic National Park? On the beach at Nome where hopeful prospectors landed through the surf by the thousands? On the snowbound upper slopes of Denali? In the antiseptic chambers of Pump Station Number One at Prudhoe Bay? In a laboratory at the University of Alaska in Fairbanks? On the banks of the Yukon River at Eagle or Circle when the ice begins breaking up? At McNeil River Falls when the bears come to feed on salmon? On the trail of the Iditarod? In a traffic jam on the Richardson Highway on a Friday evening when everyone in Anchorage tries to get out of town to visit the wilderness that first drew them to Alaska? In Glacier Bay, where icebergs are born and seals doze on ice floes?

Where is the real Alaska? Maybe the following story gives a clue.

In 1995, the Alaska Board of Game announced plans to hold a lottery to award permits for hunters to shoot bears at the McNeil River bear refuge. Outraged bear lovers quickly organized a plan to sabotage the lottery. Conservationists everywhere were urged to enter the lottery themselves, paying the ten-dollar fee. Thousands of them did indeed enter the lottery and—as reported by Dan Rather on the *CBS Evening News* on July 21, 1995—when names were drawn for the eight permits to be granted, six were the names of entrants who had declared they would not kill bears.

And I hope that something of the real Alaska is in the pages of this book.

Think of *The Reader's Companion to Alaska* as a multi-screen, time-lapse portrait of Alaska and its best-known locations.

The intention of this book, and other *Reader's Companion* volumes, is to gather eyewitness reports of a place by visitors who have brought to it a fresh eye and an inquisitive nature. The distinction between visitor and resident became a little blurred, however, when I began reading about Alaska. Margaret E. Murie first saw Alaska when she was nine years old, and she lived the rest of her life there, becoming one of Alaska's best-loved writers and strongest advocates. Poet John Haines "lived" in Alaska for extended periods over a quarter of a century. Libby

Riddles, the first woman to win the Iditarod, is an Alaskan, but how could her unique report on Alaska be omitted?

Some of the selections here are historical, going back as far as John Muir's first visit to Glacier Bay in 1879 and Frederick Schwatka's description of the Inside Passage in 1886. Today, Glacier Bay is much larger than it was in Muir's time, but the other sights of the Inside Passage, comfortably available to any passenger on a cruise vessel, remain largely unchanged from what Schwatka described more than a century ago.

But the best example here of historical perspective is, I think, the views we get of a Yukon River stern-wheeler called the *Casca*. Read Margaret Murie's description of it in 1911. Then read Pierre Berton's childhood recollections of the same ship, and his description of it today.

Despite some interesting early descriptions, there isn't much here about Anchorage and Fairbanks. People don't go to Alaska for an urban experience.

But there is plenty about the outdoors and about Alaska's great natural beauty. Jonathan Waterman climbs Denali, and Charles Kuralt spends a night on its slopes. Journalist Kris Capps explores the ice-caves beneath a glacier in the Alaska Range. Jon Krakauer hikes through the Brooks Range.

Others—Fred Hatfield, John Haines, James Ramsey—brave life in an isolated cabin in the bush. Barry Lopez makes it all the way north to Prudhoe Bay. Tim Cahill drives the Dalton Highway. Jim Christy drives the Alaska Highway. The Lindberghs fly. And *New Yorker* writer Berton Roueché braves the Bering Sea in a walrus-skin boat.

Many countries, for topographical and/or historical reasons, have a fairly standard "tourist route." So does Alaska. Most visitors today typically cruise up through the Inside Passage and then travel by train or coach from Anchorage to Denali and Fairbanks. From there, some more intrepid visitors may travel to Eagle, as Ernie Pyle did in 1937.

Some of the selections here follow the familiar "tourist route" and offer a chance to compare one's own impressions with those of others. Other selections fill in at least a little of the Alaska that lies beyond the horizon, places like Nome and

Prudhoe Bay. No tour operator is likely to urge you to explore the beauties of Sleetmute in winter; but Sleetmute is here, too.

There is an enormous and rapidly growing body of literature about Alaska, and with different selections this might have been a very different book. It might have included Thomas Merton, for example, who seriously considered living a *really* hermetic life in the bush, or something by Sally Carrighar, author of *Icebound Summer* and, my favorite of her books, *Moonlight at Midday*. But, for various reasons, it doesn't. It can't contain everything, but I do hope that it reflects Alaska's vastness and variety and the wide range of human responses to both its size and its intimate details.

Once again, I have a long list of people to thank for various expressions of help and kindness which, sometimes, they didn't even know they were providing. My warmest thanks go to Jill Bauman, Bob Booth, Diane Buchanan, John Coyne, Michael Dirda, Nancy Dunnan, Cathy Fauver, Beverly Fisher, Eleanor Garner, Leslie Hunt, Dan Kelly, Deirdre Killen, Ellen Levine, Christa Malone, Carol Doup Muller, Juana Ponce de León, Sean Ryan, Dan Shapiro, Michael Skube, Wendy Viggiano, Carolyn Warmbold, Dori Weintraub, Dave Wood, and, as in the past, all my pals at the Chariot.

Thanks also to Ann Alexander, Larry Williams, and all the staff of the Mosholu Branch of the New York Public Library; and to the Society of American Travel Writers.

ALAN RYAN
New York City
August 1996

THE INSIDE
PASSAGE

JOHN MUIR

First sight of Glacier Bay, 1879

"SUNSHINE STREAMED THROUGH THE LUMINOUS FRINGES OF THE CLOUDS AND FELL ON THE GREEN WATERS OF THE FIORD, THE GLITTERING BERGS, THE CRYSTAL BLUFFS OF THE VAST GLACIER, THE INTENSELY WHITE, FAR-SPREADING FIELDS OF ICE, AND THE INEFFABLY CHASTE AND SPIRITUAL HEIGHTS OF THE FAIRWEATHER RANGE, WHICH WERE NOW HIDDEN, NOW PARTLY REVEALED, THE WHOLE MAKING A PICTURE OF ICY WILDNESS UNSPEAKABLY PURE AND SUBLIME."

John Muir was born in Scotland in 1838, but he is respected today as a great American naturalist, explorer, and writer, the founder of the Sierra Club, and the patron saint of the conservationist movement.

He had a broad range of interests and traveled widely—his vivid description of Havana and its surroundings in 1868 is included in The Reader's Companion to Cuba—*but, for much of his life, it was glaciers that fascinated him. From the Yosemite Valley to New York City's Central Park, he had studied the tracks made by the slow movement of ancient glaciers and what they revealed about the history of the earth. And it was glaciers that brought him to Alaska.*

Muir first visited Alaska in the summer of 1879, when he was forty-one years old. He returned, in 1880, 1881, 1890, and 1899, but he didn't write Travels in Alaska *until 1914, the last year of his life. Three and a half decades after his first sight of Glacier Bay, his memories remained detailed and lively.*

The tenth chapter of Travels in Alaska *is titled "The Discovery* of Glacier Bay," but this requires some explanation. Eight decades before Muir arrived, Captain George Vancouver sailed past that very spot and recorded seeing only a solid wall of ice. There was no bay. In the intervening years, enough of the ice glacier had "calved"—great slabs and chunks of it splitting away and falling into the water—to create a deep indentation, the "bay" that Muir found. But of course he did not "discover" anything; he was taken there by local Indians working as guides. Today, Glacier Bay is a lot bigger than it was when Muir saw it, and it will be bigger still tomorrow. Watching the glacier calve is a standard attraction on cruises in the Inside Passage.

✴ FROM HERE, ON OCTOBER 24, WE SET sail for Guide Charley's ice-mountains. The handle of our heaviest axe was cracked, and as Charley declared that there was no firewood to be had in the big ice-mountain bay, we would have to load the canoe with a store for cooking at an island out in the Strait a few miles from the village. We were therefore anxious to buy or trade for a good sound axe in exchange for our broken one. Good axes are rare in rocky Alaska. Soon or late an unlucky stroke on a stone concealed in moss spoils the edge. Finally one in almost perfect condition was offered by a young Hoona for our broken-handled one and a half-dollar to boot; but when the broken axe and money were given he promptly demanded an additional twenty-five cents' worth of tobacco. The tobacco was given him, then he required a half-dollar's worth more of tobacco, which was also given; but when he still demanded something more, Charley's patience gave way and we sailed in the same condition as to axes as when we arrived. This was the only contemptible commercial affair we encountered among these Alaskan Indians.

We reached the wooded island about one o'clock, made coffee, took on a store of wood, and set sail direct for the icy country, finding it very hard indeed to believe the woodless part of Charley's description of the Icy Bay, so heavily and uniformly are all the shores forested wherever we had been. In this view we were joined by John, Kadachan, and Toyatte, none of them on all their lifelong canoe travels having ever seen a woodless country.

We held a northwesterly course until long after dark, when we reached a small inlet that sets in near the mouth of Glacier Bay, on the west side. Here we made a cold camp on a desolate snow-covered beach in stormy sleet and darkness. At daybreak I looked eagerly in every direction to learn what kind of place we were in; but gloomy rain-clouds covered the mountains, and I could see nothing that would give me a clue, while Vancouver's chart, hitherto a faithful guide, here failed us altogether. Nevertheless, we made haste to be off; and fortunately, for just as we were leaving the shore, a faint smoke was seen across the inlet, toward which Charley, who now seemed lost, gladly steered. Our sudden appearance so early that gray morning had evidently alarmed our neighbors, for as soon as we were within hailing distance an Indian with his face blackened fired a shot over our heads, and in a blunt, bellowing voice roared, "Who are you?"

Our interpreter shouted, "Friends and the Fort Wrangell missionary."

Then men, women, and children swarmed out of the hut, and awaited our approach on the beach. One of the hunters having brought his gun with him, Kadachan sternly rebuked him, asking with superb indignation whether he was not ashamed to meet a missionary with a gun in his hands. Friendly relations, however, were speedily established, and as a cold rain was falling, they invited us to enter their hut. It seemed very small and was jammed full of oily boxes and bundles; nevertheless, twenty-one persons managed to find shelter in it about a smoky fire. Our hosts proved to be Hoona seal-hunters laying in their winter stores of meat and skins. The packed hut was passably well ventilated, but its heavy, meaty smells were not the same to our noses as those we were accustomed to in the sprucy nooks of the evergreen woods. The circle of black eyes peering at us through a fog of reek and smoke made a novel picture. We were glad, however, to get within reach of information, and of course asked many questions concerning the ice-mountains and the strange bay, to most of which our inquisitive Hoona friends replied with counter-questions as to our object in coming to such a place, especially so late in the year. They had heard of Mr. Young and his work at Fort Wrangell, but could not understand what a missionary could be doing in such a place as this. Was he going to preach to the seals and gulls, they asked, or to the ice-mountains? And could they take his word? Then John explained that only the friend of the missionary was seeking ice-mountains, that Mr. Young had already preached many good words in the villages we had visited, their own among the others, that our hearts were good and every Indian was our friend. Then we gave them a little rice, sugar, tea, and tobacco, after which they began to gain confidence and to speak freely. They told us that the big bay was called by them Sit-a-da-kay, or Ice Bay; that there were many large ice-mountains in it, but no gold-mines; and that the ice-mountain they knew best was at the head of the bay, where most of the seals were found.

Notwithstanding the rain, I was anxious to push on and grope our way beneath the clouds as best we could, in case worse weather should come; but Charley was ill at ease, and wanted one of the seal-hunters to go with us, for the place was much changed. I promised to pay well for a guide, and in order to lighten the canoe proposed to leave most of our heavy stores in the hut until our return. After a long consultation one of them consented to go. His wife got ready his blanket and a piece of cedar matting for his bed, and some provisions— mostly dried salmon, and seal sausage made of strips of lean meat plaited around a core of fat. She followed us to the beach, and just as we were pushing off said with a pretty smile, "It is my husband that you are taking away. See that you bring him back."

We got under way about 10 A.M. The wind was in our favor, but a cold rain pelted us, and we could see but little of the dreary, treeless wilderness which we had now fairly entered. The bitter blast, however, gave us good speed; our bedraggled canoe rose and fell on the waves as solemnly as a big ship. Our course was northwestward, up the southwest side of the bay, near the shore of what seemed to be the mainland, smooth marble islands being on our right. About noon we discovered the first of the great glaciers, the one I afterward named for

James Geikie, the noted Scotch geologist. Its lofty blue cliffs, looming through the draggled skirts of the clouds, gave a tremendous impression of savage power, while the roar of the newborn icebergs thickened and emphasized the general roar of the storm. An hour and a half beyond the Geikie Glacier we ran into a slight harbor where the shore is low, dragged the canoe beyond the reach of drifting icebergs, and, much against my desire to push ahead, encamped, the guide insisting that the big ice-mountain at the head of the bay could not be reached before dark, that the landing there was dangerous even in daylight, and that this was the only safe harbor on the way to it. While camp was being made, I strolled along the shore to examine the rocks and the fossil timber that abounds here. All the rocks are freshly glaciated, even below the sea-level, nor have the waves as yet worn off the surface polish, much less the heavy scratches and grooves and lines of glacial contour.

The next day being Sunday, the minister wished to stay in camp; and so, on account of the weather, did the Indians. I therefore set out on an excursion, and spent the day alone on the mountain-slopes above the camp, and northward, to see what I might learn. Pushing on through rain and mud and sludgy snow, crossing many brown, boulder-choked torrents, wading, jumping, and wallowing in snow up to my shoulders was mountaineering of the most trying kind. After crouching cramped and benumbed in the canoe, poulticed in wet or damp clothing night and day, my limbs had been asleep. This day they were awakened and in the hour of trial proved that they had not lost the cunning learned on many a mountain peak of the High Sierra. I reached a height of fifteen hundred feet, on the ridge that bounds the second of the great glaciers. All the landscape was smothered in clouds and I began to fear that as far as wide views were concerned I had climbed in vain. But at length the clouds lifted a little, and beneath their gray fringes I saw the berg-filled expanse of the bay, and the feet of the mountains that stand about it, and the imposing fronts of five huge glaciers, the nearest being immediately beneath me. This was my first general view of Glacier Bay, a solitude of ice and snow and newborn rocks, dim, dreary, mysterious. I held the ground I had so dearly won for an hour or two, sheltering myself from the blast as best I could, while with benumbed fingers I sketched what I could see of the landscape, and wrote a few lines in my notebook. Then, breasting the snow again, crossing the shifting avalanche slopes and torrents, I reached camp about dark, wet and weary and glad.

While I was getting some coffee and hardtack, Mr. Young told me that the Indians were discouraged, and had been talking about turning back, fearing that I would be lost, the canoe broken, or in some other mysterious way the expedition would come to grief if I persisted in going farther. They had been asking him what possible motive I could have in climbing mountains when storms were blowing; and when he replied that I was only seeking knowledge, Toyatte said, "Muir must be a witch to seek knowledge in such a place as this and in such miserable weather."

After supper, crouching about a dull fire of fossil wood, they became still more doleful, and talked in tones that accorded well with the wind and waters and growling torrents about us, telling sad old stories of crushed canoes, drowned Indians, and hunters frozen in snowstorms. Even brave old Toyatte, dreading the treeless, forlorn appearance of the region, said that his heart was not strong, and that he feared his canoe, on the safety of which our lives depended, might be entering a skookum-house (jail) of ice, from which there might be no escape; while the Hoona guide said bluntly that if I was so fond of danger, and meant to go close up to the noses of the ice-mountains, he would not consent to go any farther; for we should all be lost, as many of his tribe had been, by the sudden rising of bergs from the bottom. They seemed to be losing heart with every howl of the wind, and, fearing that they might fail me now that I was in the midst of so grand a congregation of glaciers, I made haste to reassure them, telling them that for ten years I had wandered alone among mountains and storms, and good luck always followed me; that with me, therefore, they need fear nothing. The storm would soon cease and the sun would shine to show us the way we should go, for God cares for us and guides us as long as we are trustful and brave, therefore all childish fear must be put away. This little speech did good. Kadachan, with some show of enthusiasm, said he liked to travel with good-luck people; and dignified old Toyatte declared that now his heart was strong again, and he would venture on with me as far as I liked for my "wawa" was "delait" (my talk was very good). The old warrior even became a little sentimental, and said that even if the canoe was broken he would not greatly care, because on the way to the other world he would have good companions.

Next morning it was still raining and snowing, but the south wind swept us bravely forward and swept the bergs from our course. In about an hour we reached the second of the big glaciers, which I afterwards named for Hugh Miller. We rowed up its fiord and landed to make a slight examination of its grand frontal wall. The berg-producing portion we found to be about a mile and a half wide, and broken into an imposing array of jagged spires and pyramids, and flat-topped towers and battlements, of many shades of blue, from pale, shimmering, limpid tones in the crevasses and hollows, to the most startling, chilling, almost shrieking vitriol blue on the plain mural spaces from which bergs had just been discharged. Back from the front for a few miles the glacier rises in a series of wide steps, as if this portion of the glacier had sunk in successive sections as it reached deep water, and the sea had found its way beneath it. Beyond this it extends indefinitely in a gently rising prairie-like expanse, and branches along the slopes and cañons of the Fairweather Range.

From here a run of two hours brought us to the head of the bay, and to the mouth of the northwest fiord, at the head of which lie the Hoona sealing-grounds, and the great glacier now called the Pacific, and another called the Hoona. The fiord is about five miles long, and two miles wide at the mouth. Here our Hoona guide had a store of dry wood, which we took aboard. Then, setting sail, we were driven wildly up the fiord, as if the storm-wind were saying, "Go, then, if you will, into my icy chamber; but you shall stay in until I am ready to let you out." All this time sleety rain was falling on the bay, and snow on the mountains; but soon after we landed the sky began to open. The camp was made on a rocky bench near the front of the Pacific Glacier, and the canoe was carried beyond the reach of the bergs and berg-waves. The bergs were now crowded in a dense pack against the discharging front, as if the storm-wind had determined to make the glacier take back her crystal offspring and keep them at home.

While camp affairs were being attended to, I set out to climb a mountain for comprehensive views; and before I had reached a height of a thousand feet the rain ceased, and the clouds began to rise from the lower altitudes, slowly lifting their white skirts, and lingering in majestic, wing-shaped masses about the mountains that rise out of the broad, icy sea, the highest of all the white mountains, and the greatest of all the glaciers I had yet seen. Climbing higher for a still broader outlook, I made notes and sketched, improving the precious time while sunshine streamed through the luminous fringes of the clouds and fell on the green waters of the fiord, the glittering bergs, the crystal bluffs of the vast glacier, the intensely white, far-spreading fields of ice, and the ineffably chaste and spiritual heights of the Fairweather Range, which were now hidden, now partly revealed, the whole making a picture of icy wildness unspeakably pure and sublime.

Looking southward, a broad ice-sheet was seen extending in a gently undulating plain from the Pacific Fiord in the foreground to the horizon, dotted and ridged here and there with mountains which were as white as the snow-covered ice in which they were half, or more than half, submerged. Several of the great glaciers of the bay flow from this one grand fountain. It is an instructive example of a general glacier covering the hills and dales of a country that is not yet ready to be brought to the light of day—not only covering but creating a landscape with the features it is destined to have when, in the fullness of time, the fashioning ice-sheet shall be lifted by the sun, and the land become warm and fruitful. The view to the westward is bounded and almost filled by the glorious Fairweather Mountains, the highest among them springing aloft in sublime beauty to a height of nearly sixteen thousand feet, while from base to summit every peak and spire and dividing ridge of all the mighty host was spotless white, as if painted. It would seem that snow could never be made to lie on the steepest slopes and precipices unless plastered on when wet, and then frozen. But this snow could not have been wet. It must have been fixed by being driven and set in small particles like the storm-dust of drifts, which, when in this condition, is fixed not only on sheer cliffs, but in massive, overcurling cornices. Along the base of this majestic range sweeps the Pacific Glacier, fed by innumerable cascading tributaries, and discharging into the head of its fiord by two mouths only partly separated by the brow of an island rock about one thousand feet high, each nearly a mile wide.

Dancing down the mountain to camp, my mind glowing like the sunbeaten glaciers, I found the Indians seated around a good fire, entirely happy now that the farthest point of the journey was safely reached and the long, dark storm was cleared away. How hopefully, peacefully bright that night were the stars in the frosty sky, and how impressive was the thunder of the icebergs, rolling, swelling, reverberating through the solemn stillness! I was too happy to sleep.

About daylight next morning we crossed the fiord and landed on the south side of the rock that divides the wall of the great glacier. The whiskered faces of seals dotted the open spaces between the bergs, and I could not prevent John and Charley and Kadachan from shooting at them. Fortunately, few, if any, were hurt. Leaving the Indians in charge of the canoe, I managed to climb to the top of the wall by a good deal of step-cutting between the ice and dividing rock, and gained a good general view of the glacier. At one favorable place I descended about fifty feet below the side of the glacier, where its denuding, fashioning action was clearly shown. Pushing back from here, I found the surface crevassed and sunken in steps, like the Hugh Miller Glacier, as if it were being undermined by the action of tide-waters. For a distance of fifteen or twenty miles the river-like ice-flood is nearly level, and when it recedes, the ocean water will follow it, and thus form a long extension of the fiord, with features essentially the same as those now extending into the continent farther south, where many great glaciers once poured into the sea, though scarce a vestige of them now exists. Thus the domain of the sea has been, and is being, extended in these ice-sculptured lands, and the scenery of their shores enriched. The brow of the dividing rock is about a thousand feet high, and is hard beset by the glacier. A short time ago it was at least two thousand feet below the surface of the over-sweeping ice; and under present climatic conditions it will soon take its place as a glacier-polished island in the middle of the fiord, like a thousand others in the magnificent archipelago. Emerging from its icy sepulchre, it gives a most telling illustration of the birth of a marked feature of a landscape. In this instance it is not the mountain, but the glacier, that is in labor, and the mountain itself is being brought forth.

The Hoona Glacier enters the fiord on the south side, a short distance below the Pacific, displaying a broad and far-reaching expanse, over which many lofty peaks are seen; but the front wall, thrust into the fiord, is not nearly so interesting as that of the Pacific, and I did not observe any bergs discharged from it.

In the evening, after witnessing the unveiling of the majestic peaks and glaciers and their baptism in the down-pouring sunbeams, it seemed inconceivable that nature could have anything finer to show us. Nevertheless, compared with what was to come the next morning, all that was as nothing. The calm dawn gave no promise of anything uncommon. Its most impressive features were the frosty clearness of the sky and a deep, brooding stillness made all the more striking by the thunder of the newborn bergs. The sunrise we did not see at all, for we were beneath the shadows of the fiord cliffs; but in the midst of our studies, while the Indians were getting ready to sail, we were startled by the sudden appearance of a red light burning with a strange unearthly splendor on the topmost peak of the Fairweather Mountains. Instead of vanishing as suddenly as it had appeared, it spread and spread until the whole range down to the level of the glaciers was filled with the celestial fire. In color it was at first a vivid crimson, with a thick, furred appearance, as fine as the alpenglow, yet indescribably rich and deep—not in the least like a garment or mere external flush or bloom through which one might expect to see the rocks or snow, but every mountain apparently was glowing from the heart like molten metal fresh from a furnace. Beneath the frosty shadows of the fiord we stood hushed and awe-stricken, gazing at the holy vision; and had we seen the heavens opened and God made manifest, our attention could not have been more tremendously strained. When the highest peak began to burn, it did not seem to be steeped in sunshine, however glorious, but rather as if it had been thrust into the body of the sun itself. Then the supernal fire slowly descended, with a sharp line of demarkation separating it from the cold, shaded region beneath; peak after peak, with their spires and ridges and cascading glaciers, caught the heavenly glow, until all the mighty host stood transfigured, hushed, and thoughtful, as if awaiting the coming of the Lord. The white, rayless light of morning, seen when I was alone amid the peaks of the California Sierra, had always seemed to me the most telling of all the terrestrial manifestations of God. But here the mountains themselves were made divine, and declared His glory in terms still more impressive. How long we gazed I never knew. The glorious vision passed away in a gradual, fading change through a thousand tones of color to pale yellow and white, and then the work of the ice-world went on again in everyday beauty. The green waters of the fiord were filled with sun-spangles; the fleet of icebergs set forth on their voyages with the upspringing breeze; and on the innumerable mirrors and prisms of these bergs, and on those of the shattered crystal walls of the glaciers, common white light and rainbow light began to burn, while the mountains shone in their frosty jewelry, and loomed again in the thin azure in serene terrestrial majesty. We turned and sailed away, joining the outgoing bergs, while "Gloria in excelsis" still seemed to be sounding over all the white landscape, and our burning hearts were ready for any fate, feeling that, whatever the future might have in store, the treasures we had gained this glorious morning would enrich our lives forever.

When we arrived at the mouth of the fiord, and rounded the massive granite headland that stands guard at the entrance on the north side, another large glacier, now named the Reid, was discovered at the head of one of the northern branches of the bay. Pushing ahead into this new fiord, we found that it was not only packed with bergs, but that the spaces between the bergs were crusted with new ice, compelling us to turn back while we were yet several miles from the discharging frontal wall. But though we were not then allowed to set foot on this magnificent glacier, we obtained a fine view of it, and I made the Indians cease rowing while I sketched its principal features.

Thence, after steering northeastward a few miles, we discovered still another large glacier, now named the Carroll. But the fiord into which this glacier flows was, like the last, utterly inaccessible on account of ice, and we had to be content with a general view and sketch of it, gained as we rowed slowly past at a distance of three or four miles. The mountains back of it and on each side of its inlet are sculptured in a singularly rich and striking style of architecture, in which subordinate peaks and gables appear in wonderful profusion, and an imposing conical mountain with a wide, smooth base stands out in the main current of the glacier, a mile or two back from the discharging ice-wall.

We now turned southward down the eastern shore of the bay, and in an hour or two discovered a glacier of the second class, at the head of a comparatively short fiord that winter had not yet closed. Here we landed, and climbed across a mile or so of rough boulder-beds, and back upon the wildly broken, receding front of the glacier, which, though it descends to the level of the sea, no longer sends off bergs. Many large masses, detached from the wasting front by irregular melting, were partly buried beneath mud, sand, gravel, and boulders of the terminal moraine. Thus protected, these fossil icebergs remain unmelted for many years, some of them for a century or more, as shown by the age of trees growing above them, though there are no trees here as yet. At length melting, a pit with sloping sides is formed by the falling in of the overlying moraine material into the space at first occupied by the buried ice. In this way are formed the curious depressions in drift-covered regions called kettles or sinks. On these decaying glaciers we may also find many interesting lessons on the formation of boulders and boulder-beds, which in all glaciated countries exert a marked influence on scenery, health, and fruitfulness.

Three or four miles farther down the bay, we came to another fiord, up which we sailed in quest of more glaciers, discovering one in each of the two branches into which the fiord divides. Neither of these glaciers quite reaches tide-water. Notwithstanding the apparent fruitfulness of their fountains, they are in the first stage of decadence, the waste from melting and evaporation being greater now than the supply of new ice from their snowy fountains. We reached the one in the north branch, climbed over its wrinkled brow, and gained a good view of the trunk and some of the tributaries, and also of the sublime gray cliffs of its channel.

Then we sailed up the south branch of the inlet, but failed to reach the glacier there, on account of a thin sheet of new ice. With the tent-poles we broke a lane for the canoe for a little distance; but it was slow work, and we soon saw that we could not reach the glacier before dark. Nevertheless, we gained a fair view of it as it came sweeping down through its gigantic gateway of massive Yosemite rocks three or four thousand feet high. Here we lingered until sundown, gazing and sketching; then turned back, and encamped on a bed of cobblestones between the forks of the fiord.

We gathered a lot of fossil wood and after supper made a big fire, and as we sat around it the brightness of the sky brought on a long talk with the Indians about the stars; and their eager, childlike attention was refreshing to see as compared with the deathlike apathy of weary town-dwellers, in whom natural curiosity has been quenched in toil and care and poor shallow comfort.

After sleeping a few hours, I stole quietly out of the camp, and climbed the mountain that stands between the two glaciers. The ground was frozen, making the climbing difficult in the steepest places; but the views over the icy bay, sparkling beneath the stars, were enchanting. It seemed then a sad thing that any part of so precious a night had been lost in sleep. The starlight was so full that I distinctly saw not only the berg-filled bay, but most of the lower portions of the glaciers, lying pale and spirit-like amid the mountains. The nearest glacier in particular was so distinct that it seemed to be glowing with light that came from within itself. Not even in dark nights have I ever found any difficulty in seeing large glaciers; but on this mountain-top, amid so much ice, in the heart of so clear and frosty a night, everything was more or less luminous, and I seemed to be poised in a vast hollow between two skies of almost equal brightness. This exhilarating scramble made me glad and strong and I rejoiced that my studies called me before the glorious night succeeding so glorious a morning had been spent!

I got back to camp in time for an early breakfast, and by daylight we had everything packed and were again under way. The fiord was frozen nearly to its mouth, and though the ice was so thin it gave us but little trouble in breaking a way for the canoe, yet it showed us that the season for exploration in these waters was well-nigh over. We were in danger of being imprisoned in a jam of icebergs, for the water-spaces between them freeze rapidly, binding the floes into one mass. Across such floes it would be almost impossible to drag a canoe, however industriously we might ply the axe, as our Hoona guide took great pains to warn us. I would have kept straight down the bay from here, but the guide had to be taken home, and the provisions we left at the bark hut had to be got on board. We therefore crossed over to our Sunday storm-camp, cautiously boring a way through the bergs. We found the shore lavishly adorned with a fresh arrival of assorted bergs that had been left stranded at high tide. They were arranged in a curving row, looking intensely clear and pure on the gray sand, and, with the sunbeams pouring through them, suggested the jewel-paved streets of the New Jerusalem.

On our way down the coast, after examining the front of the beautiful Geikie Glacier, we obtained our first broad view of the great glacier afterwards named the Muir, the last of all the grand company to be seen, the stormy weather having hidden it when we first entered the bay. It was now perfectly clear, and the spacious, prairie-like glacier, with its many tributaries extending far back into the snowy recesses of its fountains, made a magnificent display of its wealth, and I was strongly tempted to go and explore it at all hazards. But winter had come, and the freezing of its fiords was an insurmountable obstacle. I had, therefore, to be content for the present with sketching and studying its main features at a distance.

When we arrived at the Hoona hunting-camp, men, women, and children came swarming out to welcome us. In the neighborhood of this camp I carefully noted the lines of demarkation between the forested and deforested regions. Several mountains here are only in part deforested, and the lines separating the bare and the forested portions are well defined. The soil, as well as the trees, had slid off the steep slopes, leaving the edge of the woods raw-looking and rugged.

At the mouth of the bay a series of moraine islands show that the trunk glacier that occupied the bay halted here for some time and deposited this island material as a terminal moraine; that more of the bay was not filled in shows that, after lingering here, it receded comparatively fast. All the level portions of trunks of glaciers occupying ocean fiords, instead of melting back gradually in times of general shrinking and recession, as inland glaciers with sloping channels do, melt almost uniformly over all the surface until they become thin enough to float. Then, of course, with each rise and fall of the tide, the sea water, with a temperature usually considerably above the freezing-point, rushes in and out beneath them, causing rapid waste of the nether surface, while the upper is being wasted by the weather, until at length the fiord portions of these great glaciers become comparatively thin and weak and are broken up and vanish almost simultaneously.

Glacier Bay is undoubtedly young as yet. Vancouver's chart, made only a century ago, shows no trace of it, though found admirably faithful in general. It seems probable, therefore, that even then the entire bay was occupied by a glacier of which all those described above, great though they are, were only tributaries. Nearly as great a change has taken place in Sum Dum Bay since Vancouver's visit, the main trunk glacier there having receded from eighteen to twenty-five miles from the line marked on his chart. Charley, who was here when a boy, said that the place had so changed that he hardly recognized it, so many new islands had been born in the mean time and so much ice had vanished. As we have seen, this Icy Bay is being still farther extended by the recession of the glaciers. That this whole system of fiords and channels was added to the domain of the sea by glacial action is to my mind certain.

We reached the island from which we had obtained our store of fuel about half-past six and camped here for the night, having spent only five days in Sitadaka, sailing round it, visiting and sketching all the six glaciers excepting the largest, though I landed only on three of them,—the Geikie, Hugh Miller, and Grand Pacific,—the freezing of the fiords in front of the others rendering them inaccessible at this late season.

FREDERICK SCHWATKA

The Inside Passage, 1886

"OUR VESSEL TOOTED ITSELF HOARSE OUTSIDE THE HARBOR TO
GET A PILOT OVER THE BAR, BUT NONE WAS TO BE HAD TILL
LATE IN THE DAY, WHEN A PILOT CAME OUT TO US SHOWING
PLAINLY BY HIS CONDITION THAT HE KNEW EVERY BAR IN AND
ABOUT VICTORIA."

*Frederick Schwatka was born in Galena, Illinois, in 1849, and
studied both law and medicine. In 1879 and 1880, he was a
member of a party that searched for the remains of the lost
Franklin expedition in the Arctic. He returned to the north
country in 1883 and was the first white man to explore the full
length of the Yukon River, a journey he described in* Along Alaska's Great River, *published in 1885. He traveled again in
Alaska in 1886, this time under the aegis of the* New York
Times. *That journey was recounted in* A Summer in Alaska,
excerpted below, which was published in 1891.

*A portion of the Brooks Range in northwest Alaska is
named the Schwatka Mountains in his honor. Elsewhere in this
book, James Ramsey recounts part of a winter he spent in those
mountains.*

*Also, when nine-year-old Margaret Murie first traveled to
Alaska in 1911, one of the boats that carried her on the Tanana
River was named the* Schwatka. *Her story begins after this selec-
tion and continues in the section on Fairbanks.*

An exception to the usual style of travel writing in his time, Schwatka wrote with unusual humor and high spirits.

"INLAND PASSAGE" TO ALASKA IS THE fjörd-like channel, resembling a great river, which extends from the northwestern part of Washington Territory, through British Columbia, into southeastern Alaska. Along this coast line for about a thousand miles stretches a vast archipelago closely hugging the mainland of the Territories named above, the southernmost important island being Vancouver, almost a diminutive continent in itself, while to the north Tchichagoff Island limits it on the seaboard.

From the little town of Olympia at the head of Puget Sound, in Washington Territory, to Chilkat, Alaska, at the head of Lynn Channel, or Canal, one sails as if on a grand river, and it is really hard to comprehend that it is a portion of the ocean unless one can imagine some deep fjörd in Norway or Greenland, so deep that he can sail on its waters for a fortnight, for the fjörd-like character is very prominent in these channels to which the name of "Inland Passage" is usually given.

These channels between the islands and mainland are strikingly uniform in width, and therefore river-like in appearance as one steams or sails through them. At occasional points they connect with the Pacific Ocean, and if there be a storm on the latter, a few rolling swells may enter at these places and disturb the equilibrium of sensitive stomachs for a brief hour, but at all other places the channel is as quiet as any broad river, whatever the weather. On the south we have the Strait of Juan de Fuca and to the north Cross Sound as the limiting channels, while between the two are found Dixon Entrance, which separates Alaska from British Columbia, Queen Charlotte Sound, and other less important outlets.

On the morning of the 24th of May we entered the Strait of Juan de Fuca, named after an explorer—if such he may be called—who never entered this beautiful sheet of water, and who owes his immortality to an audacious guess, which came so near the truth as to deceive the scientific world for many a century. To the left, as we enter, i.e., northward, is the beautiful British island of Vancouver, the name of which commemorates one of the world's most famous explorers. Its high rolling hills are covered with shaggy firs, broken near the beach into little prairies of brighter green, which are dotted here and there with pretty little white cottages, the humblest abodes we see among the industrious, British or American, who live in the far west.

The American side, to the southward, gives us the same picture backed by the high range of the Olympian Mountains, whose tops are covered with perpetual snow, and upon whose cold sides drifting clouds are condensed.

Through British Columbia the sides of this passage are covered with firs and spruce to the very tops of the steep mountains forming them, but as Northing is gained and Alaska is reached the summits are covered with snow and ice at all months of the year, and by the time we cast anchor in Chilkat Inlet, which is about the northernmost point of this great inland salt-water river, we find in many places these crowns of ice debouching in the shape of glaciers to the very water's level, and the tourist beholds, on a regular line of steamboat travel, glaciers and icebergs, and many of the wonders of arctic regions, although upon a reduced scale. Alongside the very banks and edges of these colossal rivers of ice one can gather the most beautiful of Alpine flowers and wade up to his waist in grasses that equal in luxuriance the famed fields of the pampas; while the singing of the birds from the woods and glens and the fragrance of the foliage make one easily imagine that the Arctic circle and equator have been linked together at this point.

Entering Juan de Fuca Strait a few hours were spent in the pretty little anchorage of Neah Bay, the first shelter for ships after rounding Cape Flattery, and here some merchandise was unloaded in the huge Indian canoes that came alongside, each one holding at least a ton.

Victoria, the metropolis of British Columbia, was reached the same day, and as it was the Queen's birthday we saw the town in all its bravery of beer, bunting, and banners. Our vessel tooted itself hoarse outside the harbor to get a pilot over the bar, but none was to be had till late in the day, when a pilot came out to us showing plainly by his condition that he knew every bar in and about Victoria. With the bar pilot on the bridge, so as to save insurance should an accident occur, we entered the picturesque little harbor in safety, despite the discoveries of our guide that since his last visit all the buoys had been woefully misplaced, and even the granite channel had changed its course. But Victoria has many embellishments more durable than bunting and banners, and most conspicuous among them are her well arranged and well constructed roads, in which she has no equal on the Pacific coast of North America, and but few rivals in any other part of the world.

On the 26th we crossed over to Port Townsend, the port of entry for Puget Sound, and on the 27th we headed for Alaska by way of the Inland Passage.

For purposes of description this course should have been designated the "inland passages," in the plural, for its branches are almost innumerable, running in all directions like the streets of an irregular city, although now and then they are reduced to a single channel or fjörd which the steamer is obliged to take or put out to sea. At one point in Discovery Passage leading from the Gulf of Georgia toward Queen Charlotte Sound, the inland passage is so narrow that our long vessel had to steam under a slow bell to avoid accidents, and at this place, called Seymour Narrows, there was much talk of bridging the narrow way in the grand scheme of a Canadian Pacific Railway, which should have its western terminus at Victoria. Through this contracted way the water fairly boils when at its greatest velocity, equaling ten miles an hour in spring tides, and at such times the passage is hazardous even to steamers, while all other craft avoid it until slack water. Jutting rocks increase the danger, and on one of these the United States man-of-war *Saranac* was lost just eight years before we passed through. At the northern end of this picturesque Discovery Passage you see the inland passage trending away to the eastward, with quite a bay on the left around Chatham Point, and while you are wondering in that half soliloquizing way of a traveler in new lands what you will see after you have turned to the right, the great ship swings suddenly to the left, and you find that what you took for a bay is after all the inland passage itself, which stretches once more before you like the Hudson looking upward from West Point, or the Delaware at the Water Gap. For all such little surprises must the tourist be prepared on this singular voyage.

The new bend now becomes Johnstone Strait and so continues to Queen Charlotte Sound, with which it connects by one strait, two passages, and a channel, all alike, except in name, and none much over ten miles long. At nearly every point where a new channel diverges both arms take on a new name, and they change as rapidly as the names of a Lisbon street, which seldom holds the same over a few blocks. The south side of Johnstone Strait is particularly high, rising abruptly from the water fully 5,000 feet, and in grandeur not unlike the Yellowstone Cañon. These summits were still covered with snow and probably on northern slopes snow remains the summer through. One noticeable valley was on the Vancouver Island side, with a conspicuous conical hill in its bosom that may have been over a thousand feet in height. These cone-like hills are so common in flat valleys in northwestern America that I thought it worth while to mention the fact in this place. Occasionally windrows occur through the dense coniferous forests of the inland passage, where the trees have been swept or leveled in a remarkable manner. Such as were cut vertically had been caused by an avalanche, and in these instances the work of clearing had been done as faithfully as if by the hands of man. Sometimes the bright green moss or grass had grown up in these narrow ways, and when there was more than one of about the same age there was quite a picturesque effect of stripings of two shades of green, executed on a most colossal plan. These windrows of fallen trees sometimes stretched along horizontally in varying widths, an effect undoubtedly produced by heavy gales rushing through the contracted "passage."

One's notice is attracted by a species of natural beacon which materially assists the navigator. Over almost all the shoals and submerged rocks hang fields of kelp, a growth with which the whole "passage" abounds, thus affording a timely warning badly needed where the channel has been imperfectly charted. As one might surmise the water is very bold, and these submerged and ragged rocks are in general most to be feared. Leaving Johnstone Strait we enter Queen Charlotte Sound, a channel which was named, lacking only three years, a century ago. It widens into capacious waters at once and we again felt the "throbbing of old Neptune's pulse," and those with sensitive stomachs perceived a sort of flickering of their own.

One who is acquainted merely in a general way with the history and geography of this confusing country finds many more Spanish names than he anticipates, and to his surprise, a conscientious investigation shows that even as it is the vigorous old Castilian explorers have not received all the credit to which they are entitled, for many of their discoveries in changing hands changed names as well: the Queen Charlotte Islands, a good day's run to the northwestward of us, were named in 1787 by an Englishman, who gave the group the name of his vessel, an appellation which they still retain, although as Florida Blanca they had known the banner of Castile and Leon thirteen years before. Mount Edgecumbe, so prominent in the beautiful harbor of Sitka, was once Monte San Jacinto, and a list of the same tenor might be given that would prove more voluminous than interesting. American changes in the great northwest have not been so radical. Boca de Quadra Inlet has somehow become Bouquet Inlet to those knowing it best. La Creole has degenerated into Rickreall, and so on: the foreign names have been mangled but not annihilated. We sail across Queen Charlotte Sound as if we were going to bump right into the high land ahead of us, but a little indentation over the bow becomes a valley, then a bay, and in ample time to prevent accidents widens into another salt-water river, about two miles wide and twenty times as long, called Fitzhugh Sound. Near the head of the sound we turn abruptly westward into the Lama Passage, and on its western shores we see nearly the first sign of civilization in the inland passage, the Indian village of Bella Bella, holding probably a dozen native houses and a fair looking church, while a few cattle grazing near the place had a still more civilized air.

As we steamed through Seaforth Channel, a most tortuous affair, Indians were seen paddling in their huge canoes from one island to another or along the high, rocky shores, a cheering sign of habitation not previously noticed.

The great fault of the inland passage as a resort for tourists is in the constant dread of fogs that may at any time during certain months of the year completely obscure the grand scenery that tempted the travelers thither. The waters of the Pacific Ocean on the seaboard of Alaska are but a deflected continuation of the warm equatorial current called the Kuro Siwo of the Japanese; from these waters the air is laden with moisture, which being thrown by the variable winds against the snow-clad and glacier-covered summits of the higher mountains, is precipitated as fog and light rain, and oftentimes everything is wrapped for weeks in these most annoying mists. July, with June and August, are by far the most favorable months for the traveler. The winter months are execrable, with storms of rain, snow, and sleet constantly occurring, the former along the Pacific frontage, and the latter near the channels of the mainland.

Milbank Sound gave us another taste of the ocean swells which spoiled the flavor of our food completely, for although we were only exposed for less than an hour that hour happened to come just about dinner time; after which we entered Finlayson Passage, some twenty-five miles long. This is a particularly picturesque and bold channel of water, its shores covered with shaggy conifers as high as the eye can reach, and the mountains, with their crowns of snow and ice, furnishing supplies of spray for innumerable beautiful waterfalls. At many places in the inland passage from here on, come down the steep timbered mountains the most beautiful waterfalls fed from the glaciers hidden in the fog. At every few miles we pass the mouths of inlets and channels, leading away into the mountainous country no one knows whither. There are no charts which show more than the mouths of these inlets. Out of or into these an occasional canoe speeds its silent way perchance in quest of salmon that here abound, but the secrets of their hidden paths are locked in the savage mind. How tempting they must be for exploration, and how strange that, although so easy of access, they still remain unknown. After twisting around through a few "reaches," channels and passages, we enter the straightest of them all, Grenville Channel, so straight that it almost seems to have been mapped by an Indian. As you steam through its forty or fifty miles of mathematically rectilinear exactness you think the sleepy pilot might tie his wheel, put his heels up in the spokes, draw his hat over his eyes, and take a quiet nap. In one place it seems to be not over two or three hundred yards wide, but probably is double that, the high towering banks giving a deceptive impression. The windrows through the timber of former avalanches of snow or landslides now become thicker and their effects occasionally picturesque in the very devastation created. Beyond Grenville Channel the next important stretch of salt water is Chatham Sound, which is less like a river than any yet named. Its connection with Grenville Channel is by the usual number of three or four irregular waterways dodging around fair sized islands, which had at one time, however, a certain importance because it was thought that the Canadian Pacific Railway might make Skeena Inlet off to our right its western terminus.

On the 29th of May, very early in the morning, we crossed Dixon Entrance, and were once more on American soil, that is, in a commercial sense, the United States having drawn a check for its value of $7,200,000, and the check having been honored; but in regard to government the country may be called no man's land, none existing in the territory. Dixon Entrance bore once a Spanish name in honor of its discoverer, a name which is heard no more, although a few still call the channel by its Indian name, Kaiganee. Broad Dixon Entrance contracts into the narrow Portland Inlet, which, putting back into the mainland for some seventy-five miles, forms the water boundary between Alaska and British Columbia. From here it becomes a thirty mile wide strip drawn "parallel to tide-water," which continues with a few modifications to about Mount St. Elias.

The forenoon of the same day we entered Boca de Quadra Inlet, where a pioneer company had established a salmon cannery, for which we had some freight. The cannery was about half completed and the stores were landed on a raft made of only two logs, which impressed me with the size of the Sitka cedar. The largest log was probably seventy-five feet long and fully eight feet at the butt. It is said to be impervious to the teredo, which makes such sad havoc with all other kinds of wood sunk in salt water. Owing to its fine grain and peculiar odor, handsome chests can be made of it in which that universal pest, the moth, will not live. It is purely an Alaskan tree, and even north of Quadra Inlet it is found in its densest growth. As around all white habitations in frontier lands, we found the usual number of natives, although in this case they were here for the commendable object of seeking employment in catching salmon whenever the run should commence. Their canoes are constructed of the great cedar tree, by the usual Indian method of hollowing them out to a thin shell and then boiling water in them by throwing red-hot stones in the water they hold, producing pliability of the wood by the steaming process, when by means of braces and ties they are fashioned into nautical "lines." The peaks of the prows are often fantastically carved into various insignia, usually spoken of as "totems," and painted in wild barbaric designs, the body of the boat being covered with deep black made from soot and seal oil. Crawling along under the somber shadows of the dense overhanging trees in the deep dark passages, these canoes can hardly be seen until very near, and when a flash of the water from the paddle reveals their presence, they look more like smugglers or pirates avoiding notice than anything else. The genial superintendent, Mr. Ward, spoke of his rambles up the picturesque shores of the inlet and his adventures since he had started his new enterprise. A trip of a few days before up one of the diminutive valleys drained by a little Alpine brook had rewarded him with the sight of no less than eight bears scurrying around through the woods. He had an Indian companion who was armed with a flint-lock, smooth bore Hudson Bay Company musket, while the superintendent had a shot gun for any small game that might happen along, and even with these arms they succeeded in bagging a bear apiece, both being of the black—or small—variety. Hunting the little black bear is not far removed from a good old-fashioned "coon" hunt, and not much more dangerous. The dogs, mostly the sharp-eared, sharp-nosed, and sharp-barking Indian variety, once after a bear, force him up a tree to save his hamstrings being nipped uncomfortably, and then he is shot out of it, at the hunter's leisure, and if wounded is so small and easily handled by the pack of dogs that he can hardly be called dangerous. Not so, however, with the great brown bear, or barren-ground bear of Alaska, so often spoken of in these parts as the "grizzly" from his similarity in size and savageness to "the California King of the Chapparal." Everywhere in his dismal dominions he is religiously avoided by the native Nim-rod, who declares that his meat is not fit to be eaten, that his robe is almost worthless, and that he constantly keeps the wrong end presented to his pursuers. Although he is never hunted, encounters with him are not altogether unknown, as he is savage enough to become the hunter himself at times, and over some routes the Indians will never travel unless armed so as to be fairly protected from this big Bruin. This Indian fear of the great brown bear I found to be co-extensive with all my travels in Alaska and the British North-west Territory. Mr. Ward told me that wherever the big bear was found, the little black variety made his presence scarce, as the two in no way affiliate, and the latter occupies such country as the abundance of his big brother will allow. These districts may be intermixed as much as the black and white squares on a chess-board, but they are as sharply, though not as mathematically, defined, each one remaining faithfully on his own color, so to speak. A new re-peating rifle was on our vessel consigned to the sportsman su-perintendent, and he expected to decrease the bear census during the summer, so far as his duties would allow.

About noon, after much backing and putting of lines ashore, and working on them from the donkey engines fore and aft, we succeeded in turning our long steamer in the narrow channel, the pilot remarking in reply to the captain's inquiries as to shoals that he wished he could exchange the depth for the width and he would have no trouble in turning around.

Through this part of the inland passage sea-otters are said to be found, and it was thought that one or two were seen by some of the people on board, but no one could vouch for the discovery.

The everlasting mountain scenery now commences to pall and offers nothing in the way of the picturesque except the same old high mountains, the same dense growth of timber on their steep sides, and the same salt-water canals cutting through them. A valley putting off anywhere would have been a relief, and breaks in the uniformly high mountains that looked as if they might be ravines so persistently became other arms and canals of the great networks of passage that we were anything but sorry when a fog bank settled down about two hundred feet above our eyes and cut the fjörd as sharply at that height as if it had been the crest line of a fortification extending off into miles of bastions and covered ways.

Early morning on the 30th found us at the little port of Wrangell, named after one of Russia's many famous explorers in northern regions. It was the most tumble-down looking company of cabins I ever saw, the "Chinese quarter" (every place on the Pacific coast has its "Chinese quarter" if it is only a single house) being a wrecked river vessel high and dry on the pebbly beach, which, however, was not much inferior to the rest of the town. Not far from here comes in the Stickeen river, the largest stream that cuts through the south-eastern or "tide-water strip" of Alaska. About its headwaters are the Cassiar mines of British Columbia, and as the Stickeen river is the nearest available way to reach them, although the traveler's course is against the stream of a mountain torrent, the circumstance has made something of a port of Wrangell, which nearly ten years ago was at the height of its glory of gold-dust and excitement. Even at this distance the dark green water of the deep channel is tinged with a white chalky color ground from the flanks of the calcareous hills by the eroding glaciers, then swept into the swift river and by it carried far out into the tortuous passages. Every stream, however small, in this part of the world, with glaciers along its course or upon its tributaries, carries this milk-like water in its current.

With all its rickety appearance there was no small amount of business doing in Wrangell, no less than four or five fair sized backwoods stores being there, all apparently in thrifty circumstances. Indian curiosities of all kinds were to be had, from carved spoons of the mountain goat at "two bits" (twenty-five cents) apiece to the most elaborate idols or totemic carvings. A fair market is found for these articles among the few visitors who travel in this out-of-the-way corner of the earth, and when the supply is exhausted in any line the natives will immediately set to work to satisfy the demand. One huge carved horn spoon was evidently of very ancient make and very fine workmanship, an old pioneer of these regions who had owned it for many years having refused sixty dollars for it from some curiosity collectors only the year before.

From Wrangell we debouched westward by Sumner Strait, the wide salt-water river that continues the narrow fresh-water river of Stickeen to the Pacific Ocean.

Between five and six in the afternoon we are rounding Cape Ommaney, where our pilot tells us it storms eight days in the week. It certainly gave us double rations of wind that day, and many retired early. Even the old Spanish navigators who first laid eyes upon it must have borne it a grudge to have called it *Punta Oeste de la Entrada del Principe*; all its geographical characteristics and relations being shouldered on it for a name.

Early next morning we were in the harbor of Sitka, or New Archangel, as the Russians called it when they had it for their capital of this province. The strong, bold bluffs of the interior passages now give way to gentler elevations along the Pacific seaboard, but the country gradually rises from the coast until but a few miles back the same old cloud-capped, snow-covered peaks recur, and as we stand well out to sea they look as abrupt as ever.

Sitka is a picturesque place when viewed from any point except from within the town limits. From the south-west, looking north-east, Mount Edgecumbe (of Cook) affords a beautiful background against the western sky, and when that is full of low white clouds the abrupt manner in which the point of the mountain is cut off gives it the appearance of being buried in the clouds, thus seeming several times higher than it really is.

The harbor of Sitka is so full of small islands that looking at it from a height it seems as if it could only be mapped with a pepper-box, and one wonders how any vessel can get to her wharf. Once alongside, the water seems as clear as the atmosphere above, and the smallest objects can be easily identified at the bottom, though there must have been fully thirty or forty feet of water where we made our observations.

On one of the large islands in Sitka harbor, called Japanese Island, an old Niphon junk was cast, early in the present century, and her small crew of Japanese were rescued by the Russians. Sitka has been so often described that it is unnecessary to do more than refer the reader to other accounts of the place.

Ten o'clock in the forenoon of the 31st saw us under way steaming northward, still keeping to the inland passage, and *en route* to deliver wrecking machinery at a point in Peril Straits where the *Eureka,* a small steamer of the same line to which our ship belonged, had formerly run on a submerged rock in the channel, which did not appear upon the charts. The unfortunate boat had just time to reach the shore and beach herself before she filled with water. The *Eureka*'s wreck was reached by two in the afternoon, and as our boat might be detained for some time in assisting the disabled vessel, many of us embraced the opportunity to go ashore in the wilds of the Alexander Archipelago. The walking along the beach between high and low tide was tolerable, and even agreeable for whole stretches, especially after our long confinement on the ship, where the facilities for promenading were poor. To turn inland from the shore was at once to commence the ascent of a slope that might vary from forty to eighty degrees, the climbing of which almost beggars description. The compact mass of evergreen timber had looked dense enough from the ship, but at its feet grew a denser mass of tangled undergrowth of bushes and vines, and at their roots again was a solid carpeting of moss, lichens, and ferns that often ran up the trees and underbrush for heights greater than a man's reach, and all of it moist as a sponge, the whole being absolutely tropical in luxuriance. This thick carpet of moss extends from the shore line to the edges of the glaciers on the mountain summits, and the constant melting of the ice through the warm summer supplies it with water which it absorbs like a sponge. The air is saturated with moisture from the warm ocean current, and everything you see and touch is like Mr. Mantalini's proposed body, "dem'd moist and unpleasant." It is almost impossible to conceive how heavily laden with tropical moisture the atmosphere is in this supposed sub-Arctic colony of ours. It oozes up around your feet as you walk, and drips from overhead like an April mist, and nothing is exempt from it. Even the Indians' tall, dead "totem-poles" of hemlock or spruce, which would make fine kindling wood anywhere else, bear huge clumps of dripping moss and foliage on their tops, at heights varying from ten to thirty feet above the ground. An occasional stray seed of a Sitka spruce may get caught in this elevated tangle, and make its home there just as well as if it were on the ground. It sprouts, and as its branches run up in the air, the roots crawl down the "totem-pole" until the ground is reached, when they bury themselves in it, and send up fresh sustenance to the trunk and limbs, which until then have been living a parasitic sort of life off the decayed moss. Imagine a city boy tossing a walnut from a fourth story window, and its lodging on top of a telegraph pole, there sprouting next spring, and in the course of a couple of years extending its roots down the pole, insinuating themselves in the crevices and splitting it open, then piercing the pavement; the tree continuing to grow for years until the boy, as a man, can reach out from his window and pick walnuts every fall, and the idea seems incredible; and yet the equivalent occurs quite often in the south-eastern portions of our distant colony. Nor is all this marshy softness confined to the levels or to almost level slopes, as one would imagine from one's experience at home, but it extends up the steepest places, where the climbing would be hard enough without this added obstacle. In precipitous slopes where the foot tears out a great swath of moist moss, it may reveal underneath a slippery shingle or shale where nothing but a bird could find a footing in its present condition. There is wonderful preservative power in all these conditions, for nothing seems to rot in the ground, and the accumulated timber of ages, standing and fallen, stumps, limbs, and trunks, "criss-cross and tumble-tangled," as the children say, forms a bewildering mass which, covered and intertwined as it is with a compact entanglement of underbrush and moss, makes the ascent of the steep hillsides a formidable undertaking. A fallen trunk of a tree is only indicated by a ridge of moss, and should the traveler on this narrow path deviate a little too far to the right or left, he may sink up to his arm-pits in a soft mossy trap from which he can scramble as best he may, according to his activity in the craft of "back-woodsmanship." Having once reached the tops of the lower hills—the higher ones are covered with snow and glacier ice the year round—a few small openings may be seen, which, if anything, are more boggy and treacherous to the feet than the hillsides themselves, lagoon-like morasses, covered with pond lilies and aquatic plant life, being connected by a network of sluggish canals with three or four inches of amber colored water and as many feet of soft black oozy mud, with here and there a clump of willow brake or "pussy-tails" springing above the waste of sedge and flags. In these bayou openings a hunter may now and then run across a stray deer, bear, or mountain goat, but, in general, inland hunting in south-eastern Alaska is a complete failure, owing to the scarcity of game and the labor of hunting.

The worst part of Peril Strait being ahead of us, we backed out with our long unwieldy vessel and turned westward, passing out late in the evening through Salisbury Strait to the Pacific Ocean, ours being, according to the pilot, the first steam vessel to essay the passage. A last night on the Pacific's rolling water, and early next morning we rounded Cape Ommaney, and entered the inland passage of Chatham Strait, our prow once more pointed northward, the sheet of water lying as quiet as a mill pond. About 4 P.M. we reached Killisnoo, a pretty little port in the Strait. Cod-fish abounding here in unusual numbers, a regular fishery has been established by a company for the purpose of catching and preserving the cod for the markets of the Pacific coast. Here I saw many of the Kootznahoo Indians of the place, who do the principal fishing for the white men. Their already ugly faces were plastered over with black, for which, according to the superintendent, there were two causes. A few of the Indians were clad in mourning, to which this artificial blackness is an adjunct, while the remainder followed the custom in order to protect their faces and especially their eyes from the intense glare of the sun on the water while fishing. Chatham Strait at its northern end subdivides into Icy Straits and Lynn Canal, the latter being taken as our course. At its northern end it again branches into the Chilkat and Chilkoot Inlets, the former being taken; and at its head, the highest northing we can reach in this great inland salt-water river, our voyage on the *Victoria* terminated. Icy Straits lead off to the westward and unite with the Pacific, by way of Cross Sound, the most northern of these connecting passages, which marks the point where the archipelago, and with it the inland passage, ceases, for from here northward to St. Elias and beyond a bold bad coast faces the stormy Pacific, and along its frowning cliffs of rock and ice even the amphibious Indian seldom ventures.

MARGARET E. MURIE

The Inside Passage and beyond, 1911

"THE ALASKA MOST VIVID IN MY MEMORY IS THE ONE I SAW FIRST
AS A NINE-YEAR-OLD, TRAVELING FROM SEATTLE TO FAIRBANKS
WITH MOTHER, IN SEPTEMBER, ON THE LAST TRIP BEFORE
'FREEZE-UP.' "

*Margaret E. Murie, the daughter of a sea captain, was born in
1902 in Seattle. In 1911, after a voyage recounted in the following pages, the family moved to Fairbanks, where they settled.*

*Margaret was the first woman to graduate from the Univer-
sity of Alaska. In the same year she graduated, she married
Olaus J. Murie, a biologist with the U.S. Fish and Wildlife Service. Olaus and his younger brother, Adolph, both made a life's
work of combining adventure and science. Margaret knew what
she was letting herself in for when she married him. Olaus had
already made an extensive study of the migratory routes and herd
size of caribou, had spent two summers and a winter on Hudson
Bay, and had explored the interior of Labrador by canoe, and he
and Adolph spent the fall and winter of 1922 on a dogsled trip
through the Brooks Range. Adolph, among other accomplishments, later made an important study of wolves in Mount Mc-
Kinley National Park.*

*Margaret Murie wrote several books about her life in
Alaska, including* Journeys to the Far North, Island Between,

Two in the Far North, *and* Wapiti Wilderness. *She also worked with her husband to found the Wilderness Society, of which Olaus served as director from 1946 until his death in 1963.*

In A Naturalist in Alaska, *published in 1961, she wrote, "Olaus and I cherish the hope that the Brooks Range in northern Alaska, the Alaska Range that passes through McKinley Park, and the coast ranges, and wide sweeps of intervening country, may all be kept forever wild. That the rivers may remain rivers. That the tundra, with thousands of ponds of all sizes, may be left sufficiently intact to serve in the future as nesting homes for the cranes, the many species of shore birds, the ducks, geese, and swans. All this, so that man in the future may continue to enjoy wild country."*

Margaret Murie's youthful journey to Alaska begins here. It continues in the section on Fairbanks later in this book.

The Schwatka *on which Murie traveled on the Tanana River was named in honor of explorer Frederick Schwatka, who has already made a personal appearance in this book.*

Murie's description of the Yukon stern-wheeler Casca *is especially vivid. The poet Robert Service also traveled on this ship during his days in the Klondike. And for the sad story of the Casca's fate, see the selection by Pierre Berton.*

A NINE-YEAR-OLD GIRL CAN SEE AND hear a lot. Too old to hold the center of any adult group with the charm of babyhood, too young to be considered a hazard to conversation, sturdy, round-eyed, my dark hair in a Mary Jane bob with a big butterfly bow on top, I could be quietly everywhere at once. I saw and heard.

So the Alaska most vivid in my memory is the one I saw first as a nine-year-old, traveling from Seattle to Fairbanks with Mother, in September, on the last trip before "freeze-up."

Daddy, my loved and loving stepfather, was already up there, at work on his new job as Assistant U.S. Attorney. One morning as I came downstairs to breakfast I saw a Western Union messenger boy standing with Mother in the front hall of our Seattle home. The telegram said: "Can you catch Str.

Jefferson September 15th? Last steamer to connect with last boat down the Yukon. Will meet you in Dawson."

I remember running the several blocks to the dressmaker's. "We're going to Alaska in three days and Mother wants to know can you get her a traveling dress made." In those days you didn't just go downtown and buy a dress; it was a project.

Three days. My stepfather had faith in the calm efficiency of that sweet brown-eyed woman. The dressmaker friend came and went to work in the midst of trunks and boxes. My grandmother came and flipped from room to room amid a torrent of words. "I just don't see how Millette can *expect* you to catch that boat!" And: "Minnie, do you think you should *try* to do this—in your condition?" Even while she feverishly stowed linens and clothing and dishes in the big round-topped trunks.

"In your condition"—that was a queer-sounding phrase. What condition? But then I was sent running on another errand. And finally, on the afternoon of the third day, there was Grandmother, still in a torrent of words, and between tears and laughter, sitting atop the largest round-topped trunk so the dressmaker's son could get it closed, while the dressmaker sewed on the last of the black jet buttons down the back of the brown wool "traveling dress" with garnet velvet piping around the neck and sleeves. I remember how soft to the touch that brown wool cloth was.

The boats for Alaska always sailed at nine in the evening, and it was like going to the theater—a real social occasion for the Seattle folks—going to the pier to see the steamer off to the North. Down through the great cavern of the dock warehouse, brightly lighted for sailing time, smelling of salt sea and tar and hemp and adventure. A great crowd of people, and stevedores with handcarts pushing their way through, yelling: "Gangway! Gangway!" A great wave of noise compounded of the churning of engines and the hissing of steam, and voices in every key, shouts, laughter. At last to the long opening in the side wall, and there was the ship's white side and the red-and-white gangplank.

I was dressed in my new black-and-white "shepherd check" dress with brass buttons down the front and a red collar and red cuffs, and my new red coat with black silk "frogs," and a red hat with shirred satin ribbon around the crown (and I knew the red Mary Jane hairbow would be crushed by it), and shiny black boots with patent-leather cuffs at the top and a red silk tassel. My stomach was tied in a knot of breathless, almost-not-to-be-borne sensation, and I was clutching all my going-away presents—coloring books, paper-doll books, crayons, a new volume of *Black Beauty*. Mother stood in the midst of a cluster of friends, looking so pretty in her new dress and her coat with the green velvet collar, and she too had her arms full of gifts—boxes of candy, books, the newest *Ladies' Home Journal*. All around us people were carrying or receiving packages. Going to see someone off for Alaska always meant bringing a parting gift. The first moments of letdown after the ship was under way would be brightened by the opening of packages.

For a nine-year-old, no sorrow, only excitement—being hugged all around, and nearly jumping out of my skin when the deep-throated, echoing five-minute whistle blew and set off a crescendo of squeals and shouts and admonitions from the crowd.

"Here you go!" A perkily blue-and-gold uniform sets me up onto the first cleat of the gangplank—really, really going somewhere! Step down onto the deck, find a spot at the rail. Every passenger is at the rail—why doesn't the ship roll over? Hang on to the packages. What if one should fall? From some mysterious realm above come heavy voices of authority; bells clang far down inside; down slides the gangplank to be rolled away onto the pier. That was the last tie being cut. Now it is really happening. Looking down over the ship's side, I see water, and it widens and widens, and faces are looking up, handkerchiefs waving, voices and faces fading away. "See you next June." "Don't take any wooden nickels." "Tell Joe to write." "Hope Queen Charlotte won't be too rough!"

The faces of Grandmother and all our friends are only white blurs now. We are out in the cool black windy bay and the ship is heading out and all the passengers are moving now—moving into their new little world, the Str. *Jefferson*, Gus Nord, Master.

To a nine-year-old, a ship's stateroom was a wonder of a place, such fun—the berths with their railings, the washbowl that pulled down into place, the locker seat with its red plush cushions. Our room opened into the "saloon," and that was another wonder—red plush-covered soft divans and big chairs, soft carpet underfoot, a broad stairway with a shining brass railing that curved down into the dining saloon.

There were other children aboard, and here on the carpeted floor at our mothers' feet we played our games while the women sat with their "fancy work," all of us in a cozy yet adventurous little world of our own. We children cut out paper dolls, and played Parcheesi, and colored pictures, and the women discovered one another, old Alaskans telling new ones all they knew, while fingers flew. Mother was crocheting a long black-and-white wool shawl; the huge amber crochet hook fascinated me.

A lovely routine that was over too quickly. Then, as ever, the days of ship life flew by too fast. Meals, and naps, and always the falling asleep and waking again to the sweet pulse and throb of the ship's engines and the muted hiss of water along her sides. Then racing about on deck, and hide-and-seek on the forward deck, and quiet hours in the lounge, and "dressing for dinner"—which meant, for me, being scrubbed, and having my hair brushed till it shone, and a different bow tied and fluffed into a butterfly, and either the pink challis or the shirred white China silk dress, and the "best" shoes, black patent leather with high tops of brown-calf buttoned straps. Then stepping out to wait for the musical dinner gong and to see what the three other little girls had on this time!

After four days of this delightful life there was talk of about what hour the *Jefferson* would dock at Skagway. I remember it was daytime, and we had been sliding for hours up a long channel of glass-smooth water edged on either side by the ever-present dark green forest that lay below shining white mountains.

Skagway nestled into the delta fan at the mouth of a canyon, embraced on three sides by steep wooded slopes. In front, the very blue waters of the Lynn Canal, which is not really a canal but a long fiord. A long pier extended out to deep water. The little town seemed to sparkle in the September sun. Many of the buildings were of white-painted lumber; some were half-log structures. Back toward the canyon, in a grove of cottonwood trees and spruces, stood Pullen House.

In a frontier town, the feature least frontierish is likely to be the most famous and admired. So Pullen House, looking like a southern manor, with lawns, flower beds, a pergola, a little stream flowing through the lawn and spanned by a rustic bridge. Inside, no homemade frontier furnishings, but heavy Victorian walnut and mahogany and plush, walls crowded with pictures, bric-a-brac, and souvenirs. For here was the whole history of Skagway. Pullen House was the tangible dream of a woman who had come there in the gold rush only fourteen years before, a widow with a daughter and three little sons. She had lived in a tent shack and made dried apple pies and sold them to the hordes of pie-hungry, home-hungry, adventure-hungry men of the days of '98. Thus her grubstake, and Pullen House.

Harriet Pullen, once met, could never be forgotten. She welcomed Mother as a beloved daughter come home, for she remembered Daddy from the days when the District Judge from Juneau came up to Skagway twice a year with his retinue, including his young court reporter, and held court. They always stayed, of course, at Pullen House. "Ma" Pullen, tall, red-haired, statuesque, with suffering and strength and humor in every feature—even a nine-year-old sensed this.

We slept in a room full of overpowering furniture, in a great ark of a bed with headboard reaching toward the ceiling. But this was the special room, the room many important people had occupied when traveling north. The commode had the most gorgeous basin, and a pitcher, blooming with red roses, so heavy I could not lift it.

In the morning Mrs. Pullen ushered us out into the long pantry behind the immense kitchen. "My favorite boarders always get to skim their own cream. Mr. Gillette always loved to when he stayed here," she said.

Here was the other unfrontierish feature of Skagway. Ma Pullen's great pride was a Jersey cow, the only cow in that part of the world, and in the pantry stood the blue-enameled milk pans. The guest was given a bowl and a spoon and allowed to skim off cream for his porridge and coffee. Skimming your own cream at Pullen House in the land of no cream was a ritual talked of all over the North in those days.

Being on a train for the first time provided more excitement. I had to examine every detail of the red plush-covered seats and curlicue-brass-trimmed arms, and jump from one side of the aisle to the other, trying to see everything, yet my only clear recollection from that day is looking down into Lake Bennett near the summit—such turquoise water, such golden birch trees all round it. I think all other impressions were drowned in my rapt absorption in the gorgeous uniforms of the two Northwest Mounted Policemen who came aboard to check us through at the border of the Yukon Territory.

This same impression dominates my memory of the three days traveling downriver from Whitehorse to Dawson. There was one of these gorgeous creatures aboard, and he suffered the company of an adoring small round-eyed girl. I remember sitting with him on the stern deck. I don't remember any of the conversation.

It was dusk at five o'clock, for it was late September in the Land of the Midnight Sun. The passengers on the sternwheel steamer *Casca* were all crowded at the rail on one side while the *Casca* huffed and puffed in the great surge of the Yukon and was maneuvered with uncanny skill toward the dock at Dawson. Her stern wheel chuff-chuffed rapidly in reverse, bells clanged, and with a great swoosh of water the wheel chuff-chuffed forward again. Her high-pitched, exciting whistle blew three times—a greeting to the "Queen of the Klondike" and the crowd of her citizens standing all expectant on the dock.

The *Casca*'s passengers pressed closer to the rail, straining to look, straining to recognize loved, feared, or dreaded faces. Squeezed against the white-painted iron mesh below the rail, new red hat pushed askew, heart beating fast, I stood, determined to see everything.

Mother stood quietly beside me, but I could feel her excitement too. We were both looking for the big tan Stetson hat that would tell us Daddy had managed to catch that last upriver steamer and was here to meet us.

The Yukon begins to widen at Dawson; the hills are farther apart and seem bigger and higher, and certainly more bare.

Here we were sensing a quite different world, the world of "the interior." The hill behind Dawson seemed to be sitting high above the town, with arms spread about the sprawling clot of man's hurriedly built, haphazard structures. Even then, in 1911, the gold towns had electricity, and now at dusk lights were beginning to show here and there all over the delta shape of the settlement.

The *Casca,* having chuffed upstream above the dock, was now sliding down closer in, closer in, a young Indian poised to jump with the bowline. There arose cries of "I see Jim!" "There's Mary!" And shouts from the crowd on the dock: "Hey Doc, you old so-and-so, I *knew* you'd be back!"

A bell clanged once somewhere inside the *Casca,* the engines stopped, the Indian boy jumped, for a few seconds more the great wheel turned—over and over—and then how quiet it was! Everyone seemed impressed by the silence for a moment. That is the kind of moment which lives on forever after, when you are nine and in an utterly new and so different world. Then Mother cried out: "There he is!" And there he was, indeed, right at the front, where a crew of Indian boys waited to hoist the big gangplank.

There was moose steak for dinner that night, in Dawson's famed Arcade Café. Under the white glare of the many bulbs, amid the great babble of a happy crowd, everyone talking to everyone and calling back and forth among the tables—I remember most keenly that huge thick slab of meat with a heap of fried potatoes beside it. We had arrived in the North. What the steak cost, I do not know. But that was the Yukon, that was Alaska. I think my gentle mother began to learn about the north country that night. All was costly, everything was done on a lavish scale, life was exciting and each day a story in itself, and nothing was worth worrying about. The finest things that could be hauled into this country from Outside were none too good for these pioneers who were braving the climate and the terrain of this untamable land. If all might be lost in a season in the diggings, then they would have the best while they could.

The hotel rooms reflected this spirit. The wallpaper was likely to be a Greek amphora design in gold, all fluffy with curlicues, on a deep-red ground. There might be a flowered pink

Brussels carpet on the floor, a white bedstead with more curly designs and brass knobs on each of the four posts; chairs with more fancy designs and turned legs. There was one with a lion's head carved in its back. At the windows, lace curtains which scratched your nose and neck if you wanted to part them to look down into the street.

The street. The next morning I stood looking down at it. It was full of big-hatted men, fur-capped men, men in Derby hats, men with beards, men in breeches and bright shirts and high laced boots, men in long city overcoats, men in denim parkas. Some were hurrying along, boots clattering on the boardwalk; others were standing about in small groups. There seemed to be a lot of talk and gesturing and much laughter, a feeling of excitement and of things happening. A team of big gray horses came down the dusty street to the dock drawing a load of luggage. Behind them came a team of Huskies pulling a long narrow cart on wheels, also piled with luggage. "See? They use dogs when there is no snow, too," Daddy said.

The three of us were at the window now. Across the street the carts were disappearing into the dock warehouse. The autumn stream of old-timers leaving for Outside for the winter, and of others moving in, was at its peak. One more boat from downriver was due in. It would really be the last one upriver for this season; and on it we would be going downstream, to Tanana, and from Tanana up the Tanana River to Fairbanks. "The *Sarah* should be in any time now," Daddy said. "Look downriver."

I already knew what direction that was, and over the roofs of the row of docks and warehouses, the broad brown river was there, filling our view, the brown hills beyond seeming far away. Downstream, around a sand-colored bluff, a puff of white wood smoke, then a beautiful three-toned whistle, sad and sweet and lonely. "There she is! Only she and her three sisters have that voice!" exclaimed Daddy.

In 1911 the river steamer was queen. There was a great fleet then, nearly all with feminine names, churning and chuffing their stern wheels up the rivers and sliding briskly down them. When the great two-stacker Mississippi-style steamer came in to any dock, she came like a confident southern beauty making a graceful curtsy at a ball. There were four of these on the Yukon—the *Susie,* the *Sarah,* the *Hannah,* and the *Louise*—and they lived their lives between St. Michael at the mouth of the river and Dawson, 1,600 miles upstream. That part of the Yukon is very wide all the way, with plenty of water, a great river. There was another of the big boats, bearing a masculine name, *Herman,* but "he" seemed a bit dirty and a little slower.

Now in the street below there was shouting and calling, and all the town emptied in a rush toward the dock, where the beautiful huge white *Sarah* was sliding in to make a landing.

We left Dawson early the next evening. There was still some daylight, and it seemed that all of Dawson was on the dock to see us off. Back in those times "the last trip of the year" was no meaningless phrase. It meant that all the supplies for the community, enough to last until "the first boat in the spring" came, had to be already delivered and safely stored away in the warehouses and stores—and everyone hoped he hadn't forgotten to order something important. It meant that everyone who felt he could not stand another soul-testing northern winter had better be leaving on this boat. It meant that all those who had been Outside all summer and felt they couldn't stand any more of the tinsel and heartless life of the cities Outside were there, on their way back downriver, or on beyond to Fairbanks, or to wherever they felt they belonged and could try it again. These were aboard the *Sarah.* They were mostly single men, but there were a few families, like us, going into the country to make a home, to follow a career.

How vivid that scene! Again squeezed up against, and almost under, the rail, among all those grownups, I tried hard to see and hear everything.

"Sure you got all your suitcases aboard?"

"Hope that winter dump's a good one."

"Say hello to Charlie."

"Oh, we'll winter through all right."

"See you in the spring!"

Everyone was smiling, tossing jokes back and forth. That was the way of the North always, but even a nine-year-old could sense the sad things too. Maybe we won't see you in the spring;

maybe that winter dump won't be so good; maybe this country is too tough for us. Maybe . . .

There is one thing gone forever from our world—the irrevocability of those departures, before the age of the airplane. This was the last boat, and Nature would take over from now until the middle of June. Freeze-up was coming. There would be no chance of seeing any of these faces until another year had rolled away. The *Sarah*'s stern wheel, so huge I was afraid to look at it, began to turn. The swirl and push of water, shouted commands from up above us. The young freight clerk in his navy-and-gold uniform came hurrying up the gangplank, papers in hand, always the last one aboard. A voice from up above shouted down to him: "Sure you got everything? All right, cast off!"

The big cable fell into the river with a splash that must have sent a shiver of finality down many a spine. Up came the gangplank, and the two gorgeous Mounties stood alone and calm down where its lower end had rested. The *Sarah* slid rapidly into the current, and there was a great hissing and churning as bells rang and she slowed, and turned, and straightened out into midstream. Then the three beautiful blended tones, long-drawn-out and echoing from the domed hill behind the town, and from the dock an answering chorus of shouts, and big hats waving.

The *Sarah* was even more exciting than the *Jefferson*. From all the adult conversation I listened to, I gathered that we were lucky to catch her on this last trip, that she was the queen of the fleet, that her captain "knew the river," that she "had the best food." She was, it seemed to me, enormous, both long and broad, and with a great space up front on the main deck, under the upper deck, where everyone gathered when there was anything interesting outdoors, and inside, a large "saloon" all done up in green plush and white paneling and gold trimming, like a drawing room in a fairy-tale palace. Besides this there was a card room, where the men gathered, and a ladies' lounge, where the women sat with their needlework and their talk.

To me, and to the two little boys about my own age who were the only other children on board, the card room and the big deck were the more interesting places. And here we first came in touch with the early Alaskan's attitude toward all children. Children were rare; they were a symbol of everything that many of these men had given up in heeding the call of gold and adventure; they were precious individuals. Out on the deck there were always two or three men eager to play hide-and-seek with us, with shouts and merry antics, swinging themselves about the steel poles which held up the upper deck above us. And inside we were allowed to sit beside someone at the Solo table, and play with the chips while the game went on, and because Daddy knew these men and their big hearts, we children were not forbidden any of these joys.

Life was almost more interesting than one could bear. Every day there were stops, at wood camps when the *Sarah* had to take on the many cords of birch and spruce that kept her huge boiler going. Daddy took me and the little boys ashore to walk about a bit, among the long stacks of wood cut in four-foot lengths; to watch the Indian deckhands so cheerfully going up and down the wide plank into the boiler room of the *Sarah* with their trucks loaded, racing down with a shout and a laugh with an empty truck, straining up the slant with a full one, still smiling. Life seemed a big happy game for everybody in that land. We saw red squirrels in the thick woods behind these wood piles, and sometimes had time to pick a handful of bright red low-bush cranberries before the *Sarah* sounded a short blast which meant her appetite was satisfied for now.

There were Indian villages. A row of tiny log cabins in a straggly line atop a cut bank, backed by the forest, and down below the bank, usually, on the little strip of beach, all the village dogs, chained to stakes, howling their loudest at the approach of the steamer, for it meant food thrown out from the galley for them to fight over.

Sometimes the *Sarah* pulled in to these villages to let off some prospector or trapper going into the far back country for the winter. One of these I remember well. He was called Red Rodgers, a tall, lusty, loud-voiced extrovert with flaming red hair and a long beard. His few boxes of provisions had been quickly wheeled down the plank and onto the shore, but he himself carried his gold pan and pick and shovel and with a great shout leaped from the gangplank onto the beach, and turned to shout a few last lusty, cheery words to friends aboard as the *Sarah* slipped out into the current. Behind him, black spruces stood out against a gold sunset which somehow looked cold. Even then, in my child's mind, I wondered: Did he feel a bit sad, too, as the big white ship slid away downstream?

Everybody went ashore at the towns—Eagle, with the beautiful hills near by; Circle, atop a high bank, a cluster of log buildings where not long before had been a tent city of ten thousand. We were there in the evening in a misty rain; the wide freight plank and the warehouse of the Northern Commercial Company were hung with kerosene lanterns so the freight could be unloaded. We were in the United States now, and the Law was not a beautiful red-and-blue uniform and a strong impassive face, but a jovial round face, a hearty voice, heavy brown woolen trousers, a bright plaid shirt—the U.S. Deputy Marshal. He and his pretty wife came to take us to their bright log-cabin home, and she laughed at Mother's city toe-rubbers: "Those are cheechako rubbers—they won't help you much up here!"

The two little boys and I would have gone happily on and on into the future aboard the *Sarah*; it was a perpetual birthday party. Shining white tablecloths, gleaming silver, white-coated waiters urging all kinds of goodies onto our plates. We all must have had stomachs of iron. We were even allowed to stay up sometimes for the "midnight lunch," which was served at ten in the evening. And at every town, our sourdough friends were eager to buy candy or anything else at the trading posts. My coat pocket bulged with lemon drops.

But one day in warm yet crisp September sunshine, the *Sarah* reached Tanana, where the river of that name poured a wide flood into the Yukon. From here on down to the sea the Yukon would truly be a great river, and the *Sarah* could push five barges of freight ahead of her if need be. Here those who were traveling on downriver to St. Michael and Nome and the Outside must say good-by to the rest of us, and we must say good-by to wonderful *Sarah* and go aboard the *Schwatka*, which was not really so tiny, but looked like a midget beside *Sarah*.

But the *Schwatka* had pleasure for a child which made up for her small size. It was cozy; there was only one small "saloon," and everyone gathered there. Though I had sadly waved good-by to the two little boys, who were staying in Tanana, where their father was employed at the army fort there, Fort Gibbon, some of the good sourdough friends were still aboard and always ready to play games and tell me stories (and how I wish I remembered the stories!). I was invited by the captain up into that mystical place, the pilothouse, from which I could watch the whole river at once, and the deckhands working, and the Huskies tied on the bow, and the man taking the soundings, hour after hour. For now we were in a different river world—a river swift and swirling and carrying a great load of silt and now in its autumn low-water stage, with long sand bars nearly all the way, on one side or the other.

Here river navigation was a fine and definite art. There was a certain expert sweep of the sounding pole, a certain drone to the voice: "Five" and a pause—"Five" and a pause—"and a half four"—getting more shallow—"Four" and a pause—"and a half three." And here the face would be lifted to the pilothouse. What was next? A bell, and a slowing of the engines, and the pilot leaning out the window, looking. And sometimes an awful shuddering thump. We were on the bar! Always at this point Daddy took me down out of the pilothouse. I realize now it must have been to allow the officers free rein in their language as they wrestled with the river. Sometimes they could reverse and slide off. Sometimes they sent a crew in a small boat to the other side, or to some point on the bank, to sink a great timber called a deadman; a cable was attached to the timber, and the freight winch would begin to whine, and slowly, so slowly, the *Schwatka* would be pulled off into deeper water and we could go on again for a spell.

Slow travel, in the Alaska of 1911, provided plenty of time for books and games and paper dolls, for dressing and undressing the brown teddy bear; for visiting the galley and watching the baker rolling out pies and cookies; for peering down into the engine room to watch the play of the long shaft attached to the paddle wheel, sliding forward, knuckling back, terrifying, fascinating—but so long as we heard the chuff and whoosh of that wheel, we knew all was fine, and I know, to this day, of no more soothing, competent, all-is-well sound.

To Mother, arriving in Fairbanks must have been fraught with all kinds of wondering and half fears; she must have been feeling very far away from all she had known. To me, it was just more excitement and more new faces, and new conversation to listen to, often quite interesting.

As it was the fall of the year, there wasn't enough water for the *Schwatka* in the Chena Slough, the small tributary of the Tanana on which Fairbanks had been built. So at the little village of Chena, twelve miles below the town, passengers and freight had to be loaded onto the intrepid Tanana Valley Railroad. Yes, a real train, a real engine, two cars full of people now old friends, reaching the end of a three-week journey together. Even when the train came to the end of its twelve-mile journey, we were not yet at the end of ours, for the main town was across the slough, and horse-drawn carts were at the station to meet the train. So was "Dad" Shaw, owner of the very respectable hotel of the town, the Shaw House, where Daddy had been living and where we were now welcomed as part of the family. There was a big lobby, full of men who all knew Daddy; there were some friendly women too, for on Sunday nights it was a custom with many families to take dinner at the spotless and cheerful Shaw House dining room. Some of the sourdoughs of the journey were staying here too.

Yet when Mother tucked me into a single bed in Daddy's high-ceilinged room, I felt a bit strange. What were the captain and the cook and all the rest on the *Schwatka* doing now? And how empty and quiet the little lounge must be. And where, by now, was the *Sarah*?

V. SWANSON

80 miles NW of Juneau, 1917

"COLD WEATHER NEARLY ALL MONTH OF JANUARY. LYNX ROBBED
MY MEAT CACHE UP RIVER. SALT AND TEA BUT ONCE A DAY.
GRADUALLY GETTING WEAKER."

*In the summer of 1918, two trappers working out of Dry Bay
came upon a lonely cabin in the woods. In the cabin was the
dead body of a man and the diary he had kept through the previous winter.*

The diary was first published in 1940 in A Guide to
Alaska, *part of the Federal Writers' Project series.*

The complete diary follows.

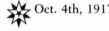 Oct. 4th, 1917. Getting sick packing, now looking for
                                      camping place. Cold in the lungs with a
                                      high fever.
          6th. Less fever, less pain, but getting weak.
          7th. Feeling better but very weak.
          9th. Getting a little stronger.

Oct. 10th. Going to build a house. Will not be able to pull canoe up this fall, got to wait for the ice.

13th. Shot a glacier bear.

14th. Shot a goat.

17th. House finished.

18th. Taking out some traps.

20th. Made a smoke house.

21st. Shot one goat.

25th. Shot one lynx.

27th. Shot a wolf and a bear cub.

28th. Winter has come. Strong wind, two feet of snow.

Nov. 4th. Shot one lynx.

6th. Made one pair of bearskin pants.

8th. Sugar is all gone.

13th. Made two pair of moccasins.

18th. Finished one fur coat of bear, wolf, and lynx.

21st. Finished one sleeping bag of bear, goat, blankets, and canvas. Rain for several days.

22nd. Left eye bothers me. Shot one goat.

26th. Shot one lynx while eating breakfast.

27th. Made one pair of bearpaw snowshoes.

Dec. 1st. Getting bad. Cold for several days, river still open.

4th. River raised six feet in 24 hours.

6th. Slush stiffening, slowly making ice.

7th. The wind is so strong that you can't stand upright. River froze except a few riffles. Too much snow and too rough for sleighing. Snow getting deeper now.

15th. Very cold and strong wind, impossible to be out without skin clothes.

19th. Snowing but still very cold. Riffles up in the bend still open. Can't travel. Don't believe there will be ice a man can run a sleigh over this winter. Very little grub, snow too deep and soft for hunting goats. Stomach balking at straight meat, especially lynx.

Dec. 21st. Shot a goat from the river.

25th. Very cold. A good Christmas dinner. Snow getting hard. River still open in places above camp.

26th. Broke through the ice. Skin clothes saved the day.

31st. Finished new roof on the house. One month of cold weather straight. Last night and today rain. Stomach getting worse.

Jan. 8th, 1918. River open as far as can be seen. Health very poor.

12th. Lynx moving down the river one or two a night; no chance to catch them.

15th. Goats moving out of reach. Using canoe on the river.

16th. One lynx. Weather getting mild.

20th. Rain today.

22nd. One lynx.

28th. One goat, been cold for a few days, no ice on river.

Feb. 1st. Cold weather nearly all month of January. Lynx robbed my meat cache up river. Salt and tea but once a day. Gradually getting weaker.

5th. Colder weather, feeling very bad. Just able to take care of myself.

10th. Milder, feeling very bad. Heavy fall of snow.

15th. Good weather continues, feeling some better.

24th. More snow. Living on dry meat and tallow.

26th. Shot one goat from the river.

Mch. 2nd. Shot one goat.

11th. Starting for Dry Bay, believing the river open. Out about one hour and struck ice. Can't go either way. Too weak to haul the canoe. Snow soft, no game here.

Mch. 25th.	Trying to get to the house. River is frozen in places, and rising. The sleigh is now only three miles from there, but open river and perpendicular cliffs keep me from getting any farther. At present cannot find anything to eat here. Eyes are getting bad.
28th.	Eyes can't stand the sun at all. Finest kind of weather.
Apr. 1st.	Got to the house with what I could carry. Wolverenes have been here eating my skins, robes, and moccasins, old meat, and also my goatskin door. They tried to run me last night, came through the stovepipe hole showing fight. Heavy fall of snow. Canoe and some traps down the river about five miles, close to Indian grave mark. Camp about halfway.
3rd.	Still snowing. Cooking my last grub, no salt, no tea.
4th.	Shot one goat, using all but three of my shells. Can't see the sights at all.
7th.	Wolverene working on camp below carrying away my things. Ate part of my bearskin pants. Packed the old .30-.30 out into the brush. Eyes getting worse again, don't even stand the snow.
10th.	Wolverenes at my bedding and one snowshoe. In the tent, getting shaky in the legs. A five-mile walk a big day's work.
12th.	Seen a fox track today. Birds are coming too. Fine weather.
15th.	The no-salt diet is hitting me pretty hard. Eyes are getting worse, in the bunk most of the time.
17th.	Rain yesterday and today.
20th.	Finest weather continues again, cooking the last grub, got to stay in bunk most of the time — my legs won't carry me very far. My eyes are useless for hunting, the rest of

my body also useless. I believe my time has come. My belongings, everything I got I give to Joseph Pellerine of Dry Bay; if not alive, to Paul Swartzkoph, Alsek River. April 22, 1918. V. Swanson.

ANCHORAGE AND BEYOND

CONSTANCE HELMERICKS

Newlyweds head north: Anchorage, 1941

"A NEIGHBOR IN THE NEXT CABIN CAME OVER AND OFFERED TO
LEND US A COUPLE OF HUNDRED FROM HIS POCKET TO GET
STARTED, WHICH WAS OUR FIRST INITIATION INTO THE ALASKAN
TRADITION, BUT WE DECLINED HIS OFFER. INSTEAD, WE LIVED
ON OATMEAL AND TURNIPS UNTIL THE FIRST PAY CHECK CAME."

Constance Helmericks knew the north well.

*Married in Arizona in 1941, she and her new husband set
out for Seward in southeastern Alaska, and later settled farther
north, in Anchorage. In 1944, with a canoe they had built themselves, they moved on to the real north, Alaska's Brooks Range,
above the Arctic Circle. They built a cabin and settled in for
nearly a year, then moved farther north again along the Colville
River until they reached the edge of the Arctic Ocean, where
they lived with Eskimos. The whole adventure lasted more than
two years.*

*Connie, as she was known, began writing about their north-
ern travels, and her first book,* We Live in the Arctic *(written by
her but published with a dual byline), appeared in 1947. The
Helmerickses quickly became celebrated as Arctic explorers and
experts; they lectured widely and were the subjects of a cover
story in* Life *magazine that same year. Two more books about
their Alaskan adventure,* Our Summer with the Eskimos *and*
Our Alaskan Winter, *followed in 1948 and 1949.*

The couple had returned home to settle in Arizona by the time their daughter Jean was born, but they went back to Alaska often, with their young daughter, to the cabin they had built on the Alatna River in the Brooks Range. After Connie was divorced, she and Jean and a younger daughter, Ann, settled in Arizona once again. But not permanently.

In 1965 and 1966, when Jean was thirteen, Connie took her and Ann off to northern Canada, where they spent two years canoeing the Peace, Slave, and Mackenzie rivers as far as the Arctic Ocean. Connie told that story in her seventh book, Down the Wild River North, *published in 1968.*

Never content to sit still for very long, Connie and her two daughters made a very different kind of trip a few years later — thousands of miles by car across the empty spaces of Australia. That trip was chronicled in Australian Adventure, *published in 1971. And at the time of her death in 1987, Connie was working on still another book, this one about her travels in Central America.*

THE MOTOR OF THE BLUE AND WHITE, six-passenger Lockheed turned over slowly as we taxied down the rough field. The pilot turned us around. At last the moment had come. Now we were rushing forward, nose down, tail up, gathering more speed at each moment. The passengers sat very straight in their seats. None would settle back and relax until we were in the air. But now the ground magically sank below us, and the snow-capped mountains of Resurrection Bay, the flaming Oriental poppies and the falling strawberry blossoms and the wee delicate forget-me-nots of full summer in Seward, Alaska, faded into a dream.

It all started for us when we were twenty-one. It might have happened while we were lingering over a Coke in the college drugstore, or meeting between classes or walking side by side along the pleasant, palm-bordered walks of the campus. Bud was wearing the loose shirt and penciled "cords" that the Engineers wore and I was in some sort of peasant swing dress, you may be sure. And we both dreamed of going to a lot of far places.

Dreams are thin things spun of air. We told everybody that we were going to go to Alaska (since that was far away!) as soon as we were married. My sorority sister and her fiancé were going to South America at that time. Everybody was going to do something unusual.

There were a few slight deviations from the trail for us, but actually at twenty-three we were married, and we left an hour after the ceremony for Seattle, the Inside Passage, and points north. It was 1941.

We had no job waiting for us in Alaska, and just what we were going there for is hard to tell. Perhaps, because we had talked about it so much, we just had to get out of town.

The early May winds, as we stood on deck watching the gulls, were cold. Even Seattle in summer had been the coldest place I had ever known, after the burning desert of the Southwest. The wheeling gulls looked cold, we thought, and we wondered why, fanning themselves through the air as they did and exposing their naked underwings and their poor bare feet, they did not turn into icicles then and there. At ten o'clock at night the cold sun sank far in the north; then we watched the endless darkened islands slide by on either hand, and jingled the sparse change in our pockets, wondering where we would go and what we would do when we reached Alaska. The lights of the warm interior of our steamboat twinkled on the water, and the sounds of music for dancing drifted out and were swallowed suddenly in darkened fjords. Some of the near-by mountain cliffs rose 15,000 feet straight up from the sea. I said to myself: "This is what you have been waiting for all your life. This is adventure. This is it." But we were on our own now, and couldn't turn back if we wanted to. We didn't have the passage back. We knew now, after two years of being bitten by the "Alaska Bug," that Alaska would exact her toll for what she gave. She would retain us for a little while on this detour—yes, longer than we had expected. To see the sights we wanted to see in the way we wanted to see them meant still further waiting and working and becoming Alaskans.

Our fellow passengers on the steamboat *Yukon* were men

on contract for labor for the new government defense projects. We had sensed vaguely that there was something stirring in Alaska, but just what we did not then know. But Alaska is changing and will never be isolated again: the "Outside" will be close to modern-minded pioneers. All but the most blind are forced to see that something altogether new and momentous is at hand. For the first time in seventy-three years, once again Alaska is at the end of an old era and the beginning of a new, like it or not.

There were a few married women, probably no single woman, on the boat, and I realized suddenly one day that there were no tourists among them. We were soon to become used to the inequalities in the population, and would almost regard it as in the normal sphere of things that the proportion of white males over twenty-one to white females of the same age group should be so different from the proportion in any other place we had seen.

Sailing the sheltered inland seas, we were wide-eyed as the vessel threaded the islands of the Alexander Archipelago. Somewhere, at the docks of some cannery long forgotten, I caught the biggest codfish of anybody on the trip.

The capital of Alaska, Juneau, was perched precariously at the foot of the mountains which threatened to push it into the sea. In this it was like several towns along this glacier-fronted coast, although it had a rainbow over it shining through a snowstorm on the peaks. But we knew at a glance that we would not want to live at the little governmental town. And it lay much, much too far south.

Cutting across the Gulf of Alaska we now left land behind us with one last glimpse of the great snowy Mt. Fairweather, over 15,000 feet tall, seventy miles away across the blue, rolling sea. Porpoises followed us.

We had a sort of great-uncle who was somewhere in Alaska. Uncle Fred was a legend. He was an Alaskan sourdough, who had run away from his home in the East to follow the sea. He had had his own fleet of fishing boats, and lost them, some said, when Ketchikan was the wickedest port on the Pacific, and he was a rough companion. It was even rumored that he had been a rum runner at one time. For the past twenty-five years, at least, he had resided in Alaska, and nobody had heard much of him.

When we docked at the end of our week's run at the long-shoring town of Seward, on Resurrection Bay, we fished out a crumpled piece of paper and went to look for Fred. Inquiry revealed that our Uncle Fred was a much-liked person by the many who knew him; that he was nearing the retirement age in the Army Signal Corps, the Territory's telegraph system; that he was now located at Anchorage, 115 miles away. Consequently we now expended a few of our remaining dollars on tickets, and embarked on the Alaska Railroad.

The train climbed slowly through forests of dwarfed arctic spruce, up over a 2,000-foot divide, and over receding Spencer Glacier. It tunneled through snowsheds over which spring freshets poured. It wound around and underneath itself in a loop which is perhaps the most scenic in the world, but we learned that not only was it in a bad state of decay which would entail several million dollars for repairs, but that it would be an inviting target to enemy saboteurs as well. Therefore another line was being built to a new port of entry, Whittier on Portage Bay, which cut off fifty miles of needless tracks. Civilians thought that the town of Seward was dying; doomed for the future.

Everybody should have an Alaskan sourdough uncle. We recall that our Uncle Fred nearly fainted when he saw us—for if anything could surprise him at his stage of life it was the sight of his great-nephew Bud arrived in this outpost of Alaska with a new bride. It seemed Fred knew he possessed many nephews, relations, and the like, but true to the type of the old-time Alaskan, the passing years had found him with less and less to say to any of them. It was all so different here from what they were used to outside. He had sent a brown bear hide and gifts of moccasins, but on returning once had found them relegated to the barn, unwanted. He had sent somebody a case of Cordova salmon and fancy minced razor clams, but his only reply had been a rebuke about forgotten postage—an oversight on the part of a messenger. Fred sent the postage. He had sent a nephew a hundred-dollar bill on his graduation from high school, but had received no reply.

Always game, however, to blow a few dollars on a man just for the satisfaction of observing humanity, Fred had replied with encouragement to Bud's general letter of inquiry two years ago. Yes, by all means come to Alaska. It was the only place to be. "But advise you not to get married, for it is better to get a stake ahead."

As what's done can't be undone, however, and we were married, Fred gave us his bed gladly and slept on a mattress on the floor of the kitchen. After a week, because Fred knew the pioneers of Anchorage, we were able to rent a cabin of our own.

Anchorage, lying on Knick Arm off of Cook Inlet, and incidentally due north of the Hawaiian Islands, was at this time the largest city in Alaska. There is no port in Anchorage because of forty-foot tides and the fact that shallow Cook Inlet is choked with ice for many months of the year. Anchorage had been a railroad town, born around 1915. By 1941 it boasted the most northern golf course in the world (very rough), a country-club swimming resort (very brief season), and the longest stretch of straight highway in Alaska, which led fifty miles inland to the town of Palmer, Matanuska Valley, and to the outlying mines in the Talkeetna Range. People had their automobiles brought up by rail from Seward just to drive them around town, gaily smashing them and beating them into wrecks within six months' time, as a rule. The road to Matanuska was like a washboard. But there were more cars at Seattle and plenty of money with which to buy them.

Because of the thousands pouring into the section around Fort Richardson and Elmendorf Field, people were living in tents and garages, and buying one-room, cardboard shacks without plumbing for $1,500 in order to have a roof overhead. To a depression-bred generation, the newcomers, it looked at first as though one could not afford to eat. Anchorage was a real frontier boom town, twentieth-century style, leading the procession of the many boom towns which were presently to pop up at quite remote points all over the earth.

Most of the newcomers, or cheechakos, came to Anchorage to make money and get out as soon as possible. Some were tough customers, the fly-by-night realtors not the least among them. Twice a month, when pay day rolled around at the Fort, certain well-dressed, prosperous-looking strangers suddenly appeared in the streets. These were the professional gamblers from Seattle, or Kodiak. Certain women who stepped from planes always had accommodations waiting for them although the wives of the town could find no suitable place to stay. This created quite a disturbance among the wives, who were sometimes forced to put up signs by their front doors: "Private Home." Vice was well organized from Seattle, two thousand miles away.

Grade school and high school were overcrowded and there was a rise in delinquency. The muddy streets thronged with strangers, few of whom ever got much acquainted with each other. Many were burdened with little children and were lonely and homesick. Some were Army wives in slacks and colored sandals, wishing, no doubt, that Anchorage was Atlantic City.

Soldier boys from home commenced to appear in great numbers. They resided at first in a tent city, which was soon to outnumber Anchorage itself in population. Everywhere one looked, Alaska was in uniform now. Congress had appropriated $200,000,000 for its defense against invasion.

Some very fine United Service Organization clubhouses, built by the boys themselves, sprang up in several Alaskan towns, and the USO Building became a much-needed focal point for community activities as a whole. Alaska wives, long dominated by an overpowering numerical masculinity and long suffering from the lack of amusement places for themselves (although there were twenty-eight rough board bars in every downtown block, so to speak), now surged forth in search of war work. The husbands as a whole were antagonistic to the policies of the USO, usually believing in the old-fashioned policy of "Let the soldiers keep to themselves." It was the women who put the USO on its feet in Alaska, as perhaps everywhere. Alaska women were great readers of the magazines and, while frequently married to slightly antisocial Alaskan men, they watched avidly the doings of their contemporaries in the States.

Among the population should also be mentioned an essential element which the newcomers saw little of in the boom towns, although they were there and had made their homes there for thirty years. These were the old-timers or pioneers.

They consisted of the Scandinavian stock of Swedes, Norwegians, and Finns; the aristocracy of the railroad staff, who at one time set the social pace in these parts; and the old people. The Outsiders didn't even know of their existence, but people past forty made up a considerable part of the Territory's population. Fred said in the old days one could see little clusters of pioneers standing and talking on the street corners in Anchorage. They had names like Moose John, Two-Story John, Benzine Bill, Horizontal Bill, Montana Bess, Alaska Nellie, Stucco Johnson, Herring Pete—names that caressed the ear and gave even to the heart of the uninitiated a strange nostalgia. But southeastern Alaska and the coast towns had changed remarkably in the last twenty years. The pioneers either died or moved away. Some of them crawled into their shells and didn't think much of the changes that were coming. Such is always the case when a change comes. The old gives way to the new only with great resistance, and sometimes personalities are broken in the process.

For that whole first year, a period of devoted and awful labors, we newlyweds lived in Anchorage in a log cabin. Water was pumped and carried from a complaining community pump (eighty-seven strokes for two buckets) over paths muddy in summer, icy in winter. It was carried out the same way and dumped from an unlovely slop bucket behind the house after it had been used. Although the city authorities harassed the landlords, neither materials nor labor was available to put in sanitary facilities—well, not until perhaps next year. Meanwhile people had to live some place. They crowded together, not in nice clean log cabins like Abe Lincoln lived in, but in sagging, hastily built log cabins with cardboard bedrooms attached, or in downtown apartments over the groceries which were veritable firetraps. There was no one available to build houses, as all were employed at the "base." The few men who cut and hauled wood to burn in the wood stoves charged eighteen dollars the cord, pile and split it yourself. It was a hard life—the crowding together as in tenements, and yet the loneliness and lack of friends; the complete lack of any place to go or anything to do for recreation; the utter sameness and drabness of life for all when the husband was working the fifty-six-hour week or the seventy-two-hour week without a single day off in the year. Yes, that is the way defense bases were built in Alaska in the emergency. Man after man who couldn't "take it" quit and returned to the States, while the next boat brought a new crowd, willing to have their chance. Even today there is no room for weaklings in Alaska. Alaska has also long been known as a great enemy of marriage, which accounts in part for the large groups of drifting, unattached men.

A neighbor in the next cabin came over and offered to lend us a couple of hundred from his pocket to get started, which was our first initiation into the Alaskan tradition, but we declined his offer. Instead, we lived on oatmeal and turnips until the first pay check came.

Bud first hefted hundred-pound cement sacks as a day laborer on an airfield construction job; but soon he had become a semiskilled sheet-metal worker and had a lot of fun handling iron, copper, and the tin for which Outside people were saving their toothpaste tubes.

Every generation must meet its destiny—the destiny of war. We were just being born during the last war, along with millions of Greek and Russian and German and Japanese and Hindu babies. Now all the babies were grown up, carefully trained in the social systems of their forebears, most of whom were dead and forgotten by this time, but their vicious systems lived on, or perhaps were even invented over again by the new generation.

It was hard for me to understand many things at the time I was married. I only knew that, having got to Alaska, I didn't like it. This, incidentally, is usually the case with women. I enjoy pleasure and luxury and have never been a particularly brave person or a particularly realistic one. It didn't affect me to know that women before me had pioneered to an extent that was inconceivable in its endurance. I was a modern woman. I could dismiss all those others with the wave of a hand. The way I thought about Alaska, why—I thought it would be nice to take the roses without the thorns.

But Alaska wasn't like that, isn't like that yet. There were none of our crowd from school to applaud the adventuring heroes now. We doubted if any of the crowd would like Alaska very well actually, except through our enthusiastic letters.

Bud is a farmer's son. He was better constituted to slide easily into the Alaskan scene. He had battled his own way since he was fourteen. In addition to working his way through school he had managed to see all of the States and parts of Mexico and Cuba, and incidentally meet a great many different people under vastly different circumstances. He was used to being alone. As he pounded copper nails bare-handed up on the roofs of the barracks that winter, his mind was with the snowclouds being whirled two thousand feet into the air from the peaks of the untrodden Chugach Mountains. Or, almost unmindful of the cold, he would wonder how the mystic green of summer would look upon those same slopes. Like many boys and young men, Bud had always cherished a desire to wander freely and unhampered through at least some of the great wilderness of the Americas as well as of other countries and continents. We agreed in this—so had I. Bud at least was well qualified to do it.

My contemplations of life in Alaska as the months passed disclosed to me presently that it wasn't only the last generation who had been uprooted and who had suffered and endured. We had thought our generation exempt. It wasn't. I began to see that I was not the only one who was undergoing or who would soon undergo a great change in methods of living.

The world was moving on, and at an accelerated pace. Following the Pearl Harbor incident the United States declared war on Japan on December 8, 1941. Germany declared war on the United States in alliance with Japan and Italy. England had been fighting for months now turning into years. The magnitude and speed of the process of adjustment to this Second World War on the part of all peoples and nations were inescapable. The activities all over the country were revolutionary in scope. They pointed two ways: to northern Europe and North Africa; and northwest through Alaska to the Orient and Japan. The legendary apathy of some of the Alaskan old-timers was being shaken. The infiltration of global war through and across Alaska, and the subjugation of Japan by the united nations from eastern Russia, would possibly necessitate a fusion of Occident and Orient which would require all of their united power and strength.

And we, insignificant, young, and very interested, were now sitting on the direct route of the main west-to-east pathway to Asia whether via the Alaska Peninsula and the Aleutians direct from the little town of Seward, or by the natural passes of the mouths of the Yukon! Alaska was the spot of the day.

Citizens of Alaska had followed Governor Ernest Gruening's advice to a large extent. The outbreak of the war found every cabin with about a year's food staples on hand, stocked as only people like Alaskans know how to do. Radios which previously had tuned chiefly to Tokyo and Mexico City, easier of contact than most stations in the States, now enjoyed in Anchorage the improved sending and receiving facilities which hooked them onto the big networks with the favorite programs that the rest of the Americans habitually enjoy—this being one of the growths, no doubt, of the war, and a real blessing. It serves to remind one of how isolated, psychologically and physically, Alaska was before the war.

Evacuation of Army wives and children and all dependents who were not residents began. There was wailing and gnashing of teeth at Anchorage by those who did not want to go. Yet for others it was a free ride, and some promptly came back after they were sent out. Many women suddenly got jobs so they would be classified as self-supporting persons vital to the lifeline of the Territory.

An interesting local phase of the war situation was the liquor traffic, which continued at increased tempo for some time. Ships docking at Seward carried hundreds of tons of beer and whisky, showing that the powerful liquor syndicates, too, were taking the governor's advice and stocking up for the future. Sometimes there was not a fresh vegetable or any other food in from Seattle because the liquor took so much room. The minority group of the housewives raged futilely to the grocers, who could do nothing about it as their orders had not been filled. Alaskans have always been good customers for liquor—a gallon of whisky per capita per month, somebody said, which is a guess. It's probably more. The Alaska Steamship Company's rates for passengers and supplies became necessarily very high as a result of the dangers of navigating the now unmarked passages of the islands wherein enemy submarines might lurk. The Company demanded a convoy, but was presently relieved of the situation when the Navy took over for the duration.

Bud and I, having survived the rigors of the long winter, were transferred, via slow freight, to Seward, there to work on Fort Raymond. That is, Bud was working on the Fort. I still had the dishes. Uncle Fred, now at Seward, finding that there were no houses to rent, bought a house and installed us in it with him temporarily. We had now resided in the Territory a year, and we were Alaskans. Digging our family bomb shelter, according to Army regulations, we kept this fact in mind and were thankful indeed.

We had been in Alaska a year when we felt we could make the break to see some of the sights which we felt we had truly earned. For instance, we had slept in sleeping bags all of the first year, just waiting to go camping, and had camped in our own home, such as it was. Now it was time for the real thing.

It was full summer in Seward when Bud approached Mr. Cox, his boss: "I've been thinking of going up to the Yukon for a while."

"The Yukon?"

"Yes, you know my wife and I haven't seen it."

"Neither have I," said Mr. Cox.

"We have read that it may be an important place now."

"Is that so?"

"And so—well, we'd just like to take a vacation and see it."

"Hold up your hands for me to see."

Bud did so, palms up and even, before Mr. Cox's kindly eye. The hands quivered uncontrollably, ever so slightly.

"Not bad, for a year," said Mr. Cox, who was nearing seventy himself and who knew the sheet-metal business thoroughly. "Well, of course you've got a month coming anyway. A vacation will do you good. See how you like it up there, if they let you go. By the way, how are you going? Going to take one of them tourist river cruises?"

"Nope. There aren't any river cruises running these days. We wouldn't want to go on one anyway. It's to be a canoe trip."

"Canoe trip! I wish I was going myself. Well, good luck to you!"

"Good luck to you, sir!"

Bud appeared at home and went immediately to the back yard. There by the bomb shelter, he was joined by myself and Uncle Fred in front of a long wooden frame erected just over the carrots and beets. Upon the frame these two weeks past had arisen magically under our hands the form of a canoe, which was to be our only home for the months to come.

JONATHAN WATERMAN

Denali: The summit in winter

"DREAMING WITH MY EYES WIDE OPEN, I SAW US STEP-KICKING
AND AX-PUNCHING IN RHYTHM UP THE SUMMIT RIDGE, HIGHER
THAN ALL OF THE CONTINENT, HIGHER THAN BIRDS FLY, HIGHER
THAN RAIN OR GRASS OR ANY BEING OF NORTH AMERICA."

*The Indians called the mountain simply "the great one" or "the
big one" in various languages. In the summer of 1896, several
parties of prospectors happened to get a look at the summit of
the mountain, which is frequently wreathed in clouds. Later,
comparing their observations, they estimated its height at about
twenty thousand feet. The leader of one of those parties named
the mountain Denali, which means "home of the sun" in the language of the Athabascan Indians, but renamed it Mount McKinley in the fall of that year to honor his political hero, William
McKinley, who was hoping to be elected to the presidency in November.*

*In 1917, Congress created Mount McKinley National Park.
In 1932, the park was enlarged to cover 3,030 square miles. In
1980, in deference to popular usage, it was officially renamed
Denali National Park. Today, the park covers an immense
7,369.9 square miles, much of it high enough to be above the
tree line.*

The prospectors' early estimate of Denali's height was very close. It is actually 20,320 feet above sea level, with two peaks. The north peak was first reached by climbers in 1910, the south in 1913. The idea of challenging Denali is pretty daunting, partly because its top two-thirds is permanently covered with snow and partly because a simple statement of its height as 20,320 feet tells only part of the story.

Denali is indeed the tallest mountain in North America. But it's more than that. Denali rises fully 18,000 feet from its base to its peak, and that is the highest uplift of any mountain on earth. (Forget Everest. Its height is over 29,000 feet, but its rise is a mere 11,000 feet from its base.)

✹ WILL AND I KNEW THAT THE FINEST mountain route in North America had long been a psychological watershed for alpinists. During the 1961 first ascent, Riccardo Cassin and his companions paid dearly. All of the team were frostbitten on the nine-thousand-foot-high Roman nose of granite that unyokes Denali's south face. On the summit they prayed for their deliverance and left a statuette of the Virgin Mary. Riccardo, veteran of numerous epics in the Andes and the Himalaya, returned to Italy with numbed fingertips and close calls burned into his long-term memory.

Six years later, several members of an expedition paid an even steeper toll for the first winter ascent of Denali: One died, and the three who made the top were frostbitten. Art Davidson wrote a book, *Minus 148 Degrees,* titled after the extremes of temperature during their 1967 ordeal. I often defended the team's decision to continue climbing after their companion's death. Certainly the book had been the headiest drug I ever absorbed as a sixteen-year-old. But after meeting the winter climbers, I thought it strange that they never climbed together again. It appeared that climbing the mountain in winter—aside from the obvious risks to fingers and toes—could also jeopardize the integrity of a partnership.

From 1971 to 1982, another dozen teams vied for the second winter ascent of Denali; no one even tried Mount Logan. These expedition-style teams stocked camps, dug in during storms, weathered high winds, and grappled with their sanity. Some lost toes; others saw God. Four Swedes bickered and split up. The soloist Johnny Mallon Waterman committed himself to an asylum. No one reached the summit.

We had a few advantages over the 1967 climb. Technology had improved climbing equipment, while changing philosophies allowed us to attempt the technically difficult Cassin Ridge alpine style, with no fixed camps or tedious load relays.

Will applied two tactics to climbing from his track and basketball years at Yale: competition and confidence. Whether at the bottom of a climb or the top of the key, Will shifted into high aerobic gear until the summit was in the bag or the ball was in the net.

In the summer of 1980, Will fell 100 feet into a hidden crevasse below the Cassin and pulled his ropemate to the brink before he stopped. Will climbed out unhurt. They retreated, although Will wanted to finish the route alone. In 1981 I, too, jumped crevasses and listened to avalanches pulverize the glacier during my first stab at the Cassin. My partner and I timorously settled for the easier west rib.

That same year, when I asked the Englishman Roger Mear to join Will and me on Mount Logan, 19,524 feet, I mentioned that the game was not only to climb it but also to get up without blackening fingers or friendships. Roger immediately agreed to go with us.

Roger called undue physical exertion "mindless graft." Nonetheless, following the tradition of the early British explorers, he flung himself on the least-traveled passages of the world. When asked about his "necky" winter climb up the north face of the Eiger, also known as the *nord wand,* he replied with typical understatement: "Right, 'twas a good climb, a wonderful place, you know?"

Roger was irreverent and mischievous. He would ridicule us as we strained at pull-ups or endured ten-mile runs. Will the Ivy Leaguer was initially piqued by Roger the queen's jester: rolling joints, pretending to lose car keys, or sleeping late. But after their uncertain initiation, they soon became an act, wholly complementing one another—and excluding me.

A month before our climb, in January of 1982, I tore ligaments in my ankle but deluded myself by casting it with a stiff double boot. Then the Canadian park authorities denied us permission to climb Logan in winter: "they didn't want to rescue us," they said; we quickly switched to Alaska's Denali. I had nightmares of falling through clouds and cartwheeling over ice cliffs with a flopping ankle. Or the wind would wrench me away from the mountain as the air exploded from my lungs and I wafted into the thin air flatter than paper. I wondered, but never asked, about Roger and Will's dreams. For consolation I returned to my visualizations, and dreaming with my eyes wide open, I saw us step-kicking and ax-punching in rhythm up the summit ridge, higher than all of the continent, higher than birds fly, higher than rain or grass or any being of North America.

For years, Will and I had argued the merits of our plans with anyone who would listen. We said that the southern ridge maximized our exposure to the sun. We told mothers, friends, and lovers—skeptics all—that we would be sheltered from the north winds that buffet the mountain in winter. With the prescience of air-conditioner salesmen badgering Eskimos, we bragged that February and March have the longest days of the dark winter, and we flaunted equipment designs that should keep us warm at sixty below. Most people, including climbers, thought us cracked.

Among ourselves, we reveled in Will's irreverent confidence, Roger's hard-core alpinism, and my willingness to suffer. We were quite willing to push one another to the ends of the earth and agreed to brook no weaknesses. Consequently, when I contracted bronchitis just before leaving, there was no turning back.

On February 17, 1982, we flew onto the Kahiltna Glacier as Will muttered about white beaches in the Caribbean. As we vaulted out of our skiplane, another team barreled into a second plane, so grim-faced after their failed winter ascent that they stared straight ahead, refusing to acknowledge our ebullient waves.

The wind poured a thirty-below-zero chill through my zippers and into my crotch like liquid ice. Since Will and Roger pretended not to notice my coughing, I pretended that the spasms were mere sneezes. True to form, Will strutted around without a hat, remarking on how warm it was; Roger discovered a *Penthouse* stashed in his haulbag by some rude joker.

We set up a tent and promptly snapped a pole. The cold would continue to break stoves and lanterns and zippers and boots and cameras. Even removing a mitten to tie a knot could cost you your fingers. Because cockiness was the only way to disguise the layers of terror in our hearts, we never discussed the cold, which shadowed us like an omniscient being.

Denali's winter mood was completely unlike the more benign and sun-kissed summer pastels. Even the sunset was violent: The orange light was plucked right off the mountain as it pulsed into abrupt nightfall. Unlike the perpetually lit summer climbing season, the sixteen-hour winter nights meant that camp chores began and ended in the dark. That night the Cassin Ridge stretched taut and arrow-straight beneath the rounded summit bow, tinted violet by stars.

In the morning we put our heads down and trudged into the relentless north wind, pulling loaded sleds ten miles toward the Cassin. We made pitiful progress. I coughed and limped behind Will and Roger on the end of the rope, tilting back a bottle of cough syrup and chewing its frozen shards. Images of hot showers, warm beaches, and an ex-girlfriend plagued me like a toothache, while my ankle rode fat and unforgettable in its double-boot cast.

On the third morning our ten-foot-long snowcave tunnel filled in with windblown snow. Feeling a burgeoning morning urgency, I slipped out of my warm sleeping bag and struggled into my climbing suit, bracing myself for the inevitable hell outside. I wormed my way into the tunnel, shoveling and kicking back chunks of snow into our living quarters.

After twenty minutes of burrowing, I poked my head up into a ground blizzard. When I stood, the wind blew me to my knees. Leaning into the gale, I staggered away from the cave and futilely searched for a windbreak. In this nether winter world where fantasy merges with reality, I imagined a toilet flushing; I yanked off my mittens, unzipped my suit, and squatted until that loathsome wind blew me over and I was back in kindergarten: shamefaced, helpless, reduced to tears as I crawled back stinking into the cave. Unwilling to bear witness, Will and Roger promptly exited and performed jumping jacks in the wind while I boiled my underpants and suit, then dried them over the stove.

I had a recurring intuition that I was going to die during the climb. Worse than the specific nightmares of falling, I was now haunted by a diurnal dread that I had stepped away from the living. Discussing my premonition with Will and Roger would only earn their scorn, and they had made it clear that the climb demanded no less than three climbers. If I turned back, Will and Roger would probably be relieved, although our defeat would rest totally on my shoulders. Because I didn't have the courage to confess my fears, I grappled with the premonition constantly.

I wondered how it would be. A brutal but quick fall like Dave Shoemaker's? A painless nodding off from hypothermia? Or maybe I'd wait patiently to meet it while trapped in a crevasse like Chris Kerrebrock. If I could have laid down money, I would have bet that the summit would equal my last day, either in a storm, as in Wilcox's expedition, or with high-altitude illness.

I became the odd man out as Roger and Will became friends. The more they came to know and trust one another, the more I was excluded from decisionmaking, route-finding, and even the nightly philosophical debates in our snowcaves. When I had been strong, my relationship with Will flourished. Now, with a sprained ankle and bronchitis and my consternation about dying (my partners sensed this), Will openly castigated my weaknesses, yelling at me to pack faster, criticizing my route selection up an icefall, and berating me for dropping his water bottle into a crevasse. It now became a dangerous game because I was determined to show Will that I would not give up.

I had rarely risked everything for a dream. Knowing that our modern, soft world has removed us from much of the suffering and physical toil of our forebears, I wanted to harness those remnant genes and live by instinct and nerve endings. In the process, I wanted insight into this magnificent mountain, but I also wanted just once to exploit all my weaknesses, and by stripping myself bare to the mountain, discover of what pith my soul was made. So on the fifth day, I buried all my wimpy thoughts about dying and cut loose from the defeatist moorings of retreat.

One night, Will tried to define the wind. As it whipped and whistled out in the tunnel, he waxed Shakespearean—a subject he had devoted considerable study to as an undergraduate. With a sweeping gesture of his arms he announced that the wind was the breath of God. I never heard anything so false in my life.

As we left the snowcave, two ravens arrived and jumped down into the tunnel. They were looking for food. In Athapaskan stories, the "Great Raven" was the creator of the world. Even in modern times, Athapaskans make prayers to ravens, because as descendants of the Great Raven, Dotson'sa, the birds are purported to carry magic. Just seeing the birds was a good omen, and these ravens had flown a long sixty miles from the nearest forest to our snowcave.

On our fifth night we dug a palatial snowcave, with a customized "quick johnnie" chamber carved into the tunnel. Inside, Will disgustedly swatted at Roger's clouds of burning dope. Roger assured him he would stop once we began climbing.

My bronchitis dried up while optimism warmed us beneath the Cassin. Below the climb, on a wind-protected glacier called the Valley of Death, the sun lulled us into naps, sprawled over avalanche debris, until the cold shadow of Denali brought us awake, shivering. Ten thousand feet above, the wind sounded like storm-driven surf. Its waves crashed and broke over the summit, swirling giant banners of foaming snow over the southwestern face. Our route, however, lay still and taunting.

Early on February 27 we emerged from a snowhole beneath the Japanese Couloir. Roger couldn't get over the *Bergschrund,* so he stood on his pack, reached over the gap, and mantled up. We hoisted the packs, chinned ourselves over, and spurred by the fear of changing weather, we pumped our legs as fast as we could. Our calves ached under the huge packs.

It was impossible to avoid knocking plates of ice onto each

other. When someone in the lead screamed "Ice!" the unhelmeted followers tried to duck beneath their packs. Four hundred feet up, Roger took a hit in the face and swore violently; his dark blood speckled the opaque ice like graffiti.

We swung our axes and kicked our feet repeatedly into the cold belly of the mountain. We were jumpy, nervous, yelling at each other to hurry. My left ankle felt good while frontpointing, but at each flat-footed twist, electrical jolts shot up my leg. I put each jolt into a little green box in my head and quantified the jolt's strength and its prickly texture and its exact relationship to my ankle, and in so doing I drifted far away from my automated climbing movements to a place inside my mind where I hid like a child. Roger and Will both remarked on my "self-absorption," and when they caught my eyes going dreamy and unfocused with the pain, they'd shout at me to climb faster.

We finished the twelve-hundred-foot gully fumbling with our headlamps. The night hung above as if it were the mid-Atlantic becalmed: vast and black and mirror-still. We tied ourselves into pitons and made our beds on a narrow rock shelf, swinging and clomping our feet over the void with great delight. Getting off the avalanche-fired glacier and coming to grips with the climbing felt so nice that we temporarily forgot the business above.

The stove's flames licked at a pot full of ice. Two hours later we slurped down freeze-dried swill, and when Will and Roger hurled my homebaked fruitcake into the void, I feigned indifference. We slept fitfully, wiggling toes and adjusting hoods, ogling the full moon as if it offered the heat of a lover.

Several hours before dawn we started melting ice for tea. Getting out of warm sleeping bags and pulling on frozen boots made us shut our eyes, clench our stomachs, and flutter our breath. Packing up was awkward with mittens, so we would take them off, make an adjustment, then rewarm our fingers in our armpits; our feet felt blocky and sore and distant.

Will and Roger raced without a rope to the east, axes squeaking in the Styrofoam-like snow; I caught up to them as they reached a rock cliff. As Roger led a hundred-foot cliff-band with down-sloping holds, Will and I looked away, cringing as we thought of Roger's seventy-pound pack. His crampons raked the rock like fingernails screeching on a blackboard. After a dutiful curse he was up.

We followed him onto a long ridge that sliced the sky and, to my delight, made the wind hum in subjugation. À *cheval* along this corniced arête, we kicked steps into the snow and ice for hours, weaving around cornices, oblivious to the space beneath. We laughed and taunted one another; I sang at belays. The mountain gave us what we had come for, and as we straddled it and held it and gently kicked it, I loved it more than I have ever loved a mountain before or since.

On such days you can see every snow crystal sparkle; at times I even thought I heard music. Some might say that we had too many endorphins rushing around in our heads or that we were surfing a tsunami and staring down at our own reef of mortality, but those people will never hug sun-warmed granite in subzero cold, gnaw icicles from their mustaches, or hazard that a mountain and its wind have become a living, breathing entity.

Our competitiveness, however, only grew, and the tension surged like a hot current along our climbing rope. If we didn't climb the Cassin quickly, we would have to answer to weather conditions beyond any of our experiences. So, fervently kicking around a cornice, then running across a knife edge, I pulled Roger off his feet behind me; snatches of blasphemy attached to my name blew past me in a fiery breeze. I now felt strong again, ready to match my partners step for step.

That night's campsite was the only flatness of the route. Instead of pitching our tiny tent, we jumped into a crevasse and chopped out a snowcave. Later, bathed in eerie ultraviolet glow, Will and Roger gagged on freeze-dried chili and dumped it into the crevasse's bowels. I forced mine down, hoarding every calorie.

As we slept, the wind gusted and swirled and shook at the cave entrance like a wolf worrying a caribou's flank. By morning our sleeping bags were frosted with snow.

There, at 13,500 feet, the climb became our only focus. We were married, chained, and bonded to Denali because a lesser dedication would have been dangerous luxury. Once we climbed higher, retreating during a winter storm, or even just surviving a storm, seemed unthinkable. We had to get up.

That day the climbing was superb, although strenuous. After stringing moves together across ice-plastered rock, I'd shout, "Boy, that'd be great with light packs!" Roger and Will replied with glowering anxiety on their faces, as if enjoying ourselves wasn't permitted. We clambered over tawny granite and gray ice, pinching rock with one hand, swinging an ax with the other. We rested on ledges, calves burning, chests heaving.

Because we couldn't afford to rest and acclimatize properly, we all had minor altitude illness. It was a question of getting pummeled by a storm, weakening to the cold, and being kited off by the wind versus dealing with headaches, weakness, and loss of appetite. We took the latter course, and if the cold had only tickled before, now we could feel its talons prickling our skin. Fear and dehydration now constipated me.

At the end of our third day of climbing, two weeks into our trip, we chopped a tent ledge into steep ice. Since it was too crowded for three, I built a separate platform with snow blocks and clipped into an ice screw. Then I lit the stove, put on a pot of ice, and hid inside my bag. Gusts of wind blew out the stove, or the pot needed more ice, so I would emerge from my embryonic cocoon, shivering and hating the cold. My fingers turned wooden, and the blood crept back all too slowly as I winced and thrust my icy fingers into my crotch.

When the northern lights first appeared, I dropped the lighter in astonishment. A single ghostly strobe swept the horizon. Then the entire sky filled with tracers. I yelled, nearly knocking off the stove, while Roger opened the tent. Outer space was raining translucent bands of jade and saffron, stealing time and the cold away from us, reeling us beyond the bounds of our banal earth. Dinner somehow got cooked but had no taste; I no longer felt the cold.

The Koyukon or Athapaskan name for northern lights, *yoyakkoyh*, means "pulsing lights in the sky." Legends tell of an ancient man, *Yoyakkoyh Dinaa* (Northern Lights Man), who broke his bow while caribou hunting and later burned up in a fire. When the lights actually illuminate the land, as they did this night on the Cassin, it means that the Northern Lights Man is shooting his arrows into the heavens.

Sleep was elusive, so I gave a running commentary of the colors to Will and Roger, burrowed inside their sleeping-bag wombs while, raving like a lunatic, I studied the flaming heavens.

I knew then that the wind is not God's breath, but Lucifer's; it is the northern lights that are the aura of the Creator. Every man-made monument—from Buddhist temples to cathedral frescoes to paintings stored in the Louvre—will remain forever artifices, forever cast into the shadow of this night and its aurora.

Although Roger and Will kept rolling onto one another inside the tilted tent, their grumbling—like the distant neon glow of Anchorage—was overshadowed by the sublime specter that blazed above and around us. I felt lifted and freed from earthly cares, while my anxiety about the climb was replaced by exhilaration and spiritual awe. Finally, the world was born anew as the northern lights dimmed into dawn.

The days began to blur into one another. We grunted up rock pitches, leaning heads and knees wearily on the ice, always guessing how much farther. I kept looking over my shoulder, wondering when the Great Fly Swatter in the sky would squash us like the insignificant insects we were.

When Roger dislodged a boulder from a long chimney, he screamed "Rock!" and I shrank under my pack. The forty-pound missile crashed a foot away and bounced fifty feet down, then crashed again and gathered more rocks, pounding down until I could no longer see them. Ozone filled my nostrils. I imagined falling with the rocks as if I had become the clipped bird of my nightmares, down past the blinking blue eyes of tottering seracs, feeling the air burst from my lungs as I cartwheeled through wreaths of cloud and bounced off slabs of pebbled granite and slammed into the maws of the crevassed glacier below, finally free.

The falling rock had come and gone in the blink of an eye, but when events move quickly and adrenaline surges through your vessels all day, you stop becoming afraid, as if you are experiencing everything from outside your body. The close call with the rock became a mere fleeting distraction. Roger shouted "Sorry!" and we cheerfully continued up the chimney together.

As the climbing became easier, we grew weaker from the altitude. The thermometer read forty below at 16,500 feet, so Roger hid our "negativity indicator" in the bottom of his pack. That night, Will dispensed sleeping pills—I did not realize that they are respiratory depressants that can predispose climbers to high-altitude pulmonary edema. The Valium allowed me to sleep soundly that night. At this point, I felt strong and healthy, with the exception of a minor headache and my anxiety about spitting in the face of the coldest winter on earth.

We wore every piece of clothing we had, and the wind still came right through our customized suits. I didn't envy Roger, who was harassed by a headache and nausea that evening, taking his turn outside the tent like a dog.

Morning fell loud and clear, but I was stuporous and still groggy from the pill. We packed the rope away and I began step-kicking up a long couloir. Will and Roger followed on my heels, grousing about the distance between my hard-won steps. So I cursed back at them—our tacit mode of climbing communication. Near the couloir's top, I felt dizzy and let them pass.

Stomach acid clung to the back of my throat. After a brief rest, panting over my ice ax, I raced upward with a pulse drumming in my head. Lost in an otherworldly spell, I stepped on a patch of windslab snow, which broke away beneath my sore ankle and started me sliding. The world flashed around me: Distant icefalls and endless peaks and cobalt sky whirled with flying saucer clouds. I jammed in my ax pick and clawed to a stop. Through the fog of my pom-pom head and my now-throbbing ankle, I forced myself to concentrate, then climb. I caught up to them at eighteen thousand feet only because they had stopped. We chopped out a platform, then set up the tent, continually looking over our shoulders at the sky.

Now everything changed. I felt ever conscious of my earlier premonition of death. I performed the only option left: Hidden inside my sleeping bag, I assumed a praying position and whispered, "Please, please, please give us one more good day." In the grip of forces beyond my control, righteousness and prayer had come to my agnostic lips as if I had been born thumping the Bible. Such alchemy is frequently denied afterward, but during the heat of action it can shrink a climber's skin with all the swiftness of a frigid baptism. No one could deny that Denali rose higher and whiter than any church on earth.

We slept deeply, and it dawned miraculously clear.

Up, up we went while the tempo of the drumbeat increased in my head. My feet turned leaden. I could not find a rhythm, let alone go more than one step at a time. Will and Roger yelled for me to hurry up, but I could barely move, so after cursing like brigands, they pulled gear out of my pack to lighten my load. Still, I stumbled back and forth, woozy with Denali's thin air, a derelict destined for the gutter.

Finally, after a paltry thousand feet, they stopped and chopped a platform. When I arrived, their anger hung indelibly, like the calm before a great storm, because they could have gone on to the summit. Bivouacs this high on the mountain are foolhardy, maybe even deadly, because bad weather or high winds would trap us. But short of being dragged, I could not go on.

We piled into the tent. I was too weak to talk. My world spun and dipped and hovered as I held my head and tried to find my breath. Will plied me with tea while Roger looked out the door and analyzed the sky; they took turns looking out the tent, as if something were coming to get us. I'll never forget their wide eyes, the creases on their foreheads, the tension that shook the tent like the wind. Even sick, I knew how worried and scared and tiny we were.

I had destroyed our speedy climbing formula, so I closed my eyes and let sickness spin me away from the bitter realities into unconsciousness. That night the tent became a frozen coffin. We tossed and turned and rolled onto each other throughout the long, long night.

Just before the dawn I dreamed of drowning. I came alive thrashing and lunging for my sleeping-bag zipper, desperate for air. I sat up and realized that fluid had infiltrated my lungs: I had pulmonary edema, and I could steal only panting breaths.

It was here. I wondered if Chris and Dave had seen it so

clearly. Death is so omnipotent that it wins merely by reducing you so low and removing all of your hope and making you so scared that you simply give up and lie back and let it take you. Will's eyes betrayed his fear as though he, too, had identified the beast beating at the door. That day if there was a discussion about leaving me I knew that Roger would never hear of it.

While the stove roared, Will diagnosed my problem as a return of bronchitis and changed his socks. His two big toes were black with frostbite, but when Roger peered closer, Will yanked the socks back on. "Oh," he said, "it's nothing."

Stuffing my sleeping bag seemed to take hours. After breakfast, Will and Roger departed the tent as if leaving a funeral home and began pulling down the tent as I zipped the door shut. I steepled my hands together and prayed for good weather and the strength to survive the coming ordeal; there were no ravens foolish enough to come this high and hear me out.

Will heard me. He knew. "You say something, Jon?"

"No," I said, my breath bubbling. "Nothing."

There was only one option now: Praying wouldn't change anything; I would have to find my own resolve to survive the coming ordeal. Backing down our steep and complex route was never discussed because going up and over was the easiest way down. I followed their steps, oblivious to the sea of clouds I would see later in the photographs, oblivious to the passage of time, and acutely aware of the irrefutable heaviness of gravity that repeatedly sent me sprawling to the snow.

After several hours Will and Roger topped out on the Cassin Ridge, dropped their packs, and strolled the anticlimactic fifty yards to the summit. Roger photographed Will holding up his ice ax and they scurried back to their packs. They were not amused to see me crawling down below.

Will jogged down and relieved me of my pack. Twenty minutes later, I finished crawling to the ridge two hundred feet below the summit. I looked briefly upward, but on this day my success would be measured in survival, not a summit. I could manage only two steps before collapsing over my ax and fighting for the privilege of breathing. The wind was mild but the cold was vivid and, despite wearing three sets of layered mittens, we couldn't touch our metal-topped axes. Somehow it registered that my toes had frozen.

We plungestepped down, and after a dozen strides I was completely winded. Even the descent of Denali's easy route was going to be tough. Roger and Will were too cold to wait, so I urged them onward. After several minutes I caught my breath, although sitting down in the hundred-below-zero windchill didn't improve my mood. I shivered violently.

I had to pace myself. Breathe twice for each step, then rest for ten breaths. Again, again, and again. I forced myself into the rhythm, eyes locked on my feet. It became a revolution not unlike our technique for speedy ice climbing, but I wondered how I could move with such diminished lung capacity. I flaunted the other option continuously, and each time I considered how easy it would be to lie down and let it take me, I berated myself for even considering it. When I gave up on cursing at myself, I deliberately twisted my ankle in my boot and felt the electricity wash over me in a salty wave that lent new definition to our short gift of time on earth with all its requisite pain and abbreviated glory and undefined love. I cried with the pain I inflicted on myself.

My partners watched and waited as long as they could in the cold. They shouted at me in shrill voices, alternately mad and caring, and after Will dispensed a tablet of Dexedrine to me, they left me behind. I swallowed the speed knowing full well it would be mere candy next to the natural adrenaline already being produced by my own body.

At Denali Pass I lay down for a long time, terrified I would even consider giving in to the demon squatting so heavily on my chest. It was a faceless, nameless presence, and just to spite the single greatest temptation I have ever been offered in my life, I contemptuously spat out a frothy green bile from my lungs and forced myself to my feet again. I tripped and tottered alone down the steep traverse known as the Autobahn, notorious for the many German climbers who fell, sped out of control, and wrecked themselves a thousand feet below.

Just before dark, I caught up to Will and Roger at seventeen thousand feet. Roger was curled outside the tent, so I crawled in with Will, thinking they might keep the temptation away if I couldn't. The tent walls shuddered with this awful presence, and inside I didn't bare my skin for more than a few seconds. Even exhausted, I could still enact my preprogrammed warming functions: Brush off snow; remove Gore-Tex suit, mittens, boots; get in bag; dry feet; warm toes with hands. I turned on my headlamp. "Wait a minute," I thought. "White toes! Frostbite?" I massaged my swollen bluish ankle and toes until I fell into a sleep racked by coughing.

Strong winds blew in daylight and clouds as we fixed cocoa in the tent. As Will dressed me ever so condescendingly, he looked me in the eyes and told me I would die if I didn't get down; then he shoved me out into the wind and I stumbled downward as they yanked apart the tent.

The sky darkened. Taking only three or four steps at a time was disheartening, but I thought I might get down. Will easily caught up and passed me while Roger stayed with me, cajoling and coaxing me downward. At 16,200 feet I Batmanned madly down the old fixed ropes, stopping constantly to catch my breath, not sure how much longer I could continue. I tried to downclimb the *Bergschrund* neatly, but in my sickened torpor I fell and landed on my back next to Will. He laughed. I'll never forget his laughter and the emptiness of our fallen friendship.

In the past, our partnership had rarely suffered because we had always been strong together. For seven years I had envisioned Will and me laughing and hurting and starving and lusting after ice-blasted mountains that no one else gave a rat's ass for. Although we would later be hounded by the media and receive letters and phone calls of congratulation, as I recoiled below the *Bergschrund* I knew our expedition possessed terrible compassionless proportions. Ours was a breakdown of humanity.

I lay gasping on my back. Maybe we were both delirious, or perhaps Will was trying to scare me into moving, but after I suggested calling a helicopter, Will suggested to Roger that they leave me. No sooner had the words left our mouths than the clouds swirled apart and we saw climbers below. The seriousness, the madness, and the isolation all disappeared as we smiled for the first time in a week.

As we stumbled down, some Brits walked uphill with congratulations and hot tea. I stared at them, speechless, exhausted, elated. They pumped our hands and we looked up at the mountain wondering if we were dreaming. Someone helped me untie from the rope. "We're alive," I said to no one in particular. Later, in their snowcave, we warmed up and the mountain disappeared. While their nurse massaged my toes, one Brit confessed that when they had first seen us they thought we were crazed because our expressions had been those of asylum escapees. The weather would not permit the Brits to reach the summit.

In the morning Will was angry, no longer willing to wait for me. His blackened toes mandated immediate descent. Fortunately, I had now recovered in the thicker air, so we roped up and raced one another down the low-angled slopes.

We reached our seventy-eight-hundred-foot cache that afternoon and dug out some food. Will apologized to me (at Roger's behest) and said his frostbite was his own fault; he had already diagnosed my own frostbite as minor. Will was denying his own actions, and I wondered how we could ever set things straight. The words froze in my mouth, so we acknowledged without speaking that this climb had wrecked our friendship.

Will announced a bout of competitive eating, and since we looked for any distraction to conceal our disappointment with one another, we glutted ourselves with canned ham and pineapples. Then Will reminded us of his toes, so with distended stomachs we packed up and trudged toward base camp in the gathering dusk.

Darkness hit quickly, and we became puppets jerking along to the pull of Will on the rope in front. Unlike Will, Roger and I had no snowshoes and often broke through the crust, floundering in deep snow. Mincing strides seemed to give us a few more yards without smashing through the crust. Sometimes we crawled, which was slow, but it prevented us from wallowing. On the final "Heartbreak Hill," Will untied from the rope and snowshoed ahead to dig out our landing-strip snowcave and fix hot drinks. Roger collapsed several times, and I went back to cajole and coax him onward. Over and over again, he murmured the name of Sir Robert Scott, who had died crawling back from the South Pole in 1912.

Recovering in the snowcave, I couldn't believe we had climbed the Cassin in winter. Roger came alive, too, so we dug out a Walkman and listened to Judy Collins while sipping steaming cocoa. The music stirred me deeply. When I realized the extent of our sensory deprivation, how much we had suffered, how far the cold and the dark and the altitude had twisted us, I ducked into my sleeping bag and let the briny tears wash my face.

When I came out, Roger was grinning contagiously, holding his breath. Smoke filled the cave and Will was coughing, trying to wave the cloud away. Will said the climb hadn't really been difficult and he had never felt extended; I half-believed him. Roger's lungs were close to bursting and his eyes were narrow slits. He offered me the joint, but I waved it off, because I could scarcely control my emotions.

By our second day of waiting, our various irritations with one another and our tardy bush pilot would no longer permit normal conversation. The cave turned into a soot-blackened repository for all of our frostbitten misery. We ached to leave this frozen hell and endlessly fantasized about the pleasures we would own once we escaped.

Unbeknownst to us, our pilot flew in three Spanish climbers on our third afternoon of waiting. Although he saw our ice axes and crampons lining the cave entrance, we could not hear his shouts, so he flew back out.

At dawn I hobbled out into the subarctic gloom and discovered the Spanish tent. At this point I no longer knew what was real, so I shuffled over, yanked off my mittens, then rubbed the tent fabric between my fingers. The Spaniards woke up, unzipped their door, and jumped back when they saw the stark and childish terror on my face.

From then on the only subject Will and Roger and I talked about with any mutual accord was our pilot's rationale in leaving us stranded in subzero anguish. Although Roger had been the only uninjured one among us, on the fifth day of waiting he fell into a crevasse and destroyed his knee cartilage so badly he could not stand. Thereafter, three derelicts grunted monosyllab-ically at one another, limping out of the cave only for matters of the toilet. Food rationing began. Will began "obsessing," ex-plaining to us that he was attempting telepathically to impart guilt in the mind of our missing bush pilot.

Fortunately, the Spaniards swore they would not begin climbing Mount Hunter until we were successfully evacuated. On the eighth day, after our *compadres* dug the word *OUT* in forty-foot-high letters, a passing bush pilot came to our rescue.

The depressive ennui that followed our unsuccessful high adventure totaled me. Out in Talkeetna Will emphasized to the reporters that I didn't go the last ridge to the summit, and I knew Will well enough to see that he was really saying that the weak or the sick didn't belong at his side.

Next to climbing Denali in winter, everything—relation-ships, work, exercise—seemed worthless. It took me months to readapt to normal living. While I recovered from my frostbite (nearly losing an infected toe) and inertia in Colorado, a friend lent me a room and a car, which I promptly crashed into the garage. Because I had squandered all on Denali, I had neither a cent nor a job.

Other climbers heard of our "success" and invited me on the big Himalayan trips I had always dreamed of. I told them that Denali had defeated me; I told them that I had quit climb-ing and I told them that summits had lost all meaning.

My inability to quit the climb, even with the red flags of injury and sickness waving in my face, can be written off to competition and the brashness of youth. But I am still haunted by the betrayal of a friend, by a cold with claws, and by a wind so corrupt I could smell its breath as it knocked me onto the glacier with my pants fouled with shit. I did not lose my inno-cence in 1964 when I saw my grandfather's corpse, nor with my first lover in 1973. I lost my innocence on the Cassin Ridge in the winter of 1982.

In the ensuing years my back stiffened as I heard about the third winter ascent of Denali. In February 1983, after Char-lie Sassara and Robert Frank had reached the summit, they be-gan descending fifty-degree ice. Both were unroped and exhausted from their accomplishment. Suddenly Frank, who was twenty feet above Sassara, yelled "Falling!" Frank knocked Sassara off. While Sassara managed to brake to a stop with his ax a hundred feet lower, Frank cartwheeled thousands of feet, spraying flecks of bone and skin and blood as he smashed his way down the west rib. Sassara picked up a two-inch chunk of his partner's flesh and descended to camp, stunned. No one ever found Frank's body.

In February 1984, the Japanese soloist Naomi Uemura disappeared after trudging down alone from the storm-washed summit on his birthday. That April I helped twenty Japanese search for Uemura's body, but we never found it.

In the winter of 1988 Vern Tejas soloed the west buttress. Tejas, who had been inspired by Uemura, not only showed the world that the mountain could be soloed in winter, but he also climbed it during a stormy February, *sans* frostbite or serious mishap. The following winter, Dave Staeli walked in to solo the Cassin. He took one look and wisely proceeded up the west rib.

Meanwhile, three Japanese alpinists, who had climbed several Himalayan giants in summer and winter, were blown off the west buttress and killed. Staeli abjectly snuck up to the summit a day later. Although the Japanese autopsies read "hypothermia," anyone who has withstood the breath of Denali in winter knows that the wind murdered them.

During these climbs, I envied the climbers not a whit; I worried about them a lot. I occasionally run into these winter survivors of Denali—Art Davidson and Dave Johnston and Charlie Sassara and Vern Tejas and Dave Staeli. But when we greet one another in Anchorage, we stop and look into each other's eyes and beam at one another with little talk. We know full well what we got away with.

Climbing changed for me because of the Cassin. Now I like to revel in the mountain's virility rather than my own. I like to say that in eleven trips, with friends and clients, I have only put the summit beneath my boot soles once, via the west rib in 1981—which feels more than fair. Certainly I have gone high on the mountain many times, but once always seemed to be plenty. Trampling the summit regularly seems part sacrilege, part conquest, and more to do with business than climbing.

I like to say that we climb because mountains are sacred

places and climbing is a form of worship. We climb because the mountains are our church. Indeed, *It*—the Chief Guide, Raven, God, the Great Fly Swatter, or Buddha—can't be greater than flaming arrows shooting into the heavens at fifty below where the wind hums over a fin of ice and the light cuts right through to your soul. Most importantly, by bringing myself over the edge and back, I discovered the passion to live my days fully, a conviction that will sustain me like sweet water on the periodically barren plain of our short lives.

CHARLES KURALT

Overnight on Denali

"FOR ONE NIGHT ONLY, WE HAD THE BEST SEATS ON THE PLANET
FOR NATURE'S MOST SPECTACULAR SHOW."

Charles Kuralt, for many years a mainstay on CBS-TV, is a kind of American folk hero. Now retired, he spent years "on the road" in an RV, exploring the hidden paths and tracks of America, seeking out both the eccentrics and the plain folks all across the nation about whom an interesting tale could be told. He found thousands.

In the following piece, he describes his one night watching the aurora borealis, the northern lights.

This atmospheric phenomenon occurs above sixty degrees latitude in both the northern and southern hemispheres. (The southern lights are properly the aurora australis.) An atmospheric disturbance related to the eleven-year cycle of sunspot activity, the visible lights take the form of colored arcs, bands, streamers, a luminous corona, clouds, fans, flames, and other shapes, all flickering and flashing across the nighttime sky, most often in late fall and early spring.

The planet Jupiter has them, too.

OF ALL THE FLYERS INTO WHOSE HANDS we have placed our lives, Don Sheldon is the one I'll always be most thankful for. We had heard of him before we met him. Everybody in south central Alaska had heard of him.

Wandering around Alaska one spring, we thought we'd make some pictures of Mount McKinley—Denali, the great mountain of the continent. On clear days, the old giant can be seen from a hundred miles or more away, but, as usual, we wanted close-ups. We drove to Talkeetna, the village that has always served as headquarters for expeditions to McKinley, and was best known as the home of Don Sheldon, the fabled mountain pilot. He turned out to be a slender, unassuming man with thinning hair. He wore a plaid shirt, army pants, and work boots. Very modest-looking, I thought, for a legend. He said he was free for a couple of days and we engaged him to fly us up to the mountain. As we helped him roll his ski-equipped, single-engine Cessna out of the hangar, he made gentle jokes about the dangers of mountain flying.

"Never know what we'll run into up there," he said, shaking his head and smiling. "You sure you boys want to do this? Well, let's fuel 'er up then."

I noticed he pumped his gas through a chamois strainer.

Light, fluffy cumulus clouds floated above the Alaska Range when we approached, Izzy riding beside Sheldon up front and a soundman named Stan Roginski strapped in behind with me. Izzy thought it would make a wonderful shot to fly through a cloud straight at the mountain with the camera rolling, so that when we came out of the cloud, the sunlit peak of McKinley would appear suddenly and dramatically.

"Let's try that cloud over there," Izzy said, and the mountain scenery tilted dizzily as Don Sheldon banked one way, then the other, to oblige. We flew toward the mountain through one cloud after another. Izzy was never satisfied that we had captured quite the desired spectacular effect. There were a lot of clouds to try, and we tried most of them. I found myself gripping the armrests and trying to keep my breakfast down each time we broke through into the sunlight, steered straight for Mount McKinley, and veered sharply away at the last minute.

"Let's try that one over there," Izzy said, pointing to yet another cloud close to the peak.

"If we try that one," Don Sheldon said, "it will ruin my reputation."

"What do you mean?" Izzy asked.

Sheldon said calmly, "That one's got rocks in it."

"Look," I said, "is there someplace we can set this thing down for a while? Maybe we need a rest."

"I know just the place," the pilot said, putting the plane over on one wing again and tilting the nose sickeningly downward. "I think I even brought along a Thermos of coffee for you boys. We'll take a little coffee break." He set the plane's skis for landing, dropped the flaps, and, a few minutes later, brought us to a bumpy stop in the snow in a big curved bowl, an ice field of the Ruth Glacier.

When Sheldon shut down the engine and we stepped out into the sunlight, I was nearly blinded by the brilliance of the white world around us. The glacier formed a vast, silent basin surrounded by massive slopes, a universe of ice and rock. Range upon range of mountains stretched before us into the measureless distance, and behind us, towering almost straight up from the ice field, rose Denali itself, with snow blowing from its summit thousands of feet overhead.

After a long silence, one of us said, "Good God!"

"Yep," Don Sheldon said, "I've always sort of liked this place myself."

We spent a long time just standing there before we remembered we were supposed to be making pictures. Don Sheldon tramped about thoughtfully in the snow while we worked.

When it was time to go, he had a little news for us.

"Good news and bad news," he said. "The good news is that the sun hasn't gone down yet and I can still get this plane out of here and back home before dark.

"The bad news is that the sun has made the snow so mushy that I can't take off with all of you on board."

I gulped. "You *can't?*"

"Nope," he said. "Too much weight. Best I can do now is take one of you back to Talkeetna, and maybe some of your gear. Two of you are going to have to spend the night up here, I'm afraid. I'll come back for you in the morning."

I looked around, imagining the nighttime temperature on the glacier. Also imagining wolves and polar bears.

"Nothing up here to hurt you," Don Sheldon said. "I'll dig a couple of sleeping bags out of the plane for you."

While he was doing so, he added, "Oh, and you won't have to be alone, either." He nodded toward a rocky outcrop about a mile away at the edge of the ice field. "You can't see it from here, but there's a cozy one-room cabin on the other side of that rock. Some of the climbers use it for a base camp. There's a Catholic priest in there now on some kind of a retreat. He's a nice guy. Father Ron is what I call him. He's been up here awhile. He won't mind a little company."

Sheldon held up the bedrolls. "Who wants these?" he asked.

I was still letting all this news sink in, about the necessity for two of us to spend the night in this wilderness, and then about there being a *cabin* in this unlikely place, and not only a cabin but also a *priest*. . . .

I heard Izzy say, "I'll stay." He shouldered his camera and the tape recorder and took one of the bedrolls. Then I heard myself say, "Sure, I'll stay, too." Don Sheldon handed me the other roll of bedding and a long length of rope.

"Better rope yourselves together when you walk over there," he said. "You know. Crevasses. See you tomorrow."

He climbed into the pilot's seat with Stan beside him, started the engine, and began his takeoff run down the glacier. The plane lifted off and turned toward home. We watched until it vanished among the mountains.

Izzy tied one end of the rope around his waist and handed me the other end, regarding my 220-pound bulk doubtfully. "If one of us falls into a hole in the ice," he said, "it better be me, I guess." We started across the glacier with the setting sun casting our shadows a hundred yards ahead of us and creating imaginary hidden crevasses every few steps.

It must have taken us nearly an hour to make it off the ice and into the rocks of the mountain. When we started up, we could see a big, red-bearded man wearing a bright parka coming down toward us, carrying a coiled rope of his own over one shoulder, and in his hand, a staff. He looked like a Biblical prophet of the mountains.

"Good afternoon, Father," I said.

"Never mind the Father blather!" he boomed cheerily. "Sorry to be late in greeting you! The truth is I wasn't expecting company! Haven't seen another soul since sometime last month! Here, let me carry some of that load for you."

He talked loudly all the way up the hill, not stopping even to ask where we had come from and what we were doing there. It had been weeks, I guess, since he had heard the sound of his own voice.

"I suppose Don Sheldon dropped you off," he said, "unless you took a wrong turn on a stroll in Anchorage and hoofed it up here. Don likes to show off his shelter. He built it himself, you know. He got tired of climbers freezing in the storms. Tough work, you know, having to fly their bodies back down and all, so he flew a few loads of lumber and nails up here— and here we are. Welcome to our humble abode!"

The cabin was small, six-sided, and half buried in snow. Inside, sleeping shelves were built up off the floor under a ring of windows. A wood stove squatted in the center of the room with a fire crackling inside. That's all there was to the place. It looked very good to me.

"I am pleased to offer you northern exposures with a view of the mountains," Father Ron said, dumping our bedrolls on the shelf. "All the exposures have a view of the mountains. The menu tonight is stew. That is the menu every night." He walked outside, dug around in the snow for a black iron pot full of beef and beans, came back in and set it on the stove. "Dinner will be served shortly," he said, "but first the cocktail hour." From his duffel bag on the floor under the shelf, he produced a bottle of Christian Brothers brandy. "We like to support the brothers in their good work," he said. He unscrewed the cap and passed the bottle ceremoniously to Izzy to drink first.

Over tin bowls of stew, Father Ron told us that he had come to Alaska seeking solitude in the loneliest place he could find. Somebody in Talkeetna had told him about the Mount McKinley shelter and he had talked Don Sheldon into flying him up here. He was escaping a critical bishop in Boston or someplace. He said this sojourn in the mountains was partly for religious reflection and partly for figuring out what to do with his life.

"Well," I said, "I guess it doesn't help your solitude much for a couple of strangers to show up at dinnertime and stay all night."

"I am very glad to have your company," Father Ron said solemnly. "I've never been alone for so long before. Let me tell you what I have discovered about being alone: it is a great gift, but it is damned lonely."

I laughed.

"Solitude is hard to come by in this world," he went on. "It is a priceless luxury. Only the very rich can afford it—and paupers like me. Everybody else in the world dreams of splendid isolation, workers from their bosses, husbands from their wives, but they can only dream, you see. They are in the grip of daily life, and daily life must be lived with others."

I said I envied him his escape from daily life.

"Yes," he said, "it offers communion with God. But about this time of day, you find yourself in need of some kind of human communion, somebody to have a drink with, or a debate. God listens well, but doesn't talk much. Moses went to the mountaintop to talk with God, but you'll remember that he came right back down again. And I have found out why. The pressure is too great up here. It is not natural to human beings to talk only with God. The tension accumulates. . . ."

We all fell silent, thinking about this.

"But now," Father Ron said, "the after-dinner show! Look over your shoulder."

In the sky behind us, a faint white light was shimmering. It grew brighter, changed to a shade of purple, then pink, and suddenly shot in a streak to the dome of the sky. Izzy and I stood up and stared through the window.

"*Aurora borealis,*" Father Ron said. "It is Latin, meaning 'the northern dawn.' "

I had seen the northern lights before, glowing dimly on some northern horizon. This was different, a display of brilliant pastels that trembled over the silhouettes of the mountains, a big Wurlitzer jukebox in the sky. Ripples of color rose in layers from bottom to top and unexpectedly sent bright streamers flying so high that we had to draw close to the windows to see where they ended above our heads.

"Charged particles from the sun entering the atmosphere of the earth," Father Ron intoned. He was used to the show.

"If you gentlemen will excuse me, I am going to retire," he said, and soon he was snoring lightly in his sleeping bag. But Izzy and I sat there on the shelf through the short subarctic night watching those bright rivers of light transform the dark world. For one night only, we had the best seats on the planet for nature's most spectacular show. It faded away only with the rising of the sun. Both of us were left awed and exhausted. Neither of us has ever been able to describe that night adequately to others, though we did our best to tell Father Ron what he had missed as soon as he wakened.

"Very good, very good," he said, with a sort of pride of ownership. "We do our best to satisfy our guests in this inn. How do you take your coffee? Black, I hope."

We were just roping ourselves together at the edge of the ice field when Don Sheldon's silver Cessna appeared overhead, turned upwind, and landed. Father Ron helped carry our gear out to the plane. He took off his mittens to shake hands. Izzy and I climbed aboard, waved once, and left the big, bearded prophet standing there on the glacier, alone again with only God to talk to. I have not seen or heard of him since. I hope he worked it all out up there in the mountains, but have no way of knowing.

"Pretty nice night?" Don Sheldon asked over the engine noise.

"It was okay," I said. "Not a very good place to sleep though, what with the lights coming in the window."

He chuckled. "I thought you might not mind it up there," he said. "I haven't seen every place, but it's the prettiest place I've ever seen."

"Well," I said, "me too. How can I ever thank you, Don?"

He said, "Don't thank me. I wanted to take you home with me last night. Thank the soft snow on that glacier."

That's what he said, but I wonder. I wonder whether Don

Sheldon sized us up as a couple of guys who thought we were in a bigger hurry than we really were and would benefit from a night to slow down and look around and think about this place where we were.

I can't ask him. Don Sheldon had cancer then, knew he had it, and died less than a year later. You can find his name on the new Geological Survey map of Mount McKinley, printed in small letters on a white patch that represents the ice field where he landed us for coffee and wouldn't take us home from until we'd spent the night, the place he said was the prettiest he'd ever seen. The beautiful big white bowl of the Ruth Glacier where the northern lights put on their show every night is forever named the Don Sheldon Amphitheater.

FRED HATFIELD

A year on Togiak Lake

"IT WAS THEN THAT A THOUGHT CAME TO MIND: THE WOLVES
WOULD PROBABLY HAVE LEFT SOMETHING. I WENT TO EACH OF
THE KILLS AND FOUND FOUR NICE LONG LEG BONES."

Among the many pleasures of being an anthologist is the good excuse it provides to search for and read books one might never know about otherwise. Fred Hatfield's North of the Sun: A Memoir of the Alaskan Wilderness, *written in an honest, plainspoken, genuinely American voice, was the best "find" in my research on Alaska.*

Togiak Lake is in southwestern Alaska, west of Anchorage and north of Bristol Bay. Hatfield's early adventures there had no lasting ill effects. He was in his eightieth year when his memoir was published in 1990.

SOMETIMES A SMALL THING WILL CHANGE the course of our lives. I bought the Anchorage paper only once that winter and an article I read in it surely changed the course of mine.

A reindeer herder had brought a large gold nugget into the small village of Dillingham in the dead of winter. He said he had found it at the head of Togiak Lake in an open creek, one that was fed by warm springs and didn't freeze over. The more I thought about it, the bigger that nugget seemed to grow. I bought a map of Alaska. Dillingham was far to the west on the Bering Sea coast and Togiak Lake was roughly west of there, and inland perhaps seventy miles. The story kept running through my head like a half-remembered song. I knew where I was going to be the following summer.

Spring finally arrived and my mind was still on Togiak and gold. I boarded the train for Anchorage one day and was on my way; the train passed Grandview and I wondered how Mack was making out. Finally we reached a place called Summit where the grade was so steep that even with two engines pulling we had to stop at the bottom and everyone had to get off and walk behind the train. At the top of Summit we climbed back aboard.

Anchorage at that time wasn't a big town: Fourth Avenue was the one main street. In all of Alaska then, even though all distant travel was by air, there were fewer than seventy commercial aircraft scattered over the entire Territory, and most of those were small bush planes. Star Airways had an office on Fourth Avenue. I went there and told them where I wanted to go and learned that a pilot would be showing up soon who could fly me to Dillingham.

I hung around the office most of the time but I had plenty of leisure to look the town over. One thing puzzled me. In the restaurant windows there were signs: No Natives Allowed or No Natives Wanted. It puzzled me because in Seward I had known many native people. I had been in their homes and they were my friends. There had been no signs in the restaurants there. I didn't like what I saw in Anchorage.

On the third day my pilot arrived. We left Anchorage next morning and set down in Dillingham that afternoon. It was small, just a fishing village at the mouth of the Nushagak River. I bought my supplies at the trading store and wished I had a little more money; the plane fare had made quite a hole in my pocket.

Togiak Lake was about seventy miles northwest of Dillingham, an hour's flying time the next morning. We landed at the mouth of a river flowing into the lake and unloaded my supplies. The pilot told me that when I wanted to get out I could follow the lake, fifteen miles of it, then follow the river that emptied out of it. About ninety miles would put me on the coast of the Bering Sea. He gunned his engine and the plane was out of sight in minutes. I stared at the mountain pass where I had last seen him and it was then that I realized I was finally out in the wilderness.

The Togiak valley was not more than five miles wide. A mountain range running north to south formed the west side, with the same type of range laid to the east. Twenty miles north of me they joined together, forming an almost up-and-down jagged barrier. South was the lake, of course, and beyond that what looked like an unlimited stretch of nothing extending to an empty horizon. To either side of this, in the far distance, were the tops of two mountain peaks. I had an idea they marked the end of the mountain ranges and that the Bering Sea couldn't be far beyond.

Locating a cabin site was my first job and it was an unpleasant surprise to find that the pilot had landed me on the wrong side of the river: north as far as I could see there was nothing but alder brush. I was too far west for any spruce timber, but on the other side of the river a nice stand of cottonwood extended for a long way. The lake shore was littered with dry drift logs and it didn't take me long to tie a raft together, load my supplies, and paddle around the river mouth to the other side. Walking ashore, I eventually found a flat area that looked as though it had never been under water and decided to build there. I had a small tarpaulin to hang for a temporary shelter and I started back to the lake shore to get it. A coughing grunt and a crash in the brush took my mind off that and I hustled instead for my rifle. I came back and after a slow, careful stalk found the tracks of a black bear. That didn't pose any problem. Black bears are quite shy and peaceful unless they are disturbed when their young are with them, and I knew this was too far west to be grizzly country.

I made my cabin ten feet square: I didn't need much room. I covered the roof logs with a thick layer of moss and over that put a layer of sod to hold everything in place. I had forgotten that a small pane of glass would be nice for a window. I had also forgotten that a good supply of candles could make things a little more cheerful at night. Still, there were plenty of porcupine around at that time of year and I cooked the fat from those. The result was a thick soupy grease that gave off a red flame. There wasn't much light but it sure produced plenty of black smoke.

The lake and streams were alive with trout. Mallard and teal were everywhere. I lived like a king and was eager to see what my country was like. One day I left the cabin, headed north, and found a game trail close to the mountains. It was a good eight feet wide and at one time had been a migration route for caribou. Small trees about four inches in diameter were growing across it now, showing that it hadn't been used by game for a long time. The settlement of a number of people on the Kuskokwim River to the west had been too much for them.

Ten miles up the valley I came to a low pass opening from the west. The game trail turned into it and so did I. All that day there was nothing to see except a good-sized creek far below me; it followed the pass and emptied into the river, north of my cabin. I made camp that night in a small canyon, grateful for the shelter it gave me from the wind that never seemed to stop blowing. There was dry cottonwood in the bottom for a fire.

The next day I came to a high rise and stopped to look around. There was nothing that looked like gold country, but on the far side of the creek I could see a small herd of reindeer. I knew them for reindeer because of the color variations; some of them were black and white, some were brown, and they were being herded by a pearl-white bull. I traveled down the slope and crossed the creek with no trouble. Reindeer are almost a domesticated animal and I had no difficulty getting within easy range. I shot the white bull and a small black calf. I wanted the thin hide of the calf for a window—fleshed well on both sides, it would be almost transparent. The rest of the herd moved off westwards; they had strayed from a much larger herd somewhere on the Kuskokwim and now they were headed back.

I dressed my meat and carried it all down to the creek bottom, where I made camp. I was lucky to have the tarpaulin: it rained day and night for five days. The meat soured and except for what I had eaten, I lost all of it. The creek had swollen from the long rain and if I wanted to get across and back on to the caribou trail I knew I was going to get wet. I kept my boots on but removed all my clothing and tied it on top of the pack and started straight across. About ten feet from shore the water boiled up around my chest and I felt my boots slipping on the smooth stones in the creek bottom. About twenty yards behind me it entered a canyon with sheer rock walls fifty feet high. I knew if I went into that I'd never come out. Fighting the current and wrestling with the pack, I made my feet slide sideways as the water forced me backwards and slowly I made knee-deep water and got back more or less to where I'd started.

I walked up the shoreline, looking for a wider, shallower place to cross, and at the mouth of a small side creek a small cabin showed ahead of me. It had been there a long time: the roof poles were still in place but all the moss and sod were gone. I walked inside. It was bare, with nothing to show that anyone had ever lived there. I didn't realize it at the time, but whoever built that cabin had worked there, and there was only one kind of work in that pass. A man had lived there and mined the small creek.

I was twenty-four years old and I must have been stupid. I had come into this country looking for gold and why I didn't check that creek, I'll never know. Instead I kept on going and finally came to a wide shallow spot where a creek came in from the other side and I could wade across with no trouble. There was an odd formation a short way up the creek: a dike or ridge had been cut through by the water and there was a small growth of cottonwood, enough for a shelter and wood for a fire to dry my boots and socks. As I pulled my clothes on I noticed plenty of quartz in the creek and dug the gold pan out of my pack. The very first pan of gravel gave me fairly coarse placer gold and a nugget the size of a small marble. During the rest of the day I took eight ounces of gold from the top of the gravel bar.

That evening I had oatmeal for supper. It had become damp during the long rain and didn't taste too good. Tired, I remembered I had a fish line in my pack and as it was still light enough I tried the main creek for trout. There was nothing. I bedded down for the night and in the morning tried several other places for fish and finally knew there were none.

I was on a good, paying creek, though, and I knew that. I had thought that finding gold would be the difficult thing but it hadn't turned out that way: my gold was in a hungry place and working that creek would be the problem. The need to find food had moved into first place. There was no game in the pass and the reindeer I had seen were well on their way back to where they came from. I had no choice so I broke camp and headed back to the lake. I would have to get the right kind of food to take in to the creek, food that would keep and not turn sour from damp weather. It meant a tent and a small Yukon stove. I would have to make the money to pay for them by trapping. Perhaps it would work out for me next year.

When I saw a glimpse of my cabin through the cottonwoods it looked like home. Salmon were beginning to show up in the streams ready to spawn, and soon they were so plentiful I could flip them out of the water with a stick. I worked on the calf hide for my window, scraping every trace of flesh away. Then I tied a rope to it, threw it out into the lake, and made the end fast. After five days of soaking I pulled the skin from the water and wiped off all the hair. Scraping the hair side with my knife, I soon had it thin and almost transparent. I cut a square opening in my cabin wall and tacked the hide in place. It let in plenty of light.

I had never seen what the lower end of the lake looked like and decided to make myself a new raft, complete with crude oarlocks. On a fine clear morning I set out to have a look. It took me some time to make the fifteen miles, but the raft worked well. Just before I reached the lake's end I spotted a large brown animal on the tundra. I couldn't make out what it was so I beached my raft and made my way up the slope; all of it was small ridges with shallow dips in between. Ridge after ridge was the same. Nothing in sight. I had one fervent hope, that I wasn't stalking a grizzly, not like this.

I eased to the top of a ridge and an Osborne caribou was looking me square in the eye, not more than twenty feet away. I shot him in the chest and he ran downhill and fell on the lake shore, less than ten yards from my raft. An Osborne is big and this one was almost as large as a three-year-old moose. Feeling lucky, I dressed and loaded the meat on my raft and headed back up the lake.

A month passed and the weather turned chilly. I set out a trapline for mink and did well. The duck had been gone for some time but there was still plenty of trout, so I didn't lack for food, though I missed having salmon to eat—they had spawned and died. Then, one morning, I stepped out the cabin door and saw something that didn't look too pleasant. The lake had frozen over in a thin sheet of ice.

I went to fish in the river and streams but the trout had gone to the lake when the water got cold and I caught nothing. I believe it was then that I began to have serious thoughts about the coming winter.

The caribou I had shot had weighed well over three hundred pounds. I could have cut much of that into thin strips and smoked it for winter, for my cabin was the perfect smokehouse. A small fire made in a circular hole in the center of the earth floor and fed with dry cottonwood would have given me just the right amount of clean, dry smoke. I could have smoked enough meat and trout and salmon to feed ten men. I had done nothing right.

The lake finally froze over enough for me to walk on it, and I fished through the ice in many places but caught nothing. I didn't know then that in winter the fish go to the deep places in the lake where the water is warmer. I stopped trapping altogether and hunted just for food. The only thing I found was a porcupine once in a while, and then they too were gone. Snow came now, and soon I was in a white, frozen world.

I realized a hard truth at that time. Nature in the summer months is bountiful and generous—birds singing in the trees, ducks in the stream and along the lake shore, busy talking back and forth and looking after their young, fish and game there every day for the taking. Now the only sounds I heard were the loud cracks as ice gave way to pressure, or the wind howling out of the north, bringing more snow. I had wasted the summer and now I knew I was going to be hungry for a long time.

I hunted hard for porcupine now and occasionally I managed to find one that I had missed in early winter. It was barely enough to keep me from starving. The deep snow brought the ptarmigan down from the high slopes but they stayed in the willow growths along the shore and were difficult to get close to. Once in a while I was lucky. Hunger is a good teacher. One day I discovered that when the birds were ready to bed down for the night they would burrow into the snow until they were completely covered. After a while their body heat and breath would form a small round air hole, and if I could get close enough without disturbing them I could put my snowshoe down over the hole, reach in, and catch my breakfast. It was slow, cold, wet work, but I got very good at it—and then one morning my food supply wasn't there. I covered many miles on snowshoes and found nothing. I learned much later that ptarmigan feed on willow buds and move on when they have exhausted the supply.

The hard winter brought me some unwanted visitors: I was regularly plagued by shrews, who began to use my cabin as their home. They were so numerous I could sit quietly on the bunk and watch them; sometimes at night while I was asleep they would nibble my neck or hand. Eventually I got tired of the damage they did in the cabin, so I worked on a way to rid myself of their nuisance. I had an empty coffee can and this I buried in the dirt floor so that the top was level with the surface. At night I fastened a small round stick across it but left it loose enough to roll and turn. In the middle of the stick I tied a small piece of porcupine meat. The shrews would run out along the stick but their weight would turn it over, dropping them into the can. There was never more than one live shrew in the can for very long. When the second shrew fell in, it was a fight to the finish and the winner ate the loser and it didn't take long. In the morning there would be a pile of fur, many small bones, and one live shrew in the can. I have read since then that a shrew can eat twenty-four hours a day and I believe it. I managed to keep them under control.

On the first of March something happened that gave me a choice of two things, and neither of them looked good.

I was carrying a piece of firewood back to the cabin. I had it on my shoulder and somehow I fell, twisting my knee badly. I crawled inside but I knew it would be days before I could walk, still less hunt. I was fortunate in one respect—I had just found what I'll swear was the last porcupine in the entire valley. I rationed myself to one small piece of meat a day, but when I was able to stand on my leg again the only thing in my cabin, in the way of food, was plenty of tea.

Prolonged hunger is an insidious thing. Against your will, it assumes control of your mind. Every thought is of something to eat. Ever-present, gnawing hunger governs every judgment.

I thought about staying where I was, trying to hold out until spring. The ice would be gone then and I could raft all the way to the coast. But I wasn't sure I could last that long. I had to leave for the coast now, while I had enough stamina left to make it. I worried what to take with me, what to leave behind. The furs I had taken had no weight to worry about, but my rifle, the Krag, was heavy and the thought of it hanging from my shoulder decided me: it would have to stay. In any case, there had been no game and I was sure I would find none on the journey. My tarpaulin was heavy, too, and I left that.

It was midnight in the middle of March when I was ready to leave. The moon was full and bright. I stood for a time outside the closed cabin door. There was warmth and shelter there and I hated to leave it, but hunger was there too. I had my furs and my one blanket. I had tea and matches, a camp axe and a small coil of rope.

The silence was so intense it seemed an invisible threat. The mountain ranges to either side were pale shadows. The cold crept through my clothing and told me to move on and I did, the only sound the whisper of my snowshoes as they slid across the soft surface.

After a time, the coming daylight pushed the night away

and the mountains were sharp silhouettes against the sky. I reached the end of the lake just as the sun cast a golden promise on the horizon. It was going to be a fine day and what I saw next filled me with joy. The river was wide open. It meant an easy ride on a raft, clear to the coast.

I didn't waste any time. I crossed to a stand of cottonwood with plenty of dead, dry trees. I cut down and limbed all I would need for a good raft and dragged them to the edge of the river. It didn't seem to matter that my knee ached, for I'd soon be riding the raft. I cut a last long, slender pole to push and steer with, lashed my small pack to the raft securely, and pushed away from shore.

The current wasn't very fast but that was because I was still close to the lake. I knew the current would pick up once I moved down the river and got into its turns and bends. After two hours of slow drifting, I went around a sharp turn and my raft came to rest against solid ice. I knew at once the river would be impassable clear to the coast.

The knowledge came to me like a physical blow. I pushed the raft to shore and tossed my pack on the bank. I was angry at the river and I was worn out. I took my pole and pushed the raft as far out in the water as I could and threw the pole after it. I made a fire and rested while I boiled some water. Sipping hot tea took some of the ache out of my bones. It was still early in the day and I decided to set out again. Whenever I came to a ravine with willows growing in it, I stopped and picked a handful of buds. They were dry and hard but they were something to put in my stomach. Every night my bed was the same, a trench scooped out in the snow, some branches laid in the bottom to keep me dry, and a little snow caved in from the sides to cover my blanket. I was warm enough. I lost track of the days, but I believe it was on the fifth day that I went down into a fairly steep ravine. The sun had melted the snow from the bottom and it looked warm down there. A stream trickled along between sandy stretches. I took my snowshoes off and it felt good to walk on bare ground.

There were small footprints in the sand ahead of me. For a few seconds they meant nothing to me and then I realized, with a shock, that I wasn't alone. I knelt down and traced the marks with my fingers. They were so fresh that sand was falling into them from the sides. They went up the steep slope of snow and I crawled after them. As my head reached the top of the slope, I saw four pairs of *mukluk*-clad legs not more than inches from my face.

I looked up and saw the little girl who had made the foot-prints. Beside her was a young man and a young woman, and an older woman, all of them dressed in fur parkas.

The man reached down, put his hands under my shoulders, and helped me to my feet.

"You come slow to this place."

"I travel slow. My knee is bad."

He took my pack and snowshoes.

"You come and you eat." He didn't waste any words. He spoke briefly in Eskimo to the older woman and turned back to me.

"My mother, you go with her."

She smiled and took me by my arm and led me to the tunnel entrance of a small sod hut. There was another hut further off. The entrance to an Eskimo hut always faces south, a rounded tunnel about four feet high and six feet long. An abrupt right turn and another tunnel of the same size and shape brings you to the door. They are made this way to cut the driving force of the wind. It was the first time I had ever been inside a native hut. It was lit by a small seal-gut skylight, the floor was hard-packed dirt, and the sod walls had been pounded smooth. There was a wood-burning cook-stove, a small hand-hewn table, and a large block of hard-looking wood. A wide pole bunk covered with hay and laced-down reindeer skins had been built against one wall. Everything except the stove was hand-made.

I must have looked tired for the mother took me to the bed and sat me down. She knelt and unlaced my boots and pulled them off and then she pulled my parka off. Smiling, she said something to me and left. She came back soon, carrying a slab of frozen reindeer meat. Putting it on the block and using a hatchet, she chopped off small pieces and tossed them in a pot of boiling water on the stove. It wasn't long before she poured all of it, meat and juice, into a big bowl and gave me a spoon.

It was the best food I ever tasted. She took the empty bowl and motioned me to lie down. I was asleep before I had time to think how lucky this day had been.

When I woke it was dark. Someone had covered me with a soft, tanned reindeer skin. I slept again. Next time I woke it was daylight and the mother was there. She smiled and spoke to me and I knew she was saying good morning. I watched as she mixed flour and water in a bowl and cooked pancakes in a skillet. After I had eaten, I asked her about Togiak. I knew the word Togiak would let her know what I meant. She went outside and soon her son came in. He sat down on the bed by me.

"When you come, you look bad. You stay one more day. You eat and sleep."

"Tell me, how far is Togiak?"

"For you, maybe five, six days. You go slow. Where did you come from?"

"Togiak Lake."

"You hunt fur?"

"Yes, I trapped. Tell me, you live here where the wind is strong—no trees, just open tundra. Down in the river bottom you could have trees, you could make log houses."

He nodded. "Yes, it is bad here now. One time, maybe my father's father's time, there was plenty caribou. They could see them far off. They see them come and they wait. When the snow is gone, I think maybe we go to the coast. Some of my people there. We live there, hunt the seal and the walrus." He got to his feet. "One more day, maybe you feel good."

He left me then. I thought of the caribou migration trail that came down into Togiak Valley through the pass I had been in. He was right. Once this had been a good place but not now, not ever again for them. Guiltily, I realized I had said nothing about gold, but perhaps it wouldn't have interested him. I slept off and on during the day, and his mother fed me. I have been in many Eskimo huts since then but I don't believe I have ever seen people who had less than that family. Whatever they had they shared with me and I thought again of the signs I had seen in the restaurant windows in Anchorage a year ago.

I slept well that night and in the morning felt ready to travel again. I didn't look forward to the trip but I was anxious to reach the coast. I tied the thongs of my snowshoes round my ankles and slipped the straps of my pack over my shoulders. The son came to me with a piece of reindeer meat and dropped it into my pack. "This will be good tonight."

I left them and after a bit I looked back. They were still watching me and they waved. I raised my hand in the air and kept on going. I never even learned their names.

When the daylight began to fade I made camp, boiled the meat in the tea can, and ate it. My eyes were smarting and felt irritated, and I knew they were suffering from the bright sun on the snow and the acrid smoke from my alder wood fire. The next day was sunny and bright again and I made a good distance, but my eyes were giving me quite a bit of trouble. They felt as though sand had been thrown in them. That evening I came upon a herd of at least two thousand reindeer, the main Togiak herd, as I learned later. I wished then that I had not left my rifle back at the cabin. I made a cold camp that night. There was no brush anywhere for shelter or heat and as far as I could see, there was no ravine. I scooped out a trench in the snow long enough for me, pulled my blanket round me, and lay down, dropping the parka hood over my face. The wind had picked up and I caved the sides of the trench in, enough to give me a good cover. I packed the snow, pushing it away from my face, and pulled back the parka hood. I had a clear space for my face, I was secure, and I was warm. Some time that night, I woke up to the sound of wolves howling. I knew they were after the reindeer. Before very long, everything was quiet again. At daybreak I could see three patches of bloody snow. The wolves had taken what they needed for food and the reindeer had moved up the valley. I hoped the friends I had left would see them.

It was then that a thought came to mind: the wolves would probably have left something. I went to each of the kills and found four nice long leg bones. They had been cleaned of meat but what I wanted was inside. I put the bones in my pack and started on again. It was another day of bright sun and by mid-afternoon I was almost snow-blind. If I had known to rub charcoal under my eyes it would have prevented that, but there were many things then that I didn't know. Towards evening, I stopped at the first wooded ravine I came to. I built a big fire, for I wanted a good bed of coals. After the fire burned down I took the bones the wolves had left me and laid them side by side on the glowing coals and waited anxiously. It took some time and then there was a sharp crack. One of the bones had split its entire length. With a little help from my axe, I soon had it laid wide open, and the rich marrow was there. Bone marrow is good at any time, but for me, then, it was something special. I cleaned out all four and settled down to sleep.

The next morning my eyes were still bad. A night's rest hadn't helped them much. I kept my direction the best way I knew, by holding the sun on my left side; that would keep me heading south. By mid-afternoon, with the sun on my right side now, I came on a sod hut. I went inside and it looked as though no one had been there for a long time. I decided to go no further that day and to spend the night inside. Wondering how much further I would have to travel to reach the coast, I walked out of the hut. The top of it looked warm and dry so I climbed up and sat there for some time. I heard a sound then, a sound I hadn't heard in a long time. Somewhere, dogs were barking, but almost at once the sound stopped.

I rose to my feet and shouted as loud as I could. I heard the sound of sled runners slicing over the snow. The dogs stopped close by and I slid down the side of the hut and walked over. An Eskimo boy was the driver. He smiled.

"I didn't know what you were until you stood up. Your eyes are bad from the sun. Where did you come from?"

"From the lake, at the head of the river. Did you come from the coast?"

"Yes, I live on the coast. My name is Wasilly."

"What are you doing way out here?"

"I'm looking for reindeer. The wolves keep them moving."

"With your dogs, maybe three hours back that way where I came from, there are plenty of reindeer. The wolves are with them now."

"I'll tell my father and we'll come back."

"My name is Fred. Can I ride with you?"

"Of course. You will come home with me."

We put my pack and snowshoes in the sled. I stood on one runner and Wasilly stood on the other; we each had a handle to hang on to. He spoke to his dogs, they tightened the traces, and we were off.

KRIS CAPPS

Ice-caving Beneath the Castner Glacier, Alaska Range

"AMONG HIS HELPFUL SAFETY TIPS, DICK SUGGESTS THREE
PEOPLE AS AN IDEAL GROUP SIZE. 'THAT WAY, IF YOU GET IN
TROUBLE, YOU HAVE SOMEONE TO EAT.' "

*The snowcapped volcanic peaks of the Alaska Range are in
south-central Alaska, west of Anchorage.*

*Kris Capps is a journalist who lives in Alaska. While others
prefer to climb up and over Alaska's mountains, she went exploring inside them. Her article was first published in* Alaska *magazine.*

WE'VE ALL COME PREPARED TO BE SLIMED,
wearing our grungiest clothes, including rain gear, hip waders, crampons, and overmitts. Two men wear kneepads; by midday the rest of us will wish we had them as well. Most
important, we carry three sources of light, plus extra batteries.
The only light in the caves will be the light we carry.

Outside, it is an early winter day with below-zero temperatures. In the ice caves beneath the glacier, the temperature

hovers between 31 and 33 degrees F, and the air is extremely humid.

Our leader is Dick Flaharty, a Fairbanks man who's often visited the depths of this glacier's belly, usually with a novice in tow. In an active year, Dick visits ice caves up to 15 times. All told, in the last nine years, he's explored more than 100 caves.

"I feel like I'm a glacial proctologist," he jokes.

We slog a mile to the cave entrance, which yawns a dark greeting in the snowy hillside. A glacial river spills from its mouth.

The caves are easily accessible in the glaciers of the Alaska Range, south of Delta Junction and just a short hike from the road.

Ice caving seems to be something people try once, then say, "That was fun. Thanks. Don't think I'll do it again."

Wilda Whitaker of Fairbanks once spent a spring day ice caving with Dick and described it as "two hours of controlled panic."

"The thing that amazed me was, we'd be in there for just a matter of minutes, and our breath would start changing it," she said. "It would start melting. Things would start falling on your head."

She never returned.

Years ago, my husband Joe Durrenberger and friend Mark Fedor came here with Dick on a bitterly cold winter day. After exploring caves, they discovered Dick's car had died. Joe and Mark made the 150-mile trip back home to Fairbanks hitchhiking in the back of an open pickup truck at 30 degrees below zero. Amazingly enough, here they were again, back for more. Just like me.

The last time I explored caves with Dick, we crawled on our bellies alongside an underground river that abruptly disappeared into a hole in the ground. My heart pounded relentlessly, and my breath came in short gasps when I realized there wasn't room to turn around. We crawled backward to retreat, and I tried desperately to control my thoughts and remain calm. I didn't want to think about how easily we could be trapped. An earthquake, a flash flood, a cave-in—any of those are possible at any time. I didn't want to be reminded of the time Dick fell off an ice block in a cave and cracked a rib, or about the time he sliced his hand open on a ridge of ice sharp as a knife.

Dick knows the caves can be dangerous. He doesn't dwell on the danger, but he doesn't downplay it either. They should be investigated only by people with extensive glacial travel experience, he says.

"You have to be able to recognize bad ice and know when not to walk through it," he says. "It's the equivalent of avalanche awareness. You have to pay attention to the objective hazards."

Among his helpful safety tips, Dick suggests three people as an ideal group size. "That way, if you get in trouble, you have someone to eat," he says, raising one eyebrow.

We stare at the entrance, wondering what lies ahead. Mark breaks the silence. "How come you never get anyone to come back here with you twice, Dick?" he asks. "All those other cavers are probably still inside," jokes Joe.

Dick smiles wickedly, "Yeah, you'll get a chance to meet all those people."

We laugh a little nervously, but it's hard to take Dick too seriously. Wearing his neoprene cap and headlamp, he looks like a glacial worm. Also, he must have felt this would be a safe trip—safe enough to bring along his 9-year-old son, Tyson.

I consciously push all trepidation aside and walk into the waiting darkness. With each step, the light dims, and the sound of the river grows louder. As the ceiling lowers, we walk, hunched over, down the middle of the river. The current pulls at our legs, and small waves splash above our waders.

Earlier, I had mentally chastised Dick for not carrying a daypack with extra food and clothes. Now I wished I wasn't wearing one myself. Those extra inches on my back prevent me from partially straightening my legs, forcing me to walk hunched over, squatting and waddling. I lean on the ice ax for balance, trying to keep my butt out of the water.

"The ceiling has dropped a foot since last weekend," Dick announces loudly. In this cave, the rushing river rumbles and echoes, making conversation difficult. We all cock our heads to inspect the ceiling and exchange concerned glances, knowing 400 to 800 feet of ice and rock press down upon us.

"Thank you for sharing that with us, Dick," I think, but keep it to myself. For I know that the harder conditions get, the better Dick likes it.

"I really enjoy a challenging environment," he once told me. "Since I was a kid, I've always liked real cold, high winds. It makes you focus on what you're doing. It makes you lose the option for screwing up. You screw up, you get hurt."

He even turned his love of cold into a profession. As owner of an outdoor clothing and gear manufacturing business in Fairbanks, he tests most of his products himself to know whether they work in harsh conditions.

He's had plenty of opportunity. There was the time he and a buddy tried to climb Mount Hesperus in the Revelation Mountains in southeastern Alaska. A wet snowstorm forced them off the mountain and drenched all their gear. Then temperatures promptly dropped to between 40 and 55 below zero for the next three and a half weeks.

Or there was the time he biked the 30-mile Pinnell Mountain Trail, north of Fairbanks, in two days, carrying only a water filter, a quarter-pound of chocolate-covered coffee beans, and a garbage bag to sleep in.

Now he looks like one of a swarm of prehistoric bugs, moving awkwardly up the channel. One person duck-walks. Another scurries forward in short bursts of speed, then stops to rest. A third crouches, squats, then crouches again. Each follows the bobbing light of a headlamp.

Although Dick's son, Tyson, boasts this trip is "about my 40th time," it's really his seventh ice-caving expedition. The way he takes the lead, it may as well be his 40th time.

A duplicate of his father, with the added advantage of smaller size and limitless energy, he worms through tight spots, then calls to the rest of us, "It's easy!" When we seem reluctant to follow, he prods us forward by proudly pointing out what we already know: "My Dad did it."

As we move deeper into the cave, the air is warmer and more humid. The ceiling drops so low, we can continue only by sliding forward on our bellies. Once-frozen mud now clings to my mitts in clumps of black goo. Muck that Dick calls "baby poop mud" smears our rain gear, top to bottom.

The claustrophobia unfurls slowly, like a creature waking and stretching after a long sleep. The ceiling scrapes our heads, even while we lie flat. The air seems thinner and steamier. Rushing water flows inches from our elbows, carrying our strained grunts and groans back to the cave entrance.

Like last time, an iron door clangs shut in my mind, closing off all thought of things that can go wrong. I find myself thinking about fresh air and daylight and standing up, and I wonder why we press on. I almost turn back, but decide to hang in there just a little bit longer.

We are about 400 yards into the cave, when Mark, who's always ready to push on and see what's around the next corner, comments on how little room we have left to maneuver.

I solemnly agree, trying not to sound too relieved that someone finally has voiced what I've been thinking for some time. We all agree that it's time to turn around—although I try not to appear too eager in my retreat.

We wiggle back the way we came, anxious to explore a different cave—maybe one with a little more headroom.

Caves in the same glacier can be vastly different, and they can change daily. The caves are formed by water running off the surface of the glacier, down cracks and crevices. The water collects in a stream that eventually flows out the terminus. As the water flows downward through the ice, caves of varying sizes are formed.

Constant melting and movement of the glacier creates bizarre shapes and intriguing pathways. Huge rocks jut precariously out of the ceiling or walls, waiting for the ice to move or melt and drop them to the ground.

Depending upon the time of year, water inside the caves can pose a deadly hazard. On warm, sunny days, the top of the glacier melts and all the water runs down into the caves. Dick enthusiastically describes climbing down into the vertical shaft of a nearby glacier. He had donned a wetsuit and rappelled down the shaft, mid-waterfall, landing in a deep pool of water

60 feet inside the glacier. From there, he swam 15 feet to the edge of the pool, then rappelled another 10 feet to a second deep pool.

"That water was cold," he says. "I think it was 32.1 degrees."

An underground flash flood can easily fill a whole tunnel— kind of like the tunnel we are in.

We climb into the second cave through its collapsed ceiling on the top of the glacier. Carefully stepping down a steep mud cone, we gingerly avoid slipping into the abyss on the sides and front of the cone.

A chasm blocks our way. We worm around it by scooting along a narrow shelf with a low ceiling. Slowly inching forward, we curse every sharp rock that bites into our sides.

The shelf opens into a wondrous, translucent ice tunnel.

While the other cave had been primarily gravel and mud, this cave sparkles from ice above and all around us. Our headlamps reveal bubbles of air trapped in the walls. Here's an ice bench, a convenient spot to sit and rest. There's a wall of delicate crystal sculpture. The tunnel glows in our reflected headlamp beams.

We can even stand upright, but not always straight. The ice tube twists, requiring us to lean against one side and face the other, trusting our crampons not to slide out from under us.

At each turn, intricate icicle formations cover the walls. Some are small and delicate. A few icicles have formed, melted, then frozen again at a new angle, bent as if they are rubber.

The tunnel winds like a cold artery through the glacier's massive body, and the temperature rises as we probe deeper. Eventually, we break through thin ice at our feet and slosh through about 8 inches of water.

Ice soon gives way to a jumble of rocks. We clamber over shelves and boulders, and find ourselves in a cavernous, multilevel room.

I look up to see Dick lying on his side on the third tier, head resting in his hand over a propped elbow. If I didn't know better, I'd swear he was relaxing in a sauna. Mark stands on the main level, and Tyson sits on another shelf.

Our headlamps explore corners of the cavern. Then, for a moment, we turn off all the lights. There is no trickling of water, no creaking of ice. Only the sound of our breathing. Dark. Quiet.

Enough. We switch on the lights and head for the exit.

One by one, our heads poke up over the lips of the glacier and into the cold air. Night has fallen, but bright stars make the sky lighter than the black of the cave.

In moments, our mitts freeze. Our packs, covered with glacier mud, also freeze.

We rip off our crampons, switch to winter boots, and slog back to the highway. Icy winds blast our faces and obliterate the trail from earlier in the day. But the air feels refreshing after the humid caves.

No one had panicked as the walls and ceiling closed in, and no one had gotten stuck, or gone swimming in any glacial pools.

But the trip wasn't over just yet.

During the drive home Dick tells me about a never-ending ice tube that trapped him in this very glacier three years ago.

Deep inside the Castner Glacier, Dick had wiggled through a narrow tunnel, an ice tube so tight he'd had to empty his chest of air before he could push himself forward. He'd stuck his arms up ahead of him and suddenly realized that he could not move—forward or backward.

Then he'd discovered his crampons were embedded in the ice. Normally those spikes helped him negotiate through the ice. Now they'd stopped him cold. "I had a brief bit of panic," he recalled. "My crampons were stuck, and I couldn't turn my head. I couldn't even take a deep breath."

Nor could he communicate with his partner back in the main cave. The rushing water of an underground river made too much noise. All thoughts of excavating a trench to ease passage through this tight spot vanished in that moment. All he'd wanted to do was move.

"It took an hour to get everything under control," Dick says. "First I thought only about my foot and tried to work it. I did that, working all the way up my body. It took three hours.

By then I was really cold, and my body had cramped up. I got out of that, and it was still a long way to the entrance.

"I crawled through tube after tube. I couldn't turn on my side, so I couldn't turn around.

"And I needed to get out of there."

I realize my own mental control had gotten a workout in two fairly easy ice caves. How would I have reacted if I were in Dick's place in that tube? I don't even want to speculate. I do know if I ever go ice caving again, I will work hard to banish that story from my mind. I'm glad he saved it for last.

RICHARD ADAMS CAREY

Summer at Kuskokwim Bay

"MY PARTNER FIRED AWAY WITHOUT COMPUNCTION, AND TWO OF
THE SWANS FELL HEAVILY TO THE GROUND, DROPPING LIKE BAGS
OF SAND OUT OF A THEATER'S RAFTERS. AT THE END OF THE DAY
HE WAS MORE GLAD OF THAT MEAT THAN OF ANY OF THE MANY
DUCKS WE'D TAKEN."

*Richard Adams Carey first traveled from Massachusetts to Alaska
in 1977 to teach high school English.* Raven's Children, *his
memoir of the experience, was published in 1992.*

*"In Kongiganak," he writes, "the ordinary gestures of every-
day life—at least to me—are in equal parts familiar and
strange, like signposts in garbled spelling. They point in their
enigmatic manner to a past of such depth and scale, of such dis-
course between forgotten generations, as scarcely to be imagined,
yet one as immanent as yesterday's weather. I blink, and all the
buildings just that quickly revert to grass. In my mind's eye the
old village and the new begin to blur together, and I conceive of
them as each the complement and the destiny of the other. They
blur even into destinies such as my own, and in these knotted
grasses, among these shifting sloughs, I don't think I know any
longer exactly where the boundary exists."*

ONLY YESTERDAY OSCAR ACTIVE LAUGHED, his single front tooth like a sliver of quartz in his gum, when he told me that I'd been enrolled in his school of cussing for the summer. Now I get my first real lesson as we find that the tide is out in the Kongiganak River and that the *Crazy J*'s anchor rests beneath the keel of another wooden skiff. This other boat rests high and dry on exposed riverbed, and is too heavy to be lifted. So Oscar cusses at the top of his lungs, dispensing his expertise abroad, not only to me and his family but also to the half-dozen houses that line this portion of the riverbank, their windows thrown open to the weather today. Still cussing, he goes down into the mud to tunnel the anchor out, while his brother Charlie and I haul on its line. Elsie and Margaret and the four children and their cousin line the bank above us, staring silently down at the progress of this project, and the clouds above their heads are high and white and dreamy.

Today is the next to last day of May 1989. Breakup came a couple of weeks ago to this part of southwestern Alaska, but this is the first day that really feels like spring. Delayed by weeks of chilling rain and high winds off Kuskokwim Bay, the hordes of shorebirds and waterfowl that migrate each year to the Yukon-Kuskokwim Delta are finally nesting. Similarly, at Cape Avinof, forty miles west of here, shoals of persistent shelf ice have delayed the herring spawn, and so also the opening of the commercial herring fishery.

Oscar Active is a fisherman, and he knows that agents for the Alaska Department of Fish & Game are at this very moment performing their test fishings over at the cape. Today the winds have died, and a sky so vast that on many days it's honey-combed into several discrete weather systems is ruled all at once by a single blue and breathless clarity. Oscar raises his head, just as his mother and wife and all the children start down the riverbank, just as the anchor pops loose like a seed and Charlie nearly falls over backward. Oscar peers up at the sky first and then down the river, reminding himself, I'm sure, that the fishery could conceivably open at any moment now and that this would be a perfect day for him and Charlie and me to be traveling over to Cape Avinof in the *Crazy J*. He cusses again, under his breath this time, then glances up in his wife Margaret's direction.

The *Crazy J* is twenty-four feet long and broad-beamed, painted slate blue with a crisp black trim. It seems huge compared to the little aluminum skiff that Oscar and Charlie fished in last summer, and Oscar himself, as he stands at the steering console that he has bolted to the stern thwart, seems no less huge. Yesterday in Bethel, the big town seventy miles inland up the Kuskokwim River, a *kass'aq* running the cash register in a hamburger joint nodded familiarly to Oscar, and Oscar laughed, but with an embarrassed edge to it, as the clerk pointed to a group of strange teenagers playing an arcade game and said, "I'm telling all these white kids what it's gonna be like here this summer with all the crazy drunk Eskimos, and you're just what we need, Oscar—a big one. One look at you—I'll tell 'em what you're like—and they'll be buying tickets home faster than they can sell 'em."

Charlie is a big one too; indeed, all of the natural brothers in the Active family are big, astonishingly so for Eskimos. But Oscar is the biggest, the most physically imposing: something over six feet tall, something beyond 260 pounds, most of it square and thick, bone and hard muscle, though in recent years his belt buckle has been safely out of the weather. This morning, in a little house on the opposite side of the village, Oscar sat at his breakfast like a great bear come wandering inside and tamed. But his mother, Elsie, impressed by his fiery temperament and mane of wild black hair (already graying in streaks), prefers to call him Oscar the Lion. I heard her murmur that to herself a moment ago, conceding in frank admiration, while Oscar swore and dug at the anchor, "He's even louder than I am." Older fans of *Sesame Street*, when they're teasing him, call him Oscar the Grouch.

Now, grouchily, Oscar looks back over his shoulder at the eighty-horse outboard motor. His two little boys are the last to clamber into the boat; Margaret rinses their feet in the river before they set their rubber boots down on the clean floorboards. When Oscar kicks the Evinrude into life, the boat ponderously faces upstream, lifting toward its skeg. Oscar Junior and Clayton, aged four and three, settle themselves on the boat's middle thwart, on either side of their mother, and stare in wonder at the banks gathering speed, then blurring past. Up from the village the crests of the banks are lined by sedge meadows, and Junior stands to point at the dozens of ducks that flush from their midst as we flash by: northern pintail, mallard, American widgeon.

The Kongiganak's channel is a narrow and silty trough, coiled and accordioned and then pressed like a gutter into the level plain of the tundra, and today Elsie enjoys even the pull of these crazy veers and loops. The old woman squints like Popeye through her one good eye and laughs, making a swirling motion with her hands. Then she gestures forward to the dwindling image of the village, which by now has appeared at one time or another over all quarters of the boat—bow, stern, port, and starboard. She shouts above the roar of the motor, "This is a seal-intestine river! Shaped like seal intestines!" She laughs again, her mouth hollow and toothless, her short white hair trailing straight in the wind.

Oscar's mother still lives in Bethel, where Oscar grew up, where in fact she raised all of her six sons, and where Charlie has made his home once again since his divorce a few years ago from the Kongiganak girl he married. But the foraging is no longer so good in the vicinity of populous Bethel, which has grown to a town of four thousand, and a good portion of the old woman's food now, by necessity—and to her distaste—is the *kass'aq* food that she has to buy at the supermarkets. But down here on the coast the foraging is still very good, and in fact subsistence hunting and fishing remain the chief economic activity in villages such as Kongiganak, providing explanation enough for their existence and location, just as they did for all those centuries prior to the appearance of the Russians. Elsie is delighted to be headed upstream like this, to devote an entire day to searching out the eggs of the nesting wild birds, and it was precisely for this, and the promise of fresh spring food, that she came down from Bethel with Oscar and Charlie and me in this boat.

Margaret and all the children are delighted too: serious-minded Elizabeth, who is twelve years old and has her father's pouting lower lip; eight-year-old Janet, the exuberant one, whom Oscar named this boat after, and who answers as often to her nickname, Crazy; the two little brothers; and their ten-year-old cousin, Aaron Paul. This morning, after Oscar had un-expectedly agreed to the foray, Janet danced in sweet joy throughout the tiny house, her brown feet bare, one of them labeled FOOT with a felt-tip marker and the other labeled FEET.

But Margaret didn't say a word then, and she continues to be as silent as Elsie is effervescent. She sits with her back to Oscar, facing into the wind, and I watch as she lifts her face to the sky a moment and flares her nostrils, drinking in the brackish scent of the quickening marshes. Her cheeks are high and round, her brow smooth. Her shoulders hunch slightly in the chill. Behind her glasses her face is like water at the bottom of a well: clear, pure, betraying nothing.

Half an hour after leaving the village, we reach an area where the river twists past a covey of meltwater lakes. Oscar throws the Evinrude into neutral and then kills it, allowing the boat to skim into a portion of the bank where swaths of under-cut sod have split and fallen into a sort of stairway up the in-cline to the surrounding tableland. Charlie pulls the hard-won anchor out of the bow and then climbs stiffly up the bank, dig-ging its tines into the parched grass above us. The rest of us empty out of the boat, Elsie skipping nimbly as a goat up the steps of sod. Oscar and Margaret climb up separately, still with-out sharing a glance, and I doubt that they've so much as ex-changed a word all day.

At the top of the bank we stand in a row and look out upon a huge, unportioned field of chalky greens and wintry yellows and browns, the lakes in the distance winking cobalt blue in the sunlight. Now that the big motor has stopped, the quiet is almost palpable. But slowly that ringing silence is overcome, and overwhelmed, by another sort of ringing, almost a roar, startling in its pervasiveness and the breadth of its register: a sourceless, throbbing cacophony of bird cries, a sound like the morning of the fifth day of creation.

Oscar grunts as he drives the sharp end of a broken oar into the grass at the top of the bank so that it stands upright like a fence post, marking the position of the boat. He stands there for a moment with his lips pressed together, hard and white, just as he did while he stood at his window earlier this morning, staring into the light glancing off the smooth surface of the bay.

Then, without a word or gesture to one another, we fan singly and in pairs out into the tundra.

I watch Oscar move off upriver with Junior's hand in his, a bear, or maybe a lion, and his cub, while Charlie takes off alone in the opposite direction, a twelve-gauge shotgun cradled in his arms. Others depart at angles between these extremes: Margaret and Crazy toward an area of rolling frost heaves; Elizabeth, with Clayton on her shoulders, in the direction of some marshes covered over with horsetail; Elsie, by herself, toward one of the lakes. The nephew, Aaron, stays with me. Dressed in a brown leather flight jacket with Army Air Force arm patches, the boy is as lean as a willow switch, and his skin seems to have been brushed like varnish over the planes of his face.

We stand in the midst of a landscape more peculiar than mere tundra. About twenty miles east of here stretches the wide mouth of the Kuskokwim River. The Kuskokwim is the chief artery into the interior for this part of Alaska, twisting more than 700 miles from the foothills of the Alaska Range to this remote and soggy coast, draining (along with its tributaries) an area of more than 50,000 square miles. Far to the north, about 150 miles distant, lies the mouth of the Yukon, the Kuskokwim's more glamorous and storied sister. But in southwestern Alaska the rivers argue to be taken on equal terms. They approach within twenty-five miles of each other at Kalskag, a Kuskokwim village seventy-five miles above Bethel and once the site of an important portage between the two. There, though the Yukon then swings sharply north to empty into Norton Sound, the two rivers' flood plains begin to open out and blend together, finally combining into a single immense alluvial fan roughly the size of Wisconsin. The coastal fringe of the Yukon-Kuskokwim Delta runs 250 miles up the coast of Alaska, from Cape Newenham to Saint Michael, and the saturated tundra of this fringe and its interior, with its seal-intestine sloughs and meltwater lakes, provides summer breeding grounds for some 24 million migratory shorebirds and waterfowl.

In its own way, I suspect, the Yukon-Kuskokwim Delta is a natural wonder on the order of, say, the Grand Canyon or Yellowstone, though of an entirely inverted sort. Just as the Grand Canyon is a monument to the erosive power of running water unconfused by other natural processes, and Yellowstone to the might of Pleistocene ice in a similarly pure application, this hybrid planet of water and silt is a monument to the converse tendency of filling in and leveling off—a monument, over the millennia, to nothing but the long and single-minded exercise of sedimentation, its motions flash-frozen each fall, then sluggishly renewed in the spring over its underlying pan of permafrost. Here this process is played out on what seems a universal scale, the flooding and silting simply swallowing up, like the sea, whatever topography lies beneath it, every hint of the kind of relief that so distinguishes those other monuments, or indeed is characteristic, on a lesser scale, of any other landscape.

The birds that so relish this wetland converge in seasonal streams from the Pacific, Asia, and all over the Americas—converge in a place so vast and uncut, however, as to absorb them even in all their millions, scattering their nests like motes of dust, providing flyways as widely spaced across this sky as the weather systems. I don't think much of my own chances of finding any eggs here, and in fact I've been foraging like this many times around Kongiganak in the spring—once before in this very area—and have never on any occasion found more than a few broken bits of shell, and never any eggs. So instead I go back to the boat to get my shotgun out of the bow, as Charlie did. Aaron looks pleased. He points straight ahead to the lakes maybe a mile distant, in a bearing only slightly off from Elsie's, and then dances ahead of me.

The river disappears as we move away from it. Underfoot the ground is spongy beneath its cover of reindeer moss, cassiope, Labrador tea, and crowberry; this will end with surprising crispness at the margins of the lakes and ponds, and from the air it looks as though the beds of the lakes have been stamped through the mat with cookie cutters. From any ground-level perspective, however, the breadth and uniformity of this cover swallow up all other features, so the river simply vanishes as we move a short distance away from it, the matching planes of its banks blending in sight, the landmark oar the only sign to indicate that a division exists. From this distance the lakes appear as little more than sequined blue threads teased through a carpet of burlap. Aaron, who prefers Yupik to English, though he speaks both languages, points ahead to a set of white pinpoints strung like rice along a portion of one such thread. "*Qugyuut— pissurlapuk!*" he says. "Swans—let's hunt them!"

These big, straight-necked tundra swans, also known as whistling swans, are the chief ingredient of a delicious soup prepared by Margaret's grandmother, though it has taken time for me to superimpose the image of game bird on my received *kass'aq* perceptions of swans. And to see them stirring in their bright, numberless flocks here among the barrens is in fact arresting in a way that surpasses the stirrings of any other bird. Once I went hunting in the fall near here with a man named Tommy Andrew as my partner. That time I just dropped the muzzle of my gun and let squadrons of the swans pass over my head unmolested, even as Tommy called them in my direction. He had placed himself on the other side of a lake from me, and in following his call the birds flew over his position as well. My partner fired away without compunction, and two of the swans fell heavily to the ground, dropping like bags of sand out of a theater's rafters. At the end of the day he was more glad of that meat than of any of the many ducks we'd taken.

But here the swans are alert and difficult to approach as they feed on the sago pondweed growing along the bottoms of the lakes. Aaron and I stalk them, alternately crouching and crawling, skirting the rims of intervening ponds. But the birds always sense us and rise from the water in whooping, spiraling clouds long before I've gotten my shotgun in range. Then they gather and circle off toward the ocean, sometimes swinging near enough for Aaron to exhort in Yupik, "They're close. Try and shoot!" I don't think so myself, but twice I try such mortar shots anyway—to no effect on the birds, which disappear to the south with powerful bell-beats of their wings.

A short while later Aaron takes an opposite path to mine around a lake, and when he joins me he proudly pulls from his pocket a seagull egg as big as his hand. "*Elpet pikan*, it's yours," he says, presenting it to me with a white smile creasing his face, his eyes just creases themselves. Then he points suddenly to a pair of pintails skimming rapidly toward us from the east, their wings weaving flashes of violet and bronze and green. I shoot between them and drop the female into the margin of the same pond that yielded the seagull egg. Heartbreakingly, the male veers back and lands beside his dying mate. Reluctantly I take him as well, watching down my barrel as he explodes from the midst of the pellets hailing about him, the slender plume of his long black tailfeathers trailing, and falls into the pond.

Later, when Aaron and I join the others for lunch back at the boat, Oscar the Grouch tells me that the swans were out of range and spares hardly a glance for the two ducks. "Don't shoot pintails now," he scolds. "They're too damn skinny."

Elsie pinches their breasts between her fingers and says, "They're good." She thrusts out her chin, as she does habitually when she contradicts Oscar, or anybody else, and her face, with one eye closed off, looks as nicked and creased as a prizefighter's. She says she lost the eye years ago in an accident when she was taking care of her kids, and is reluctant otherwise to talk about it. I know the pintails will be eaten, skinny or not, for Margaret wouldn't discard wild meat, though Oscar might complain about having to eat meat so lean. After lunch, however, I leave my twelve-gauge in the boat and concentrate fully on the gentler task of finding eggs.

But this is worse for me than stalking swans. Aaron goes off on his own into the lakes, and I begin an erratic drift across the wavelike peat ridges and around the borders of the ponds. Sometimes I'm tantalized by bits of broken shell, or occasional feathers, or an owl pellet, or the mere presence in my ears, like surf or the echo in a seashell, of all the thrumming bird cries. But the calls come distantly, from off toward the horizon, as though these lakes had entirely emptied, and my eyes tire quickly from the monotony of the groundcover, from the memory of similar long afternoons.

This time, however, my circuits start to intersect with those of a more experienced egg-finder, and I learn from watching Margaret that it pays better to rely on the birds and their behavior than on the thin odds of coming across a nest by chance.

When a black-bellied plover shows signs of distress, whistling plaintively and floating in its colors of charcoal and old leaves from frost heave to frost heave in a circle around me, I drop to my hands and knees and scour the immediate area for its nest. Margaret glances at the bird, approaches, and finds the nest in only a minute.

Later I notice a tiny western sandpiper trailing like Tom Thumb in the wake of my boots and cheeping frantically in agitation. When I turn, the bird hops away as though flightless, flitting as needed just beyond my reach. Again the nest eludes me, and when Margaret can't quickly find it either, she drives the bird away and sits on a driftwood stump some distance removed. Margaret grew up in the neighboring village of Kwigillingok, eleven miles to the west, and as a little girl she was badly mauled by a loose sled dog. In this bright sun the faint scar that she still bears on her cheek looks like the track of a bird. She turns in my direction, her eyes drawing slowly over the ridges, and the scar disappears.

"Where's that bird?" she wonders in English. "Did you see it come back?" Then a smile plays about her lips, betrays her thoughts. She thinks mischievously about Hannah, her grandparents' adopted teenage daughter, who has left her two-year-old with the old couple and gone off to Bethel. "It must be Hannah's grandmother, abandoning her children like that."

But then the sandpiper reappears, landing and settling into a patch of bog cranberry thirty or forty feet away. Margaret rises from her stump and goes directly to the spot. The little bird's four tiny eggs are maroon and slate gray, sharply pointed and full of promise. "We should take them all," Margaret says. "That way she'll be fooled into laying another clutch, if they're not too old. But she won't if there's even just one egg left."

Others find eggs as well. Oscar locates a yellowleg's nest when the long-beaked bird nearly scares the wits out of him by exploding like a ptarmigan from right under his feet, but then he calls Crazy over and lets her find the eggs. Elsie finds a dozen eggs of various sorts by foraging skillfully on her own among the lakes, but she falls on the tundra coming back to the boat, and four of them break. Elizabeth finds a lesser golden plover's nest, but Margaret has been watching, and she discourages the girl from taking the eggs. The plover was too aggressive in the way it pursued and harassed Elizabeth, Margaret says, and probably the eggs are too far along.

No one's eggs are welcomed more delightedly, however, than those that tiny Clayton finds. Elizabeth can hardly tell the story, she laughs so hard. "I was carrying him up on my shoulders, you know, and one of his boots fell off. And then just while I'm bending down to pick it up, right then, he points down into that grass and tells me, 'Look.' Gee, I couldn't believe it."

The semipalmated sandpiper eggs that result from this precocious foraging won't be eaten immediately, like the rest. Instead Margaret will boil them and keep them in the cool of the entryway at her house. Then, later this summer, she'll throw these eggs, along with candy and other foods, some household and toilet items, and a number of cut strips of cloth and yarn, to a shrieking and laughing assembly of women—the grandmothers and mothers of any girl in the village that Clayton might conceivably marry. This will be his *uqiquq,* his seal party, a centuries-old observance that marks a male's new status as a provider—an event happening singularly early in Clayton's case.

The Yupik term *uqiquq* relates to seal oil and refers to the taking of a bearded seal, an animal not only rich in that nutritious commodity but charged with a peculiar spiritual power in the ideology that still informs and supports this hunting economy. Once a boy or young man captures one of these great seals, the *uqiquq* that is given for him formally welcomes him to the village's pool of marriageable males. But an *uqiquq* may also be mounted to commemorate the first harvest of any wild food, including sandpiper eggs. In a number of the villages upriver on the Kuskokwim, and around Bethel, these seal parties are rarely or never celebrated anymore, though I remember that Elsie attended one near her home last week. In Kongiganak and other coastal communities, however, they are still performed, much as Susie Chanigkak, Margaret's grandmother, has always performed them, and they are even enjoying something of a renaissance, with daughters now occasionally feted in the same manner.

Clayton sits in the boat and sips at a can of orange soda, heedless of his renown, the pop trickling down his chin. Elizabeth places the eggs in a plastic bucket floored with moss and then sets the bucket up on the boat's forward thwart. "Put that bucket down, stupid!" Oscar booms. "Them eggs'll fall and break. What you doing, putting it up so high?"

Elizabeth cringes as though struck, lifting the eggs down to the floorboards. I prop my back against that same thwart and start to nod off; I find that by now the thunder of Oscar's edginess, his suspicion that this egg-hunting may be a costly mistake, registers hardly at all on a sensibility grown more diffuse than in even a three-year-old like Clayton. I'm leg-sore from all my walking, wind-burned, drowsy, and everything seems to come at me at once in the avian frenzy of this world, almost as if in a dream: the distant rattle of the sandhill cranes; the brief, busy flights of the black-bibbed Lapland longspurs whisking from rise to rise; the little dunlins rocking like hunchbacked sailors along the shores of the lakes; the striking scarlet flush on the necks of the breeding phalaropes; the strange, whiffling thrum of the common snipes as they lay their tailfeathers like sounding boards against the air in courtship.

I absorb all this now as I have all day, and just as I always have: with hardly a hint of a subsistence hunter's focal purpose, a forager's attention to relevant minutiae, even when I try consciously to assume that stance. Young Aaron sees the big flocks of game birds approaching from the horizons long before I do. Tiny Clayton almost falls on his face into a clutch of eggs, while I need help to cash in on my own near misses. For brief periods, maybe, I exist here almost as pointedly as Margaret does, or Elsie, or Oscar when he's not thinking of everything he's already sunk into this commercial fishing season and everything that's already gone wrong, or promises to; but then I find myself distracted by something as extraneous as the sight of a stilt-legged dowitcher prospecting through a bed of goose grass, and I'm lost to my own purposes here, like a child unable to concentrate long enough to learn simple addition. Instead I meander casually through a world that has become a pleasant art form, and I find the hunter's task of asserting any firm place for myself in its motions and flux as puzzling as Arabic. The effort to separate and anticipate its stirrings ends up tiring me, frustrating me, and I come back empty-handed, too proud to pretend that the seagull egg Aaron gave me was mine.

The stern of the *Crazy J* is heavy with water that leaked in through the bow while we were gone, and Oscar starts his little electric bilge pump by touching the bare end of a wire to a battery post. The water gurgles over the side as though through a faucet. I don't remember ever hearing Charlie fire his shotgun; I watch through half-open eyes as he returns with no game, stows the gun beneath the boat's small foredeck, and then stands at Oscar's side behind the stern thwart. Crazy fetches the bucket that contains Clayton's eggs and shows it to him. Charlie smiles as he looks into the bucket, his teeth splayed and chipped like broken crockery, his upper lip wisped by fine black hairs. His eyes are sleepy and vacant as he looks up again from the eggs, and his cheeks hang like curtains down the length of his face.

The other eggs as well are secured safely in the boat, and Oscar starts the motor. Before I dropped down the bank and into the boat twenty minutes ago, I turned and saw the women trailing reluctantly back, looking like a band of gypsies: Margaret advancing prettily across the peat ridges in her flowered cotton parka cover, her *qaspeq*, the two boys holding on to her hands, and Elsie some distance behind them in her green nylon jacket and bright bandanna, carrying her eight unbroken eggs in her pockets. The old woman's mouth was open in a laugh again, and her legs were so bowed that she rocked back and forth like a dunlin as she walked.

Elsie is still laughing, astonished at breaking those eggs, but the mask on Margaret's face is firmly in place once more. Margaret sits on the middle thwart as the boat swings downstream, her back to the bow this time, her eyes gazing emptily between the two brothers.

Oscar and Charlie and I sit around the converted telephone cable spool that serves as the Actives' supper table, and Oscar laughs as he describes what it was like commercial fishing with Charlie a few summers ago at Quinhagak, a village on the southern side of Kuskokwim Bay. "That summer Charlie had pneumonia, but we went down from Bethel anyway," he says. "He steered the boat, and I hauled the nets and did all the work. But then I got a pinched nerve in my back, and I couldn't hardly move. But Charlie was feeling a little bit better by then, so I just started steering, and Charlie did all the work."

Charlie shakes his head and says, "It was stormy down there that year, man. One day we spent the whole time just surfing down those waves."

"Yep, they were as high as the roof on that *lagyaq* there," Oscar adds, pointing out the window to the little shed where Margaret and her grandmother cut and store their fresh meat.

Charlie looks at the *lagyaq* and still can't believe that he got talked into going out into weather like that. "Gambling with our lives," he says.

Oscar laughs again. "It's a good gamble when you survive."

Margaret clears our plates away, taking them to a sink where water is contained in a plastic basin and clean dishes and mugs are piled in perilous architecture in a drying rack on the counter, and I wonder what she thinks of Oscar's gambling this year. On our way up to the nesting grounds this morning, Junior pointed out to me various items of the boat's cargo—the Styrofoam grub box, the broken oar, the VHF radio, and the new marine battery and the propane camp stove, both of which Oscar had just bought in Bethel out of his and Margaret's income tax refund—and after each item set himself in front of me and said in his stentorian voice, "It's not yours!" Finally he took hold of the boat itself, latching onto the starboard gunwale with both tiny fists, reminding me that even the *Crazy J* itself wasn't mine.

Margaret knew that—knew that for better or for worse, the big wooden boat now belonged to her husband. Oscar had just bought it from Jerry Demientieff, an old school buddy of his, promising to pay Jerry $1,000 for it at the end of the fishing season. Last night he told Margaret, "It'll pay for itself no sweat. It won't fill up with fish as fast as that little aluminum boat I been borrowing from Joe Brown, and I won't have to be running back and forth to the tenders all the time making deliveries. Instead I'll just keep my net in the water—save time, save gas—and get more fish, you know?"

Margaret nodded, though I doubt that Oscar's assurances quite quelled her concern. I'm sure it's already occurred to her, as it has to me, that maybe there is too much that belongs to Oscar this summer, that quite possibly he's put too much in the pot and is already overextended. Besides this new used boat, with its $1,000 price tag, and besides the Skidoo Safari snow machine that he wants to buy from me in the fall, and besides the gear that he has already bought for this boat, there is the new thirty-horse Nissan outboard that he bought last month from Swanson's Marina in Bethel. Margaret had to arrange for a $1,500 loan from the First National Bank in order to buy that motor, and they still have eleven more payments to make on the loan.

Of course, the herring are coming to Cape Avinof, if they're not there already, though they don't appear to have arrived just yet. Oscar's brother Buzzo now lives in Kipnuk, the village closest to Cape Avinof, and Buzzo called this morning to say that there was still too much ice off the cape and that Fish & Game wouldn't be opening the fishery immediately. On the strength of that, Oscar agreed to take the family egg-hunting, though no sooner had he done so than he began to get nervous, and to start thinking that maybe he should be traveling instead, especially with everything he's got riding on this season.

Though potentially lucrative, the herring season is a short one, and it's not until the various species of Pacific salmon start swimming in waves up the Kuskokwim River that the real money crop of southwestern Alaska finally arrives. The salmon will be there all summer long, available to fishermen three to four times each week in periods set aside exclusively for commercial—as opposed to subsistence—fishing. But given the commitments that Oscar presently supports, and given the sort of money that he could realistically hope to make this summer anyway, from both the Cape Avinof and the Kuskokwim fisheries, he can scarcely afford to have a single thing go wrong—and a couple of things already have.

Jerry Demientieff now lives in Kasigluk, a village about thirty miles northwest of Bethel, and last week Oscar and I went up there in the borrowed aluminum skiff—with the Nissan on its back—to pick up the wooden boat. We traveled on the Johnson River, a tributary to the Kuskokwim, and on the way back to Bethel, as I followed in the skiff behind the newly christened *Crazy J*, the Nissan just stopped dead in my hands. Oscar towed the skiff to Bethel and then left the motor at the marina, saying, "I don't know what's wrong with that thing, but I hope the warranty covers it. If it don't, I don't know what I'm gonna do."

Then Oscar discovered some cracked ribs in the bow of the *Crazy J*. Yesterday, in fact, he was afraid that the boat might break up beneath us in some heavy weather on the Kuskokwim, and the cussing that he then gave to Jerry, who had never said anything about those cracked ribs, was what later suggested to Oscar that he might legitimately teach the art to those less skilled. Now, if it's at all possible, he wants to be in Kipnuk at least a full day before the herring season opens, both for the margin of safety a day would provide and for the purpose of repairing his damaged boat. "The buyers don't want the herring anyway, just the roe," he told me. "And roe counts are gonna be real high when Fish & Game finally opens it up. So I want to get over to Kipnuk ahead of time, get Buzzo's help with fixing that damn leak, and be ready."

Finally, there is this other brother, Charlie, the youngest, Oscar's long-time fishing partner and also an alcoholic. Oscar himself has vowed that he's on the wagon now, that he isn't going to do any more drinking in Bethel, not this fishing season nor anytime after that. It seems also that he's been using my presence this summer to encourage a similar resolve in Charlie. Before we left for Kasigluk last week, Oscar and I rendezvoused in Bethel at the little efficiency his mother now rents. Charlie showed up drunk at Elsie's that afternoon, his slumberous eyes lit up, his arms and legs in spastic motion from the rocket fuel running through them. He said to me, "Oscar told me not to do any drinking this summer 'cause you were gonna be hanging around. But I'll tell you something, Rick, I don't stop drinking for nobody—not you, not the great Oscar Active, not George Bush, not the pope, not nobody. If anybody's gonna stop me from drinking, it's gotta be me, myself. That's the only way it's gonna start happening. You know what I'm saying?"

Then Charlie laughed and said, "Oscar, you remember that time Rick got drunk with all of us? That was after that basketball tournament in Napakiak. When was that? Maybe in seventy-nine?" He clapped his hands and slid down from his seat to the shag rug, down on all fours, his legs suddenly watery, a drunk imitating a drunk. "He couldn't even stand, man." He grinned up at Elsie, who just ignored him, and said, "Ma, you shoulda seen him. He was yellin' out, 'Help me up! Please somebody help me up!' "

Oscar wanted to get out on the water that day before the tide got too low on the Johnson, before we ran the risk of bending a propeller on the ice still frozen fast to the river bottom. He didn't like being delayed by Charlie, but even he had to smile as Charlie rolled about on the rug. "That was the year that bench-warmer hit that long shot at the end of the third overtime, or we woulda won that tournament," Oscar said. "Gee, I couldn't believe he made that shot."

"But we won a lot of other tournaments, Oscar," Charlie said. "We were the best, you know that? The Kongiganak Hunters, man—there wasn't nobody could beat us."

"Yep, then we got old," Oscar said.

The only vow that Charlie took that day was that he wasn't going to fish with Oscar at Cape Avinof, as he has in years past. "Them herring are too filthy, Oscar," he said. "I'm retired from herring fishing. You're gonna have to find someone else be your herring captain this year." Oscar didn't say a word, just set his lips and looked away, like he did this morning after he drove the oar into the bank of the river and prepared to set off with Junior.

But of course here Charlie is after all, maybe because he felt he actually owed Oscar the help, especially considering all his brother's bills, or because he was flat broke himself and needed the money, or because, with his bootleg vodka all drunk up, he was just too hung over to argue when Oscar went to his house to get him yesterday. At Cape Avinof, Oscar only needs skilled help, the sort that Charlie can provide. Later, on the Kuskokwim, he will also need the commercial salmon fishing permit that only Charlie possesses. Certainly that's part of what makes Oscar afraid now, contributing to that sense of gambling with his life again, though in a different way. I'm sure it makes him wonder sometimes how he got here from where he was, from the way things were in those days before he got old.

Now Oscar goes out to the front steps to smoke a cigarette while Margaret fetches bags of wet laundry from both of the little bedrooms. She places these first in a pile beside the mail-order shelves that hold the TV, the children's books, the family photo albums, and the various basketball trophies, and then starts carrying them one by one to the clotheslines outside. The sky above her is slowly filling with clouds like bolts of dirty linen, and the wind is blowing crisp and cold again off the bay.

ANNE MORROW LINDBERGH

Nome

"A CAR! A ROAD! WE HAD NOT SEEN A ROAD FOR SO LONG THAT
I HARDLY RECOGNIZED ONE."

*Anne Morrow met Charles Lindbergh while she was living with
her family in Mexico, where her father, Dwight Morrow, was
U.S. ambassador in the late 1920s. Dwight Morrow served with
considerable distinction, never missing an opportunity to advance American interests, and showing a special taste for cultural matters—he even commissioned extensive mural paintings
by Diego Rivera—and for public relations.*

*After Charles Lindbergh's historic solo flight across the
Atlantic in 1927 and the tumultuous reception he was accorded
on his return to the U.S., Morrow invited him to be similarly
feted in Mexico City. Morrow and the capital's government organized a grand parade and reception.*

*When the festivities were over, Morrow invited Lindbergh
to stay for a while to rest. The young hero and the ambassador's
daughter were quickly attracted to each other, and he courted
her with long and thrilling flights around the peaks of the two
volcanoes that tower on Mexico City's horizon.*

Other dramas were to follow in their lives, of course, and among them was an air trip they made together in 1931 from the east coast of the United States to Tokyo, Japan, via the great circle route over the Arctic zone. The purpose of the trip was to scout out this northern route and the conditions to be encountered on it, with an eye toward establishing regular Arctic air routes for commercial flights.

The Lindberghs took off, amid a flurry of reporters, on July 27, 1931, from College Point, Long Island. Their first destination was to the south, Washington, D.C., where they picked up passports and travel papers. On the 29th, they were heading north again, first to New York and then on to North Haven, Maine, where they stopped for a few hours so Anne could say good-bye to friends.

From Maine, they flew westward to Ottawa, then northwest to Moose Factory, on the southernmost point of Hudson Bay, on to Churchill, on the western edge of Hudson Bay, and from there northward to Baker Lake. Then they had a long westward flight to Aklavik, on Mackenzie Bay, and then another long and fog-shrouded flight northwest along the edge of the Arctic Ocean to Point Barrow, in the Alaska Territory.

The Lindberghs flew in a two-person aircraft named the Sirius. It had a 600-horsepower engine, fuel tanks that gave it a range of two thousand miles, and pontoons for landing on lakes and coastlines along their entire route to Japan. Their equipment included "instruments for blind flying and night flying; radio and direction-finding apparatus; facilities for fueling and for anchoring." They had food, medicine, and, within the plane's weight limitations, gear for every sort of condition or emergency, from warm boots to an insect-proof tent.

The Lindberghs' visit to the small town of Nome, on the Bering Sea, followed their stopover at Barrow, even farther north, on the Arctic Ocean coast of Alaska. For more about that portion of their trip, see the headnote to the selection about Barrow by Mrs. Lindbergh elsewhere in this volume.

When the Lindberghs visited, Nome had a population of fewer than 1,500 people. Located only 150 miles south of the Arctic Circle, Nome has direct sunlight for all but about two hours of the day in summer, when the Lindberghs were there.

No roads or railways reach Nome from other settlements,

so flying in is one of only three ways to get there. Another is to mush there behind a team of huskies. Suitably enough, the town's Front Street, facing the sea, is the finish line of the 1,049-mile Iditarod race from Anchorage. For more about the Iditarod, see the selection by Libby Riddles. The third way to reach Nome is by sea, but you'd have to land through the surf onto the beach, as thousands of hopeful prospectors did after gold was discovered nearby in 1898. For a sense of what that might have been like, look at the beach scenes in the John Wayne movie North to Alaska.

For more about the King Island Eskimos, see the selection by Berton Roueché, which appears last in this book.

ESKIMO SPORTS
Tomorrow Afternoon at 4 P.M.
At Barracks Sq. and Water Front
ESKIMO "WOLF DANCE" IN COSTUME
At Arctic Brotherhood Hall 8 P.M.
Public Invited
LINDBERGHS' BE GUESTS OF HONOR

THE NUGGET, NOME'S DAILY TELEGRAPH bulletin, lay on the table, its front page announcing the day's entertainment. We had arrived in this old Alaskan mining town after a short flight from Shishmaref Inlet. The night mists had melted when we woke the morning after our adventure with the duck hunters. In front of us glistened a promised land. This was the Alaska we had read of. Snow-capped mountains climbed ahead of us instead of flat wastes. Green valleys cut the morning light. And the sea, the Bering Sea, rising in the gap between two hills as we approached, burned brilliant blue. We followed the beach, a gleaming white line, toward Safety Harbor. A second white line ran parallel to the shore, like foam or scattered flowers. As we came nearer I saw it to be a tangled trail of driftwood, polished white by the surf after its long journey down the Yukon River, out into Norton Sound, and up the coast to Nome. Pounding, dancing, tossing, all the way they had come, these white arms, these branches from an alien forest, to flower on a bare coast that had never known a tree. They were as startling to see here as the waxen stems of Indian pipe in the heart of green woods, ghostly visitors from another world.

No trees yet. We had come far south from Barrow, but there were still no trees on these green hills falling to the water's edge. A broad trail cut its way over the slope, rippling up and down, like a whip cracking in the air. An Eskimo trail, I supposed, until I saw a black beetle crawl around the corner. A car! A road! We had not seen a road for so long that I hardly recognized one.

A little later we were bumping along the same road on our way into town. It had been a trail in the Gold Rush days. Old roadhouses were stationed along the side, a day's dog-team journey apart over winter snow; we had already passed the second one in forty minutes. Dilapidated shingled buildings they were, fast becoming useless; for the airplane on skiis is replacing the dog team. It is cheaper per pound to fly.

Nome has changed since the Gold Rush days when in the 1890's the precious metal was discovered in creeks and on the coast, and the great trail of prospectors swarmed over the mountains to that far cape of Alaska; when all the beach for miles—that white line we had seen from the air—was black with men sifting gold from the sand; when banks, hotels, theaters, and shops sprang up overnight and busy crowds thronged up and down the plank streets. Twenty thousand people once filled the town; now there are hardly more than a thousand.

But there were still signs of the old life. We passed a deserted mining shack by a stream. Fireweed, yarrow, and monkshood sprawled over the rusted machinery. On the beach two men were shoveling sand down long wooden sluice boxes, "washing" gold.

"Just about manage a day's wage that way," explained our host as we passed. Ahead was a gold dredge in action; the water pipes or "points" plunged deep into the ground to thaw it out before dredging.

The banks, the hotels, the shops, were still there as we rattled over the plank streets of Nome. Empty shells of buildings, many of them, gray, weather-beaten, sagging like an old stage set, tattered banners of a better day. But Nome was still busy. Besides a number of stores selling drugs and provisions, there were little shops showing moccasins and ivory work. One large window was a mass of climbing nasturtiums grown from a window box. There were boats coming in, trade and tourists. There was the loading and unloading of lighters in the harbor. That was what brought the King Islanders.

This Eskimo tribe from King Island in the north came to Nome in the summer to get what work they could as longshoremen and, perhaps, selling trinkets to tourists. They paddled eighty miles down the coast in huge "umiaks," walrus-skin boats holding twenty-five or thirty people. When they put to shore they tipped their boats upside down and made tents of them. Here under a curved roof they sat—those of the tribe who were not working in the harbor—and filed away at walrus-tusk ivory, making bracelets and cigarette holders.

Not today though. Today they were all down at the wharf, as we were, to see their Chief win the kyak race. For, of course, he would win. That was why he was Chief. He was taller and stronger and stood better and danced better and hunted better than anyone else in the tribe. When he ceased to excel, he would cease to be Chief. I wondered, looking at him, if he had to be browner than the rest of them, too. He stood quite near us on the dock, shaking his head and sturdy shoulders into a kind of raincoat, a hooded parka made of the gut of seals. His head emerging from the opening showed a streak of white across the dark crop of hair, and, looking at his face, one was shocked to see the same splash of white on the side of brow and cheek, as though the usual Eskimo brown were rubbing off. It was not a birthmark, they told me, but some strange disease which was slowly changing the color of his skin. Would it detract from his superiority or increase it? He seemed quite invincible as he stood there, his broad shoulders thrown back, his head well set. Even his features were stronger than those of his men; firmer mouth, more pronounced cheekbones, unusually deep-set eyes. He belonged to those born rulers of the earth.

The three men who were to race squeezed into their kyaks (a native boat entirely sealskin-covered except for a hole where the man sits). Each one then tied the skirt of his parka around the wooden rim of the opening so that no water could enter. Man and boat were one, like Greek centaurs. Then they were launched. A cold rain was driving in our faces and the bay was choppy, but the three kyaks, far more delicately balanced than canoes, rode through the waves like porpoises. It was difficult to follow the race. Sometimes the waves hid a boat from view, or breaking over one, covered it with spray. But the Chief won, of course. The crowd on the beach shouted. He did not come in; merely shook the water from his face and started to turn his kyak over in a side somersault. A little flip with the paddle and he was upside down. "That's how easily they turn over," I thought. For one horrible second the boat bobbed there in the surf, bottom up, like one of those annoying come-back toys with the weight stuck in the wrong end. A gasp from the crowd. Then, "A-a-ah!" everyone sighed with relief. He flipped right side up, smiled, shook the water off his face. What was he thinking as he shoved in to shore after that triumph? He had won. He had turned a complete somersault in rough water. No one else could do it as well. He was Chief of the King Islanders.

We saw him again at night. The bare raftered hall was jammed with the Eskimo and white inhabitants of Nome. Around the walls, as in an old-fashioned dancing school, sat a row of Eskimo mothers. Leaning over their calico skirts they peered at the audience and at the same time kept watch of their black-eyed children who sprawled in and out among the slat chairs. There was much giggling and rustling of paper programs. As the curtain rose one noticed first the back wall hung with furs, one huge white bearskin in the center. The stage itself was empty except for a long box, like a large birdhouse, in which were five portholes. On top of the box over each hole squatted an Eskimo in everyday dress: skin trousers, boots, and parka. Out of the holes suddenly popped five wolves' heads. Ears erect, fangs bared, yellow eyes gleaming, the heads nodded at us. Nodded, nodded, nodded, insanely like a dream, this way and that, to the rhythmic beat of a drum. For now in the background of the stage sat some Eskimo women and a few old men chanting and pounding out the rhythm of those heads. Every little while when a head became awry, the Eskimo on top leaned over and jerked it straight by pulling at an ear. The snarling heads began to look childish. Weren't those squatting figures just like the nurses in Central Park? "Tony! Anne! Christopher! come here—what have you done to your coat? Look where your hat is! There now—go along." They apparently had no part in the drama, these nurses. Like the black-hooded figures who run in and out on the Japanese stage, they were, I assumed, supposed to be invisible, and only there for convenience.

Pound, pound, pound—out of the holes leaped the wolves (who were dressed in long white woolen underwear below their fierce heads). On all fours they stared at us. Pound, pound, pound—they nodded this way, that way, this way, that way, unceasingly, like a child who is entranced with a new trick and cannot shake himself free of it, but repeats it again and again, a refrain to his life. Pound, pound, pound—they were on their feet and shaking their bangled gauntlets this way and that. The wolf in the center tossed his head and glared at us—the Chief of the King Islanders. Pound, pound, pound, the nodding went on and on. Pound, pound, pound, their movements were sudden and elastic, like animals. There was more repose in their movement than in their stillness, which was that of a crouching panther, or of a taut bow. One waited, tense, for the inevitable spring. Action was relief. Pound, pound, pound—legs in the air and a backward leap. They had all popped into the holes, disappeared completely. The cross-legged nurses merely nodded approval. And the curtain fell.

The Chief of the King Islanders came out from a door to the left of the stage. The wolf's head lay limp in his hand. Sweat ran down his face. He stood a head above the rest of the group and had that air of being looked at which is quite free from any self-consciousness, as though stares could reflect themselves on the face of the person beheld even when he is unconscious of them. The Chief did not notice the eyes turned toward him, for he was watching the sports now beginning in the hall.

Chairs pushed back, the Eskimo boys were kicking, with both feet together, at a large ball suspended from the rafters. Their toes often higher than their heads, they doubled up in a marvelously precise fashion like a jackknife. Now the girls' competition. The ball was lowered from the ceiling to meet their height. A thin strip of a girl was running down the aisle, her black braids tossing arrogantly. Stop, leap, and kick—the ball shot into the air and spun dizzily. That was an easy one. "The Chief's daughter," someone whispered to me. The ball was raised; the contestants fell out; one fat girl tried and sat down on the floor; everyone laughed.

There were only two left now. A run, a jump, and a leap— the ball floated serenely out of reach. Three times and out. Only the Chief's daughter left. A run, a jump, and a leap—the ball gleamed untouched. She missed it. She ran back shaking her braids. The ball was still. Several people coughed, rustled their programs. I saw her sullen little face as she turned. A run, a jump, and a leap. We could not see her touch it but the ball quivered slightly and began to spin. She had grazed it. "Hi! Hi!" shouted the Eskimos, and the crowd clapped. Her expression did not change as she wriggled back into her seat. But the Chief of the King Islanders was smiling, an easy, arrogant smile.

The next morning we walked down the plank streets of Nome to the King Islanders' camp. The town was quiet after the excitement of the night before. Life in camp was going on as usual. In the shade of their long curved "umiaks" sat whole families, mothers nursing their babies, old men filing at ivory tusks, while near by were young men curing fish, hanging long lines of them up to dry in the sun. We stopped and talked to one of the ivory filers. He had a half-finished match box in his hand. A pile of white dust lay at his feet. He was, we were to discover, the Chief's brother.

"That was a wonderful dance of yours last night." A broad smile accentuated his high cheekbones. Then gravely he looked up at us.

"My," he said simply.

" 'My,' " we echoed. "What do you mean?"

"*My*," he repeated with emphasis, putting down his file, "*my* brother, *my* son, *my* nephews—" He took a long breath. "*My.*"

That was it, I thought, as we walked back. That was what the Chief of the King Islanders felt, shaking the water from his face after the somersault. That was what he thought tossing his wolf's head. That was what he meant by that smile when his daughter made the ball quiver—simply, "*My.*"

LIBBY RIDDLES AND TIM JONES

Running the Iditarod

"NOTHING DAMPENED THE DOGS' ENTHUSIASM TO GO CATCH THOSE OTHER TEAMS. I HUNG ON FOR ALL I WAS WORTH WHILE THEY DRAGGED ME THROUGH THE DEEP SNOW ON THE TRAIL. MY GRIP ON THE ROPE WAS WEAKENING ALL THE TIME, THEN I LOST IT. I STOPPED, FACE IN THE SNOW, MY FIFTEEN MIGHTY HUSKIES LOPING OFF INTO THE NIGHT WITHOUT ME."

The dog most people think of as the Alaskan husky is the malamute, a breed of working dog originally developed by an Alaskan tribe of that name. It is often crossbred with wolves, to whom it is related. The slightly larger male usually weighs between sixty-five and eighty-five pounds. Malamutes are broad and strong in the chest and shoulders and have a thick coat that protects them from the cold. They are typically used as sled dogs.

A sled dog, however, may be of any breed at all. The requirements are straightforward. They need to be physically strong, have great endurance, be able to withstand severe cold, have a powerful will to win, have good social skills (in order to work as part of a team), and like fish (since chinook salmon will be a major item of diet). Gender doesn't matter.

Between 1910 and 1912, there was a gold rush in the interior town of Iditarod. At that time, a sled trail was cut from Seward to Iditarod and then on to the Yukon River, where it joined an older sled trail to Nome. In 1967, a husky breeder in the region named Joe Redington began lobbying for a long-distance dogsled race on the old Iditarod Trail. By 1972, he had convinced the U.S. Army Corps of Engineers to clear and mark the trail. The first race was run in 1973 with twenty-two dog teams competing. The race has grown in popularity, news coverage, and size since then; at times, more than a thousand dogs have taken part, with a maximum of eighteen per team. Because of occasional controversies over the treatment of dogs, strict controls have been put in place and there are severe penalties for contestants whose treatment of their animals doesn't conform.

The race begins on the first Saturday in March from Fourth Street in downtown Anchorage. The route is traditionally said to be 1,049 miles in length, but it actually covers 1,150 miles. The trail is marked and has twenty-two checkpoints. Mushers must send ahead the supplies they'll need, which might include as much as 2,500 pounds of food for a team of dogs. Eleven days plus a couple of hours later, the race ends at Front Street in Nome. First one there is the winner.

Two fine books about dogs, sleds, snow, and the Iditarod are Libby Riddles's Race Across Alaska (1988) and Alastair Scott's Tracks Across Alaska: A Dog Sled Journey (1990).

In 1985, Riddles was the first woman to win the Iditarod. She had entered twice before, finishing nineteenth and twentieth. At the finish line in 1985, a reporter asked her how she felt. "What I feel is," she said, "if I died right now, it'd be okay."

March 2, 1985   Mostly sunny, high 25° and low 14°, with winds averaging 6 to 7 knots.

MY BROTHER MIKE DROVE. IN THE DARK-ness we saw other dog trucks on the highway—big plywood boxes in the beds, little doors cut in the boxes, and here and there a dog's nose testing the breezes. Our beat-up old Dodge was no match for some of the fancy rigs. New pickups with freshly painted dog boxes and signs naming the mushers and their sponsors kept disappearing ahead of us into traffic. I had to remind myself that it isn't trucks that win the Iditarod.

We stopped once to check on two dogs we'd had to double up in one compartment. They were already arguing.

We worked our way to a staging area, where race officials would assign parking spots on Fourth Avenue for the start of the race. Just a hint of morning lit the place where we sat waiting. A call came over the loudspeaker asking for anyone who carried an Emergency Medical Technician card. Joe had completed his EMT training the previous summer and headed toward the official's car—if you don't answer a call, you can even face charges. This would be his first emergency. But then the voice announced that the situation was under control, and Joe got back into the truck, relieved. On a day like this you have enough emergencies of your own.

Joe Garnie was my partner. At our home in Teller, seventy miles north of Nome, on the coast of the Bering Sea, we had bred and trained dogs to run the Iditarod, Alaska's most famous marathon for sled dog teams. If we had done our jobs, these fifteen dogs would take me the twelve hundred miles from Anchorage to Nome. If we had done our jobs well, and if I had the will and the stamina, I might finish in the top ten. But what I really wanted was to win.

We sat in the truck, Mike blowing his cigarette smoke out the window as the Dodge idled. We tried to figure out whose dog truck was whose. Our Dodge made its own statement. The faded dog boxes sported no sponsors' names or even our kennel name, and the sides were blank. Now and then we could feel the dogs shuffling in their boxes, and we'd hear an occasional growl from the grouchier ones. At last somebody called, "Number forty-six."

We drove a couple of blocks to our spot on Fourth Avenue, one of the main east-west streets of Anchorage. Starting here would be a new experience. In my first two races we had started from Mulcahy Park, not downtown. Trucks were arranged by number along each side of the avenue, lowest numbers closest to the starting line, so that as each team took off toward the start, the dogs wouldn't have to weave through other teams on the way. Snow had been trucked in and spread on the street for the race.

A banner stretched across the street proclaimed the start of the 1985 Iditarod Trail Sled Dog Race, big red letters outlined in yellow. Far beyond, the Chugach mountains seemed to block the end of the street; their outline never ceases to awe me, especially when they reflect a sunrise or sunset. The winter sun, still behind the ridge, was beginning to spread its light over the city.

Now the work could begin. We piled out of the truck and strung a tie-out chain, first around the truck and then back to a couple of parking meters to give us room for all the dogs. A snowfence lined the street from meter to meter, protecting the dogs and spectators from each other. Some of the racers toward the front were already putting dogs in harness. With sixty-four racers and fourteen to eighteen dogs per team, the area was noisy.

We started taking the dogs out of the boxes, in order. First out was Sister, a dog of Joe's who was so ornery we tied her to a parking meter as far away as possible. She was the oldest dog in the team and probably figured her seniority should bring her respect. She would mix it up with any other dog, male or female. She might have been so mean because she was so darned ugly—mostly white with a few washed-out gray spots, built square like a Mack truck, with scars all over her muzzle from her various encounters. The pigment in one eye was pink. But there wasn't a trace of quit in her, and I knew I could rely on her as a spare leader if things got tough.

In a few minutes she was ripping the snowfence slats to shreds. In the dog barn at home she had a special stall made of corrugated tin. If we left her behind when we went on a training run, she would try to demolish anything within her reach, especially dog houses, and if she couldn't reach anything destructible, she'd start digging up the snow with her front paws, then tearing up the ground with her teeth. Other times she'd bark and squeal and jump straight in the air, "four off the floor." Did we want to buy the city a new snowfence? We put Sister back in the truck.

The next dog out was Minnow. She was a big dog, about fifty-five pounds. Her sister Tip was even bigger. The two dogs looked so much alike I occasionally mistook one for the other when they were tied in the dark dog barn and I could see only their faces and not the kink in Minnow's tail. The similarity could be a major nuisance because I could let Minnow run a little, knowing she would honor my "come" command. But Tip liked to explore the neighborhood, and she always took her time before submitting to being caught. If I mistook Tip for Minnow and let her go, I'd end up chasing her around the village. Today, Minnow was in heat, and we let her out for only a few minutes for her own comfort. Then she, too, had to go back into the truck, where she would be safe from amorous advances.

Two out, two back in; so far, about normal.

The only rookie in the team was Stripe. All the others had raced Iditarod at least once. Stripe was white and liver-colored with a pink nose on a face only a mother could love—and his mother was Sister. Stripe was also tough and liked to let the others know it. He wasn't as tough as his mother, but then, he wasn't as ugly, either. He had die-hard drive and a good attitude, a good head.

Whitey was his littermate, but in personality she was his opposite. Her favorite trick was to try to be invisible whenever there was any type of commotion. Like most huskies, she liked to work, to cover miles, but she also held rest in high esteem, and given any chance, she'd plop down in the snow. These were both Joe's dogs.

Joe's pride and joy was his leader, Dusty, a stout little red dog, his color suggesting more golden Lab than husky. Dusty was a giveaway pup from our neighbor Albert Oquillik. He would do figure-eights and back flips for Joe, and although he would lead for me in training, he was never as happy with me. I guess he was a one-person dog. He was fast, though, and even if I didn't trust him as much as my own leaders, he could be put out front to give them a rest. As for team dogs, there weren't many better than Dusty.

Four brothers were the core of my team: Dugan, Axle, Bugs, and Binga. Dugan would be the main leader for the race with Binga and maybe Axle to help out, along with Dusty and Sister.

Two more of Joe's dogs came out of the truck to the picket line, Brownie and Socks. Littermates, they were pups of Joe's retired leader, Ugly. Brownie had a flying trot and a tendency not to lope. He always seemed composed, self-contained, and didn't seem to care if I ever petted him. I'd pet him anyway. Joe had been trying to make him into a leader, and he was beginning to pick up the idea.

Socks was the smallest dog in the team, but built solid and strong. She could have been a bit faster, but somehow with her short legs she got the job done, and she was consistent. She was the only dog on the team who had a reputation as a chewer and I intended to keep a sharp eye on her. All I needed was for Socks to chew through one of the lines and let all the dogs in front of her take off down the trail, leaving me and the sled behind.

Another dog of Joe's I was taking was Stewpot, a real one-of-a-kind dog. He looked like a collie crossed with a white arctic wolf, and he was almost as big as a wolf. Joe and I had feuded over which was the bigger dog, his Stewpot or my Bad Dog Bane, the father of Tip and Minnow. We never did weigh or measure them. That would have taken all the fun out of it. As a pup, Stewpot had had a fancy name, Sewlik, Eskimo for northern pike. When he was a couple of years old, we lent him to our friend Ray Lang, a dentist in Nome who used him in the All-Alaska Sweepstakes. Ray never could remember the dog's name, so he started calling him Stewpot. The dog was a big old pot-licker anyway. Stewpot was going to be my main wheel dog, right in front of the sled.

My favorite of the dogs from Joe's lot was Penny. She was the fastest and most consistent, and I also liked her pleasant manners. She did her work in the team and minded her own business. I hardly ever had to look at her when I was on the move—an invisible dog. Penny had perfect Siberian markings of gray and white. Her radar ears were always in constant motion as she high-stepped down the trail. If she heard any sound, her ears would swivel in its direction. If a dog in the team received a scolding, Penny's ears would lay back in submission.

The last dog out of the box was a coal-black female named Inca. She was a half-sister to Tip and Minnow. Inca had been born on my birthday three years earlier. She had a strong desire to please and would obey me better than most of the other dogs. Inca was loyal, a dog I could let loose. At home in training, I always cut her loose from her chain and let her follow me. She'd run ahead, then run back to me and jump up, sometimes throwing her whole body on me. I usually had to have an arm free to block her exuberant assaults. I used Inca for a herder when I took pups for walks, and if the pups got carried away with their temporary freedom, I'd just call Inca back, and the pups would follow along behind.

There was little to do once the dogs were out. I stood and regarded my team. For the next two weeks we would eat, sleep, and labor across more than a thousand miles of Alaska. I had high hopes for this pack of mutts. I wasn't one of the famous mushers, one of the people the press hung around and talked and wrote about, but I thought these dogs could even win the race if I could handle them right. I sure wanted to give them every opportunity, but there were a lot of miles and a lot of variables on the trail between Anchorage and Nome.

A few days before the race, Joe had been down at the Knik Bar with a group that included some racers.

"Don't you think you'd be right up there if you were driving that team instead?" they kept asking.

"You guys," said Joe, "are going to screw around and screw around and underestimate her and she's going to pass you up."

But what others were thinking didn't affect me too much. I had learned that in sled dog racing, as in most other things, respect must be earned. I'd run the Kuskokwim 300 twice since my last Iditarod and managed to beat some teams I'd never beaten before. Some of the racers had to know I was serious. And only two teams had been able to beat our dogs in the previous year's race.

Susan Ogle and Kelley Weaverling came by with egg burgers and coffee. They had helped me organize my airdrops of food and supplies for the checkpoints along the trail. To make my burlap bags distinctive, so that I could pick them out of a pile, Kelley had spray-painted them green and purple. We began hauling down sleds and gear from the top of the dog boxes and stretching out the gangline and preparing harnesses. Another friend stopped by and gave me an orange for the trail. Elwin Johnson and Katrine Zosel offered their services as dog handlers. Other people were stopping to wish me luck and look over my dogs. When neither of us was racing, I had been one of the walkers, wishing favorites well, strolling and looking at all the dogs. This year I had eyes for no dogs but my own.

A special friend arrived—Patty Friend. She had given me not only some of her dogs and a lead on a summer job, but also inspiration. In 1979, running the Cantwell 180 sled dog race, she had sprinted to the finish half a minute ahead of the competition and become the first woman—at least in modern times—to win a long-distance sled dog race.

Kelley and Mike went to work putting the new bindings on my fancy new Sherpa snowshoes. I had purchased them just a day before the race. I couldn't quite afford them, but they were lighter and smaller than the regular wood and rawhide snowshoes, and they packed a lot easier into the sled. I'd been sure I could jury-rig bindings, but these high-tech snowshoes would work only with the real thing, the expensive real thing.

I started sorting gear. When we had finished, a race official checked over the mandatory equipment for the sled and counted the dogs. Volunteers followed with cans of paint to mark each dog on top of its head, a way to make sure racers wouldn't add dogs to their teams. Mine got purple. I resented having the sticky paint on my animals' fine pelts, but I accepted it as a necessary evil.

Just after Minnow got her splash of purple, I stepped a little too close. She jumped and spread a nice blotch of purple all over my brand new L. L. Bean Thinsulate jacket.

All the time, the loudspeaker down the avenue was announcing one team after another as the racers left the starting line. Police were holding traffic. Part of the dogs' training was to get them used to crowds, but you don't find many crowds where we live. As it turned out, our dogs were so intent on chasing the teams ahead of them, they hardly seemed to notice the people.

On the first day of a race, dogs are usually pretty excited by the presence of the other teams and the overall commotion. They're also fresh, and fifteen dogs in the peak of condition can be mighty difficult to stop if they set their minds on going somewhere. And if you go down the wrong trail and have to turn around, you have to untangle a lively mess of dogs while other teams pass by. After a few days on the trail, the dogs would settle into a routine and be more inclined to behave themselves. I wondered whether the other racers dreaded the first days as much as I did.

The teams in front of us disappeared down Fourth Avenue one by one. I waited until the last minute to put my dogs in harness to keep them from going wild. Once they're in harness they reach an almost fever pitch in their excitement, yipping and yowling, lunging and jumping forward. They don't like being left behind. My old Bad Dog Bane used to grab the gangline in his teeth and pull back on it, pulling the other dogs with it. Then he'd let go, and the dogs taking up the slack and lunging forward would help him in his attempt to be on his way. Pretty slick.

Over the morning I'd collected quite a few handlers: Mike, Susan, Kelley, Patty, Dennis Lozano, Jack and Nancy Studer. Nancy was one of my strongest suppliers of moral support.

When the race officials told me we had fifteen minutes to go, we got busy. Sister and Minnow came back out of the truck, and I put all my handlers to work, showing them which dogs to put where. I had to resort to my list to make sure. For the first part of the race, officials wanted us to take a handler along to help with tangles and supply added weight to slow the dogs. Some handlers rode in the sled. We had decided Joe would ride a second sled, which we had borrowed from Jack Schultheis.

For the tight work of maneuvering through town I would use my two best leaders, Dugan and Bugs. Bugs especially was my "power steering" for this work. Behind them we put Inca and Binga. Behind them came Axle and Dusty, Sister and Penny, Tip and Minnow, Stripe and Socks, Whitey and Brownie. In wheel we put Stewpot by himself.

At last we received the signal. Each handler grabbed a tandem of dogs, Joe took the leaders, and I rode the sled and the brake. The dogs surged ahead impatiently, dragging their handlers, but we managed to stop for the countdown.

All the preparations had come down to this. I was at the starting line, the dogs stretched out front facing the high white mountains at the end of the street. Race officials and photographers surrounded the sled. Some helped hold it so the dogs wouldn't pull us over the line in their screaming lunges to chase the other teams. The announcer made some cracks about Joe being in the second sled and noticed our single wheel dog. The countdown began. "Ten . . . nine . . ." Joe stood on the second sled behind me. At "two" I motioned the handlers away. I wanted a clear shot; I didn't want a tangle with the dogs running over somebody; I wanted the dogs to see where they were going. I glanced over my shoulder at Joe. He was ready. "One . . . GO!"

Big crowds leaned into the snowfences on both sides of the street as we sped down Fourth Avenue. We passed the spot where years before I'd watched my first race. I could hear the muffled roar made by the clapping of hundreds of gloved and mittened hands. I kept my eyes on the team.

We went about half a dozen blocks and then made a right turn. Earl Norris was right in front of us. He'd been running dogs around Anchorage since the 1940s but this was his first Iditarod. We passed him and then went over the hill and down Cordova Street. We took a curve around Mulcahy Park, where the race used to start, and went out of sight of the crowds.

The day warmed as we went along, the temperature rising to uncomfortable heat for the dogs. We let them stop frequently for a few minutes to cool off and bite a little snow. We crossed through a long meadow and reached a stand of trees on the far side, the lead dogs disappearing into the bushes around a sharp corner. As the sled came closer I could hear someone cussing up a storm. We stopped and Joe held the team while I went up to see what was happening.

One of the racers was crashing through the underbrush, pulling lines and lifting dogs, untangling a team that had wrapped itself around half a dozen trees. Worse, I hadn't stopped in time, and the front end of my own team was tangled in the same trees. I unwound them and they came free just as the team ahead pulled away. I went back to the sled, gritted my teeth, and prepared to negotiate what remained of the turn and keep the rest of my team on the trail.

But instead of following the trail around, the dogs went flying through the alders, bouncing our sleds off trees until at last we hit the trail again and returned to business. I made myself a note to come back one day and personally chainsaw that patch of alders.

From there the trail was good, alternating wide stretches and narrow portages.

Then Dugan and Bugs started down some sort of narrow trail, following a couple of sets of tracks. By the time I saw this new adventure, it was already too late. Two by two the dogs jumped over an old wringer washing machine iced into the trail. The sled hit it and I flew over the top. I heard Joe shout just as he was knocked off the second sled and then my sled went over. I hung on to the drive bow while the dogs dragged me until I righted the sled and regained the runners and stopped. I set the hook into the snow and waited for Joe to catch up. He'd slammed into a tree and banged his knuckle badly. I shook my head and shrugged. A washing machine in the trail, of all things.

Less than an hour into the race and already my expectations and fears for the first day were starting to fulfill themselves. For a while we continued along a fairly normal trail, some sort of road, but then I spied half a dozen boulders dead ahead. I figured the boulders kept cars off the road. Someone had removed one boulder, leaving a space between the side of a bank and the second boulder for us to pass. The space was only about four feet wide—not a lot of maneuvering room for a sled skidding on a slippery surface. We had fast trail, and with the dogs so fresh and excited we were doing about twenty miles an hour.

Joe shouted, "Get off your brake and steer."

I always figure that if I'm going to crash, I'd rather crash going slowly, so I laid into the brake. That takes away some maneuvering ability, however, so I compromised, letting off the brake just as we came to the opening. My heart rate accelerated a little and my breath stopped but we slipped nicely between the boulder and the bank. Later I heard that some other racers hadn't fared so well. Armen Khatchikian broke his collarbone there and had to drop out of the race at Eagle River. Joe Redington, Sr., also crashed there and hurt his arm badly. I don't imagine anybody had fun going through there.

Beyond the rocks, the trail smoothed out, and we had an easy time into Eagle River. We passed quite a few teams, and a few passed us while we rested the dogs in the heat. I was in no hurry. I wanted to go easy on the dogs during the warm part of the day. It was a long, long way to Nome, and the way the day was going, I didn't even want to think about how far it was. Soon the last few miles of energy in those egg burgers wore out. I was starting to get that shaky feeling that comes from hunger. I remembered the candy bar Dennis Lozano had slipped me back on Fourth Avenue and dug it out of my pocket. I made my second note of the day. Maybe even before I chain-sawed the alders I'd thank Dennis.

We pulled up a long hill into the chute at Eagle River and I could see my pit crew already there waiting to haul us by truck across open water and a tangle of roads to the restart at Settler's Bay. We made our way through crowds past the VFW post that was being used as the checkpoint. The old Dodge was parked just around a corner.

The dogs looked hot and dry when we rolled in, and though my own hunger and thirst were wearing at me, from now on the dogs had to come first. We gave them water out of a cooler in the truck, and most of them drank quite a bit. An old friend, Penny Moore, popped out of the crowd. I hadn't seen her since the last Iditarod, and we talked, catching up, but I was distracted. Now the race was going and I had to keep track of my time. The crew agreed to watch over the dogs while they rested so that I could grab a bite to eat.

The VFW volunteers had cooked a big batch of stew and made corn bread, along with coffee and other snacks for the racers. I took advantage and wolfed down as much as I could. When I'd thoroughly stuffed myself, I thanked the women there and headed back to the truck. We loaded up the dogs and started out to drive the forty miles to Settler's Bay, the restart and, at last, the release from the city to the comfort of the open trail away from crowds and traffic.

We didn't stop anywhere, counting on fierce traffic all the way. The previous year we'd stopped at Palmer to change the runners on Joe's sled, and he had barely made it on time. By race rules, drivers can leave exactly three hours after arriving in Eagle River, and I didn't want to stay a minute extra. We were on race time now.

It looked like all of Anchorage had emptied out to go watch the restart and we settled into the flow. Settler's Bay is a development of recreational and residential homes on the west side of Cook Inlet just across the bay and a little north of Anchorage. Its golf course provides good open country for the race, with plenty of room for spectators. We followed signs and arrows pointing the way for racers to find the staging area, where officials directed us to a parking lot. Stakes in the snow held paper plates with the mushers' numbers on them. All manner of vehicles were scattered through the area: dog trucks, motor homes, pickups, a few cars. A forest bordered one side of the parking lot, and there we found Number 46.

We backed in toward the woods and strung our picket cables in the trees. This put the dogs where they wouldn't be bothered so much by the knots of spectators wandering through. Once we had the dogs out of the truck, we hauled down the racing toboggan sled and started packing for real. I had thought of picking up some of my gear at the next checkpoint, which was Knik, about seven miles or so away and the last stop on the road system. But I decided I didn't want to waste any time there—once we were gone, I wanted to stay going. Besides, the trail committee might consider that planned help, a disqualifying offense.

I put the heavy cooler full of dog food in first, toward the back of the basket. The sled steers better with the weight in back. The food in it was cooked and all ready for our first real stop down the trail. Then I put in the new snowshoes, tied together. The sleeping bag and the cooker went in next. Dog pans went up in the front. I tied the axe in its leather sheath to the outside of the sled bag, where I could grab it easily. I had a smaller bag tied between the back supports of the sled, below the drive bow, for personal items: dry gloves, snacks, headlight, goggles, sunglasses. While I was packing, friends came by, talking when we could. Dan and Karen Owens visited. I usually see them for an hour or so each year at Settler's Bay for the restart and that's about all, even though they've been friends of mine probably longer than just about anybody I know in the state.

Several other friends came by, talked for a moment or two,

and left. Susan and Kelley brought more burgers. I wasn't hungry but I figured it might be several hours before I could eat again, so I tried to stuff one down.

A checker from the race committee looked over my gear, checking the mandatory equipment. At least we didn't have to sign in at this checkpoint this year. The previous year one driver had neglected to sign the sheet at Settler's Bay. Faced with returning seventy miles to the checkpoint to sign or being disqualified, he withdrew.

Three old friends from my days at the Bureau of Land Management stopped to talk. LaDonna Westfall, Charlene Montague, and Nancy Reagan had all helped the last time I raced, preparing some of my personal food. They took some pictures and wished me luck again, saying they wanted me to know they were still behind me.

LaDonna pulled me to one side. The night before, she said, she'd been inspired to write something for me. She handed me an envelope marked "Libby." I tucked it into a pocket, its message unread. This was something to save. Somewhere down the trail, I was going to need a little boost and the time would be right to take out that envelope. Then the three of them faded back into the crowd.

Time passed quickly in the bustle of packing and organizing and visiting, and when I finally checked my watch, I had only fifteen minutes left. For some time Joe had wanted me to hook up, but again I didn't want the dogs to wait long in harness, expending energy in their excitement. With fifteen minutes to go, though, we were getting down to the wire and I gave the go-ahead.

With all the help experienced by this time, the dogs were harnessed and hooked into the gangline in no time and we were just about to go to the starting line when a woman with two children in tow came up. I recognized her face right away even though it had probably been twenty years since I'd seen her. She was my cousin Phoebe, who'd just moved to Anchorage from Wisconsin.

The team was more than ready to go, and with close to a dozen handlers, we edged through the trees to the restart line.

I stood under a banner again, this time looking up a long hill, the trail lined by snowfence, the snowfence lined by people. The run to Eagle River had tamed the dogs some, but they were still lively, and I was nervous.

While waiting for the countdown, I asked about the trail ahead. Somebody warned me about a corner at the bottom of a big hill, but that only added to the nervousness. My first goal was to get to Knik, six or eight miles, and then take it step by step from there.

We took off through a snowfence chute and climbed the long hill. People cheered, and I couldn't help waving as I passed along the fence. For a mile or two we cruised the golf course, past spectators taking pictures and calling out their good luck wishes. At last I was alone with the dogs. We approached a split in the trail with no markings for which way to go. Two photographers were standing there and when with unfailing accuracy I picked the trail that turned out not to have sled tracks, I had to call them for assistance. Once the team was stopped, the dogs had to be turned 180 degrees in a narrow trail—one of the best ways to tie forty feet of ropes and fifteen frisky dogs into a knot. Luckily for me, the two photographers were willing to help. I asked one to stand on the snow hook and hold the sled; the other helped me turn the dogs. I was ordering both of them around, perfect strangers, but I had to get out of that mess.

Every one of the dogs was tangled somehow. The lines were so tight I couldn't even get them loose. If people hadn't been around to help, I might have lost a dog. Minnow was caught in a nasty knot and almost choked. Her expression was pitiful. All the other dogs were straining forward, making her situation worse. The photographer pulled back on the other dogs so that I could free Minnow from the stranglehold. The rest of the team grew increasingly impatient to be on the way, jumping, barking, lunging, and doing anything else difficult they could think of. It was all the two men could do to hang on to the sled while I worked with the rats' nest of dogs. After a couple of quarts of sweat, I finally managed to free them and line out for the proper trail. When I was finally ready, I thanked my rescuers profusely and then geared my mind toward whatever disaster might be in store for me next. The day was fulfilling my worst expectations.

We were approaching the steep hill I'd been warned about. An old boat lay rotting in the snow at the bottom of the hill, and beyond it, the trail swung sharply to the right. I stood on my brake with both feet trying to keep my speed at a minimum in anticipation of the corner. A roostertail of snow kicked up behind me. We swept around the corner beautifully, and through the curve we came out onto the tidal flats of Knik Arm. Now and then I touched or rode my brake to keep control over rougher parts.

I began to feel some looseness in the brake when I pressed down. At first I tried to ignore it: "It can't be what I think it is." When I finally did look down, I saw that the bar, a half-inch-thick bar of steel, had snapped at one of the rounded corners. It was broken clean through. I looked at it several more times in disbelief.

Panic turned to anxiety. I had to get it fixed. I was within a couple of miles of Knik, but I wasn't sure how I was going to repair it. For the time, I had to concentrate on those next few miles and then somehow stop the dogs and park them without the use of a brake. I had no idea whether my pit crew had been able to fight the traffic and reach Knik. I might be alone there, with no brake and no way to get a new one or fix the old one. And going on without it was out of the question.

Near Knik the trail wound through thicker woods, then rose sharply to the road, where volunteers were stopping traffic. Across the road we dropped into the parking lot at the Knik Bar and into a sort of picnic area next to Knik Lake. As soon as I came up over the road, I hollered for help, since I had no brake to help me stop. Several people, including some of my pit crew—they had made it after all—managed to grab the team and guide us over to some trees where I could tie the dogs. Joe and Mike figured there was a good chance someone in the crowd might have the same type of sled, and maybe we could borrow or buy a brake for my sled.

Dean Osmar, who had won the race the year before and was helping his son, Tim, this year, offered a brake, but it was too short. Raymie Redington's handler, Gary Longley, an old friend of ours from Nome, said he had one we could use. There was some confusion as to whether it was Raymie's or Gary's brake, but I wasn't being too particular at the moment. I got it bolted into place and we were ready to go. In all, we'd lost only about twenty minutes.

If that brake had snapped any farther down the trail, I'd have had to backtrack to Knik, and by the time I returned to Knik, no one would have been there. I might have spent hours tracking someone down to find another brake. No way would I have headed up into the mountains without a brake. My luck had been good bad luck.

I gave Joe a last hug. It would be the last I'd see him until Nome.

"Wish me luck," I said. "If this keeps up, I'm going to need it."

We tore off down the lake and then climbed the bank onto the trail I'd been using for training over the past couple of weeks to keep the dogs in shape. Debbie Altermatt's house, where we had stayed, was just three miles away, and I started to worry that my leaders might try to head back to her house. Dugan, good as he was, had a stubborn streak, and if he had it in mind we were going back to Debbie's dog yard to eat a big dinner and sleep on fresh straw, he'd try it.

Fortunately, Debbie and a friend had chosen that intersection to watch the race, and they were in position when Dugan made his dive. His attempt was only half-hearted, however. I think the dog really knew that we were Nomeward bound, he was just making sure I didn't want to change my mind.

I finally felt like I was really on the way to Nome. A great weight had lifted and I recalled the same feelings of relief the other two times I had raced. All the busywork and preparation for the race were over. The hassle of the city and the start were behind us. Before us the quiet trail opened up to Rabbit Lake, and beyond, so far ahead I didn't even want to think about it, Nome.

Somehow this year was different. All of my energy was focused on the team and the trail. I was deadly serious about racing this year, and in my concentration I was looking ahead to each mile of trail, mile by mile, instead of the grand experience of the whole. Nothing I'd heard about the upcoming trail did anything to make me feel relaxed or complacent.

This first, familiar, stretch of trail wound through a forest of birch and spruce. At one turn I recognized Jack Schultheis taking pictures along the trail, and I hollered my thanks for the borrowed sled. Except at checkpoints, we wouldn't see too many more people standing along the trail from here on, and we settled into an easy pace, eating up the miles.

I'd raced twice before and had a good idea of the time schedule I'd need. But it was critical to be flexible, to fit the schedule according to the dogs and the weather. I wasn't going to burn up the trail—and burn out the dogs—in the first part of the race, just to keep within sight of the front runners. Still, I didn't want to be any more than six hours behind in those first few days; less would be better. Closer to Nome, I wouldn't be able to let anyone get more than an hour in front.

With all the teams in front of us, the trail was pretty chewed up. Brakes left deep furrows on the downhill stretches. The dogs and sleds and mushers left behind a trail of loose snow, making it tough going for the dogs while we twisted through the forest. We easily passed the obstacles I knew about, a big birch on an inside corner, and then, beyond two lakes, a rock on a forty-five-degree turn that could catch a sled runner. At the rock, thick alders on each side of the trail complicated matters. I hopped off the sled and ran around that corner, taking away any chance of tipping over.

I pulled a can of Squirt from the sled bag and swigged it down between trail bumps in about three swallows. Not even twenty-four hours into the race and already I felt dehydrated.

The trail curved around a few big hills through thick woods, then across a big open area of frozen marsh and small ponds and onto another road. That was as far as I'd gone on my training runs. From then on, the trail would be new to us, and the time had come to pay even more attention. The dogs took the winding trail smoothly without mishap and we passed the miles with no problems finding the proper trail. About twenty-five miles out of Knik I thought it was time to give the dogs a little breather and let them snack on some of the treats in the sled. I began looking for a good place to stop, where I could anchor the team to something sturdy and wouldn't interfere with teams coming up from behind.

I stopped by a fairly sturdy scrub spruce and tied the sled to it with a heavy-duty rope about fifteen feet long. I pounded the snow hook down, too, even though in four feet of powder it couldn't gain much purchase.

I had to unload most of the sled to reach the cooler. I gave each dog a scoop of food and repacked. I wanted to let them rest a little bit, twenty minutes or so, but they were restless. When they're tired, they dig a little nest or circle around until their ground is just right and then curl up. If they're not tired, they just sit or lick their paws or stand and look at me. Today the dogs were too restless even for that. But if I let them run too much, they'd be sore and tired the next day.

A couple of teams passed while we were resting: Bob Bright, Terry Adkins, and Victor Katongan. They were all good teams, but I tried especially to get a look at Victor's. It was a tough outfit he had, and he was a determined driver.

My dogs watched those teams go by, too. They were jealous, barking and whining, trying to give chase. They didn't care to watch others go down the trail, leaving them behind. They began barking and jumping up and down, even doing a couple of four-off-the-floors. They lurched forward once, and again, and all of a sudden they snapped the little tree I had them tied to. The couple of feet they gained fired their efforts. They started yapping and throwing themselves forward in their harnesses, gaining on the tree little by little. The tree held, but my faithful, easy-to-untie, hitch-the-dogs-up knot was now underneath, and the knot cinched so tight I couldn't budge it.

Hindsight tells me if I had had a brain in my head, I would have waited to get help from another driver. But one of the ideas of the race is to take care of yourself, and that's what I proceeded to do.

The dogs kept their pressure forward, so there was little chance of untying the knot. I would need that rope every time I camped, so I wasn't keen on cutting it. I decided instead to take a few chops at the tree with my axe and then make a grab for my sled. Trouble was, by this time the sled was about seven feet from the tree, farther than I could reach if I chopped through the tree and it let go. I chopped at the tree a couple of times and then stepped onto the runners and encouraged the dogs forward, thinking they might break it. No luck. So I went back and tried to pull the knot again. After my encouragement the dogs were almost frothing at their mouths with excitement, jumping and leaping forward. I decided to take a couple more chops at the tree. On the third swing, the dogs jumped and broke free. I grabbed for the only thing I could see, and that was the hunk of tree flying by, still tied to my snub line. I held on to the axe with my other hand, gripping both for dear life. The axe was mandatory equipment, and so were the dogs and sled.

Axe in hand, I was sledding along the trail on my face at twenty miles an hour, pulled by fifteen wired-up dogs, hollering while I tried to dig my boots into the snow to bring the team under control.

"Whoa, dammit!" I yelled.

But nothing dampened the dogs' enthusiasm to go catch those other teams. I hung on for all I was worth while they dragged me through the deep snow on the trail. My grip on the rope was weakening all the time, then I lost it. I stopped, face in the snow, my fifteen mighty huskies loping off into the night without me.

It was too cruel. My dogs could get tangled in an alder path, maybe choked to death. My race was down the drain. All the months, the years of preparation, the money, all the people who had helped . . . In anger and frustration and fear I picked up and chased after them, glad no one was close enough to hear me as I ran after them, cursing and hollering, wavering, slowing to walk, close to tears.

"Come back here, you miserable dogs! Oh please, *please* stop."

For fifteen or twenty minutes I slogged through deep snow, running and walking, hollering and unzipping layers of clothing as I heated up. I'd lost my whole outfit, but I still had that crazy axe, for all the good it would do me now. A headlight came through the trees behind me and I flagged the driver. I was out of breath but tried in quick bursts to explain. The stranger got the point quickly and told me to hop onto the sled; we'd go look for my team.

He introduced himself as Chuck Schaeffer. I'd never met him before and I couldn't even see his face in the dark, but I knew he was from up north in Kotzebue. He had less trouble figuring out who I was—there were just a handful of women in the race. I felt guilty for imposing my extra weight on this racer's dogs, but he said it was no problem giving me a lift. That's one of the great things about the Iditarod. Even if drivers are expected to keep their own acts together, even though they're all competing, if you ever need help, someone's always glad to oblige.

Chuck's dogs kept up a steady pace as I sat on his sled, clutching my axe and mumbling about my doggone dogs. After half an hour we saw something ahead reflecting our lights. I had two strips of reflective tape on my sled, but I didn't really believe it was my team until we got closer and I could see the dogs' eyes reflecting the light. There they were, all lying down resting. The gangline was tied off in three places and the sled turned upside down, so even if they had gotten loose, the sled would have slowed them down. Somebody had done a fine job of rescuing my team for me. I didn't know who, but I vowed to find out and buy him a couple drinks at the end of the trail.

I tried hard to be mad at my dogs, let them know what bad dogs they were for ditching me, but I couldn't quite pull it off. I moved along the team, checking them for injury. They all looked at me so innocently, their expressions seeming to say, "Aw, we were just funnin' ya." And truly, what they'd done was instinctive. Although I was drenched with perspiration from running and shaken by the whole experience, my thoughts were positive. I had my team back, and my chance at the race came back with them.

I begged Chuck to stay until I got the dogs ready. He helped me untie them from the trees and get their tuglines hitched, which took a while because whoever had tied the dogs had done it well. I righted the sled, never once letting go of it, and sent them off.

I lose my team maybe once every season, and although I'd had several nightmares about that, even during the summer, before training started, I'd never lost them in a race. Still, I felt a little relieved. Everything bad that could happen had already happened to me. I wasn't even worried about moose: I'd already received more than my share of bad luck. I don't tangle with moose, I don't get lost, I just lose my team.

About ten miles along I came upon a campfire and stopped to find out how far it was to the Rabbit Lake checkpoint. A man and a woman were sitting by the fire and I poured out my story about losing the team. They turned out to be friends of Dennis Lozano's whom I'd met before. I couldn't stay long. I'd left my team in the trail and I didn't want to block it for anyone coming from behind. When Chuck pulled in, I moved on through the darkness and eventually found my way to Rabbit Lake a bit after one in the morning.

FAIRBANKS AND
THE INTERIOR

MARGARET E. MURIE

Winter in Fairbanks, 1911

"DADDY FOUND ONE VACANT HOUSE—ONE WAY OUT ON THE EDGE
OF TOWN, EIGHT BLOCKS FROM THE RIVER, THE LAST HOUSE ON
THE LAST STREET OF THE FAIRBANKS OF THAT YEAR."

*The following passage continues Margaret E. Murie's story of
her arrival in Alaska, begun in the section of this book on the
Inside Passage.*

*Fairbanks, 120 miles south of the Arctic Circle, grew out of
a mining camp at a bend of the Chena River around 1901, so
the town was only a decade or so old when she first saw it. Many
of its oldest streets, along the river, and some homes from early
in the twentieth century remain intact.*

FREEZE-UP

Such a final sound—"the last boat," "the freeze-up." But
in Fairbanks that year it was an unusually late, mild, sunny
autumn. Daddy knew everyone, it seemed, and there were even
some picnics with his friends who had horses and buggies, driving out through the golden birch woods and the green spruce
forest which extended thick and untouched behind the town,
out to the Tanana River, four miles south, a marvelous place of

sand and stones and bleached logs to sit on and serve lunch on and clamber over.

After a few days of this exciting life (and without school too!) Daddy found one vacant house—one way out on the edge of town, eight blocks from the river, the last house on the last street of the Fairbanks of that year. It was log of course, and sturdy, but with only four rooms: a living-dining room about sixteen by twenty; behind it a bedroom and a kitchen; and off at one side, a lean-to bedroom built of slab wood. This cabin was home for ten years.

The back door opened into a woodshed-storage place. All such places were called caches, and off one corner of this was what in those days sufficed for sanitary convenience. That was one of the first phenomena of the northern towns. Late in the night on certain nights we might be awakened by a clatter out there. The most heroic soul on the frontier was emptying the can. Lying curled down warm in the middle of my bed in the lean-to bedroom, I would hear the stamping and clatter, the jingle of harness, the low "giddap" to the horses, the creaking of sled runners on the snow, out there in the cold dark.

Added to this was the problem of water. I know Mother really wondered about this life sometimes! Oh, there was a well, and a hand pump in the kitchen sink (the sink drained into a slop bucket which had to be carried outdoors). But the water was so terrifically red and rusty and hard and smelling of iron that Mother could not use it. So we had a big whiskey barrel, with a cover, just inside the kitchen door, and "Fred the Water-man" came every day with his tank wagon or sleigh. First he looked at the kitchen window, to see if the square blue card said two or four, then filled the buckets hanging at the back of his tank—five gallon oil cans fitted with handles of thick copper wire; after this he quickly hooked them onto the hooks of his wooden yoke and came stamping in. "Cold today, yah, yah." Fred's last name was Musjgherd—nobody ever tried to pronounce it. Nobody knew his nationality or how he had come to this far place. But he owned a well which poured forth clear, sweet water, and this directed his life. He was our friend, Fred the Waterman, and his black horses the fattest, sleekest, best-cared-for in town.

So that was the water situation. As for the rest, Mother by some magic touch made it home—colorful and warm and somehow, with everything we owned in those four rooms, still uncluttered.

Neighbors told Mother of how the living room had looked before. The house had belonged to a Mrs. Jackson, a nervous woman with a background of luxurious city life, who had brought her city furnishings along. True, she didn't belong on the Alaskan frontier, and now was gone, but she had not taken it all with her. Even Mother was dismayed about the wallpaper in the living room. As in all the cabins of those days, over the log walls was tacked "house lining"—unbleached muslin cloth—which was also stretched across from eave to eave, making a low ceiling, called a "balloon ceiling." Then the whole was covered with wallpaper. In this case Mrs. Jackson had consented to have *some* light, and the ceiling was white with a "watered silk" silvery overlay, very popular then for ceilings. But the walls jumped at you. They were of a deep red paper with a sort of coat-of-arms figure about a foot high—in gold! The tall front window and the little square ones on each side were curtained in what was called scrim, in a very fancy pattern in red, blue, and tan. On the floor was a Brussels carpet, all roses on a tan background; in one corner was a wide couch "cozy corner" affair, the mattress covered with red rep; in another corner a tall corner cupboard, the bottom part hung with red-and-white-striped material. Mrs. Jackson, the neighbors said, had had this filled with hand-painted china—altogether a lively room. As soon as possible, Mother had the walls covered with light-tan burlap.

I think my mother felt the unspeakable isolation more than she would ever say. She kept it locked away inside, while she went serenely about the task that was hers—adapting her very civilized self to creating a home and bringing up a family on this far frontier, with the man she loved. I realize now that I felt this in her, even while not feeling it myself at all. To an eager, curious child, everything was interesting here.

One thing I remember is that Mother could hardly stand the howling of the dogs. Not too far from our house, across the fields and beyond a slough and some spruce woods, was the dog pound, down on the river. Alaska was a dog country then; there were always plenty of strays, or whole teams being "boarded out" there, so whenever that famous six-o'clock whistle blew there was a chorus not to be ignored—it was too close to our little log house—and Mother thought they "sounded so mournful." To me it was just an interesting noise. The trouble was that the "six-o'clock whistle" blew at six A.M. and seven A.M. and at noon and one P.M. and finally at six P.M., and the chorus was just as great each time, to say nothing of the frenzied tune when that awful fire siren stopped us all in our tracks. That one was enough to make any dog howl; it made all of us want to, besides stabbing us with cold fear each time. Perhaps to the dogs those whistles signified the ancestor of all wolves howling to them. They had to respond. Anyway, I am sure that later, when we moved down close in to town, Mother was glad to have put some distance between herself and that opera.

She had enough to do, that first winter, to adjust to this new life. I can see clearly now that things that were of no thought and little trouble to me, a child, were a daily series of battles for her, gentle and sweet and straight from the city and expecting my first half sister in the spring, and with Daddy gone through Christmas and far into January, traveling by dog team on the Yukon from village to village, for he was the field man for the U.S. Attorney, and the Law had but recently come to this part of the wild North.

Temperatures, and stoves. On one side of the living room stood the indispensable stove of the North, a Cole Airtight Heater. This took in big heavy chunks of spruce wood. In the kitchen, close to the back window, we had the big wood range. This took endless feeding with split spruce. When the thermometer went down to minus 20, and 30, and 50, and sometimes stayed there for weeks, the pattern of life was set—feeding the stoves. But, since the houses were small and low-ceilinged, and had storm windows and "bankings" of earth about three feet high all around the outside walls (where a riot of sweet peas grew in the summer), we were warm. But Mother's feet were always cold. She would go busily about her housework for a half hour, then open the oven door and sit with her feet in the oven for a few minutes, then back to work. Thank heaven for the nine cords of good spruce wood all neatly ricked up in the back yard. And for the cellar under the kitchen, where all the supplies were stored—vegetables and canned goods, jams and jellies. And out in the cache, in a special cupboard, we had cuts of moose and caribou, all wrapped and frozen oh so solid, and bundles of frozen whitefish. We were fairly self-contained, in a little bastion against the 50-below-zero world outside.

We did have some helpful things: electric lights, so Mother could use her new electric iron, and a telephone, so that during those very cold spells she could talk to her friends—and there were fine friends, but most of them lived on the other side of town.

The house nearest us was vacant that first year. (Later our wonderful friends Jess and Clara Rust moved into it.) Across the street there was only one house, and after Daddy left for his long winter journey that house became a source of worry to Mother. One day we saw six enormous mustachioed, fur-coated, fur-capped men moving their gear into that house—six of them! They were what Fairbanks called "Bohunks"—Slavic men of some kind—tremendous in stature and strength. They worked in the mines in the summer. I don't think Mother had ever seen such huge men before. For weeks the only sound from them was the terrific noise they made late each night, coming home from an evening in town, stamping the snow from their boots at their front door, which sounded as though they were stamping on *our* front doorstep and coming right on in. Then one day there was a gentle knock at our back door. I opened it and there stood one of these giants. He looked at me solemnly and said one word: "Ax!"

I flew in terror to Mother, but when she came, the giant made her understand by a few gestures that he would like to cut some wood for us. And he did. After that the stomping and the singing in Russian, or something, meant only that *our friends* were home from a convivial evening on Front Street.

THE TOWN

Every one of the gold-rush towns had to be unusual. All the factors which combined to produce them were unusual.

First, the presence of gold in the earth—call that providential or geologic as you will. Second, the character, the climate, the topography, of the land itself; a land more difficult to conquer could hardly be imagined. Third, the people—the many kinds of people who would be attracted to the promise and the challenge of the gold and the land.

Most important to the story of Fairbanks is a consideration of the conglomeration of people who *stayed* in the country. For it was a conglomeration—it was more than merely an assortment. It was a mixture which made the town like no other perhaps, and in that era, from 1902 to 1922, the town was all theirs.

Growing up in Fairbanks, one knew no other town. There were no others nearer than eight days by horse sleigh or ten days by river steamer. So we children of Fairbanks were early accustomed to all the kinds of people—they were taken for granted, part of the environment we knew. Not until I was nearly grown and at last went Outside to school did I begin to realize that our town was indeed different.

Fairbanks in 1911. Of course it was built on the river bank, the bank of Chena Slough, that offshoot of the mighty Tanana, which swept on four miles behind the town. The story is that Captain Barnette, bound for the upper Tanana, with his new flat-bottomed boat *Isabelle* loaded with supplies, to establish a new trading post where the trail of the Klondike gold seekers from Valdez crossed the Tanana, got into the Chena Slough, got stuck in the shallow water, and at the same time met two or three prospectors who gave him the news that Felix Pedro had just made a strike on a nearby creek. Here was the place for his trade goods, here was the site of a new camp, and since Barnette's friend James Wickersham, then federal judge for that part of Alaska, had asked him to name his trading post after his friend Senator Fairbanks, of Indiana, the new camp was named accordingly.

The slough was navigable except in low water. Out in the States it would be quite a river, but Alaska is a land laced with great rivers. The slough drew a great shallow curve here; the first street of the new camp followed that curve, so that the pattern of the whole town reflected it, with streets slightly bent.

Along Front Street there was a long row of false-front business houses, built of green native lumber, painted white, and green, and ruddy ocher trimmed in red. Opposite these, on the very bank of the slough, a few warehouses on piles, where the steamers tied up just below the bridge. There were more of the same kind of buildings on Second Avenue and a few on Third. That made up the main part of the town. Beyond these, spreading out into the great slightly curved half circle, the buildings diminished from a few two-story frame houses to the low log ones in which most of the people lived.

As though they were the first things the early settlers thought of, the saloons were nearly all on Front Street, some twenty-three of them! The real ladies of the town never walked up Front Street; they turned down and walked on Second. Here and on Third and along Cushman, the main street that bisected the avenues, were the respectable shops.

And then, in the very center of the town, beginning at Fourth and Cushman and extending downstream two or three blocks, was the red-light district, known as "the Row." I guess it was there before many families arrived. With the coming of wives, and churches and schools, a feeble attempt was made to put a respectable face on the town. A high solid board fence, with gates in it, was built right across the street, one on Fourth where it left Cushman, and one across Fourth where it emerged on Barnette, two blocks down, and the big dance hall on Third and Cushman was closed and turned into a dry-goods emporium. Immediately beyond the Row on Fifth and Sixth and Seventh, especially along Cushman, lived the elite, the very respectable leading citizens, in two-story houses which tried to look almost like conservative middle-class homes back in the States.

In the first place, the miners were the source of life. Amazingly soon after them came the followers, to cater to every real or imagined need of those hardy diggers and to share in their diggings. First the traders, who set up stores—grocers, butchers, hardware merchants (who dealt in all the heavy tools and machinery of placer mining), dry-goods dealers, saloon keepers—and, right along with them, gamblers and prostitutes. Restaurants and bakeries and laundries came next, and two newspapers, and all the while anyone who could put two boards together and would stay in town and do that instead of going prospecting was in great demand. And by this time, to keep all these interests in worse or better order, but in any case to make a living from them all, came the lawyers, and in Fairbanks these made a colorful story.

Eventually these energetic pioneers realized they must take time to set up a government of some kind and to accept some representatives of the federal government. After all, the town did belong to the United States. So the next thing they knew they had all helped build a monstrosity of a courthouse on Second and Cushman, right in the heart of the town and just a block and a half from the Row. A monstrosity built in the only style known to the frontier it seemed, a straight box, two tall stories high, of native lumber, with a recessed entrance porch on one corner. To make it supremely attractive it was painted a sickly muddy olive green, and Justice was set up in business in the Far North. In the front corner of the second story of this building was the suite of offices of the U.S. Attorney, Mr. James Crossley, and his three assistants. They were supposed to enforce virtue and observance of the law throughout the Fourth Judicial Division of the Territory of Alaska, an area of 220,000 square miles!

Not surprising either that, as "the Creeks," the mining district around Fairbanks, kept on producing, two banks should soon be established and housed, in cracker boxes not so tall, near the Courthouse. Banks, drugstores, grocery stores—above them the doctors, the lawyers, the dentists, yes, even real estate men and public accountants. This town was pretty solidly built up now. It had five churches and two hospitals. And all this just nine years after Captain Barnette's *Isabelle* got stuck on the bar and Felix Pedro found a certain spot in the tundra wilderness.

Busy place. Happy-go-lucky place. No place for too much concern over morals—plenty of room for all the characters.

So there you have Fairbanks in 1911. It was a place to draw questions from nine-year-olds—"Why does that part of town have a fence around it?"—and it held various terrors for me.

Soon after our arrival a friend of Daddy's gave me a beautiful, sweet-tempered Husky named Major. He was my companion and protector. He could lick any dog in town. I had a long rope tied to his collar, and if we met a loose dog and there was a fight, I merely stood holding the end of the rope, well out of the way, and waited until the other dog went off whimpering; then Major and I went on about our business. He and I, with the little sled, were sent on all the errands for Mother.

Well, I was forbidden to go up Front Street because of the saloons. I was supposed to go up Second or Third, but each of them held a fear for me which I would never confess to Mother. On Second, the back part of the big corrugated-iron buildings of the Northern Commercial Company housed the town power plant and was the home of the big deep "six-o'clock whistle" and the terrifying fire siren. I had almost a pathological terror of loud sounds, and if I did force myself to go up Second Avenue, I fairly scuttled past, sure the siren was going to blow just as Major and I came abreast of the huge open doors and the terrifying sound of the big dynamos.

The Fire Department fronted on Third Avenue, in the two-story City Hall, whose back door opened into the Row. At street level were the two great double doors, and I was sure that when I reached the exact middle of those doors the alarm would sound within, the doors would fly open, and both teams of huge gray horses would dash out, over my prone body.

So I went clear up to Fifth Avenue and hurried along those two blocks behind the Row—not too fast to cast fearful yet wondering glances at the backs of all those close-ranked little log cabins—and emerged on Cushman Street, and its open, harmless, respectable stores, with a deep breath of relief.

I suppose it's the good women who do it. On the frontier, before the wives arrived I don't think Society was organized. They were a motley group of men, all there for the same two things—adventure and gold, or gold and adventure—and their spare hours were spent in whatever bunch, in whatever saloon, they happened to wander into.

But soon, almost immediately in Fairbanks, there were women, and churchmen, and thus the whole mixed-up population began to fall away into groups—Presbyterian church,

Episcopal church, Ladies' Aid, Guild. Also whist clubs, sewing clubs, a Women's Civic Club. They gave the men the fever too. Masons became very active, and along with them, Eastern Star, then Eagles and Lady Eagles, Moose and Lady Moose. And in those early days throughout the North there flourished two strictly indigenous lodges, the Arctic Brotherhood and the Pioneers of Alaska.

The A.B. was quite a plushy lodge. Their functions were examples of how much luxury can be laid over the wilderness. All the "best people" were there. An A.B. dance was a top social event; the ladies' gowns were described in the Fairbanks *News-Miner* the next day. One of the sharp, ecstatic memories is of Mother, ready for one of these balls, in pale blue marquisette over Alice-blue satin, a sprinkling of gold sequins over the bodice, black velvet ribbon about the waist; and then, next day, listening wide-eyed while Daddy read the whole account from the paper, with chortles and dramatic expression. I remember he was so impressed by the fact that every other gown was "a creation," and he had a way of reading "crepe de Chine" that made it sound like the silliest, most ridiculous kind of stuff imaginable.

All that crepe de Chine at the A.B. New Year's ball of 1913 turned into a family joke which has persisted through the years. "Mrs. J. J. Crossley was radiant in a creation of pale pink crepe de Chine with black velvet streamers." To a ten-year-old, every word was straight from the mysterious world of grown-up doings. Mother had to tell me every little detail—how at midnight the orchestra played "Auld Lang Syne" and they formed a great circle about the big Eagles Hall, hands clasping hands clear around; how she found herself clasping the hand of Jack Robarts, a local newspaperman, and how they both remarked how far they had come on this New Year's Eve from their native New Brunswick, and how that got her to thinking about all the others, from what far distant places they had all come. Here was this gay scene, this little huddle of homes, one little working, whirring piece of civilization set down in almost the exact center of this enormous land, the great wilderness, thousands of miles of it, surrounding that tiny, whirring, alive spot. It was as though a great clock somewhere had exploded, and one little cogwheel had been flung through space, landed in the arctic tundra, and continued spinning.

But of course, Mother told me, while this queer thought was running through her mind they were all trooping upstairs to the dining hall, where a real "collation" was spread. These people on the little cogwheel were of the strongest, most alive, most carefree breed—"Eat, drink, and be merry! We've come a long way; we're different from the stodgy folk; let's take all we can get from life."

DOROTHY LAWRENCE MINKLER

Valdez to Fairbanks, by bicycle, 1941

"WE ARRIVED IN FAIRBANKS THE NEXT DAY. IT IS A SMALL TOWN
WITH A BUSINESS SECTION JUST ONE BLOCK LONG."

*In the summer of 1941, two friends from New Jersey, Dorothy
Lawrence and Elsie Smith, set themselves an ambitious goal.
They meant to see Alaska by bicycle. And they did.*

*Dot's account of the trip was set to be published in De-
cember 1941, when more dramatic news from Pearl Harbor
squeezed it from its spot. For the next half century and more,
her manuscript languished in the bottom of a trunk. When she
finally dug it out and showed it to a few people, all her friends
demanded copies. It was published, at long last, in the July
1995 issue of* Alaska *magazine.*

*In Alaska, Dot took every opportunity to send postcards
back to her folks in Gloucester, New Jersey. One of those cards,
postmarked in Fairbanks on July 22, 1941, is reproduced with
the magazine article and reads in part, "Had a wonderful 42
mile bike ride today. Climbed 5 miles to Summit lake. Passed
Summit glacier and Rainbow mountain. . . . It was so beautiful. . . . Everything wonderful."*

Alaska magazine is probably the only publication of its kind

*that includes a page of obituaries—titled "End of the Trail"—in
every issue. In the same issue in which Dorothy Minkler's article
was published, "End of the Trail" featured a lengthy obituary of
LaDessa Hall Nordale, a Fairbanks resident for seventy-two
years, who had passed away on February 22, 1995, at the age
of ninety-five.*

*Mrs. Nordale had served Alaska well, as a teacher at the
Alaska Agricultural College and School of Mines (now the University of Alaska—Fairbanks) and at Fairbanks High School,
and she also served as U.S. Territorial Commissioner in 1952
and as Commissioner of Revenue in 1963.*

*But perhaps most interesting is something she did many
years earlier. She arrived in Fairbanks in 1923 to teach at the
college. The following year, she returned to the States to get her
automobile, loaded it on a steamship, and brought it back to Valdez. From there, she drove it north to Fairbanks, becoming the
first woman to drive this difficult route alone. Her daring trip
was big news, and operators of the U.S. Signal Corps reported
her progress along the way. One report read, "She just went by
here driving like hell. She must have been doing 20 miles an
hour!"*

*LaDessa Hall's 1924 route from Valdez to Fairbanks was
the primitive Richardson Highway, the same route (because it's
the only route through Thompson Pass) taken by Dot and Elsie
on their bicycles seventeen years later, in 1941.*

IT WAS 1:30 A.M. ON A RAINY SUMMER
night in 1941 when the ship *Alaska* docked at Valdez. After
traveling across the country by rail and up the Inside Passage
and through the stormy Gulf of Alaska by steamer, my friend,
Elsie Smith, and I were very excited as we stood on the dock,
ready to begin our bicycle trip across Alaska.

Unfortunately, we had made no reservations for the night.
The fact that we would leave the boat in the middle of the night
had never entered our heads, and now we stood on the dock,
in the rain, with our bicycles.

We had packed away our suitcases and given them to the

ship's purser to check in Seward to await us at the end of our journey. We planned to cycle 371 miles north to Fairbanks, cross the Arctic Circle, visit Fort Yukon, then come south by bicycle and rail to Anchorage and the Kenai Peninsula. With us when we left the boat were our sleeping bags, grub kits, and saddlebags. The saddlebags each contained a dress, a raincoat, towel, washcloth, toilet articles, pajamas, socks, and three changes of underwear.

We were traveling under our own power, so we tried to avoid any added weight. With a camera over the handlebars and the extra pack on the back of the bicycle, we each had about 25 pounds of equipment and ourselves to get over the mountainous country through which we expected to pedal.

We had the dilemma of being in a strange country at such an hour in the morning in the rain, but as we were strapping our equipment on our bicycles, we were approached by Rev. F. G. Phillips of Valdez, who had come down to meet the boat. He smiled at our predicament, and because he knew there was no available space at the hotel, invited us to the parsonage.

The next morning, Rev. Phillips took us to the local post office for mail and then to the store for supplies. We bought hardtack, canned ham, beans, oatmeal, prunes, sugar, canned milk, and cheese for our lunches.

Our trip to Fairbanks was marked on the map. There was no other road to take, so we couldn't possibly get lost. We said goodbye to the reverend and his family, and started north. It was still pouring rain.

Valdez is surrounded by beautiful, snowcapped mountains. In order to travel north, we had to follow the Richardson Highway through Thompson Pass.

To a person who has lived in southern New Jersey, a highway is usually a long white ribbon, carefully laid across the countryside. Sometimes it may be black but it is always smooth with a surface like a clean-swept floor, and traffic rolls along in the plainly marked lanes. This highway was gravel, and at times it was too narrow for two cars to pass. There were large rocks and little sunken troughs and gullies that were now being filled with rain. As the road wound around the mountain peaks it seemed less definite and even more rocky.

The lack of guardrails made the view from the top of the mountain more breathtaking. We were thrilled by the rugged beauty of the country and the feeling of youthful strength that was characteristic of the high, jagged mountain peaks and the powerful waterfalls along the highway.

We had cycled about 12 miles when we heard the growling rumble of a truck as it came up the mountainside. With the road getting steeper and the rain getting heavier and colder, we gratefully accepted the invitation of the truck driver to ride over the mountains.

We stopped and had dinner at Tonsina, a roadhouse where travelers may stop to eat or sleep. We found these log cabin lodges anywhere from 25 to 50 miles apart on the highway. Dinner was $1 and well worth it. It was all good home-cooking, and homemade bread and pies. Before long, we learned that all meals cost $1, breakfast and lunch as well as dinner.

After dinner we rode on to Gulkana and decided to stay the night at the roadhouse there, again for the price of $1. In our room was an old-fashioned potbellied stove, an old iron bed, and the usual basin and pitcher that served for any washing that had to be done. There were candles if any light was necessary.

Back on our bikes the next day, we pedaled north. The mosquitoes were many and vicious. We stopped several times to get them out of our eyes and finally donned black glasses as a protection against them. Conversation was impossible because as soon as we would try to say anything the mosquitoes choked us. Try riding a bicycle for 40 miles sometime with your lips tightly closed.

We crossed the Tanana River in a cable boat. A large sign by the landing said, "Ring the bell for the ferry," and was to be heeded if the ferry was on the wrong side of the river. The bargelike ferry carried Elsie and me across for nothing, but trucks have to pay $1.

Hansen's Lodge was there by the river, so we stopped for the day. Mary Hansen is famous for her dog racing, and Elsie and I had fun petting her dogs. They were very friendly and playful. That evening we learned that on the following day we would cycle through Richardson and that the most fascinating character of the locality lived there. We should by all means stop to see him.

So in the morning we went along, wondering where we might meet Galen Fry, an old-timer who had come to Alaska in the Gold Rush days 43 years earlier. As we neared Richardson, coasting comfortably down a hill, someone called, "Hello." We stopped to find the greeting came from just the man we were hoping to meet.

Galen Fry invited us into his "igloo," as he called his small but comfortable cabin. After he served us a lunch that was more like a banquet, Galen suggested we visit two friends of his. He said the "kids," as he called them, would show us how to pan for gold.

The "kids" lived four miles off the main road, so we went by car through the woods. When we pulled up to the cabin, Galen called out, "Hi ya, kids, I brought you some company." Two men appeared, one with a huge gray beard. One was 95 and the other 75 years old. But that means nothing in Alaska— their agility and spryness were remarkable. The younger man took us for a walk along the mile-and-a-half ditch they had dug along their claim. He seemed not in the least tired.

The men are quite independent. They have a small vegetable garden to care for, they bake their own bread, prepare meat from animals they kill, and cook their meals. When they are not busy at the mine, they have a masculine way of mending their clothes and doing the housekeeping that is absolutely essential to existence. This does not include the care of starched doilies or curtains.

The older man had made a spoon from the first gold he found. He told us that he lost his utensils in the mad rush of the early days, so necessity had created his strange tableware, elegant in material and crudely simple in design.

That evening the "kids" returned with us to Mr. Fry's cabin. Elsie and I helped to cook the dinner. We heard tales of the mines and miners who had lived and died, failed miserably or succeeded to fabulous wealth.

We arrived in Fairbanks the next day. It is a small town with a business section just one block long. It was a typical downtown, one store after another with appropriately decorated windows, but Elsie and I cycled up and down that square several times. The secret of our interest and the satisfied smiles on our faces was the paved road that stretched before us for one whole square. It felt like a carpet of velvet to us traveling by bicycle after the dirt and gravel roads.

In four days we saw Fairbanks not only from the road but from the air. Flying is very popular in Alaska, and one of the main means of transportation for long-distance traveling. Dog teams are used in the winter for journeys that are not too long.

Now we were ready to resume our bicycle trip toward the Arctic Circle. It was 162 miles to Circle City over the Steese Highway. In the first day we made Chatanika, 30 miles from Fairbanks, with rain dripping from us, our saddle bags and sleeping bags.

Helen Patton greeted us in the general store and said we would have to stay that night with her because the mining town had no accommodations for travelers. We rested, dried out, and then had dinner. While we were eating, we heard the news commentator on the radio tell about two girls seeing Alaska by bicycle. Until now, everyone we met had been very hospitable, pleasant, and helpful, but from now on they were looking for us to come and they made us feel more than welcome.

Twelve miles farther, at Long Creek, we met Leonhard Seppala, the famous dog racer. We watched him while he fed his dogs, and then Elsie and I received a special invitation from the cook in the mining mess hall to have lunch with them.

At Circle City, we had expected to take the riverboat, better known as the sternwheeler in Alaska, to Fort Yukon. We rode into the deserted-looking village and went to the general store for information. We were greatly deflated when Fred Powers, the man who managed the store, told us the riverboat would sail in a week. Circle City did not look like a place where we wanted to stay for a week. There were only 75 people, and food prices were very high.

To help us out, Mr. Powers offered to lend us his rowboat and assured us we could row the 85 miles to Fort Yukon in 14 to 16 hours. Without a second thought, Elsie and I said we would do it. We immediately bought a day's supply of food, and Mr. Powers put the rowboat in the river for us. We left our bicycles to be shipped back to Fairbanks.

We were all ready to leave at 6 in the morning. All the guests at the roadhouse came down to see us off. We found the river to be very wide, anywhere from seven miles to 20 miles wide according to a book, and full of small islands and sandbars. We were going with the current, so when it became difficult to find the channel we would pull in the oars and drift in whatever direction the stream carried us. Finding our way down the river was like going through a maze.

We rowed steadily all morning in a drizzling rain. The weather had been most disappointing now for several weeks. It took one of us to row while the other one bailed out the water that swished around our feet. At noon we were glad to see a huge woodpile near which was a small cabin. We pulled into shore and spent a few minutes talking to Tom Lewis, the woodchopper. He kept a supply of wood for the riverboat, which used it for fuel.

Once we got caught on a sandbar, and Elsie had to get out and push us off. At other times we were successful in rocking ourselves off. We rowed out of the main channel to avoid a whirlpool that was formed by the water flowing around an island in the middle of the stream.

It began to get late, and we ached in various places. We didn't worry about darkness coming on because the sun was below the horizon for just half an hour at this time of the year. Feeling like real pioneers, we arrived at Fort Yukon at 11 o'clock that evening. Our hands were so blistered we couldn't tie up the boat. The Indians did it for us as we staggered up the bank to find the roadhouse.

A man greeted us with, "So there you are. That was good time." He was Dr. La Rue, the flying dentist, who flies from point to point to fix teeth. He had been in Circle City earlier in the day, and Mr. Powers told him about the girls who were rowing to Fort Yukon. He told us he was going to fly out and look for us if we didn't get in by midnight. All day Elsie and I had thought if we got lost no one would miss us for days.

We were now above the Arctic Circle, sipping coffee in

order to overcome the chills we were experiencing in our damp clothes. I almost choked on one swallow when Dr. La Rue asked us if we planned to attend the local dance. When I was able to speak, I said, "How could anyone, after 17 hours of rowing, think of dancing, and besides, it's now midnight and the dance would be about over." His response was that the dance had just begun.

Elsie was exhausted and went right to bed. I was feeling tired, but accepted Dr. La Rue's invitation to the dance because I knew I would never rest now that I knew there was something more to be seen.

We were the only white people present. With the top layer of mud scraped off my saddle oxfords, and in rain-washed slacks, I danced until 2 in the morning to the music of a violin and a banjo. Then I enjoyed some homemade ice cream with a few fur trappers and decided I was more than ready for bed.

While staying in Fort Yukon we made friends with Dorothy Howe, a native of the fort, and when a plane flew into the village, the three of us jumped into the back of the only truck to ride out to meet it. The field, which looked like a small, hilly cow pasture, was on the other side of a rushing stream, so we had to get out of the truck and walk across a rope footbridge that swayed high above the water.

A Canadian Mountie, who was to be a passenger on the plane, made walking almost impossible by standing on one end of the bridge and jumping us up and down. To make matters worse, we all got the giggles. We looked like four crazy people desperately trying to balance ourselves on the very flimsy bridge. When we waved goodbye, as the airplane sped down the field, I had the feeling that here I was among my friends and it was too bad the Canadian Mountie had to go away and leave us.

The next morning, it was our turn to leave on the sternwheeler. Elsie and I almost had tears in our eyes when the boat pulled away from the bank of the river. There stood Dot and all the others we had known for only a day, but seemed to know so well. We waved and waved until we couldn't see them or Fort Yukon.

We paid $11 for our tickets back to Circle City and $5 to

haul that very familiar-looking rowboat. It was a beautiful day, so we sat on the deck and appreciated the comfort of the warm sun and our dry clothes.

We spent an hour in the pilot house. The pilot said he wanted us to see the river from a fairly high point, and he congratulated us on being able to find our way down such a waterway. He also showed us an aerial map of the Yukon. We were glad we hadn't seen it before we started on our rowing expedition or we never would have attempted it.

From Circle City we took the stage back to Fairbanks, where the people we had met earlier in the summer made us feel like successful explorers returning home. We washed our clothes, wore dresses, ate sundaes, and went to the movies. We ate regularly and had a definite place to sleep for several days. When we boarded the train for Mount McKinley Park, we were leaving many friends.

Although we spent several days in the park, we did not get a clear view of Mount McKinley, the highest peak in North America. It had been raining here for one month. After a three-day stay, we left by train, the only means of transportation to and from the park.

That night we stopped at Curry, not because we wanted to, but because there were no Pullman accommodations on the Alaska train. Curry is a hotel in the wilderness where the passengers stay overnight. Early in the morning the train blows its whistle, and people stream from the hotel to the train and everyone is again on his way.

We left the train in Wasilla and cycled to Palmer, the center of the Matanuska Valley. The valley is a government project peopled by farmers from various regions of the United States who were sent to Alaska and supplied with material to build their farms. It was very hard work and many hardships were endured; however, the prospector who ventured into Alaska before them not only paid his own way but had no one to supply the things he needed. That is why the prospectors called these people the "cream-puff" farmers.

The community is run on a cooperative basis, and the farmers are gradually overcoming difficulties. The valley promises to be a successful farm country. Elsie and I cycled out to several farms and saw cabbages that weighed 40 pounds apiece.

We stayed over a day to climb Bodenburg Butte and, as usual, it rained. When we reached the top we could see very little because of the low clouds. The saying, "Now, if it were a clear day we could see so much more," became a standing joke.

There were no rooms to be had in Anchorage, so Father Fenn very graciously let us spread our sleeping bags in the basement of the Episcopal Church. This town, site of an Army base, grew from a population of 2,500 to 10,000 in one year. Anything was slapped up for a home, and the whole place looked as though it were built on the wrong side of the tracks.

There was no road south from Anchorage, so again we boarded the train. As we moved south we were rather glad we had to ride, because the train huffed and puffed up many mountains, and it was a pleasure to listen to something besides ourselves struggle uphill.

We stepped from the train at Moose Pass because we knew there was a road from there to Seward, the coastal town where we were to get the boat. On our final day of riding, Elsie and I sang a peppy tune and pedaled to its rhythm. Everything was so beautiful. The mountains were high and austere. We seemed so small, but we felt so good that all this greatness was at our command.

We sailed away from Seward on the S.S. *Columbia* feeling well-satisfied with our journey, but a bit sad because it was over and the time had come to leave Alaska.

By the time we returned home, we had covered 12,000 miles by bike, train, truck, and ship in two months and six days. I still say that if you want some fun, many unusual experiences, and excitement, do your sightseeing by bicycle. Shall I add rowboat, too?

JIM CHRISTY

The Alaska Highway: Whitehorse to Fairbanks

"I HAVE, NO LIE, SEEN MEN DRIVE THROUGH CUSTOMS, STOP BY
THE SIDE OF THE ROAD, AND KISS THE ALASKAN ASPHALT."

*Jim Christy's book about driving the Alaska Highway, from
which the following selection is taken, is called, with some justice,* Rough Road to the North.

*After December 1941, when the United States realized with
a shock that distance alone did not make a nation invulnerable,
the territory of Alaska was suddenly seen as strategic ground. For
one thing, it was a convenient staging point for air forces. For
another, it was uncomfortably close to the northern part of the
Pacific Ocean. Indeed, the Aleutian Islands saw some action during the war; in June of 1942, Japanese forces actually occupied
two of the islands, Attu and Kiska, and did not surrender them
until the following year.*

*This sudden realization brought fast action. By March of
1942, the Army Corps of Engineers, with the help of some private contractors and the cooperation of the Canadian government, had begun building a supply road through the uncharted
wilderness of Canada's Yukon Territory and northwestward to
Fairbanks, in Alaska.*

Speed was the primary requirement, and the first object was an access road through the forests. Once that road was completed, in November of 1942, other teams, primarily private contractors, took over the work of constructing a permanent road, more or less parallel to the access road, and this time with permanent bridges across the streams and rivers. Usage was restricted to the military. Known first as the Alcan Highway, the Alaska Highway stretches 1,506 miles from Dawson Creek, in British Columbia, to Fairbanks. It was opened to civilian traffic in 1948.

The two-lane highway is kept open all year, but even in good weather it's a road that requires forethought. Smart drivers take the same sort of precautions they would take to cross the Mojave Desert in August, especially if they're hauling a trailer, as many are. The motorist's Bible here is Alaska Mileposts; updated regularly, it provides detailed information on features and facilities.

Shortly after crossing the U.S.-Canada border, the Alaska Highway brings drivers to Tok, a junction that actually offers a choice of three routes—a pretty exciting prospect after 1,500 miles of forest. One road goes south toward Anchorage and Valdez, on the coast. Another goes north toward Eagle, on the Yukon River. And the Alaska Highway itself, now become one with the old Richardson Highway, heads northwest to Fairbanks. For most travelers, the choice is obvious.

✸ WE DROVE OUT OF WHITEHORSE THROUGH the old copper mining country northwest of town. The mountains there are rounded and gray and they watched over their wooded plains and late August meadows alive with delicate blue Jacob's-ladder with little yellow eyes in the flower and, of course, the pink and yellow fireweed which the Indians call the consolation flower because it appears after a forest fire and remains in old burns. It was this same flower that grew in London among the rubble of bombed buildings.

On to Haines Junction, nestled below the towering peaks of the St. Elias Range. They stand in iron-gray majesty above the little town and the icy trails through the passes mark the path of moist Pacific air like fingers of melted white candle wax. We stop at Mother's Cozy Corner set in the mountain shadows.

SMALL IN SIZE
BUT
BIG IN HOSPITALITY

We order pie and coffee and in comes an elderly couple, from Texas according to the plates on their camper. She is a buxom, graying nonstop monologist and her husband bears an expression of resigned irritation. She comes through the screen door like a television announcer: "Oh my, what a cute little place. There are pies on the counter and they look so fresh. Hmm, now I wonder if we can get a glass of water here. I could really go for a glass of water and I *am* hungry. I haven't had anything to eat since that town a while back, what was it? Whitehorse, yes. Of course, I *could* just have an itsy-bitsy piece of pie and wait till we get to Alaska. Are there any Cheezies in the car, dear? No, never mind. I'll have a meal. Where's the waiter, where's the menu? Oh, look at the cute little signs on the wall."

They finally sit down after she has announced the contents and decor of the restaurant and the waiter, who has tensed as soon as he saw them come in the door, tries to take their order, but it all turns into a complicated rigmarole which Mif and I observe bemusedly. The waiter glances at us and rolls his eyes.

When the ordering is over we get into a conversation with her, or rather we listen as she tells us what Amarillo is like and what her children are like and what her husband does for a living. He, meanwhile, sits there pretending he doesn't know her and that it is just some weird twist of fate that finds him sitting at the same table. As she is talking, a brand-new magenta Coupe de Ville with a snow-white padded vinyl top and an opera window pulls up out front with Washington plates. Through the screen door comes a middle-aged man with gray coiffed hair wearing a tailored and sequined suit, see-through shirt open to his hairy chest, silver and jade bracelets on his wrists; accompanied by two women in high heels and short shorts, one of them sporting an ankle bracelet and blond Afro wig, the other wearing a glitter halter top and reeking of Charlie.

The lady from Amarillo looks up and actually drops a syllable. "Well, ah dee-clayuh!"

Burwash Lodge, Mile 1103 . . . We spend the first night out of Whitehorse at Mr. Allinger's lodge, a veritable cliché of a mountain hostelry set right on Kluane Lake and at night from your window you can hear the thupping of the water as it hits shore and washes the gravel with a shoosh like brushes on a cymbal. At dawn and dusk the mountains on the other side of the lake are black cut-out forms against the dark pink-tinged sky. The cool lake air carries a hint of early fall wood smoke.

Before turning in we have a few drinks in the lodge's linoleum-floored bar where two helicopter pilots are getting too drunk to fly and one kid from Newfoundland keeps interrupting them to brag of his many fistic exploits, how he kicked this one and that one insensible. An old Indian man sits quietly sipping his beer and watching Mif and me.

After a while he smiles and nods his head at us, invites us to join him. When we are seated he remains absolutely still and silent for a couple of minutes and then he says, "I want to tell you a story about something that happened years back to my cousin. This cousin, he owed lots of money to the trading post here at this place here, called Burwash. He was an honest man my cousin, just like me and hard-working too. Not very much like me. The trader, he knew my cousin was honest and so he give him more credit. But my cousin he could not make any money no matter what he done and to make it worse his old wife dies in the middle of the winter. He was very sad but because it is winter he could not dig a hole to bury her. So he hauled her body up into a tree. When he did this it made all the animals come around. All the animals in the forest come to the tree to prowl there in the nighttime and sniff at the body. So my cousin he set his traps there by the tree and he had his best season ever. He made enough money to pay the trapper and he had plenty left over. And that's what happened to my cousin."

America!

Alaska!

Where the future is.

No sooner do they finish building one pipeline than they start on another one. Land of the six-thousand-dollar-a-month welding job. Waitresses who dabble in real estate. Gold nugget watches on the arms of boys a year off the farm. Fairbanks! One of the few places on God's earth where you will find Eskimo men wearing mascara. Money, oil, gas, snow, whores, and Teamsters.

And to think that the American Secretary of State got Alaska from Russia for $7,200,000 and they laughed at him. Called it Seward's Folly. It was pigeonholed as Indian territory and promptly forgotten about until the Gold Rush. Why, in 1868 the people of Sitka, fearing a native uprising, had to call on the Canadian Government for help.

What a wonderful, heartrending feeling it must be to stand just over the border and look off across the broad plateau into the horizon with Fairbanks just beyond and to know you've driven that nine-year-old Fury all the way from Alabam where things had ceased to look so grand in Birmingham; you, the missus, the three kids, the furniture in a U-Haul and roped to the roof. The springs of the Fury groan under the weight of human hopeful flesh and the impedimenta of living.

I have, no lie, seen men drive through customs, stop by the side of the road, and kiss the Alaskan asphalt.

They are thinking, We made it, sweet goddamn. Maybe *this* time we'll find it. If it's anywhere it has got to be here. The missus is thinking the same thing despite her previous doubts through the rough unpaved Canadian passage. The words of a song keep echoing in her head, the ones about following him to Utah and Nebraska and it never working out, and finally reaching Alaska where there was sure to be a gold mine.

It is just like the Okie migrations to California in the thirties. Old cars with southern plates loaded down with hope. Tired of being busted down and busted out, working in the sawmill, working in the fields, working on the line. Fresh out of the Army, fresh out of jail. Looking for a new start. During the main rush to Alaska, at the height of the North Slope Pipeline project, grown men were getting paid $2.50 an hour in the southern states and in California too, where the minimum wage had not increased in over ten years. In 1979 it is $2.65.

You see the old jalopies wedged in between tourist Winnebagos in the summertime. Whole families asleep in blankets or patched canvas tents far enough off the road to avoid the dust. Families with serious purpose. Young kids off on a lark, out for big bucks and a good time, and waiting down on Second Avenue are hookers who take charge cards.

The road for the rest of the journey cuts through the broad plateau between the Wrangell, Nutsotin, and Alaska mountains with the Brooks Range far to the north. The mountains seem to lurk on all sides, often just faintly visible on the horizon but always felt, always there in the distant haze, as if to not let you forget your own humble human insignificance, tiny specks inching across the vast floor of the Tanana River Valley. The many creeks form crevices in the bottom of the valley bowl and it is here in the fissures that the alder and the cottonwood, the willow and the aspen, proliferate. Stream margins with water hemlock and purple violets. Between the creeks and rivers buck brush dominates and the sunlit meadows are brilliant with yellow milk vetch and blue gentian. Even the old Alcan drainage ditches seem to be on fire with thousands of tall yellow duster flowers.

Tetlin Junction, Mile 1311, the cutoff for the Top of the World Highway to Eagle, Alaska, and Dawson City, Yukon. There is a lodge and truck stop here and four log cabins with wood-burning stoves. The truck stop features the world's coolest gas station attendant. A thin, curious Inuit hipster with a pencil-thin mustache and a low, wise voice. "Wow. Say, man, where you headed? . . . Fairbanks, hmmmm . . . well, groovy."

He glides around the gas pumps, head bowed, humming to himself. He fills the tank and snaps his fingers. I go around to watch him. He is—I don't believe it, so I lean close—he is scat singing. "Shoobee, dewop, skiddy op, shoo bop."

What is *he* doing here? Or rather, what is he *doing* here? What's his story? I wish I had the month to stick around and find out. I try to engage him in conversation. "I'm hip. I'm hip," he assures me.

He is well into his forties, looks like a gaunt old-fashioned junkie. I can just picture it: as a kid he probably attended a Catholic mission school in some place like Barrow and his life was changed irrevocably when one night creeping around the rectory log cabin he overheard one of the good father's bop records on the wind-up Victrola. He recognized immediately the similarity with old Eskimo songs, same atonal polyrhythmic sound. He started singing to himself improvisations of the old songs, like Lester Young turned loose on seal-hunting chants. He asked questions and the father told him stories. "Right this very moment somewhere far away in the mainland a cat with a tenor is standing on a stage and everybody is going wild listening to him make this music, same as you're listening to now."

He decided right then to head out for LA to see palm trees and hear Wardell Grey. Maybe he made it and bought a zoot suit and fell by clubs on Central Avenue posing as mulatto. Listened to cool jazz, bought a tenor with sticky valves and smudged adhesive tape over the cracks, practiced in his hotel room, and when he was good enough decided to go back to the Arctic barrens and start a weird bop Eskimo band.

But for some reason he never made it past Tetlin Junction. He lives in one of the log cabins back of the restaurant, moth-eaten zoot suit packed away in a duffel bag stored under the bed, and blows his tenor late at night when he is all alone out by the gas pumps.

Crazy.

In the restaurant: big mugs of coffee, homemade cinnamon buns and apple pie, greasy large portions of food, and a huge woman cook in filthy apron. The truck drivers keep segregated from the car drivers. They discuss their routes, their companies, that idiot in a Volkswagen camper that stopped in the middle of the highway down in Sedro Woolley, and the flash of beaver on the four-lane outside of Anchorage.

In the men's washroom, written on a wall:

God made that road out there to punish truckers

and

Driving for K&W is like friggin a hog
It ain't too bad but
You just don't like to talk about it.

On the other side of the café at a table are an elderly gent and a young boy and it is plain to see that they are enjoying themselves immensely. Mif and I start talking to them. Grand-dad and a kid. They're coming from Indiana—what a trip—just the two of them in an eleven-year-old Falcon, trunk filled with fishing gear and camping equipment, glove compartment crammed with maps and marshmallows, dashboard cluttered with sunglasses, Life Savers, chocolate bars, and cookies. The old man laughs all the time and tells stories while the kid looks at him with the utmost admiration and flat-out adulation. "Took me three years to convince his Mom and Dad to let me take him along. Especially since my wife wanted no part of the trip."

No wife to keep the old man reined in. No parents to mete out discipline and worry about where to stop, and to divide the kid's attention. They are buddies and equals, the way fathers and sons can never be. The old man begins a story about a bear that hung around their cabin in British Columbia and it dove-tails into a yarn about when he used to raise pigs back in Indiana, seventy miles from the Indianapolis Speedway. The kid interjects about the honest-to-God Mountie they saw back in the Yukon and the old man sputters, "Mountie, yep that's right. And the bear. Don't forget the bear. Big old bear he was too. Yes. Heh, heh. Wanna milkshake? That's right!"

They stop jabbering long enough to pay the bill and the old man says good-bye and to the kid, "Let's go do some fishin'," and off they go, tumbling into the old car. Driving off, the old man talking himself blue in the face, sputtering chocolate chip cookie crumbs all over the dashboard. The kid proud as can be because the old man is the world's greatest fisherman and woodsman and buddy and absolutely the No. 1 Granddad.

Mile 1314 . . . Tok, Alaska . . . A roadhouse Saturday night. Rockabilly and raucous behavior going on in Young's Husky Lounge. The band is wailing, the dance floor is crowded, and they're wedged four deep at the bar, hands pass along money and beer in aluminum cans like at a ball game. The men are construction workers, oil men, dog mushers, and breeders. The women work in local lounges and restaurants or actually live here all year around and have regular homes and families. Tok is dog-raising country. People talk dogs or nostalgia. The action and conversation start the minute you walk in the door, and don't stop until you leave. A little bit of culture shock after a thousand miles of Canadian waterholes where unless people are totally drunk they tend to be reserved. This is the kind of place where someone is going to talk to you and for no reason other than a little companionship. The guy on the next stool is either going to turn out to be your best buddy or take a swing at you. Either way, you will know you're alive.

Mif has been asked to dance ten times before she can finish her first drink and I've already made a couple of great friends and taken down a few addresses. "You ever come through El Paso, you look me up, hear?"

The fellow on the stool in front of me, whom I can't help leaning against from time to time in the general jostle and activity, looks like Lloyd Bridges and tells me he's a construction foreman. Buys me a Schlitz and allows as how he's homesick for Michigan. Can't wait until January and shutdown time so he can get back home. "I got ten acres with the nicest little house on it and the best trout stream in the world running through the middle of the property. Boy, oh boy!"

Trout! Lord, man! This is the *land* of trout streams. But nostalgia is the best fishing hole of all. Nothing like a trout caught back home in the land of big two-hearted rivers. Hem fishing the dark pools in the early morning.

Our words on fishing back home start the big guy on the other side of me talking about his home, which is a farm in Iowa, and as a matter of fact he looks like Central Casting's Iowa farmboy. Looks like Randy Quaid, which is the same thing. Tall, husky, round-faced and jug-eared, an expression of simple concerns, wide-eyed, wearing a cap with a Purolator badge. He's a salesman of oil filters and travels all around Alaska. Used to be a tackle on the high school football team.

Someone comes over and insists on introducing me to his boss and his wife. A huge Indian drapes his arm over my shoulder and swears we worked together on a job somewhere and insists on buying me another Schlitz to remember the occasion.

The band keeps working. The beer keeps flowing. Backs are being slapped. It's a good-time scene save for one fellow brooding over by the doorway, a weight-lifter, obviously. Sleeves cut out of his tight sweater, he flexes his muscles and glares at any male who catches his eye. Everyone ignores him and he slinks off into the night.

Mif and I dance long into the early hours of the morning and leave at 3 A.M. and outside a man we never saw before says he hopes we had a good time.

The Sunday morning-after breakfast takes place at the little log cabin diner at the Glenn Highway Intersection. I recognize people from the bar. There is a serious nursing of hangovers going on at some tables: bowed heads, red eyes, trembling cups of coffee, hands fumbling in shirt pockets for cigarettes. Unmindful of this sober adult state of affairs, three teen-aged workers with Texas accents come in laughing and kidding each other about what they did the night before and all the time mock-groaning, "Man, I got me a bee-ug haid this mawnin'."

They order huge breakfasts of hotcakes, bacon, eggs, and hash browns, and on top of the mound of food dump blobs of ketchup, causing grown men to look away.

"Hay-ul, I thought chew was gittin' sweet on at lil blonde last nide, Larry."

"Damn, Warren, he warn't neither. Din't you see him makin' up to that ole squaw?"

Outside, kids are lining up in the morning hitchhiking positions. At the junction is Dennie's Speed Kleen, a laundromat in the form of a monstrous, three-story-high washtub. The Texans finish breakfast and have to get to work. They are all overgrown and gawky and coordination hasn't caught up with them. They rush out bumping into tables and chairs like overeager puppies, climb into two low-slung Fords with glass pac mufflers, and pull away, spraying gravel on Ma and Pa's camper.

Johnson River, Mile 1380 . . . After driving the '67 Chevy 300 miles over rocky rutted Canadian road, it decides it can't take the smooth asphalt of civilization (relative) and blows a tire. The jack is rusted and useless. We sit by the river and wait for someone to come along.

A vehicle appears after half an hour, a yellow Datsun pick-up, and I wave it down. Two long-haired, bearded, back-to-earth types in their mid-thirties get out in overalls and rubber boots. I borrow their jack and set to work while Mif tries to engage them in some conversation. They are not unfriendly but as taciturn as a pair of elderly New England farm brothers.

One eventually breaks the string of "Yeps" and "Nopes" to allow as how the pipeline is ruining Alaska by bringing in too many people and if there is one thing he hates, it is too many people. When I'm finished I thank them and they nod and drive away ever so much like a cooled-out version of the Freak Brothers.

Twenty miles farther on, way back off the highway down a muddy lane, I spy a cluster of trailers and a barn-like garage surrounded by twenty or so junk cars. I turn down, half thinking I might get a tire off one of the wrecks and half out of curiosity. In front of the garage is a craggy-faced man in permanently begrimed coveralls trying to get a school bus started. He emerges from inside and plunges his hands into the innards of the bus motor. Blackened, swollen hands, grease that will never come out from the cracks in his fingers. He tells me he came to Alaska from the countryside near Covington, Kentucky, worked on the pipeline for a year, taking but a day or two off, and bought this place with his earnings. His two little boys hang around handing him tools and asking questions. A tall and jolly, florid-faced fat man comes over, nipping at a back-pocket pint of Bourbon, and bends to study my Yukon license plate. "Lawd, lawd," he drawls, "a Canadian boy. You don't *look* Canadian."

He laughs and I wonder what the hell he means by that.

"What the hell you mean by that?" I ask.

He finds my question even funnier and says, "Just never you mind. Never you mind."

I take the proper size tire off a dead Fairlane and note that some of the junked cars are from Illinois and Georgia. They had penetrated far enough into the land of the future that when they expired their owners could not be too angry, just gave them a final push into the woods or else, broke, their drivers pulled in here and sold them for bus fare into Fairbanks. Where do they start their auto-biographies, these old wrecks all lachrymose in junkyards, once fine sedans, squatting ignominiously in the roadside weeds?

Delta Junction, a town that vigorously insists it, and not Fairbanks, 101 miles away, is the end of the Alaska Highway. It is here that the Alaska Highway joins the Richardson, Alaska's first highway, for the final leg into Fairbanks. The U.S. Army Corps of Engineers did not have to build past Delta Junction, therefore, claim the town fathers, we are obviously the end of the road. On the other hand, the Alcan wherever possible was built over previously existing trails and stretches of actual road. And furthermore the goal of the project was Fairbanks and the dramatic factor must prevail and declare for it and not Delta Junction.

The town, which stretches for miles along the highway, began in 1919 as a work camp for the Richardson, itself built over an old sixteen-foot-wide pack trail connecting Valdez on Prince William Sound with the gold fields at Eagle and Fairbanks. Bison from Montana were imported here in the twenties and the settlement was known until the building of the Alcan as Buffalo Center.

Rainier and Olympia beer signs are glowing in the window of the Club Evergreen hard by Mary's House of Beauty (*"Ladies Fresh Up! It's the End of the Alcan"*) and inviting us to enter.

Now what better way to meet the people and get the true feel of these little communities than by visiting the local watering holes, which are the social and business centers after all? Drinking is a big part of the life of the North, some would say the biggest part, and a teetotaler knows not the land of the midnight sun. Belly up to the bar if only for a coffee or a club soda. Had you not stopped, you would fail to be introduced to any of the gallimaufry of types known as Alaskans and proud of it.

Jeanie the bartender, for instance, of the push-'em-up bra, blond bouffant hair, and painted green eyelids.

"I'm from Arkansas, Little Rock, but I consider myself to be an Alaskan now. I spend my winters here."

She rode the bus North but ran out of money when she got to Calgary, where she had to "Um, work for a while." When she had enough together she bought another bus ticket, this one to Fairbanks.

"The bus stopped for half an hour at a place called Pink Mountain in British Columbia. The lady there waiting on tables was pregnant and I could see right away that she was feeling sick. She fainted right in the middle of serving a whole busload of passengers. Her husband was taking care of her and I just got up, found an apron, and went to work. Stayed four months."

When she got to Delta Junction she fell in love with it and decided she was going no farther. "I wouldn't go back to the States for anything." She is a splendid bartender and can earn a lot of money. "Besides, it's so much fun dancing at all the lodges hidden away in the woods on the lakes. Tourists don't know about them. In the winter we all get plastered and play snowshoe baseball. You ain't an Alaskan unless you've played snowshoe baseball."

I order another Wild Turkey. Soldiers from Fort Greely are shooting pool. A young girl comes in assisting her father, a man in his sixties crippled by arthritis. She helps him onto a bar stool, kisses him on the cheek, and leaves him there. It is obviously a daily ritual. "The usual, Jeanie."

She brings him a Southern Comfort. We get to talking and he tells us that he arrived a year ago from Vincennes, Indiana, to be near his two sons, one a minister in Fairbanks, the other a pipeline worker. The skin on his hands is drawn tightly over the misshapen knuckles, the veins stand out vulnerable and blue. He cradles the glass in a clawlike grip. He begins to talk about music and as it turns out he used to be a bass player in Les Brown's Band of Renown. "I wanted to make music my life but . . ." he sighs, looks at his hands, and leaves the sentence unfinished.

Tanana River . . . an Alyeska Pipeline camp. The welders are up on high scaffolding fitting a giant elbow pipe into place. Little kids watch them from behind the chain-link barbed-wire-topped fence. On the shore people are beaching their Alaska river boats—thirty-foot-long freighter canoes with huge twin Mercury outboard engines. An American Colette, a lady with pancake makeup, rouged cheeks, garish kohl eyes, and henna hair, sits in the passenger seat of a camper stroking a Siamese cat with robin's-egg-blue eyes.

The Tanana River is the inspiration for the great Alaskan annual betting classic with one hundred thousand dollars in prizes for those who guess the day, hour, and minute that the river ice will break up and start to move downstream.

Twenty miles along the road is the Richardson Roadhouse, which advertises it has "sassy help." It is one of the original log cabin inns that were built every twenty miles along the old trail. The prospectors and trappers would stop here, traveling by horse, foot, bicycle, dog team, or in old Studebaker sleighs with carbon heaters at the foot.

Twenty miles from Harding Lake and just past the Boondox Bar there is a curious two-story building whose walls bear a forest mural with bear cubs shimmying up a tree and fish jumping in the streams. The shades are drawn over the windows. What could it be? We stop to explore.

A strange lady appears and invites us in for coffee. She has a severely lined face, eyelids like walnuts, and her iron-gray hair is arranged in a disconcerting Veronica Lake peek-a-boo style. She is in her middle fifties, diminutive, active, speaks out of the corner of her mouth. She says the place is for the elderly.

"Where are they?"

"That's the problem, sweetie. I run it for the old people but the city has stuck it way out here twenty-five miles from town where the rent is cheaper but where the old people can't get to it. They don't give me any money for upkeep. I haven't gotten paid for two months. But if I don't do it, who the hell will? Personally, I make out. I got a place down the road. I raise dogs."

She chain-smokes Camels, slits her eyes to exhale smoke through her nostrils. She tells us she came from St. Louis in the early forties with her new husband who was a Navy pilot. "He had the choice of here or Hawaii. I wanted him to take Hawaii. But, no, he was fascinated by the Jack London bit. We were here three months and he died in a crash over the Aleutians. The poor bastard. I just stayed on."

We talked and drank coffee with her for another hour and

left her there sitting alone in the darkened old folks' social center on the other side of the forest walls.

North Pole . . . the last community before Fairbanks. Originally a homestead site, it was bought out by a development company that named it in the hope of coaxing a toy manufacturer to relocate because of the advantage of a North Pole address. The ploy worked. A man named Con Miller runs Santa Claus House and is widely known and well loved because he not only sends Christmas gifts to poor children in remote Alaskan settlements but also answers all those letters kids from around the world write to "Santa Claus, North Pole."

Nevertheless, the little community seems dedicated to the motto: When you've got a good theme, flog it. Homes and businesses are decorated for Christmas twelve months of the year. There is the Snowflake Laundry, North Pole Trading Post *("Santa's Christmas Home")*, Arctic Acres subdivision, KJNP Radio *("The Gospel Station at the Top of the Nation")* whose staff live free in log cabins in "Jesus Town." And on the local pop station Roy Helms' "Jingle Bell Rock" is in the top forty all year round.

Four miles from Fairbanks a line of gray fighter planes stand poised and ready before their hangars at Fort Wainwright.

Then the outskirts of town, a cluttered jumble of pre-fab and franchise, a miasma of drive-ins, shopping centers, warehouses, motels, and vacant lots—once parcels of the Tanana Valley wilderness, now civilized with oil cans, tin cans, McDonald's wrappers, old tires, last month's centerfold, and the remains of a microbus from Mississippi—all making the city limits vaguely reminiscent of the back of an old radio.

The Alaska Highway runs into Cushman Street and on into town. On Second Avenue black hookers in blond Afro wigs parade, shaking the shakable, showing the stuff, licking frosted lips with pink tongues, and offering fake lascivious leers to short-haired, fresh-faced soldier boys. The pimps are draped over the bar in places like The Mecca and The Golden Nugget. The big parking lot is filled with dented Jeeps, mud-splattered campers, hillbilly Fords, old Volvos owned by geologists, and long cream-colored Coupe de Villes. Kids lie around in sleeping bags, their heads propped against tires. Over in a corner of the lot behind a van a couple of people are completing a deal of some kind while Eskimos pass around a bottle of California port a few feet away. Three pipeliners with beards and long hair and ample bellies commandeer the middle of the sidewalk, drinking beer and smoking cigarettes, tossing each dead Oly can into the street, vying with one another in exclaiming what they'd like to do to their section foreman. Down the street, tourists take photos of gold nugget watches in a jewelry store window and Indians in tattered clothes sprawl on the curb in front of them.

Several years ago, pre-pipeline, Fairbanks was acclaimed as an All-American city. Farther back, a hundred years pre-pipeline, the land on which it sits, the land that it litters, had never even been viewed by the white man's eyes.

Arthur Harper, a prospector, was the first white man down the Chena River, arriving in 1873. He found evidence of gold but he neither stuck around nor returned to the country because the gold would have been too expensive to bring out. Fifteen years later Lieutenant H. T. Allen went up the Copper River to explore the area for the United States Government and in 1898 Lieutenant Caster arrived at the mouth of the Volmar River and after four days into the country, determined that perhaps as many as ten men lived in the entire Chena Slough.

In 1901 Ebenezer T. Barnette of St. Michael traveled up the Chena in a little steamer, the *Lavelle Young,* with the intention of trading with the Indians. Five miles from the river's junction with the Tanana, Barnette put to shore to cut wood for the stoves. It just so happened that an immigrant Italian prospector named Felix Pedro was in the hills above and saw the smoke rising from the river. Pedro hiked down and made the acquaintance of Barnette. They were an unlikely pair. Barnette was a crook, an embezzler, a man whose name would become synonymous in Alaska with the more sneaky of swindles. Pedro had been put to work in the coal mines of his native Bologna when he was seven years old. The mines were all he knew—those in France and southern Illinois—until he reached the Cariboo gold fields in the 1890s. From there he drifted to Dawson and got out when it became too crowded.

Pedro told Barnette he felt in his bones that there was gold in the immediate vicinity of where they stood talking. Barnette had intended to establish his trading post at Tanana Crossing but he allowed Pedro to change his mind. For those who are familiar with Barnette's future and his past, it might seem out of character for him to trust in another man. Not so. If there was gold, there would be men to find it and, thus, men to steal it from.

It is Felix Pedro who is considered the founder of Fairbanks although its first name was Barnette's Cache. Pedro indeed found his gold the next year on a creek that feeds the Chena.

The area fell under the jurisdiction of Judge James J. Wickersham of St. Michael who named the town, which he had never seen, after his good buddy back home in Indiana, a senator and future Vice President of the United States, Charles Warren Fairbanks. In the spring of 1903 Wickersham felt it incumbent on him to take a look at the little settlement that was beginning to draw the gold-hungry from Outside. He journeyed by dogsled from St. Michael and found "sourdoughs and cheechakos, miners, gamblers, Indians, Negroes, Japanese, digs, prostitutes, music, drinking! It's rough but healthy—the beginning—I *hope* of an American Dawson."

In 1903, forty thousand dollars in gold was taken out and the Rush began. Dawson and Nome were drained. The real death knell for Dawson as a gold town was sounded when Cheechako Lil saw the writing on the wall and deserted for Fairbanks, where she set up shop on Second Avenue, thus beginning the city's proud tradition of prostitution.

Further strikes were made on Fairbanks Creek and Fox Gulch, at Chatman and Cleary, where a fair-sized town grew up. This was the first modern boom. Roads were built to the creeks and a telephone system installed. Towns arose at Dome and Ester. The Tanana River Railroad built track to Ester Junction and down to Fairbanks in 1905. A telegraph line connected Fairbanks and Valdez and a trail was built over the Thompson Pass through the Copper River Valley, a trail that eventually became the Richardson Highway and a hundred miles of the Alcan.

The next year, on May 22, 1906, most of the little city, the "largest log town in the world," went up in flames. But so great was civic pride that the rebuilding had begun before the last ember died. The day after the fire, surviving businesses advertised *"Genuine Fire Sale."* The town was rebuilt in a month!

There was a spirit of friendliness uniting the people that helped such hardships to be endured. Although, as Wickersham noted, the people came from everywhere, no one cared about whatever deeds lurked in their neighbor's past. As Rex Beach wrote in *The Spoilers:* "You was in trouble—that's unfortunate; we help you—that's natural; no questions asked—that's Alaska."

Now the descendants of these Tanana Valley pioneers can only sit and shrug and sigh at the antics of the new breed. Long-haired rednecks from Texas who put their pointy-toed boots to the hirsute heads of other rednecks just because they happen to hail from Oklahoma. Why, this fellow in the short-sleeve nylon shirt with the wrinkled face of an old Alaska hand got his gold nugget watchband in '47 before some of these new people were born. "They come up from the lower forty-eight and leave their broken-down cars on my lawn. They cry and complain and vow to kick ass because their union-ordained coffee break was cut short twenty-three seconds. I nursed my pick-up, ancient when I got it, for fifteen years and these characters tear the gears out of sixty-thousand-dollar Cats and walk away laughing. They don't give a good goddamn because they're working a cost-plus project. And all the parasites that are living off this money they make! The whores. Nothing I got against whores. Far from it. Whoring has always been a way of life in Fairbanks. But it's a different class of hooker up here. Like this summer you've probably seen that Winnebago with the Florida plates? Well, it's making the rounds of the camps along the Richardson from Valdez to here. Driven by two wops with shades from Miami and in the back they got four women, blond, brunette, redhead, black hair. All they want is your money and get out. Used to be an Alaska whore had a heart of gold. I remember the poem my daddy used to recite when he'd had a few; about a whore, it was.

> *"Lottie went to the diggings;*
> *With Lottie we must be just:*

If she didn't shovel tailings—
Where did Lottie get her dust?

"See it was all good-natured back in the old days, which aren't so long gone actually. It was prostitution and some might call it sinful but it was *personal*. Now it is in there and out, not a second to spare, *im*personal like everything else. But they do take your *personal* check or your American Express card.

"Ah, these people, what do they care for this country? They'll make their twenty-four dollars an hour for as long as they can take it, and get out. Good riddance, but they leave mementos of their presence all about; each one of them has destroyed a little of Alaska before they leave. And what they done to the Indians. I used to go out on the trapline and work with them people. My life depended on them and theirs on me. We got along fine. They lived and made do beautifully out there in the back country. Now they lie on the floor in the washrooms of the white man's bars. Try and find one that could live out in the forests. Talk about whores, the white man turned the Indian woman into a whore and then they couldn't even earn money that way because the black women came up from Detroit and Seattle and drove the Indian woman off the street. Like that song by Jerry Mac and Mike Dunham says—'Alaska Soul,' it's called:

> "*I see the drunken Native now and know why*
> *he thinks drinking's fun*
> *'Cause booze sure helps to blind your eyes*
> *to what the white man's done.*
> *I'm going to Second Avenue, get drunk,*
> *forget the pain.*
> *Alaska! Alaska! Oh why'd they make you change?*

"Lord, lord, ain't it the truth."
Are you listening, Yukon?

Mif and I were sitting in Herb's Bar while a fat fellow in his early thirties bragged to us about his numerous adventures and incredible exploits. He had served two rounds of duty in

Vietnam and killed "about a thousand gooks" and fought as a mercenary in Africa, assisting " 'bout the same number of niggers" out of this world. Then he had run his own charter-boat enterprise in Newport News, Virginia, after which he made a million dollars in real estate. Which all made it curious, to my mind, what he was doing working as a mere cook, even though his employer was "Alaska's best restaurant."

"It's the greatest and the best but nobody much knows about it 'cause we keep it a secret. Don't want the pimps and the pipeliners to find out about it. It's in a castle back in the woods and you got to fly in there by helicopter, dig it?"

"Uh huh."

"Lots of famous people come in there. Last month the Fonz, you know, Henry Winkler, was in there. He was up to do some big-game hunting. I took him out hunting with me 'cause I told him the local hunters and guides weren't worth shit. I took him out, made a man out of him. Showed him how to shoot a .303. Then I brought him into town and got him some dark meat."

"Uh huh."

He continued in this vein for another few minutes and then, unfortunately, he had to go off somewhere to "see someone about a big deal I'm putting over." A round of drinks appeared and I asked the bartender, the Vietnamese war bride of a Green Beret, who had sent them over.

"Why, Bennie did," she said in a tone that implied I was dumb for having to ask.

"Who's he?" I asked, looking around the bar.

"Oh, he juss leff. He say give you anything you want long as you here."

I inquired of the fellow next to me who this Bennie was. "Why, he's one stone-crazy dude from down around Paraguay way. Has so much money he don't know what to do with it. Makes ten thousand dollars a month on the pipe and may the Lord strike me dead right now if I'm not telling you the truth. Just the other evening fellow in here said a few words to him in Spanish. Bennie, he was so glad to hear his own language, he stuffed a handful of tens and twenties into that fellow's pocket."

Now I had the idea I might stay in Herb's as long as it took for Bennie to return. After all, the funds were running low, that old Chevy had gone through two tires and numerous quarts of oil getting here from Whitehorse, and I *can* speak a bit of his language and he *is* buying. Lo and behold, he did arrive an hour later but, alas, he was falling-down drunk. I threw some South American slang at him, he giggled, seemed to reach for his pocket, and passed out, crumbling to the floor.

Ah well. I went into the washroom and on the wall read this sentiment:

Texans aren't all bad
I met one last year
that wasn't a faggot

From my pocket I took my magic marker and underneath these words scrawled:

. . . Rex Beach.

Motel on Lacey Street . . . lobby filled with soldiers and oil men; women of shady repute hang around outside the doors. As we walked to our room we heard a radio playing country songs, the door was open, and a man was sitting on the edge of the bed with his elbows on his knees and he was staring at a spot on the rug between his feet. Beside him the desk with the peeling veneer top; in front of the mirror were gilt-framed photos of a woman and some children. I thought of the poem by Kenneth Rexroth, *Blue Sunday:*

The radio is breaking
Somebody's heart somewhere
In a dirty bedroom.

Around four in the morning I was awakened by a female voice screaming in the night. I got up and looked out the window. There was the sound of a truck door slamming and heels clacking. The voice cried out, "If you think I'm going to give you a blow job you're crazy!"

Fairbanks!

More pollution than Los Angeles!

Home of the world's busiest McDonald's!

Modern shopping malls and housing projects alongside wooden false-front buildings and turn-of-the-century log cabins. Five highways besides the Alcan end here, as well as the Alaska Railroad. There is a flight a day from New York. A flight a day from Tokyo.

We drifted through hotel lobbies, sat in bars and cafés, drove down little back streets, and peeked around corners and wherever we went we encountered displaced persons after the big buck.

A young Eskimo boy with teased hair and painted eyes swishing down the midnight avenue. The North Carolina couple picking each other apart in the fantastic Mexican restaurant. The hordes of dirty-clothes working men. Oldtimers bemoaning passing time, remembering a long-dead Alaska. Okies pumping gas. The Jewish man running the Vienna Delicatessen with Aleut waiters. A crowd of Eskimos gesticulating under a street lamp outside a Bingo parlor. Men in Fairbanks formal attire—leisure suits—plotting big deals with Arabs and Japanese in the basement restaurant of the Chena View Hotel. Cottages with three-foot-high cabbages in the garden. Sad parking lots. And always the whores: young ones working the streets and lobbies; old ones turned to waitressing in greasy luncheonettes.

There it is at the foot of Cushman across the street from the Arctic Café on the banks of the Chena River: the final Alaska Highway marker. Before it are the same tourists you probably saw in Dawson Creek. Fairbanks, the terminus to the Alcan. The All-American town smack dab in the middle of the tawdry future.

The beginning of the Dream and the end of the Road.

JOE McGINNISS

The pipeline, Pump Station Eight, winter

"IT WAS 35 BELOW AT PUMP STATION EIGHT. THE SUN WAS
SHINING. WE ATE LUNCH, POLISH SAUSAGE AND RICE, IN A
BRIGHT PLASTIC CAFETERIA. LOTS OF PASTRY AND PIE FOR
DESSERT. LIQUOR AND DRUGS WERE SUPPOSEDLY PROHIBITED
IN PIPELINE CAMPS, AND THE WORKERS WERE FED SWEETS
INSTEAD."

*In the last two decades, there has been an avalanche of books
about Alaska, but none have matched in popularity John
McPhee's 1977* Coming into the Country *and Joe McGinniss's
1980* Going to Extremes.

*McGinniss travels through Alaska wondering, as travelers
should everywhere, what it's like to live there. It's the people
who interest him. In the following excerpt from* Going to Extremes, *covering a day's flying visit to Pump Station Eight on
the pipeline, Pump Station Eight and the pipeline get only two
brief and perfunctory paragraphs. The doughnuts are much
more memorable.*

THE ALARM WENT OFF AT FIVE-THIRTY.
I dressed quickly but carefully, trying to remember every
layer. Long underwear first, top and bottom. Cotton socks, then
heavy woolen socks. Then I went to the bathroom and brushed

my teeth. Too early to shave. Too cold and too dark. I didn't want to get wet; didn't want to be any more awake than I had to be. Back to the bedroom. Jeans on over the thermal underwear. Then a flannel shirt, and a woolen shirt over that. My Pendleton wool shirt from Eddie Bauer. Check for mittens, notebooks, sharpened pencils. Not pens. In Fairbanks, in December, ball-point pens had a tendency to freeze.

I stepped into my Snowpacks and went out into the dark to start the Travel-All. There were a couple of inches of fresh snow on the ground, squeaking against the soles of the boots.

The Travel-All was parked on the street, fifty feet in front of Tom and Marnie's house. There was an electric heater attached to the engine block. A short cord that led from the heater was connected to a long extension cord that ran from the basement of the house to the curb. The Travel-All had been plugged in overnight, in order that it might start in the morning. This arrangement was quite common in Anchorage.

The engine started easily. There was heavy frost on the windshield. I put the defroster on and went back inside to drink some juice. In the bedroom I laced the Snowpacks up tight, and slipped into my Eddie Bauer maximum-strength, ultimate, super-warm Arctic parka. It had a hood with fur around the edge. When the parka was zipped tight and the hood was pulled forward all the way, there was created, for three or four inches in front of the nose, a little tunnel that warmed the air before you breathed it. Not necessary, or even desirable, at zero or 5 below, but in Fairbanks, in December, who could tell?

The Travel-All defroster was not working well. I scraped the windshield. At 6 A.M. in December there were no other headlights to be seen; no other house lights yet lit. It was still a clear and starry night. I put the Travel-All in gear. The tires made fresh tracks through the snow. The temperature was 3 below.

Out through Spenard. Not much traffic, even on Spenard Road, at 6 A.M. Spenard was the most raucous section of the city. The rowdiest bars. The highest concentration of massage parlors per square mile. The bars had been closed for an hour. The massage parlors had not. They were open twenty-four hours a day.

I reached the airport at six-twenty, parked and locked the Travel-All. The terminal was modern, brightly lit. There were glass cases containing stuffed moose, wolves, and bears. The lobby was almost empty: just one large, ragged cluster of men, mostly bearded, mostly overweight, and mostly dressed in flannel or woolen shirts. They were bunched around the gate from which the seven o'clock Wien Air Alaska flight to Fairbanks would depart. There were only two or three people in suits and ties. Only two or three women. Not exactly the Washington shuttle from La Guardia.

Wien Air Alaska was one of the two major airlines in the state, the other being Alaska Airlines, which flew mostly to southeastern Alaska and which, in fact, was based in Seattle. Wien did not fly to southeastern Alaska but went to almost all other parts of the state. It was the airline founded by the Wien brothers, immigrants from Minnesota, who were among the first people to fly airplanes in Alaska. It had been Noel Wien, in fact, who made the first flight ever from Anchorage to Fairbanks, in 1924, as aviation brought the concept of relativity to Alaska: space and time suddenly being perceived as less than absolute.

There was a rumor that the plane might not go. The weather in Fairbanks had been very cold, and ice fog had set in. No flights at all had made it yesterday. Only two or three the day before. Ice fog was produced when pollution in the air—particularly exhaust from motor vehicles—began to freeze and turned solid. This happened in Fairbanks when the temperature reached 35 or 40 below.

The plane did take off, half an hour late. A Boeing 727, with every seat filled. Some people had been trying to reach Fairbanks for several days.

It would have been possible to drive, of course: an all-day trip, over an icy, snowy, two-lane road, with only about four hours of daylight. Or it would have been possible to take the train. But in winter the train ran only two days a week and took twelve hours to get from Anchorage to Fairbanks—without problems. And in winter there were very few trips without problems. An avalanche, perhaps, or maybe a moose on the tracks. Moose liked the railroad tracks because they were kept plowed and it was easier for the animals to move along them than through the deep snow in the woods.

I wound up in a middle seat between two bearded men who reeked of alcohol. Immediately, they went to sleep. We flew north in the dark past Mount McKinley.

After forty-five minutes, the pilot came on the intercom. He said he was going to begin circling Fairbanks. If a break came in the fog, he would land. There was enough fuel to permit ninety minutes of circling. If he was not able to land in that time, we would return to Anchorage.

A first, faint gray light now appeared. My seatmate stirred and glanced out the window. The engines droned as the plane banked and turned once again.

"What do you think?"

"Fuck, I don't know. I don't even care, man. Either way, as long as we walk off this baby. I don't care if it's Fairbanks or Anchorage, or fucking Paris, France." He shut his eyes and went back to sleep.

Circling and circling and the pilot back on the intercom, saying twenty more minutes and we'll have to turn back, and the gray light stronger now, and seeing low hills, pine-covered, snow-covered, no signs of an actual city, and then a flat, impenetrable gray cloud beneath us: Fairbanks, the airport, the ice fog.

The No Smoking sign flashes on. There is a change in the pitch of the engines. The plane plunges into the fog. No visibility now, just the feeling of going down fast. High-pitched scream of the engines, a little tipping motion back and forth, seats into the full upright position, the gum chewers chewing a little faster, the armrest grippers gripping a little tighter, a sudden swirling gray outside the window, land right there, snow, pine trees, fog again, see nothing, then ground below, only ten feet below, five feet, inches, a bump, a roar, and the plane is down, fog all around, can't even see the terminal building, the pilot leaning on the reverse thrust to slow us on the bumpy, icy runway, blue lights flickering past, we're in Fairbanks.

A cheer goes up.

The pilot comes back on the intercom. Announces that the temperature in Fairbanks is 49 below.

At first, the cold was less of a shock than expected. With no wind, the fog, initially, asserted itself more. It was gritty, metallic: not so much an odor as a taste. A fog made not of moisture, but of microscopic particles of foulness; a blanket of frozen filth.

There was, at first, a sense of numbness rather than a feeling of being cold. With parka zipped tight, hood forward, and no wind, there was little direct contact with the cold. The difference from Anchorage—the difference between minus 3 and minus 49—seemed not so much physical, at first, as metaphysical. A deep chill in the marrow of the soul. A sense of not belonging; an awareness that this was not a part of the world—of the universe—that man was intended to inhabit.

I took a cab downtown. There was snow piled high on both sides of the road, much more than in Anchorage. If Anchorage had been the edge, then this seemed the capital, the heart, of the bleak and foreign world that lay beyond. The icy, fogbound essence of Alaska.

Neon glowed, then vanished in the fog. The cab inched toward downtown at no more than fifteen miles an hour. Already, my eyes stung from the poisonous fog and from the cold. Forty-nine below. At 9:30 A.M. It would not be light yet in Fairbanks even if there had not been any fog.

"Forty-nine below," the cab driver said. "That don't sound too bad if you say it fast enough."

Then he laughed. In Fairbanks, they made jokes about the cold. They were proud of it. It was their greatest natural resource.

The driver said he had kept the engine of his taxi running all night, parked outside his house.

"What does it cost me? Five bucks in gas? I'll make that back on this trip." A lot of the taxis in Fairbanks had not started this morning. At 49 below, even plugging in was not enough.

The thought occurred that this was, in a sense, nature fighting back. The cold was, after all, in Alaska, the strongest weapon nature had. With Fairbanks—with all of Alaska—under brutal technological assault, here, for the first time, was evidence that it would not succumb without a fight.

In this sort of cold you did not think of normal things—upset stomach, fatigue, financial problems, whether there was life after death. You were able to think only of the cold: it monopolized every facet of your being; like first love, or news of a death in the family. Actually, the first time, it was a marvelous novelty. For the visitor, the Arctic dilettante, the cold was fun.

The cab reached downtown. At least the driver said it was downtown. In the ice fog there was no way to be sure. There was a sense of multi-story buildings nearby, but you could not actually see them through the fog. There were supposed to be four hours and twenty-seven minutes of daylight in Fairbanks on this date, but with the ice fog there would not be any daylight at all.

Out of the cab, it was as if I were no longer on earth, but on a distant, foreign planet; a planet that was much farther from the sun.

The pipeline public relations office was one flight up, in a shabby old building across the street from the Chena Bar. That was the one sign I could read through the ice fog. A neon sign. Chena Bar. With only the *R*—the last letter—lit. CHENA BAR. ENTERTAINMENT NIGHTLY. GIRLS GIRLS GIRLS.

In the office, there was classical music on an FM radio station, the University of Alaska campus station. They were playing Rachmaninoff. At 49 below, with the *R* of CHENA BAR flashing pink. In Fairbanks, in winter, they played a lot of music by Russian composers.

A pipeline public relations man was going to drive me to Pump Station Eight, so I could see how the pipeline would work. This was something I had arranged in Anchorage the week before. The public relations man was not happy. He was sick of Pump Station Eight, sick of the pipeline, sick of leading writers and photographers around by the nose. Besides, he was tired and cold: he had been up most of the night with his girlfriend in Anchorage, flying back to Fairbanks on the plane which I took; having to come back only because I was coming. Before the pipeline, he had worked for the Fairbanks newspaper. The pipeline was getting them all: the newsmen, the policemen, the short-order cooks. The trap was, first you fell in love with Alaska; then you had to work for the enemy—for the pipeline, for the oil companies, for the forces that were destroying what you loved—just to be able to remain.

For the PR man, all this would be over in a year. Then he would be able to move to London and to live for a year without even having to work. Just living off the money he was making now. But that would be next year. This was now. Forty-nine below. Heavy ice fog. And he had to drive, once again, out to Pump Station Eight, instead of remaining in his office with Rachmaninoff.

We rode for ten minutes, then went up a slight grade toward what turned out to be the edge of town. Suddenly it was a brilliant, clear day. A beautiful day. Soft, rolling hills, studded with evergreens, through the snow. The sky so bright it was painful. The sun, in late morning, low on the horizon to the south. Open land, uninhabited, rolling free, toward the sky, in all directions. From ice fog to no ice fog instantaneously. As if someone had pushed a projector button and changed a slide.

Pump Station Eight was thirty miles out of town, and still under construction. There were 170 men there working twelve hours a day, seven days a week, eight weeks at a stretch, then two weeks off. Earning up to $2,500 a week.

The pipeline was going to run almost 800 miles, from Prudhoe Bay, in the Arctic, to Valdez. There were going to be twelve pump stations along the way. The oil would flow in, get pumped, flow out. Something like that. To tell the truth, it was the cold I was interested in, more than the pipeline.

It was 35 below at Pump Station Eight. The sun was shining. We ate lunch, Polish sausage and rice, in a bright plastic cafeteria. Lots of pastry and pie for dessert. Liquor and drugs were supposedly prohibited in pipeline camps, and the workers were fed sweets instead.

After lunch, I climbed some winding metal stairs to the top of an oil-storage tank. It was the highest point for miles around. Thirty-five below, a slight wind starting to rise, and, from the top of the tank, I could see the distant, flat sun setting over faraway mountains. There was a bright orange glare, then the onset of twilight, and a quick blue darkening of the pine trees and the snow. Then cold and stillness everywhere. Except for the machinery in the foreground. Except for the pipeline.

My feet got cold, even in the Snowpacks. I went back inside to the pump station manager's office. He was eating a cream-filled chocolate-covered doughnut. And why not? It had been almost an hour since his lunch. He smiled at me, at my red nose and at the frost on my hair. He offered a doughnut. I declined. He took another. The buttons of his flannel shirt were stretched tight across a stomach that had not been there, in such dimension, a few months earlier. He had a good job. As part of management, he did not have to live in the barracks. He drove back and forth to Fairbanks every day, one of the more exotic commuting routes in North America. He explained to me how the pipeline was a miracle of modern technology. He was quite sincere, quite proud of the work he was doing. I had met army officers like him in Vietnam. The pipeline, he told me, would be able to withstand an earthquake that registered eight on the Richter scale; it would be 99 percent operable even if hit by an earthquake that registered nine. Every valve on every pump could be remote-controlled from Valdez. He went into great detail about the purpose and function and virtual perfection of Pump Station Eight. Quite clearly, he had long ago convinced himself. Now he just about convinced me. What the hell, for eight billion dollars it should work.

But eighteen months later, when the first oil would finally flow toward Valdez, it would be here, at Pump Station Eight, that the most serious mishap would occur. Someone would forget to throw a switch, and the mechanical backup system would fail, too, and a spark would ignite oil and the whole place would blow sky high. The whole pump station. One man would be killed, a dozen would be injured, and thousands of gallons of oil would spill out, across the tundra.

It was dark now, and colder. The manager had work to get back to. My tour guide was eager to leave. We returned to Fairbanks at high speed. Through clear, brilliant night air; then, suddenly, back into the fog; swirling, stinking, bitter fog. I would be tasting it in the back of my throat for a week.

We parked behind the pipeline office, across from the Chena Bar, which, by now, was filled with drinkers. Fairbanks was a sub-Arctic blue-collar town. A town—even more so than Anchorage—of Teamsters and drunkards and pimps. And a lot of people getting rich quick. The population had gone from 12,000 to 60,000 in three years. Two-bedroom apartments were renting for $700 a month. There was virtually no police force left in the city. The cops had all quit to work pipeline security, at four and five times their previous wage. There were drugs and whores and trailer camps, and disputes among residents were less likely to be settled in small-claims court than by small-caliber—or large-caliber—pistol. Compared to Fairbanks, Anchorage seemed like San Francisco.

The pipeline man drove me to the airport, slowly, carefully, through the fog. It had warmed up to 46 below. No telling if the plane would get in.

The airport was a madhouse. People trapped by the ice fog had been trying to get out for days. And discovering that trying to get out of Fairbanks could drive you much crazier than simply not being able to get in.

My luck held. My plane came in, and I got my seat. A middle seat again, but I did not complain. There were people at the gate offering two hundred dollars for boarding passes. For a seat which cost forty-six dollars.

I was back in Anchorage by dinnertime, feeling like I had just returned to earth. It was only 5 below at the airport and the air was clear and I walked to the Travel-All with my parka unzipped.

TOM KIZZIA

Sleetmute: Winter of the soul

"A VISITOR WOULDN'T HAVE GUESSED THAT SLEETMUTE'S
REPUTATION FOR EPIDEMIC ALCOHOLISM, BROKEN FAMILIES, AND
VIOLENT DEATH HAD MARKED IT AS ONE OF THE MOST MISERABLE
PLACES IN THE ALASKA BUSH."

*The number of people who have ever heard of Sleetmute is se-
verely limited. Only faithful viewers of* Northern Exposure, *one
of the best series American television has ever offered viewers,
might think they once heard the name somewhere.* Northern Exposure *was set in the fictional town of Cicely, Alaska, a place
whose own location was deliberately left vague in the scripts.
The only references to the fictional locale were occasional mentions of its distance from somewhere else. A few of those noted
that it was so many miles or so many hours—such mentions
were never consistent—from Sleetmute, which certainly did
little to put either Sleetmute or Cicely on the map for anybody.*

*Those of us who live at less dramatic latitudes must be fasci-
nated by the extremes of "night" and "day" in the far north. I've
taken photographs and read a book by daylight in the middle of
a summer "night" in Iceland and other northern countries. But
it's the long, dark winter that is most interesting, and most troubling. A few years ago, on a longish visit to Denmark and Swe-
den, I asked residents of Copenhagen and Stockholm about this.*

*Since they were born and raised and lived their lives here, un-
der these annually recurring conditions, did they become accustomed to the months-long night of winter? These were educated
and resourceful people (and residents of Copenhagen in particular must be among the world's jolliest), living in sophisticated,
modern cities, a far cry from isolated Sleetmute. No, they said,
every one of them.*

✺ A PART OF ME HADN'T WANTED TO GO TO
the bush in winter. I could have happily restricted my travels to the season of long daylight and riverboats and returning
salmon. January in the villages conjured a different sort of
place, the primitive Alaska I would have imagined the one or
two times, as a boy, when the place might have crossed my
mind: a land of igloos and shivering, starving people. To judge
from the stories I'd heard of hard drinking and violence, winter
in the bush could indeed mean a struggle to survive. There was
little hunting, especially among the young, and there were no
jobs; nothing to divert the mind from a long dark turning inward. The season played to the weakness of life in an empty
place, and I didn't want to look—fearing, I suppose, to find
that when the rivers freeze and animals disappear, exalted ties
to landscape don't count for much.

But summer in the bush was only half the story, and so
one morning I found myself gazing down on the eerie stillness
of the frozen Kuskokwim River, turned inward already, floating
on my own soft cloud of goosedown. The cold had sent me
smartly in retreat the moment I stepped from the Aniak air terminal into the morning darkness. The air had spent the night
out at thirty below, and at the first gulp my throat choked shut.
I pressed my lips together and my nostril hairs turned brittle
with ice. Inside the mail plane, I pulled my knees up toward
my chest. The drone of the engine and the faintly nauseating
exhaust shut down my other senses. I wore earplugs now after
a summer in small planes, and a balaclava of thick gray wool
was pulled to my earlobes. I did my best to burrow into a place
where nothing could touch me.

Dawn came slowly as we flew through the Kuskokwim

Mountains. Above the wing, rounded Appalachian ridges rose to wind-crusted knobs where snow picked up the first blue tinge of day. It was getting on toward midmorning—in Anchorage the rush hour would be over, stores and offices would be busy. In the river canyon below nothing moved.

Snow, cold, cold, snow—January weighed on me as a single heavy fact, a bloc impossible to break apart and examine. I longed to have at my service a multitude of nuanced Yup'ik expressions, sharp as ice picks, but part of me wanted to stay bundled up and forget the whole thing.

I looked again at the canyon's snaking course. There was life in the landscape, I told myself bravely. Beneath that frozen track, a great river moved.

Outside Alaska, the Kuskokwim is virtually unknown. It lacks the epic historical resonance of the famous river running parallel to the north, yet among Alaskan rivers, the Kuskokwim is second in size only to the Yukon and its tributaries. Its source is in the glaciers that run west from Mount McKinley. High-power Creek, Swift Fork, Windy Fork, Big River—silty rough-and-tumble tributaries carry the ground-up Alaska Range southwest into a broad interior valley, where new rivers—the Stony, the Holitna, and the Hoholitna—come up from mountains to the south. Fully assembled at last, the Kuskokwim pushes into these aging mountains where the names on my map were mostly the names of ghost towns: Ophir, Tolstoi, Iditarod, Flat. From Mount McKinley to the canyon where I was flying, and on, all the way through the mountains and out across the delta to the sea, in 724 miles the Kuskokwim never passes a dam or a bridge or even the dead-end turnaround of a road. The Kuskokwim retains an intact wildness the Yukon can no longer claim. In an overcataloged age, its obscurity seemed a sign of grace.

The most remarkable feature of the Kuskokwim is its delta, a vast tundra plain that the river shares with the Yukon. More than four hundred fifty miles of coastline wrap around a marshy plain the size of South Carolina. The region's one big town is Bethel (1985 population: 3,681), which sits atop the river's long tidal mouth, but there are more than fifty small Yup'ik Eskimo villages scattered across the delta and up the river canyons, among them some of the most isolated and traditional communities in Alaska. When Knud Rasmussen finished his crossing of the Arctic in 1924, he was intrigued by what little he saw of the Yukon-Kuskokwim delta. The whaling fleet had passed its shallow coast by, he wrote, schools and missionaries had hardly penetrated the pagan country, and "as a result the people there are most interesting." The delta remains home to the largest concentration of Eskimos in the world. It had also become the center for a growing "self-determination" movement whose aim, so far as I had been able to make out from Anchorage, was to go back to living by ancient Yup'ik precepts without sacrificing the right to be a people of the modern world. In a week the villages that called themselves the Yupiit Nation were going to meet in the delta settlement of Akiachak. I planned to be there, but first I wanted to spend some time on the Kuskokwim, traveling downstream through this traditional part of Alaska. In winter.

We flew into a basin filled with sun: the Holitna River valley. The Holitna fastens onto the Kuskokwim in a braid of channels, and on the first big bend below we flew above the small village of Sleetmute.

Yup'ik hunters had been pushing into this Ingalik Indian valley just when Russian fur traders from Bristol Bay arrived in 1830. All three cultures left parts of themselves in Sleetmute. Russians crossing the mountains from the Nushagak had built the first fort on the Kuskokwim close by. Within the unsteady grid of Sleetmute's houses and log cabins, I picked out the tin roof of a Russian Orthodox church.

We buzzed the snowy airstrip to make sure it was clear, and banked sharply. A beguiling thread of chimney smoke across the river told a story of peace and wintry contentment. A visitor wouldn't have guessed that Sleetmute's reputation for epidemic alcoholism, broken families, and violent death had marked it as one of the most miserable places in the Alaska bush.

"One year there was a husband and wife who were drinking hard," said the mayor of Sleetmute. "They pushed their skiff into the river and started up the outboard too fast. He had a cast on his arm. They both fell in and the boat was just going around in circles. Their six kids were standing there on the shore, watching."

Andrew Fredericks, the mayor, and Pete Zauker, the traditional chief, were surprisingly eager to talk about the village's problem. There were a hundred people in the village altogether. They could name only two families who kept away from alcohol. Everyone else drank to get drunk. Sometimes it seemed like everyone in the village was drinking at once.

"They look right at you but they won't know who you are," Andrew Fredericks said. "When everyone is drinking you wouldn't want to be here."

Pete Zauker said he stopped drinking a few years earlier after he saw that his oldest son was afraid of him.

They told of rapes, beatings, suicides, deaths by hypothermia, all owing to alcohol. In one family the father had been sent to prison, the mother stayed drunk, and the children had been taken by the state. Six months earlier at a party, a young man had shot his uncle to death with a rifle. The year before an older man froze to death in a skiff, wrapped against the cold in a sheet of clear plastic.

Such stories were not unique to Sleetmute. As they spoke, I stretched their stories over a familiar skeleton of statistics. Alaska Natives, 16 percent of the state's population, accounted for 34 percent of state prison inmates—and for nearly every serious crime in the bush linked by state troopers to drinking. If the bush was a dangerous place to be around when people were drinking, it was even more dangerous a place to be drunk. There were so many violent "accidental" deaths and injuries that the state epidemiologist called them "our new plague," and statisticians were being forced to redefine the category of "suicide." Even under the standard definition, the suicide rate among young Alaska Native males was ten times the national average. Alcohol was working its curse down the generations not just in broken families but in the birth defects and mental retardation of fetal alcohol syndrome, found among Alaska Natives at a rate two and a half times the rate in Seattle.

In Anchorage you could see lost faces in the crowds outside the Fourth Avenue bars, and it was easy to feel sympathy as you drove by. In the bush, however, sympathy gave way to fear in the presence of open liquor bottles. I remembered a night in Fort Yukon when I'd been invited into a small trashed-out house to share a plastic bottle of whiskey with six Indian teenagers. I took in the eyes back in the shadows, fumbled a lame excuse, and fled—for once, I had no wish to see the world from their side.

What the general theories about the boredom of the unemployed and loss of self-respect in a community funded by welfare checks failed to account for was how twists of fate and geography allowed some villages to rise above the troubles and consigned others to unending misery. I was surprised, when I sought out Sleetmute's leaders, to hear them spill their stories so readily. A natural reticence compounded by grief and embarrassment makes the subject difficult for many rural people to talk about, even among themselves. The traditional way of handling deviant behavior through silent disapproval and social shunning had poorly prepared Native people for epidemic alcoholism. But a sobriety movement was beginning to spread, with dozens of villages voting to ban sale or importation of alcohol. There was even talk of a new state law that would allow villages to vote in prohibition and ban possession.

Then I realized that perhaps the leaders of Sleetmute were so ready to talk because they had an explanation for their troubles. They started to tell me about Red Devil.

It happened that the biggest liquor store outside an incorporated town in the bush was located two bends down the Kuskokwim. There were only a few dozen people living in Red Devil, an old mining camp named for the ore that had produced mercury. The Mercury Inn opened as a bar and package store to serve the mine thirty years ago. After the mining stopped in the early 1970s the bar closed, but booze continued to flow through the Red Devil package store to the communities of the middle Kuskokwim.

The village of Sleetmute had voted itself "dry"; people weren't supposed to bring in booze. But the liquor store was only twenty minutes away, and the chiefs said they couldn't check every skiff or snowmachine coming up the river.

Recently they'd put together a list of all the alcohol-related deaths in the past thirty years in the tiny communities along the middle Kuskokwim—Crooked Creek, Red Devil, Sleet-mute, Stony River—and came up with eighty-five names. The closer a community was to Red Devil, the more violent crimes and deaths it had. Thirty-one of the dead had come from Sleet-mute.

This winter had been one of the calmest in a long time, Sleetmute's leaders said. They attributed the improvement to the dry law, but more to an airplane accident that resulted in the Red Devil store being shut down for a while.

"Why do they keep selling it, even though so many died, so many are in jail, so many families are broken up?" asked Moxie Alexie, a younger man and staunch former drinker who had joined us upstairs in the village's two-story office. "The only people that can answer it is them."

Sleetmute's leaders wanted the state alcohol board to revoke Red Devil's liquor license, though apparently not everyone agreed with them. Someone was circulating a petition in Sleet-mute to overturn the village dry law. They already had thirty signatures.

"People who just got out of prison for alcohol-related offenses, who are still on probation, signed the petition," Alexie said. "It makes you wonder what they are thinking."

They said there was no binge in the village at the moment, but there was a plane coming in that afternoon from McGrath they weren't sure about—it might have a load.

When I asked about a place to sleep, they suggested the lodge across the river.

I walked around the cold lanes of the village for an hour, terrorizing myself. In each smiling stranger I thought I perceived, if not an assailant's glare, at least a threatening glint of an unpleasant truth. I stayed burrowed in that place where nothing could touch me—I myself might as well have been drinking. I spoke at length to no one and learned nothing more about Sleetmute than I could divine from my own heart.

I caught a ride on the back of a snowmachine as the snowy hills were turning pink. The quick trip across a half mile of ice turned my cheeks the same color. The temperature, already below zero, was sinking fast.

Nixe Mellick lived in self-imposed exile in a small cluster of wooden buildings opposite the village. His father was from Yugoslavia and had owned the trading post in Sleetmute, and his mother was a local Native. Nixe was active in the local Native corporation and ran a fishing and hunting lodge in summer, flying his customers himself. Because the Holitna entered the Kuskokwim just above his lodge, his side of the silty river ran clear in summer.

His guest cabins were deep in snow and closed for winter, but he invited me to stay in his comfortable home and share dinner with the family.

After the meal his wife and kids faded from the room, and we sat up talking past midnight. Nixe was a big-featured man with thick black eyebrows and an air of self-assurance. He told me of an old Eskimo from the area who'd had a window seat on his first flight out to the Lower Forty-eight: when the jet banked, he turned to his seatmate and said, "We're passing the moon." The last two truly traditional people in the region, he said, were an old woman on the Holitna who still trapped for a living and a shaman who had successfully sweated his own cure for his kidney problem.

Showing me a collection of prehistoric artifacts that he kept in a glass case, he made the region's early Natives sound more like mysterious and fascinating strangers than his own ancestors. Nixe was an amateur archeologist. He helped researchers in the area, locating old village sites along slough channels of the Kuskokwim that were now filled in, visible only from a small plane—"You've got to go way up high. I tried to tell them but at first they wouldn't believe me."

He told me how early Native hunters were able to kill a bear with a spear: walk right up to the bear, stare him in the eye, let him know you're going to kill him. Then show a sudden flash of fear, to make the bear drop his guard, and that's when you make your thrust. Hunters wrapped leather around the spear handle at a bear's arm's length from the point, so they would know not to let their hand slip too close. But Nixe said he, too, believed animals could talk to you, and if one outsmarts him on a hunt he lets it go.

He was disappointed I knew nothing about his newest interest, the forced collectivization of Siberian Natives as described in H. P. Smolka's 1937 book, *40,000 Against the Arctic.*

Nixe was an active Republican—in the Democratic bush, it seemed a further way of disassociating himself. But he defended the local state legislator, a homesteader from up the Holitna River who had been mocked in the press after billing the state $13,000 in moving costs when he returned from Juneau with fifty sheets of plywood, three outboard motors, three airplane wheels, and a bathtub.

Occasionally Nixe lifted his empty coffee cup in the air and his wife appeared with a refill.

Nixe described himself as a social drinker. It was his opinion that every village should have its own bar: better to have drinking in the open than behind closed doors.

I doubted his idea had much future, given the bush's spreading prohibitionism.

"A bar you can control," he insisted. "A package store you can't. We've had too many people fall out of boats between here and Red Devil. My brother was one. He disappeared in the fall. There was a lot of ice running on the river at the time."

Later I learned that Nixe's own son, a pilot like him, had been buzzing boats on the river and crashed into a bluff two years earlier. He and a passenger were killed. The autopsy showed his son had been drinking.

"You know, I owned the trading post at Red Devil for a few years back in the sixties," Nixe said. "One night I had a Tin City miner who died at the bar—fell asleep with his head in his arms and never woke up. Another old gal left and we found her the next day, froze by the door. I sold the place soon after that. It was a hard way to make a living."

He gazed into his glass reliquary.

"You've got to be able to live with yourself," he said.

The last census of Red Devil had put the population at thirty-nine, mostly non-Native. The post office was on the closed-in porch of somebody's cabin. A young woman behind the counter said she'd taken my message over the village phone and passed it on to the Vanderpools. I'd called to be sure they were around when I stopped by. It was a mistake.

She told me how to find the Mercury Inn. A road passed through the piles of plowed snow by the airstrip and followed the river. The morning was clear and still, the temperature twenty-one below. Snow squeaked beneath my boots. When I reached the two red buildings at the end of the road and knocked at the trading post, nobody was inside. A hand-scribbled note said the store would be closed all day "for inventory."

The other building appeared to be a lodge, shut for winter, with the door to a private home on the right. A Sesame Street swing set was covered with snow. I pulled off my outer mitts, knocked at the door to the house, waited, knocked again. The curtains were drawn, but I could hear people moving around inside. I shifted from foot to foot for ten minutes, knocking occasionally. Finally I walked back to the river to take a photo of the store.

The door to the house flew open.

"What the heck are you doing?" a dark, heavy woman called out. "I don't want any pictures taken of my store. Give me the film."

With a practiced naïveté, I ignored her request and called out that I was looking for the Vanderpools. Was she Mrs. Vanderpool? She said no.

I asked if I could talk to her.

"My kids are sick. I don't want to talk to anybody today," she said, and slammed the door, forgetting about the film.

Bob Vanderpool had been flying, mining, and trapping in the Kuskokwim Mountains since the 1940s. He'd owned a local flying service and had gone out of his way to help people through the years, and they remembered. Everybody in Sleetmute praised his character, even as they did what they could to put him out of business. He'd owned the Mercury Inn since 1967. The Vanderpools lived alone in the mining ghost town of Georgetown; the trading post was being run by their son, Robert, and Robert's wife. That must have been Gail you talked to, said the young woman at the post office, an itinerant special-education teacher who traveled by dogsled between villages on the middle Kuskokwim.

"Gail probably didn't want to talk to any visitors after the accident," she said. "Every time somebody died they closed down the liquor store for a while, but this time they've had it closed most of the winter. This was the worst because it happened right here in Red Devil and people saw it."

In Bethel, one hundred forty miles away, sale of alcohol is illegal, as it is all over the Yukon-Kuskokwim delta. Red Devil is the last liquor store before the Bering Sea. The plane that flew up from Bethel that summer night had four people on board. The pilot woke up the storekeepers and bought four bottles of scotch and four boxes of wine. Investigators said he already had a blood alcohol level more than three times the legal limit for driving a car.

There was a heavy fog by the time the plane took off. Apparently the plane got into the air and made it a little way down the river, turning before it hit the trees. The pilot's daughter was the only one who lived long enough to crawl away from the wreckage, though she'd had one leg torn off. No one heard the crash. The next morning another pilot spotted the wreckage.

There was still plenty of daylight when the mail plane came through to take me down the Kuskokwim.

PIERRE BERTON

On the Yukon River

"NEAR LOWER LABERGE, THE HULL OF THE OLD *CASCA*, LIKE A
VAST, WOODEN WHALE, LOOMS OUT OF THE WILLOWS. IT IS
HARD TO CONNECT THIS ROTTING HULL WITH THE PROUD
STERNWHEELER, PENNANTS FLYING, WHISTLE SOUNDING, PADDLE
WHEEL WHIRLING, THAT ROUNDED THE DAWSON BLUFFS IN MY
CHILDHOOD."

Canadian writer Pierre Berton provides a very different perspec-
tive on the storied Yukon River from others in this book. The
wrecked Casca *he describes is, alas, the same proud stern-*
wheeler so vividly recalled by Margaret E. Murie in the section
of this book on the Inside Passage.

When Berton's essay first appeared in 1994 in Writing
Away: The PEN Canada Travel Anthology, *edited by Constance*
Rooke, it was titled, suitably, "River of Ghosts."

THE RIVER OF MY CHILDHOOD IS A DEVI-
ous river. it rises in the peaks of the Coastal Range, just
fifteen miles from the Pacific Ocean, and then, like a prospector desperately seeking paydirt, embarks on a long search for
that same Pacific water, coiling in a vast 2,200-mile arc over
the entire Yukon and Alaska before spending itself in the Bering
Sea.

Every river has a personality, but the Yukon has more than most, because its character changes as it grows, broadening and maturing on its long journey to the ocean. The Mackenzie is a bore. It flows directly into the Arctic almost in a straight line, with scarcely a curve and rarely a twist, moving resolutely on beside a long line of mountains. It is much the same with the St. Lawrence and the Saskatchewan, which define the horizontal nature of our country. But the Yukon is more human. It has moments of uncertainty and frivolity, as it changes from baby blue near its source to a sullen grey at its delta. It skitters back and forth, hesitates, changes its mind, charges forward, then retreats. There are few dull moments on the Yukon. New vistas open up at every bend.

It is not practical to travel the Yukon River in a single season. My own advice for cheechakos is to settle for the first four hundred miles—the stretch from Whitehorse to Dawson—and to drift with the current, watching the forest unfold. The trip need not take longer than ten days or two weeks. Outfitters in Whitehorse can supply rubber Zodiacs, which are the safest and most comfortable method of travel. On this stretch the river moves through history, for this is the water highway of the gold-seekers of 1898, and the marks of their passage are everywhere.

The river of my childhood is also a river of ghosts. You can travel for twenty-four hours and never encounter a single human being. Moose raise their snouts from the marshes at the mouths of tributary creeks; black bears scuttle up the hillsides; lynx peer out from the willows at the river's edge like big tawny cats. But the signs of human passage all belong to the past—to the days when the river was the only highway to the city of gold. Ghost towns are dotted along the entire length of the Yukon—ghost cabins, ghost steamboats rotting in the willows, ghostly cemeteries, and, of course, the artifacts left by those who came before.

I can remember sitting on the bank one evening, looking out on the empty river and on the endless hills drifting off to the north, ridge upon ridge, all the way to the sullen Arctic. There was no hint of man—no boat upon those swift waters, golden now in the rays of the late evening sun, no smudge of smoke staining the far horizon, where the spiky spruces met the pale sky, not even a clearing in the forest or an old blaze on a tree. But there, hidden in the mosses, I spotted a little aluminum pot complete with handle, and recalled that the previous day we had come upon a wooden rocking horse in the woods.

On a deserted bank near the ghost settlement of Lower Laberge, I spotted a little white table sitting all by itself as if waiting for guests to arrive. Furniture in the wilderness! One finds it all along the Yukon.

For fifty years, before the Alaska Highway changed the pattern, this was steamboat country. The ghosts of those brave days still haunt the Yukon valley. Near Lower Laberge, the hull of the old *Casca,* like a vast, wooden whale, looms out of the willows. It is hard to connect this rotting hull with the proud sternwheeler, pennants flying, whistle sounding, paddle wheel whirling, that rounded the Dawson bluffs in my childhood. On an island near the mouth of the Teslin River, the remains of another steamer, the *Evelyn,* can still be seen. She has been sitting there, slowly rotting away, since 1922. And five miles downriver from the ghost community of Big Salmon, the original *Klondike* lies in its watery grave, nothing more than a hull-shaped ripple in the whispering river. (A newer *Klondike* is now a monument in Whitehorse.)

At Little Salmon—an Indian village wiped out by the influenza epidemic of 1919—the rotting cabins rise out of a blaze of fireweed. Here, the graves are as numerous as the cabins. They are, in fact, like small dwellings, a village of spirit-houses with sloping roofs, glass windows, and curtains, containing dried flowers, teapots, and plates for the use of the dead.

Some communities have vanished without a trace. Only the presence of tall blue delphiniums and bright Arctic poppies spattering the grass tells us that there was a time when families lived here, and men and women tended flourishing gardens.

The one live community left on the river is Carmacks, now nothing more than a truck stop at the point where the Alaska Highway touches the Yukon. This, too, is historic ground, named for George Carmack, who ran a trading post here and mined soft coal before he found the nugget that touched off the great stampede. The seams of coal can still be seen on the riverbank, just before the famous Five Fingers rapids. Here, the river, caught between two cliffs, seems to be blocked by a wall of broken rock. Through that barrier, the water has torn five narrow channels or "fingers." The rock itself is conglomerate, composed of various small shales forced together like bricks by the pressure of time. These four pinnacles, jagged and misshapen, are rendered more grotesque by the trees and shrubs that grow out from them. Between and around these flower-pot islands, the river races savagely. In the old days, the steamboats on the downstream run used to slip through the right-hand channel and over the ledge of rock in a matter of minutes, but the struggle upriver, especially in low water, was a different matter. It took hours to winch the boat through, so slowly that it seemed to make no headway at all in its struggle with the ten-mile current.

Five Fingers rapids is the only real impediment on the Yukon for all of its 2,200 miles. The easiest way through is by the steamboat passage on the right. On the high bank above, you can see a white smear about a foot beneath the topsoil, uncovered by erosion. This is a layer of volcanic ash, about a foot deep, known locally as Sam McGee's Ashes. It runs for many miles through the great valley of the Yukon. Centuries ago this entire region was smothered in ash from what must have been an awesome volcanic explosion.

Geologically, the Yukon valley is very ancient. The interior plateau was too dry to support much rainfall, most of which fell on the other side of the Coastal Mountains. Thus the Ice Age, which covered so much of the country, did not intrude upon the Yukon. The original drainage pattern is still to be seen in the series of terraces that rise like gigantic steps from the river to the hilltops. Ages ago, when the Yukon was young and these great valleys did not yet exist, this was unstable land, forever tilting, heaving, and rumbling. These various upheavals produced the wonder of the present broad valley, where the benchland drops off in successive steps. Looking up at the hills through half-closed eyes, one seems to be gazing on a gigantic staircase.

On the old steamboat charts, every bend in the river has a

name—Vanmeter Bend, Keno Bend, Fourth of July Bend, Steamboat Bend. This last bend coils around a long peninsula, and here, in the old days, the steamboat would stop to let off those passengers who wanted to cross the neck of the peninsula, pick flowers, and enjoy the fresh air. An hour or so later they would join the steamboat on the far side.

There is something new to see around every bend, for the river itself changes and shifts from year to year. Islands vanish, reappear, change shape, diminish, or join onto others, depending on the vagaries of the weather, the current, or the season. At Fourth of July Bend there is an immense escarpment—Dutch Bluff—and at the mouth of the Pelly, a spectacular wall of rock—a sheer cliff of columnar basalt that rises 450 feet to a poplar-topped plateau. It runs for eighteen miles downriver to Twin Falls, looking as if it were fashioned by some monstrous hand.

The oldest community on the river is found at the point where the tawny Pelly pours into the Yukon. Founded as a Hudson's Bay Company post in 1848 by Robert Campbell, Fort Selkirk was destroyed by the Chilkat Indians in 1852, forcing Campbell to make the longest snowshoe journey on record—three thousand miles to the railhead at Crow Wing, Minnesota. The post was never rebuilt, but in my day Selkirk was a lively community. Today, the police post, the Taylor and Drury store, two abandoned churches, and a mission school are still standing. It was to this point in 1898 that the Yukon Field Force of 203 soldiers was dispatched by the Canadian government to show the flag and prevent the Yukon territory from falling into American hands. The outlines of the old parade square can still be found, and the military cemetery not far away is kept in good condition.

The Yukon, which was once light green upriver from Whitehorse, and then baby blue, becomes a rich brown after the Pelly joins it. It changes colour again when the White River pours in on the left. This great stream is choked, as its name implies, with glacial silt and probably volcanic ash from the Kluane Range of mountains. The mouth of the White is blocked by islands formed from that same silt, their wet and colourless flanks encumbered by the bleached trunks and branches of dead trees swept downstream in the high water and left in heaps on the sandbars. These "snags" clog the river for miles, a menace to small boats, some of which have been caught in their clutches and swamped. The same danger can also occur at the mouth of the Stewart, which pours in from the right. What remains of Stewart City—a thriving settlement in the days when steamboats pushed barges of silver ore down from the mines at Keno Hill—can be found on an island in the main stream. I remember when Stewart had a Northern Commercial store, a post office, a telegraph station, servicing facilities, and a cluster of trappers' cabins. But the river has eaten away half of the island—the buildings that have survived have been moved well back from the crumbling bank—and the population is down to four.

Dawson City lies a day's journey downriver from Stewart City. Beneath the boat one now hears a rasping, hissing sound, as if some strange river creature was whispering to itself beneath the waters. In reality, it's the sound of the silt scraping softly against the bottom of the Zodiac. It adds to the spectral quality of the river.

In Dawson, the old buildings still stand, teetering like drunken miners along the main streets. A good many, however, have been restored by the federal government, for Dawson City itself has become a heritage site. It is, in my view, the single most interesting community in Canada, but then I am biased, for it was here that I was raised, in the days when the river was a broad highway linking us to the outside world, when the familiar sound of the steamboat whistle echoed over the rounded hills, when the *chug-chug* of the paddle wheel was as soothing as a lullaby, and no ghosts yet haunted the river of my childhood.

ERNIE PYLE

Dateline: Eagle

"AS THE STORY GOES, NIMROD WAS AN ALASKAN WOODSMAN WHO
LOST HIS TEETH. SO HE KILLED A BEAR, TOOK THE BEAR'S TEETH
AND FASHIONED A CRUDE PLATE FOR HIMSELF, THEN ATE THE
BEAR WITH ITS OWN TEETH."

*The town of Eagle, east of Fairbanks on the Yukon River, is in
the Yukon-Charley Rivers National Preserve. In 1881, there was
only a single log cabin on this spot on the bank of the Yukon,
ten miles from the border with Canada. In gold rush days, in
1898, its population rocketed to 1,700. By the 1930s it had
dropped to fewer than 60, but has now climbed up to nearly
200.*

*Small as it is, Eagle deserves its place on any map of
Alaska. It is a major access point for much of the interior of the
state, and it has a considerable history for a place so small and
remote.*

*In December 1905, a foreigner came mushing into Eagle,
telling an unclear story about a ship sailing through northern
waters. The visitor remained in Eagle for a few weeks, a garbled
version of his story appeared in some newspapers in the United
States, and then he left, heading back to the north. The visitor
was the Norwegian explorer Roald Amundsen, whose sloop Gjöa
had found the long-sought "northwest passage" from the Atlantic*

Ocean to the Pacific. Amundsen, eager to tell his story to the world, had crossed five hundred miles of winter wilderness alone by dogsled. The full story, including his discovery of the location of the north magnetic pole, came out the following summer when his ship finally reached Seattle.

Ernie Pyle was born in Indiana in 1900. By 1935, he was managing editor of the Washington Daily News. Then, in the summer of that year, the Scripps-Howard Newspapers moved him out of that deskbound job and sent him on the road. His assignment was staggering: he was to drive around the country, seeking out interesting characters and stories, and file six articles, each a thousand words in length, every week, to run in twenty-four Scripps-Howard newspapers under the heading "Hoosier Vagabond." On his first trip, traveling with his wife, Jerry, in a Ford coupe, he covered six thousand miles in eight weeks, visiting the northeast states and moving on to Nova Scotia, Québec, and Ontario.

Over the next seven years, Pyle also reported from Hawaii, Mexico, and Central and South America. During those years, millions of Americans turned to his column first every morning, wondering where he'd gotten to and what he'd found there. His journalistic wanderings established a tradition worthily preserved in later years by Charles Kuralt.

Kuralt has paid his own tribute to Pyle. "Ernie Pyle was there first," he has written. "He showed everybody else the way. He wrote plain pieces about plain people, never straining to find lofty significance in their lives, rarely analyzing them or trying to make them fit into a big picture. He was not a sociologist. He was a reporter.

"He was a hell of a reporter."

During World War II, Pyle reported from England (covering the bombing of London in 1940), Europe, and the Pacific. On the tiny island of Ie Shima, just off the coast of Okinawa, in the East China Sea, a monument marks the exact spot where Pyle was killed by a sniper's bullet in April 1945. My son Sean has visited there, paying his and my respects.

Pyle's straightforward American writing style was genuine. While he was in Alaska in 1937, he wrote a letter to an old friend in which he said, "I haven't had any mail for three weeks, *and haven't seen a newspaper or heard a radio for a week, so I don't know what's going on in the world and furthermore don't give a shit."*

MAKING HIS WAY IN WILD COUNTRY

EAGLE, ALASKA — Adolph Biederman is the sort of man we in the States think of when we think of Alaska.

He's a small man, brown as leather, and wiry, and he walks with a *thump-thump*. He speaks with an accent, and with that jumpy, hard-to-follow narrative style you frequently hear in the speech of transplanted foreigners.

Biederman is the winter mailman between Circle and Eagle. For thirty-five years he has driven the dog-team mail routes of bitter central Alaska. He's sixty-eight and tough as nails. He was born in Bohemia, and came to this country when he was thirteen. He wound up in Alaska at the turn of the century, and has never been out since. He never intends to leave.

He married an Indian woman and has eight children. Some are grown, and other are tiny kids. He lives in a log cabin, stays up all night when the boat is in. He has a summer camp downriver where he catches fish for his dogs.

Biederman loves Alaska. He says he loves it because you're so free. That's what they all say, and I ask them, "Free from *what*, free to do *what*?" I've yet to get a good answer.

The things Biederman has been through would fill a book. I suppose no man knows more about sled dogs, or winter weather, or making his way alone in wild country. He walks with that *thump-thump* because the front half of each foot is gone. It happened twelve years ago. He let himself get caught, after twenty-five years of knowing better.

It happened because he lost his regular dogs. Captain McCann, the skipper of our boat, accuses himself of causing Biederman to lose his feet. Biederman's dogs were coming upriver on a barge that Captain McCann's boat was pushing. They hit a rock and the barge upset and drowned all the dogs.

So Biederman had to borrow a team and start the winter mail run with green dogs. His sled got stuck in an overflow spot. His regular dogs would have circled it. The new ones didn't. Biederman's feet got wet. It was forty-two below zero, and his moccasins were frozen on him before he could cut them off.

He knew he was in for it. He had frozen his feet before, but this time he knew it was for good. He got to an empty cabin not far away. He built a fire, and got his boots and moccasins off. And then he went outside, at forty-two below, and walked around in the snow in his bare feet. But it was too late. He couldn't feel anything. He sat down and pulled his big toe way over to one side, and it stayed there. Then blisters came on his feet, and the flesh was all black.

He was in the cabin four days. When they found him, they sledded him back to Eagle and later to Circle, where a doctor amputated the fore parts of his feet, a little at a time. He was running the mail again the next winter.

Biederman wears regular shoes in summer, and has phonograph springs in them to keep the toes from flying up. In winter he wears three pairs of socks, and stuffs the toes full of rabbit fur. And over these he wears moccasins.

It is a hundred and sixty-two miles from Eagle to Circle. The winter mail makes the round trip every two weeks—thirteen round trips during the winter—forty-two hundred miles of mushing behind huskies every winter. Biederman has cabins strung along the route, twenty-five to twenty-eight miles apart. Sometimes he makes it from one cabin to another in four hours; sometimes it takes as long as eighteen hours, depending on the weather.

When it gets under forty below it's almost impossible to go on, because dogs perspire through their tongues, and if a dog sticks its tongue out at fifty or sixty below, the tongue freezes. And, too, the sled's runners stick at that temperature, and it's like trying to pull a sled over bare ground.

I went out to see Biederman's sled dogs. They were corralled in a nearby woods, each chained to a separate tree, and you never heard such a din as they set up. But you never saw twenty-eight such beautiful dogs—each one an individual face, all part wolf.

Biederman's sons have grown up now, and they run the

mail most of the time. Horace brings it halfway, and Charlie sleds it on in. They are steely, brown, half-breed boys, wiry and bashful and strong.

I asked Biederman if he rode the sleds, or mushed behind all the way. He laughed and said, "Well, I never ride the slide, but I'll have to say my boys do. I don't know whether they're lazier or smarter than I am, but they ride the runners most of the time."

Biederman knows everybody in eastern Alaska, and everybody knows him. He has a great deal of humor, and talks a lot, although there's a northern grimness about him, too. He cusses mightily, but doesn't drink or smoke. He quit drinking twenty-eight years ago, because he got drunk and missed collecting a hundred and ninety dollars somebody owed him. He quit smoking because it was hurting his wind.

He used to wear a mustache to cover up his bad teeth. Now that he has false teeth he still wears it. He says it frosts over in winter and protects his mouth.

July 14, 1937

NIMROD'S TEETH

EAGLE, ALASKA —All the way from Seattle to Eagle I've been hearing about Nimrod. Everybody in Alaska knows about Nimrod and the bear's teeth.

As the story goes, Nimrod was an Alaskan woodsman who lost his teeth. So he killed a bear, took the bear's teeth and fashioned a crude plate for himself, then ate the bear with its own teeth.

I went to sit at the feet of the great Nimrod and to hear the epic yarn from his own storied lips. I found the story true in its larger elements, but its purveyors had neglected a number of small things.

They neglected, for instance, to say that Nimrod, instead of being an uncouth creature of the wilds, is a cultured gentleman from Maine who still speaks with a Boston drawing-room accent after thirty-nine years in northern isolation. And they didn't mention that Nimrod is an experienced artisan who can do any sort of mechanical work with his hands. Making a set of false teeth was no great task for him.

Nimrod was living way up the creek out of Eagle, he and his partner, working at a little gold and cutting some wood. The year was 1905. That winter the wolves got in and destroyed their cache of meat, leaving them with nothing but vegetables and canned foods. Nimrod got scurvy.

Within a few months there wasn't a tooth left in his head. So he decided to make himself some teeth. He knew how.

For the front ones he used mountain-sheep teeth. He says they are almost like human teeth, except longer, so he just filed them down. Back of these, four on each side, he used caribou teeth. And for the grinding molars he used bear's teeth. Just one on each side—a bear's back tooth is so large it takes the place of two human teeth.

He made the plate of aluminum, drilled out holes for the teeth, set them in, and then worked the warm aluminum back over to hold them tight. It took him a month. He made two sets, uppers and lowers. And he wore them for nearly twenty-five years.

About seven years ago, a Seattle dentist offered to make him a set of real teeth in exchange for these homemade ones. So Nimrod sent in his specifications, and back came the store teeth. He's still wearing them today, and the teeth he made are on display in a Seattle dental shop.

As the story is told outside, Nimrod ate the bear with the bear's own teeth. He says he ate a lot of bear meat with them, but not the bear the teeth came from.

Nimrod's real name is Ervin Robertson. He was nicknamed Nimrod when he was a boy in New England because he was such a good fisherman. He was a jeweler by trade for fifteen years in the East before he made the break for Alaska in the '98 days.

For more than a third of a century he lived "up the crick" from here, in a cabin. He hunted and fished and cut wood and played at gold. Nothing much ever came from anything.

Today he lives in a tiny old log cabin in this streetless riverbank village of eighty-five people, not more than a dozen of them whites.

Nimrod is one of those perplexing human question marks you find now and then in far spots of isolation—buried by choice. Why he came here, and why he stayed for nearly forty years, is something that Nimrod himself probably doesn't understand.

He is a man of acutely fine instincts, and a genius for craftsmanship. He has never let himself slip into shoddy ways, as most self-exiles do. His speech is professorially precise. He wears a neatly laundered gray shirt, with long collar points, and blue trousers with belt and suspenders. He is freshly shaved, and meticulously clean. He apologizes for his appearance, says he hasn't cleaned up today, and stands while he talks.

His ancestral tree goes back to Scotland, and he still has the family crest between tissue in a cardboard folder. He has scads of relatives in New England, and corresponds with them regularly.

I asked him why he came here in the first place, and he said he joined the gold stampede in the hope of making a thousand dollars. He needed that much to develop his ideas for an airplane. "If I had had a thousand dollars I'd have flown long before the other fellows," he says. "But I'm not much nearer to my accomplishment than I was forty years ago." He laughs as he says it, but the culture in his voice of failure makes it a poignant thing.

Nimrod makes his living now by creating small things. He fashions beautiful hunting knives, and fine gold-wire puzzle rings, and he repairs watches. He is a crack rifle shot, and an ardent hunter. He says he hasn't hunted much in the last year because he has been so busy in the shop. The truth is, he hasn't been able. Constantly he makes these little excuses. It's perfectly obvious to you as he makes them, but you wouldn't let on for anything.

Nimrod has been outside Alaska only once in forty years. He probably will never go again. But forty years of isolation have not corroded him. He is still just as polite, just as gay, just as neat, just as gentle, as he was the day he arrived hoping to make a thousand dollars.

And so he sits in his little shop—the man with the dreams to do fine things, but who achieved his fame by putting bear's teeth in his mouth—he sits, still telling you of what he is going to do someday.

July 15, 1937

DAMNED GLAD NOT TO BE IN CHICAGO

SHEEP CREEK, ALASKA—The Yukon very nearly killed Heinie Miller this spring, and yet you couldn't get him out of this spot in the wilderness, where Sheep Creek runs into the Yukon. He has lived here alone in a cabin for thirty-seven years, with nothing around but trees and Indians and wild animals and the big outdoors. And him originally a city fellow, too, born and raised in Chicago.

Heinie has never been outside since the day he came. "Hell, no, and I ain't goin' out," he said. "I didn't lose nothin' down in the States I have to go back after."

Our boat stopped at Heinie's woodpile along the riverbank early in the morning. We had heard about his catastrophe before we got there. The ice breakup had played havoc with his home and his woodpile. They were still a mess, just as the surging waters had left them.

Heinie and the Indians who work for him cut about seven hundred cords of wood each winter. They stack it on the riverbank, to feed the fireboxes of the Yukon steamers during the summer. By spring their year's work is done—piled in beautiful rows along the riverbank.

But this year nature took a hand. The breaking ice was pushed far up the bank, and then floodwaters came rushing out on top of it, and crushed everything before them. Heinie saw the flood break, and started running. He got less than a hundred yards before it was up to his waist, so he climbed a tree.

He stayed in the tree two hours. Then the tree started to go. Heinie got down and waded in water up to his shoulders, toward the woodpile. "It was *cold!*" he said. He made the top of the woodpile, and there he was marooned for sixteen hours. It was just above freezing, and pouring rain. Ten feet of water all around him, and the wood liable to go floating down the river any minute.

The water suddenly went down, though, as fast as it had risen, and Heinie got off the woodpile at four A.M. He started walking to a trapper's cabin, two-and-a-half miles away. He was so tired it took him six hours. He thought sure he'd catch pneumonia and die. He dried out and stayed with the trapper two days. "And damned if I even got a cough out of it," he said.

But even so, nature served Heinie pretty badly. He lost a hundred cords of wood—at eight dollars a cord—and his new log house, which he had just finished last year, was swept off its foundation and tipped over. His radio was ruined, and his icebox and stove and all his tools. He says he never will find lots of his belongings. It will take all summer to rebuild his cabin.

One of the pilots on our boat said, "You'd better move out and go to California to live." And Heinie said, with a dose of his backwoods profanity, "By ——— ——— no, I love this country and I'm gonna stay right here and die right here."

He says getting washed out is all in a day's work, and he loves it up here because you're so free. "This country's so damn big and there's so few people in it," he says. "That's what makes it so free."

Heinie is getting along in years. His clothes are old and not too clean, which could be said of almost everybody who lives in the woods. He needs a shave, and a large brown string of tobacco juice trickles down each side of his whiskery chin. His eyes are as blue as the sky, as I've noticed about so many of these men up here. But Heinie's eyes are going bad. He said he couldn't see our boat until it got right up close to shore. He has a cataract, and he's scared he'll have to go to Seattle for an operation.

One morning a couple of years ago Heinie dreamed he was back in Chicago. He woke up and sat up in bed, still thinking he was in Chicago, and wondered, "What the hell am I doing here?" And then he realized he wasn't in Chicago at all. "Damn, but I was glad," he says. And yet Heinie subscribes to the *Chicago Tribune*. He was a newsboy for the paper when he was a kid, and he has had it sent up here for over thirty years. He says he can't read it anymore, but he still takes it.

There are trappers and Indians scattered through this country, and they get around a lot, by snowshoe and boat. Whenever anybody shows up, it's food and drink time. "The Indians eat me out of house and home," Heinie says. "They always show up at mealtime, and I can't say no. I've been trying to say no for twenty years, but I can't do it."

An Indian named Willie drives Heinie's Caterpillar tractor, dragging the logs down from the hills. Apparently it's quite something for an Indian to be driving a Cat. "Hell, them Indians come all the way from Dawson, a hundred miles, to watch Willie drive the Cat," Heinie says, "and I have to feed 'em."

Every couple of years Heinie takes the boat up to Dawson, and three days later he has shed about nine hundred dollars and is weak and weary from too much celebrating, and ready to go back to his cabin on the riverbank among the trees and the mosquitoes.

July 17, 1937

TRAPPER WOMEN

FORT YUKON, ALASKA —This is probably the strangest story I will find in Alaska. No matter how far you might wander the earth, looking for examples of great strength of character, I doubt that you would find a more remarkable specimen than this one.

Nine years ago the world had come to an end for a woman in this mosquito-infested village. She had had more than she could take. She led her four children down to the riverbank. "Come on, let's go for a little ride in the canoe," she said. It would be easy. Over the side with them, and herself over last. You live only a minute in the Yukon River. The cold water stops your heart.

Two of her boys had just been buried—mysteriously

drowned in the Yukon. The husband had quit cold on the family. Everything was on her shoulders. And they had grown too weary, from fifteen years of half-living and scraping and scratching in the Arctic woods and villages. It was time to quit. Nobody cared anyhow.

They were at the riverbank, ready to step into the canoe. An old man with long whiskers came and tapped the woman on the shoulder. "Come walk up to my cabin," he said. "I want to talk to you." She barely knew the man.

But she walked. And the man said, "I know you don't want to go onto charity. You can make a living on the trap line. It won't be easy, but it will be an opportunity for you to support yourself and the children."

So she turned trapper. She bundled her four children into a gas-powered boat. The old man went with them. For two weeks they chugged up the Porcupine and its tributaries. The baby boy died on the way. They buried him, and went on. They chugged up the Black River, and up a river that runs into the Black.

Now, Fort Yukon itself is north of the Arctic Circle and about three quarters of a mile beyond the end of the earth. But they didn't stop until they were two hundred and eighty miles beyond Fort Yukon. And then they camped on the bank of a river, under a mountain slope. They built a log house, and fixed it up with stuff they had brought—on two thousand borrowed dollars.

That was nine years ago. The three little girls are now young women. The two thousand dollars has been paid back. There is a little in the bank. And they go on trapping.

Only nine times in nine years have Mrs. Maud Berglund and her three daughters been back to Fort Yukon. Eleven months of the year they do not see another living soul. They live alone, among snow and wolves and moose and mountains. Just after the spring ice-break they get into their two gasoline boats and come downriver with their pelts, on a combined vacation and business trip. They sell their furs at auction, and they load their boats with a year's supply of staples.

The round trip takes them two weeks. They tarry in Fort

Yukon a couple of weeks. They are gone from home just a month. I was lucky enough to catch the Berglunds on their annual trip here. I spent an evening in their log cabin, and a forenoon with them. I shot their guns at targets and rubbed their homemade salve on my mosquito bites. And they told me about themselves. . . .

Mrs. Berglund is a handsome, gray-haired woman—fine of feature, refined in speech, easy and gentle in her manner. I don't know her early story, but I do know she came to Alaska twenty-five years ago from Oregon. The rough life seems not to have touched her personality at all.

But her three daughters are children of nature. They are brownly tanned, their hands show hard work, and their shoulders and legs are strong like a man's. They are Marion Hazel, Evelyn Maud, and Elsie May. They range in age from fourteen to twenty-one.

These girls grew up in the woods. Elsie May was carried over the trap line by dogsled for two years before she was big enough to make it herself. All their education has been given them by their mother. They know no life but the life of the trapper.

They have never been south of Fort Yukon, never seen a village with real streets or brick buildings. They have no conception of what a city is like. They don't know much about men. They have never drunk or smoked, or danced or played cards. They wear men's clothes eleven months of the year. But they only have to shoot once at a running moose, and they can freeze their feet without crying.

Their hobby, their amusement, their recreation, their joy is all in one thing: their dog teams. Each girl has her own team, her own sled, her own rifles. They'll talk dog to you until you're black in the face. They love their dogs above all else.

The girls, although they do not know our world, are smart. They are zestful and eager. Their conversation flows like a torrent, and their eyes shine. They accept new acquaintances at face value; after the first few minutes of bashfulness, they speak forward in a flood of enthusiastic recountings. Out come guns and wolf skins to show you, and moose antlers, and little incidents in excited snatches. These three girls are the freshest in spirit of any women I have ever seen.

July 21, 1937

FORT YUKON, ALASKA — . . . For nearly a decade, the years have gone like this for Mrs. Berglund and her three daughters:

As soon as they return from Fort Yukon to their cabin, they start a busy season of picking and canning berries and wild fruit. They catch salmon with a fish wheel, and dry it and store it for winter feed for the dogs. They repair their dogsleds, and the harnesses, and get the traps in order, and store and pack the four tons of supplies they purchased in Fort Yukon.

When the fall freeze-up comes, they cut ice from the river and store it in the ice well. They kill a moose apiece, and fry steaks, and then freeze the steaks. And then in the late fall, when the snow is on and the season opens, they'll start their winter's work—five months of lonely running of trap lines.

They have more than two hundred miles of trap lines, along which are scattered some four hundred traps. They run the line with five dog teams, hitched to five sleds. Each sled carries traps, bait, guns, dog feed, tents and sleeping bags, and frozen food.

John Roberts and one girl travel together. Mr. Roberts is the long-whiskered old man who tapped Mrs. Berglund on the shoulder and gave her the opportunity to do something besides drowning her children and herself in the Yukon River. He has trapped with them for nine years, and although he is now aged and shaky, he can shoot as straight as a G-man and tramp behind the dogs all day.

Mrs. Berglund and the two other girls go in the opposite direction. They set traps as they go. Only a trapper could tell you why they set them where they do, but they can tell, by tracks and trails and gnawed bark and other little things, where to put them each year.

Every fifteen miles or so they have a log cabin. It is only about ten feet square, and the door is so low you have to crawl in. They try to reach a cabin each night, but sometimes they don't. Every cabin has a stove, and a couple of bunks. They use candles for light.

Frequently a branch line of traps is laid, at right angles to the main line. When doing this, mother and girls separate, so a good part of their winter is spent traveling absolutely alone. They are away from home four to ten days each trip. And on the return visits at home they stay only a day or two. The majority of their winter nights are spent in tiny candle-lit cabins, alone, scores of miles from home, hundreds of miles from other humans. . . .

And what do the four women trappers make from all this work? Here is last winter's catch: twelve mink, fifteen lynx, eleven wolves, two ermine, thirty-one marten, and one wolverine. These brought about sixteen hundred dollars. Their supplies for the coming year ran them about six hundred dollars. They made a profit of a thousand dollars. Some years they do a little better; other years they barely make "grubstake," as they call it. But on the whole, they're keeping well ahead of the game. . . .

July 22, 1937

FORT YUKON, ALASKA —What will eventually happen to four white women, living alone eleven months of the year in the cold Far North, trapping wild animals?

I asked Mrs. Berglund if she supposed her three girls would ever marry. "That's something that will have to take care of itself when the time comes," she said. "They don't know anything about the other life. I don't expect they will ever go outside. It would be a mistake to try to make them live in a city."

I asked the girls, "Do you ever look at pictures of people or scenes in the cities?" One of them said, "Yes, we've seen pictures of New York and places like that. But we don't know anything about what it's like, and I don't think we'd ever want to go there. We've got too much freedom up here."

"Are you so busy that you don't have time to get lonesome?" I asked Mrs. Berglund.

"Well, we're busy all right. And we don't get lonesome much anymore. But when we first went up, I would get in these black sloughs, and I couldn't see daylight for days. The girls are a reflection of my mood, and when I got down we'd all get down. But the radio has helped that a lot. We've got two radios now, and when we get low we turn on the radio, and we're soon out of it."

In their home cabin they have gasoline lamps, which make good reading lights. They pick up books and magazines on their annual visits to town. But the girls don't care much for reading; they turn on the radio instead. They have a camera, and on this trip out they brought four rolls of film to be developed. . . .

I said to Mrs. Berglund, "You speak so often of the cabin up there as being your real home. Do you expect to stay there forever?"

"No," she said, "we'll stay till the price of furs or the run of pelts drops so that we can't break even. Then we'll come out. I expect we'll live on the south coast somewhere. But we'll never leave Alaska. We've been here too long.

"Sometimes I like it up there, and sometimes I feel I can't bear it another minute. My health hasn't been good for the last two years. We've eaten too much meat. I've lost thirty pounds in two years. We all have too much meat in our diet. And I've got so I suffer so from the cold." . . .

Just before our boat left, Mrs. Berglund told me a secret. It's not a secret by now, so it's all right to tell it. "Mr. Roberts and I are going to be married," she said. "He'll just be in his overalls and me in a calico dress. There won't be any fuss. And in a couple of weeks we'll be on our way back in again. Nobody will ever know how big his heart is, or what he's done for us. He was the only one who sensed what I had come to that day nine years ago down by the riverbank." . . .

You don't burn up with this thing called love, I guess, when you're knocking at the gates of threescore and more. But there is a deep thing called gratitude, and there is another thing known as human companionship, and the two put together sometimes do just as well as love, I guess, or maybe even a little better.

July 24, 1937

JEAN ASPEN

Fort Yukon and Venetie: Heading for the bush

"EVERY MILE BECAME TOUGHER UNTIL EACH YARD WAS A BATTLE WITH THE QUICKENING RIVER. . . . OUR PROGRESS SHRANK TO LESS THAN FIVE MILES A DAY AS, ON FOOT NOW, WE HAULED OUR STUBBORN CANOE AND HER HALF TON OF DREAMS UP THE RAPIDS."

When Jean Aspen set out to spend a year or more in the Arctic with her longtime friend and companion, Phil, she was facing a new challenge, but she was not a stranger to northern lands. She is the daughter of Constance Helmericks, some of whose own adventures in Alaska are included elsewhere in this book.

So when Jean headed north to Alaska in 1972—she was twenty-one and her friend, Phil, was a year older—she had before her the image of her mother's adventurous spirit and her example of capturing the adventure in words.

"I have been asked," Jean writes in the first chapter of her book, Arctic Daughter: A Wilderness Journey, *"why I would undertake such a journey. Why, I might counter, would any young person choose instead a mortgage and forty-hour-a-week job when they could be free to explore a wild and beautiful land?"*

The day after final exams at the end of her junior year of college, Jean, Phil, and a friend set out for Alaska in Phil's old pickup truck. The friend came along to drive the pickup back to

*Tucson. It took them ten days to reach the town of Circle, on
the Yukon River. They pulled into town just as the June sun was
rising, at about two in the morning.*

*Their ultimate goal was the Chandalar River, across the
Arctic Circle in the Brooks Range. They still had weeks of hard
travel ahead of them.*

*As quickly as possible, they transferred their gear—a
nineteen-foot aluminum canoe and half a ton of supplies and
equipment, including a seven-gallon kettle nicknamed "Mightypot"—and around midnight, under an orange and purple sunset, slipped into the river and headed for their first target, the
settlement at Fort Yukon, still several days away.*

BEFORE I WAS BORN, MY PARENTS HAD
wintered in a small cabin in the Brooks Range, much as
Phil and I intended. The following year they crossed the Continental Divide and floated down to the Arctic Ocean. There they
met a truly wild people, Eskimos living much as their ancestors
had for hundreds of years. Life on the tundra is very different
from the forest. The people were nomadic, following the seasonal migrations of game. They took my parents in, and without
their help, my parents would never have survived the winter.

My mother told me stories of these people. There was an
old man who had never owned a rifle. He caught seals in a
hand-made net under the ice. He was eaten by a polar bear.
Another old man had only an ancient single-shot .22 rifle to
hunt grizzly with. He would lie on his stomach on the tundra
in the path of the browsing bear and move his hands to imitate
ground squirrels. He once told my mother that he had seen
"many babies left in the snow." These were good people who
loved their children, but they were realists too. They knew that
in a bad year the entire family would starve if there were too
many of them.

Alaskan Indians were different from the Eskimos in many
ways, but they shared a common heritage of recent primitive
existence in this wild northern land. Life close to nature can be
a tough teacher.

———

When we arrived in Fort Yukon, we nosed our canoe among a group of flat-bottomed boats. I jumped ashore with a line and stood ankle deep in thick mud, holding the bow.

"Is it okay to leave our outfit here?" Phil called to the small solitary figure leaning against the general store and watching a fish wheel revolve in the current.

The man was an older Indian, dressed in dark and dusty street clothes and beaded moose-hide moccasins. The visor of his blue baseball cap was flipped back to reveal a stubble of salt-and-pepper hair and obliquely observant eyes creased between wrinkles.

His mouth moved in what may have been a smile as he shook his head. "They steal everything here."

The summer sun stood hot and high in the early morning, reflecting off a string of big boats that rocked in a backwater of floating debris. The smell of the river mingled with a fishy odor. Not a hint of breeze stirred the muggy air. Behind us the featureless blue sky was separated from its reflection by a ragged thread of green islands.

I tied the bow painter fast to the covey of boats and lumbered up the bank, pulling each foot free with an audible "ssssssluck." Running a self-conscious hand over my wispy braids, I grinned at the quiet little man.

"Is this your fish wheel?" I asked him. "Are you catching any? Could we buy some?" A fish wheel is a wonder of simple technology. Turned by the current, it scoops the migrating salmon into a basket.

He smiled down at his feet saying in a low voice, "No good for fish here."

Why put a fish wheel where there were no fish? I wondered. From atop the bank I could see a rambling clutter of wooden buildings and log cabins, some leaning at unusual angles.

"I think you'd better stay with the canoe while I try to buy a few things," Phil said, coming up behind me.

I settled myself on the grassy bank a few feet above the canoe just as a river boat loaded with shouting Indians zoomed past a hundred feet from shore. Momentarily caught up in their speed, I watched them skim over a shallow bar, noting how they could raise their motor vertically to avoid hitting ground. The engine seemed to be mounted on a lift. The lift and the shallow draft of the big flat-bottomed boat formed a practical combination for rapid river travel. I felt a twinge of envy, followed by alarm as their bow waves struck our canoe, causing it to wallow deeply in the heaving muddy water.

"Where you going?" came the soft voice behind me. I turned in surprise and saw the old man watching the bucking canoe, his face carefully neutral. I hadn't expected him to speak.

I explained our plans to him, feeling foolish. It was obvious, even to me, that we didn't really know what we were doing. At length the old gentleman ventured tactfully, "Chandalar very fast river. Many rocks."

"How will we find it?" I asked, eager to meet someone who had actually been there. Somehow we had imagined ourselves drifting downstream until we spotted the tributary entering from the north. Now we were beginning to realize the complexity of the Yukon.

"That side," he motioned with the flat of his hand. "You stay always that side."

The boat shot by again and I stared at the rocking canoe in hypnotic fascination, afraid it would sink before the town.

"Isaiah Daniel," he answered when I asked his name. Isaiah Daniel from Venetie. He was visiting friends here in Fort Yukon. Could we buy gas in Venetie? Yes.

"How far is it to Venetie from here?"

He shrugged. "One drum of gas."

Fifty-five gallons. How could we have forgotten that map? I chided myself. The one we had didn't start until somewhere north of Venetie.

The Indians returned, swinging recklessly into the tethered boats which shied and bucked in ringing confusion. Isaiah turned contemptuously to stare at the fish wheel as it creaked through endless cycles.

"Why do they keep a fish wheel here?" I inquired of his austere back, my mind still on food. "If this isn't a good place?"

He glanced at me in amusement, then dropped his gaze. "Tourists."

Before long Phil returned, surprising me with an expensive cola and a drooping chocolate bar. Then he took my seat on the grass while I set off to explore.

It was a shanty town of variety: sagging cabins, oil drums, and new pickup trucks—despite the fact that there were only a few miles of road. A horse-drawn road grader rusted beside the pieces of a modern one. A discarded bicycle lay in a heap of cans and bottles. Racks of moose antlers were nailed over doorways. And everywhere were playing children and chained dogs.

A flavor of leisure wafted from the dusty roads. It seemed an easy integration of life styles and cultures. There were a few modern government buildings including a Native Center where people could wash clothes or see a movie, but the rest of the town lacked indoor plumbing. The town's electrical generator supplied power to homes, but water was delivered by truck to white and Native alike.

Thoughtfully I circled back to Phil, the canoe, and the shimmering plain of river.

"You look as melted as the chocolate," I said, coming up behind him.

"All done?" he asked, getting to his feet and brushing off his trousers. "Get some pictures?"

I nodded.

"Let's get going."

The Indians were still cavorting in the skittish boats. Standing there, I was inspired to sneak a photo of them. "Go ahead," I heard my mother's voice from somewhere in my past, "get the picture. You'll never see these people again." Covertly I aimed my telephoto in their direction only to confront a dark face scowling back up the lens at me. Unsteadily the men boiled from the boat and surged up the bank. A pockmarked face pushed close, raging, "Goddamn, smart-ass tourists!"

The man was short and heavy with a mop of coarse black hair overhanging scared, muddy eyes, bleary with drink. I caught a look of helpless anger as his face withdrew.

This was our introduction to Amos and Bertha Fred of Venetie. My mother was wrong about never seeing them again. I was to find that you never really leave your past behind.

The following morning I lay quietly under damp folds of down listening to the soft music of rain on the tent fly and ignoring the demands of my bladder. The light coming through the orange nylon tent was subdued by a low overcast. Phil, with his back to me, was propped on one elbow, leafing through our bird book.

"Well, it's ten o'clock," I said. "I suppose we ought to get up."

We were clothed in the night things we would wear all summer, I in light pajamas, he in a T-shirt and underpants. The cramped tent was humid from our breathing; the waterproof floor, cold and slippery where it protruded from under the ensolite pad. Phil stretched and slid his book into the journal box (an army ammunition box) and snapped the lid shut. Then he wriggled deep into our zipped-together sleeping bags and ran his cold hands up my back.

"Well, what do you want to do? Get wet or starve?" I asked.

He cocked his head and listened. "I really don't think it's raining as hard as it sounds."

"Maybe. But just think of the soggy bushes out there." I rolled over and snuggled my behind into the curve of his stomach and legs. My back ached from lying down. "What say you volunteer to go dig out the wool shirts?"

The day before we had entered a small winding slough that slithered for miles into the forest. Here we decided to try our gill net. After pitching camp, we had chosen a spot and (for want of a better idea) cut a pole, looping on as much of the net as it would hold, and hung the pole over the water.

"Come on. Here's your shirt," Phil said as he slid back into the bags and plastered his wet feet onto my calves. "Water's up since yesterday. Aren't you anxious to see if we caught any fish? Maybe the net's solid with them."

The warm scratchy wool felt good as I dressed in the confined tent and Phil curled down out of the way. Then I reached outside for my boots which were upended under a corner of the rain fly.

We emerged into a gray and scented world of bugs where bird calls echoed between black-trunked trees. Clouds clung to the ground in tenuous trails, hiding even the direction of the sun. I sniffed deeply of dripping forest and poplar smoke as I knelt on the bit of sloping mud bank to start the fire. It was a good day to lay low for out in the channel small whitecaps crowded before a blustering wind.

There were indeed fish that morning: three scaly suckers. Flavorless, mushy creatures with numerous forked ribs, they nevertheless bolstered our spirits, being our first catch. Soon it began to rain again, cold drops splattering into our tin plates. We ate and returned to bed. Lying fitfully within the sticky bags, we read aloud until nearly midnight.

The following day was not favorable for travel either. A high overcast lent a chill to the drab sky from which a cold western wind descended to kick up waves. Still, we regretted every lost day. After another fishy breakfast we packed our outfit and set off.

Even on the slough, water slopped more than occasionally over the gunwale as we crept along. Although we had eaten some of our supplies, we were still riding dangerously low. When we reentered the main Yukon we motored quietly a few feet from shore. The sullen rushing river, as faceless as the gray sky, now seemed malevolent as big waves built up over miles of open water. The river was peppered with large islands, some distinguishable from the shore only at close range where narrow channels were sucked off between the trees. On the headlands of the islands smashed the relentless current, piling up debris in a deadly trap.

Again the shore opened ahead. Beset with indecision, we watched the crisis approaching. Which way? Should we risk a small channel that could meander for miles, perhaps losing itself in thickets and log jams? Or stick with the main river and chance missing the Chandalar? We had almost decided to avoid this little offshoot when Phil spotted geese. By the time he had photographed the departing birds, we found ourselves dragged sideways into the channel.

Thus two accidents, a stiff breeze and a flock of geese, charted our course. The river we sought collides with the Yukon in a confusion of arms, most of which would have added greatly to our journey (had we found them at all). But nature has provided a way, a wandering secret way, to enter miles above that tangle, and somehow we found it.

Our path snaked swiftly inland through fields of waving willows, green and gray in the shimmering wind. The mud strand was carpeted with the rich velvet of joint grass and the elaborate print of bird tracks. At our approach, startled ducks flung themselves into the air from hidden reed beds. We caught sliding glimpses of open areas, ponds and marshes, through the shifting trees. Within the cozy safety of the slough we began to relax.

We stopped for dinner at a confluence of waterways, building our fire atop a grassy cutbank. Nearby stood three or four deserted cabins. Below us the chocolate channel plowed into a small river. It had a friendly look, this river, not unlike the slough. But where the two swept together, a slight color change persisted. My heart lightened at this brave promise from snowy peaks hundreds of miles away. Our river! We had picked it from the map and now here it was: a real wilderness river! My gaze lingered on it affectionately.

We were waiting for the wind to drop, as it generally did at night, before trying our hand at upstream travel. Eventually we would need to "line" the canoe upstream, pulling it on foot, but now hoped to put that off awhile. This was the beginning of a hard and often discouraging chapter in our new existence. Our days of floating were over.

"Someone's coming," I said, cocking one ear into the wind. I tossed my fish bones into the fire and lumbered to my feet.

Behind us a boat suddenly materialized with Amos and Bertha Fred, two of my brief photographic acquaintances. With them was a proud and well-muscled young man, beaded headband holding back his shoulder-length black hair. They sighted us and swung toward shore, almost swamping *Lady Grayling*.

I climbed down the five-foot cutbank. It was flaking off and I jumped onto soggy tussocks of grass rooted in melting mud. "Would you like some tea?" I called out in greeting as I reached for their bow line.

"No, no. We gotta get back to Venetie tonight," returned Bertha. "We just stop to see are you okay." She was a well padded woman with short dark hair, a round face, and intelligent eyes.

"Oh, we're fine!" I answered enthusiastically. "Sure you won't stop for some tea?"

Bertha shook her head resolutely. "No, we gotta get back to the village tonight." She studied our overloaded canoe in open skepticism. "You like, we can take something for you. We got lotta room. Wouldn't be no bother."

Amos said nothing.

Phil scanned our outfit with indecision. "Thanks for the offer," he replied politely, "but we'll do okay." We were beginning to tire of skeptical looks.

"You got plenty of food?" Bertha inquired with the same directness. We nodded. Amos pulled the starter rope and the young man shoved off with the butt of his rifle. I watched, intrigued as his new 30.30 sank into the ooze. Then the big engine caught with a rumble and the boat shot upstream and was gone.

That first evening was deceptively easy. By midnight the wind had stilled. We set out with our five-horse motor opening the wide bends before us. The water turned milky gray where our small bow wave broke the reflection of sky and trees as the Chandalar unrolled, taking on the look of a real river. Sitting in the front seat, I gazed at it with a new sense of excitement. There was promise on the early morning air and purpose in the smooth bends when, for the first time, we caught sight of the mountains clear and small ahead.

Cold dawn was upon us when we stopped on a sandbar to build a large driftwood fire. In the Arctic summer, the splendor of sunset-sunrise may take several hours. This river wasn't so bad after all, we concurred as we sipped steaming mugs of spice tea and watched the brilliant morning fade into day. We had come quite a ways and seen the mountains: the great Brooks Range! Mud banks of the Yukon had given way to sand and gravel. We pitched our tent in that picture-book camp and headed for bed full of the happy miles we would make on the morrow.

A few hours later we woke to flapping nylon and blasting

sand. Cold sheets of wind-borne sand thundered down the beach, obscuring the far shore and forming dunes. The stinging particles sifted into everything, filling our eyes, ears, and sleeping bags. The tent billowed and strained at its moorings, frequently ripping free. Driven forth at last by hunger, we ate a gritty oatmeal breakfast, eyes squinted against the blast, and went back to bed.

When we emerged into the still amber of evening, our calm beach had returned.

For the next few days we traveled by night to avoid the wind. Every mile became tougher until each yard was a battle with the quickening river. We discontinued use of the motor except for occasional quieter stretches, and even then used it only at the loss of many shear pins, much gas, and the edges of our propeller. Our progress shrank to less than five miles a day as, on foot now, we hauled our stubborn canoe and her half ton of dreams up the rapids.

We became discouraged as plans of starting our cabin early withered and the elusive mountains slipped ever backward at our plodding. The longest day of the year came and went, marking the annual descent back into winter. And we weren't even to Venetie yet! "We have to get back tonight," they had said. "Chandalar very fast river." The memories lilted through my brain.

But there were good signs too, as we never tired of pointing out to each other. The Yukon jungle lay behind us now, mud and all. This country had an open, healthy feel. The living water was inlaid in bars of tawny sand and polished colored stones. Although we saw no game, the shore was often marked with the tracks of bear, beaver, wolf, and moose. Trees were smaller here and spaced with patches of wild flowers: lupine, forget-me-not, fireweed, wild rose, and gentle gifts for which I have no names.

By now it was late June and the steadily dropping water was becoming clearer every day. New sandbars surfaced, growing up through the swift, shallow river like young plants. We feared that the canoe might escape while we slept, so each night she was firmly grounded out of the current and well shackled. And every morning found her high and dry. It always took considerable effort to badger her back in, but the peace of mind was worth it. This was big empty country. Phil now wore the .22 pistol, not for protection, but as a hedge against starvation should we ever lose the canoe, and we both carried matches in waterproof containers, mosquito repellent, and our pocket knives.

Energy, I was thinking. So that's what it's all about. Living in a land of bulldozers, I had never realized how fragile yet tenacious our little selves are. Think of what it means to own a mule! To travel downstream instead of up! All the work of life must be done by something: the hauling of wood and water, the building, the growing of food, the travel from place to place. And mostly it was done like this, by human muscles. No wonder people wanted to take the load off their backs and put it on machines, I thought, looking upstream. But then, I admitted, glancing back the way we had come, progress certainly means more to you this way.

Early one morning found me immersed in icy water and chill dawn breeze, tired and discouraged. Minutes before we had broken a shear pin and, paddling furiously, come ashore at the base of a crumbling gravel cutbank.

"What's taking you so long?" I snapped, holding to a sweeper with one hand, the canoe with the other. Beneath my numb feet, the relentless current sucked away the sand as I fought for balance, water to my waist.

"I dropped the goddamn shear pin!" Phil wailed. He disappeared from view and groped about blindly under water.

I shifted my grip, fighting the restless canoe. "Let's just camp. Maybe we can walk it over to that island." Together we scanned the whorls of morning-streaked river, oblivious to the song of sleepless Arctic summer. "I think we need to eat better," I said dully. "A person can't work like a mule on a handful of oatmeal." But we had caught no more fish and no rabbits.

We made camp on a flower-decked cutbank under shifting clouds. This was a young bank, composed of fine brown sand. Clumps of perennials laden with red blossoms were sprinkled between vigorous young balsam poplar trees and the tiny spruce that would eventually take over. When the first hardy plants invade a new sandbar, they transform it into a place where insects, small animals, and slower growing trees can get a foothold. But now the capricious river wanted it back. That is what cutbank means.

We had finished our starchy meal when we caught the distinct buzz of an outboard. Very soon a river boat leapt into view, spinning down current. He spotted us and careened rashly shoreward, cutting the motor at the last instant. To my astonishment, the big boat settled gently beside our canoe.

"Difference between planing and displacement hulls," Phil answered my surprise. "Besides, he's not loaded."

It was Amos and Bertha out for an evening ride. They were bundled against the wind of travel and toiled stiffly up the bank while their handsome young friend fastened the boat. He was introduced to us as Johnny Albert, his long hair tied back this time with a pink silk scarf. He grinned as I handed him a cup of mint tea.

"We was a bit worried about you," Bertha stated, holding her chapped hands out to the blaze of our fire. "Our chief, even, Isaiah Daniel, he come lookin' for you last night."

"Oh, it takes us awhile." I smiled sheepishly. "Uh . . . how far is it from here?"

"I think maybe fifteen miles?" she turned to Johnny and he nodded.

Fifteen miles! That would take us days! My face fell.

I lifted our little blackened tea pot from the fire and squatted near the cups, steam drifting back over my hand as I poured. I was embarrassed by our apparent helplessness. "Sugar?" I asked, handing her a scalding mug.

She spooned it in. "I always like lotta sugar in my tea," she grinned. "You?" she handed me the bottle.

"I prefer mine plain," I lied, thinking about our diminishing supplies.

The clouds were once more closing in. I could feel a fine spray of mist hitting my face and soon big drops were dancing in the dust around the fire.

"We can give you a ride," Bertha offered, setting her empty cup on the lid of the grub box. "We got lotta room and we just put everything in, your little boat and all."

This time we accepted with gratitude and relief. Adding three quarters of a ton slowed their progress, but we sailed right over riffles and rapids at what seemed an incredible rate to me. I shouted a happy conversation with Bertha above the roar of the engine. Already I had quite forgotten the river. It slipped by with such ease that I was surprised I had ever taken it seriously.

Morning sounds of Venetie, the discordant howl of two hundred chained dogs, woke us in our graveyard camp overlooking the village. Beginning like a distant wind, it swept upon us until all was drowned in a rush of voices.

We poked among the old grave markers for something to burn as the first guests began to arrive, their trudge up the steep hill heralded by fresh dog song. We had been assured that it was okay to camp here, for the actual cemetery had been moved because of the encroaching river. Still, there were nervous titters from our visitors about ghosts.

Our first adult visitor was the ancient patriarch of the prolific Mark family. Slowly he topped the bluff, leaning on a walking stick. He had dressed to greet us in a rumpled white shirt, black tie, and shiny black suit. He wore glasses and smoked a pipe. Atop his head was a quilted cap with a visor.

"Hi. I'm Jeanie and this is Phil," I said. I stuck out my hand and grinned. He touched it as if unaccustomed to shaking hands.

"Abraham Mark," announced the bandy-legged little man. He sat cross-legged in the dust, sipping sugary tea and conversing with Phil in broken English while his great-grandchildren swarmed about. The old fellow appeared oblivious to the shrills and giggles that engulfed us as he continued his stories.

He told us that few in the village had been far up the river, for as he explained it, "Nobody walk no more."

"Tell us about the river," I persisted.

"Many year now I have not go there." He brushed mosquitoes from his leathery neck with a small dark hand and smiled winningly. His worn suit seemed somehow in keeping with his personal dignity as he sat amicably in the dirt by our breakfast fire. "Too darn many rock, I tell you. Too fast that river." He shook his wrinkled head at some memory. "You can't take no boat there, I tell you that. Why you want go?"

"We like the woods," I answered.

He nodded eagerly in agreement. "Trap line. Lotta fur sometime. Sometime no good. That lynx, you catch him, maybe he plenty good sometime. Two year ago, rabbit everywhere." He extended his small arms to encompass the village. "Oh, plenty lynx that time," he beamed. "But nobody trap too much now. They just wait for native checks. No good, them people now days," he declared, clamping his jaw shut. "Drink, all the time drink! Venetie is a dry village. You know what that means? Nobody supposed to drink in the village. But they go down to Fort Yukon and bring it back, then everybody drink. Drink and fight! Drink and fight. No good. God as my witness, I never drink, not one time, and now I ninety-one years old. I work when I was young and I know what my life was for. What they live for? To drink and then shoot each other!"

"Gran'pa present," a child tugged at his sleeve. Old Abraham smiled angelically. "All my gran'kids love me and my great-gran'kids," he proclaimed modestly. From his pocket he fished out a crisp dollar bill. A rush ensued. Soon the kids were off down the hill to buy candy and tobacco at the village store. "My gran'son, you know him? He get lotta moose last winter with the snow-go. In the village, everybody eats lotta moose then. In Fort Yukon, they got freezers so they just keep their own moose, just hide it, put it away."

By our third day in the village we knew almost every adult on sight and a good many by name. There were perhaps 120 people in Venetie and they were friendly and curious about us. When we met Bertha returning from the airstrip where the daily mail plane had come in, Phil was carrying boxes of welfare food for one of the larger Mark families. Followed by skipping children, we dropped off the groceries and trailed after Bertha back to her cabin, each chewing on an apple.

As we passed the last cabin, old Sophie, bent double and nearly blind with the seasons, hailed us from her yard. "You want come in for whitefish? I just got good whitefish." Her cabin was large and well tended with wood stacked before her door by neighbors. The small village retained its sense of community: sometimes petty and gossipy perhaps, like any group of people living together, but still a unit that cared about its members.

"No thank you, Grandmother," I called to her. "I will come visit you this evening."

The path wound among broken and discarded equipment and the inevitable skinny dogs. Here was a culture that for years had been supported by the government. People who once lived happily with few possessions had discovered the toys of civilization. It seemed to me that by comparing themselves with others, they had also discovered poverty.

I knew that it was not a simple problem. The land once supported the Indians because they starved when game was scarce, keeping their numbers within the balance of nature. They can't go back, any more than we can return to the days of covered wagons, but if they move to cities they must give up the support of their village and their whole way of life.

My eyes lingered covetously on the boats tied along shore. How would we make it into the mountains before winter? We had offered to buy the needed fifty-five gallons of gas for anyone who would transport us upstream to the abandoned gold town of Caro beyond the first fork of the river. But no one stepped forward, and daily the river level dropped, making upstream travel more difficult.

The Freds' cabin was constructed of unpeeled, green-cut logs and papered inside with stained cardboard and pictures cut from magazines. The main room was divided by a high linoleum-topped counter. Behind the counter was a propane stove, cupboard, dish drainer, various pans, and an open five-gallon slop bucket for dog feed. Across the room stood an oil heater, a sofa, several chairs, and a gas-powered wringer washer. Over the stove rows of wires were strung for drying socks and mittens. Only the village school had electricity, and the people hauled water from the river in buckets.

Amos brooded in a corner of the dark cabin while Phil and I chatted with Bertha around the counter. Like most of the villagers, his days seemed spent in a tedium of inactivity. For hours he would sit beside the cabin, staring at the ground. He seemed a sad and lonely man and in poor health. I found the silences between us too great to span. But then I never tried.

Amos Fred, I thought, watching him covertly while I spoke with Bertha. Amos Fred, the early missionaries were wrong. A man should keep his own name.

"You want some fish?" Bertha asked, turning from the propane stove with a skillet of fried grayling. She had been more than generous, often feeding us meals or snacks of pilot bread and jam. In fact, although they seemed at a loss to understand us, the whole village treated us with kindness.

We ate in silence, each wondering what to say. Although her English was good, our backgrounds were so different that we often misunderstood one another.

"We caught some fish too," I boasted, "only they were suckers."

"Oh, we don't eat those," she told me seriously. "Too many bones."

My attention was drawn to something still bubbling mysteriously on the back burner. "Whitefish guts," she said, following my gaze. "Very good." She seemed defensive. "You try some?" So far we had eaten muskrats, boiled unskinned; and boiled geese, heads and all.

I walked over to the stove. "Sure . . ." Forking out a bit, I returned to the counter and gingerly tasted them. They were much the flavor of oysters.

"Is there anyone else we could ask?" I finally approached the subject that was on my mind.

"Maybe Bobby Mark takes you when he get back from drinkin' in Fort Yukon," Bertha replied irritably. "I worry about you," she said after a minute. "Maybe you get into lotta trouble. Two years back, this white man, he went and live by himself. We never see him again until the Trooper, he go back there in the wintertime, lookin' for him. That man, he builded himself a little house, so small he couldn't even stand up and with no real door, just canvas. And he didn't have no food. He eat up everything and then he shoot himself."

She got up and placed tea before us on the counter. "Even good Native boys, sometime they get killed. Last winter a Native boy (he know what he was doing too!) die when his snow-go break down not too far from the village." Bertha watched us, chin in hand, from her stool on the other side of the counter.

I knew that others were wondering too as they studied our little canoe or talked quietly with us. Some of the young men had borrowed *Lady Grayling* for a frolic near the shore, for none had ever been in a canoe before. "We'll be okay," I smiled reassuringly. "Next spring we'll be fat as beaver. Just call us the upstream Indians."

She looked uncomfortable for a minute and then declared, "You aren't Indians."

The door of the cabin stood open and drugged mosquitoes drifted in and out of the punk smoke. The smell of the slowly burning insecticide coil tinged my thoughts, reminding me of the Mackenzie River and other people who had entered my life briefly along those far-away banks. Outside in the bright hot sunlight, flies buzzed about the dogs. Often sadly neglected, they are kept as status symbols, a cultural hangover from the days before snowmobiles. I remember Great Slave Lake in Canada where the dogs were abandoned on small islands to survive the summer or die. In the fall, they would be gathered and fattened up for winter work.

A dog was probably the last thing we needed, but watching them from the cabin, I decided I wanted one. Phil and I both loved dogs, and I missed that relationship. Seeing the ratio of dogs to humans, I assumed we were in the ideal location to acquire a pet. We followed one lead after another around the village. People were friendly and proud, bragging about their dogs, which were all shapes, colors, and sizes, but no one wished to part with a single one.

By evening our quest brought us to young Johnny Albert.

"Just woke up," he said, swinging open the door of the small dark cabin reputed in old Abraham Mark's gossip to be the haunt of the undesirable.

"We're trying to buy a puppy," I began. "One to take up the river with us. Franky Jim told us you had some."

Reluctantly he led us around the corner of the cabin to a makeshift wire pen enclosing a dozen colorful balls of fur. "I had to put 'em in jail." He pointed to the tumbling puppies.

"They broke into Isaiah Daniel's cache and ate up all his dry salmon. And he wanted that fish for himself."

I laughed and Johnny looked up in surprise from tying on his headband. I suddenly was aware that humor takes more than a common language: it takes shared assumptions.

"I'm gonna race these dogs," he finally stated, obviously embarrassed at the request. The spring inter-village dog races are a big social occasion. "I don't want to sell none of 'em."

That evening Bobby Mark returned from Fort Yukon, his boat laden with a cow moose that he had shot along the river. After we spoke with him, he agreed to take us up to the old abandoned gold town of Caro, which was probably as far as his boat could go.

It was sprinkling fitfully the next morning as Phil and I trudged up and down the hill behind town, lugging gasoline from the airstrip. There were no vehicles, or even any real roads in town. As we broke camp, Johnny Albert appeared unexpectedly with the runty mongrel puppy I had liked. He told us that he had dreamed he would be killed in a boat accident. To prevent this, he said, we should take the dog.

So for five dollars we acquired a bundle of problems which we named Net-Chet-Siil, or "Little Girl" in the Kuchin dialect of Athabascan. She was a pretty little thing, just weaned, all honey and cream with strawberry tongue and licorice-drop nose. Her coat was thick and soft, her tummy bald and freckled, fuzzy ears flopped over her puppy-blue eyes, and her voice carried for miles.

As we loaded our outfit aboard the big river boat everyone in the village came down to see us off. With a wave of farewell we shoved into the current.

Go! Go! Go! Pleeeease! I pleaded silently as we crept up the tumbling river.

Bobby seemed surprised by our sluggish pace and I caught the words, "One time I got four moose in this boat! I chartered a plane on floats and just fly around and look for 'em!" as he shouted to Phil above the roar of the outboard. He was a fine looking, cheerful man of medium stature, about thirty and already head of a large family. Like many of his generation, tawny eyes, bronze skin, and big bones told of the infusion of white blood. He motioned to his friend, Kevin, a slender youth of seventeen, and turned the motor over to him. Then settling his back to the wind, he cupped his hands about a cigarette and opened a can of Coke.

I watched Kevin driving the powerful engine as he stood proudly in the stern, legs apart, eyes scanning the water, long black hair streaming.

Net-Chet-Siil burrowed under my red woolen coat, soft and wriggly next to my body, as I craned forward, urging the boat on. We plowed toward the foothills as rainbows and showers played over a landscape colored in nameless shades of velvet green. I saw Bobby shake his head as Kevin swung the motor up once again, avoiding sudden shelves of rock.

"I think I go back to the village and get more gas tonight," he shouted to Phil, flipping the empty Coke can overboard. "We sure use it up this way." Phil reached into his pocket and drew out our remaining cash and handed it to him. It was the last money we had in the world. Finally I crawled under the overturned canoe to get out of the drizzle.

Then we were stopping. I stuck my head out as Phil ran nimbly forward and leapt ashore with the bow line. Two tiny old men greeted us and we arranged ourselves about their smoldering fire. Like other places we had noticed along the river, this was a well used camping spot for the Indians. It was situated on a small cutbank in the protection of mature spruce, many of which had been stripped of bark. The bark, which comes away easily in large sheets in the spring, is used like plywood to cover lean-to's.

After a brief conference in their own language, one of the old men, Matthew Fred, turned to Phil with a big smile and said, "This my lucky day! I see moose over there. I shoot 'em and he swim across and die on this side. I didn't have no boat. I was just gonna eat those little fishes and I don't like 'em." He pointed to a can of sardines.

The three young men unloaded the boat and set off to retrieve the skinned and disjointed carcass of a yearling bull. This they heaved onto a bed of willows in the shade. No one seemed concerned about the flies, which will lay their eggs on meat, converting it to maggots in a short while. The two old men stood quietly by as the quarters were hefted ashore. I thought of the skill that lay in those small, veiny hands. Butchering a moose is no small chore.

We ringed their smudge fire, sipping coffee while the Indians exchanged news. Finally Bobby turned to us in English saying, "Jeremiah Daniel, Isaiah his brother. He don't speak English good. His gran'son, Niel, he was supposed to take 'em up the East Fork to their cabin. But he run out of gas and went down to Fort Yukon to drink and just leave 'em here."

Jeremiah grinned and nodded, not understanding a word. There was something gentle about this man. Like his companion, he was of slight build, dark and weathered. His almost beardless face was carved by history, as were his small, gnarled hands. In the near blindness of age he wore thick glasses. He was dressed in baggy slacks, red checked flannel shirt, and beaded moose-hide moccasins. His short-brim cap secured a flutter of gauzy material to protect his neck from bugs.

Matthew Fred offered us the interesting animal matter that was gurgling glutinously in a thick green soup over the fire. The Indians were already at work with their pocketknives stabbing long strings out of the five gallon can.

"Moose guts," said Bobby, glancing over his knife as he chewed. "The old people, they really like this stuff. They eat it when they was young." Matthew nodded and smiled.

Phil and I looked timidly at one another and dug out our knives. When in Rome. Phil leaned over and whispered, "They still have the shit in them!" I nodded and smiled. Rubbery, but not bad.

Next came boiled tenderloin. The backbone was severed with a knife at each vertebra and plunked into our large kettle. Most Native cooking seems to be geared to reducing preparation of the food, not a bad idea for people living a simple life outdoors. This was topped with the usual sugar-laced tea and the budding antlers of the young bull. Jeremiah singed the velvety skin and roasted them in the fire.

We spent the night there. After breakfast of boiled moose, I squatted on the bank, scraping the impervious tallow deposits from Mightypot with sand. Behind me, Jeremiah had a tape recorder going. It was playing Native chants sewn together with his fiddling. I listened, feeling across the cultural chasm that separated my world of science from this ancient heritage. I was intrigued and would have stayed awhile, but Bobby, who had taken most of the moose to the village and returned during the night with extra gasoline, considered the old folk dull company. He was anxious to be off.

So I hurried to pack up our camp gear and load the river boat while the recorder fiddled on and Jeremiah danced.

"You know," I said to Phil as we shoved off and the waving old men dwindled into the Arctic vastness, "in our culture we'd lock those two up someplace safe where they couldn't hurt themselves. Did you hear that old Jeremiah spends every winter alone up on the Wind River? As blind as he is too. I suppose some day he'll die out there and people will wonder why somebody didn't stop him. But he's alive now."

We hadn't been long underway when the East Fork veered off taking most of the water with it. Because of the shallows, I and half of the gear remained at the junction while Phil and the other half continued on up the diminished river.

As the sound of the engine melted into the river, I took a moment to look around. We were now actually in hilly country, able to glimpse mountains through breaks in the green. Underfoot spread a springy six-inch carpet of multi-colored sphagnum moss, lacy white reindeer lichen, and dainty sprigs of lingonberry, also known as low bush or mountain cranberry. This intricate work was woven with minute flowers and inconspicuous plants of many varieties. The scattered trees, spindly and often draped in threads of gray moss, contrasted somberly with the bright ground cover. The land seemed brilliant and fresh after the dank Yukon and dusty village.

This new country pleased me. Its very openness should enhance our chances of seeing game, I decided. As if to prove me right, my eye caught the cautious hippity-hop of a feeding snowshoe hare, brown now in its summer attire. I unsheathed my old .22 rifle and soon was cleaning the luckless rabbit, our first game. A flash through the trees drew my attention to a hole in which a pair of yellow flickers tended a brood of demanding young. Everybody is busy this time of year. I rinsed the rabbit, very unimpressive now, and was saddened that it was a nursing mother. Guiltily I tasted the milk on my bloody fingers, then washed the fluids from my hands in the river.

When the boat returned to shuttle me upstream, I was ready. Phil had camp set up by the time we arrived, and a short while later I was preparing rabbit and dumplings. The Indians were tired of our slow travel and we did our best to make them comfortable. As we sat gnawing diminutive bones and glancing casually at one another, Bobby announced that he could take his boat no further. Tomorrow they would leave us and head happily downstream hunting.

As for us, we would be left entirely to our own strength and imagination. These were the last people we would see in almost a year.

JOHN HAINES

Near Richardson, alone

"I AM LIVING OUT A DREAM IN THESE WOODS: OLD DREAMS OF THE
FAR NORTH, OLD STORIES READ AND ABSORBED: OF SNOW AND
DOGS, OF MOOSE AND LYNX, AND OF ALL THAT IS STILL NATIVE
TO THESE UNPEOPLED PLACES. NOTHING I HAVE YET DONE IN
LIFE PLEASES ME AS MUCH AS THIS."

Since Winter News, *his first book of poetry, was published in
1966, John Haines has been among America's finest poets. And
many of his poems have grown out of his experience in Alaska.
The following piece is drawn from a 1989 collection of essays,*
The Stars, the Snow, the Fire: Twenty-five Years in the Alaska
Wilderness.

*Haines first settled in Alaska—at Richardson, on the Tan-
ana River southeast of Fairbanks—in the summer of 1947. "I
remained there only until late August of the following year," he
writes in the Preface to that book. "The longest and most active
period of residence was hardly more than a dozen additional
years—from 1954 until the late 1960s. We can add to this that
for the past eight years I have again lived at Richardson, though
with extended periods of absence. So that what is implied in a
subtitle is at best a symbolic figure that stands for many arrivals
and departures."*

*Perhaps it is that history of arrivals and departures, com-
bined with a poet's sensitivity to language, that informs Haines's*

writing about living in the wilderness. Certainly he has the rare ability to see the universal in the particular deeds of daily survival.

"More than one reader of these essays and chapters has remarked on the dreamlike quality of many of the episodes," he writes in the Preface. "I think I have always been aware of certain events existing in a kind of dreamtime *in the ancient tribal sense of this. When, at one point in the narrative, I say that it was all 'far, far back in time,' this is not merely a rhetorical figure. For somehow those days in the field, those treks with the dogs over snow and grass, the long hunts, the animal killing, and the rest of it, were all part of the inmost human experience on this earth."*

I

Six o'clock on a January morning. I wake, look into the darkness overhead, and then to the half-lighted windows. I listen. No sound comes to me from the world outside. The wind is quiet.

I get out of bed, pulling the stiffness from my body. Jo is still sleeping under the big down robe, turned toward the wall. I go to the window with a flashlight and look out at the thermometer. It is minus thirty-one, clear, and no moon. It will not be light for another three hours.

I put on a jacket and pair of slippers, and go outside. The door creaks on its frosty hinges, the latch is cold to my hand. One of our dogs emerges from his house in the yard and shakes himself, rattling his chain.

The stars are bright, Orion gone down the west. The Dipper has turned, Arcturus above the hill. The sky and the snow give plenty of light, and I can easily see the outlines of the river channel below the house, and the dark crests of the hills around me. The air is sharp and clean, it will be a good day.

I gather up a few sticks of wood from the porch and go back indoors. Laying the wood on the floor beside the stove, I go to a table by the south window, find a match, and light the lamp. I turn the wick up slowly, letting the chimney warm.

Light gathers in the room, reflecting from the window glass and the white enamel of a washpan. I open the stove door and the damper in the pipe. With a long poker I reach into the big firebox and rake some of the hot coals forward. I lay kindling on them, dry slivers of spruce, and two or three dry sticks on top of these. I close the door and open the draft. Air sucks through the draft holes, and in no time the fire is burning, the wood crackling. I fill the big kettle with water from a bucket near at hand, and set it on the back of the stove. It will soon be singing.

By now Jo is awake and beginning to function. I sit on the edge of the bed, putting thoughts together. The lamp makes shadows in the small room; heat is beginning to flow from the stove.

Today I am going back to our cabin below Banner Dome, to look at my traps. I have not been out for over a week, and must surely have caught something by now. While Jo makes breakfast, I begin to dress. We talk a little; the mornings here are quiet, the days also.

I put on heavy wool trousers over my underwear, and two wool shirts. Over the wool trousers I sometimes wear another light cotton pair to break the wind or to keep off the snow. I put on socks—three pair of wool, and the felt oversock; two pair of insoles, and last the moosehide moccasins. I tie them at the top; they are a loose fit, soft and light on my feet. I made them six years ago from the hide of a big moose, and though worn by now, they are still the best I have.

I go out to the storehouse, find my big basket, and begin to pack. I will need my small axe, a few traps, and perhaps a few snares. That piece of dried moose paunch I have been saving—it is strong-smelling and will make good bait. What else? Something needed for the cabin—a candle, some kerosene in a bottle. I put it all together in the basket.

We eat our breakfast slowly, there is no hurry. Half-frozen blueberries with milk, oatmeal, bread, and plenty of coffee. We listen to the stove, to the kettle buzzing. How many winters have gone by like this? Each morning that begins in the same quiet way—the darkness, the fire, the lamp, the stirring within. We talk a little, what she will do when I am gone. Food will have to be cooked for the dogs, there is plenty of wood. I am not sure when I will return; in three days, maybe.

By seven-thirty I am ready. I get my stuff together—into the basket now goes a light lunch, some bread for the cabin. I put on my old green army parka with its alpaca lining buttoned into it. It is heavily patched, and by now almost a homemade thing, the hood sewn large and trimmed with fur to shield my face from the wind. I take two wool caps, one for my head, and another in the basket in case I should need it. My big mittens also go into the pack; to start with, I will need only a pair of canvas gloves.

I say goodbye at the door, and walk up the hill. The dogs think that they may be going too, and the four of them begin to bark, waiting for the harness and tugging at their chains. But today I am going on foot; I want to take my time, to look around and set new traps. My dogs are too much in a hurry.

I begin the long climb through the birchwoods to the ridge. The trail goes steeply the first few hundred yards, but it soon takes an easier grade, turning north and away from the river. The woods are still dark, but there is light in the snow, and perhaps a brightening in the sky above the trees. Morning and evening come on slowly this time of year, a gradual twilight. I carry a light walking stick made of birch in one hand as I go along. It comes in handy, to knock snow off the brush, to test the ice when I cross a creek, or to kill an animal with when I find one alive in a trap.

It is a winter of light snowfall, with barely ten inches on the ground, and I do not need my snowshoes. The trail is packed hard underfoot, and is easy walking, but away in the woods the snow is still loose and powdery under a thin crust; in the dim light I see that it is littered with dry, curled leaves and small, winged seeds from the alders and birches.

The air is sharp on my face, and it pinches my nose, but I soon begin to feel warm from climbing. I open my parka and push the cap back on my head; I take off my gloves and put them into one of my pockets. It won't do to get overheated.

Behind me now I hear an occasional mournful howl from one of our dogs, sunken and distant in the timber. Otherwise, there is not a sound in the woods this morning, and no air moving in the trees; but now and then the quiet snap of something contracting or expanding in the frost. At other times I have walked this trail in deep snow and bright moonlight, when the birch shadows made another transparent forest on the snow. There were shadows within the shadows, and now and then something would seem to move there—rabbit or lynx, or only a shape in my mind.

Partway up the hill I come to a marten set. Earlier in the season I caught a marten here, close to home, but there is nothing in the trap this morning. In the grey light I see that nothing has come to it, and all the tracks in the snow around it are old.

Frost bristles on the trap, a dense white fur over the jaws, the pan, and the trigger. I put my gloves back on, spring the trap, and bang it a couple of times against the pole to knock the frost from it.

I have two ways of setting traps for marten—one on the snow, and the other on a pole above the snow. This is a pole set. To make it, I have cut down a young birch four feet above the snow, and drawn the trunk of the tree forward a couple of feet to rest in the vee of the stump. I split the end of it to take a piece of bait, and the trap is set back a short space on top of the pole and held in place with a piece of light wire or string. It is a good way in heavy snow; once caught, the marten will always be found hanging from the pole.

Satisfied that the trap is working properly, I reset it, tying the wire loosely in place again. I go on, walking at a steady pace as the trail levels and climbs, winding among the birches.

Within half an hour I come out of the trees and into the open on the long, cleared ridge that rises behind the homestead. Light is stronger here, and I can see the cold, blue height of Banner Dome to the north beyond a range of hills. I have a long ways to go.

I begin to cool off now that I am on top, so I wear my gloves and button the front of my parka. As I stride along in the lightly drifted snow, I savor once more the cold stillness of this winter morning—my breath blown in a long plume before me, and no sound but the soft crunch of my moccasins, and the grating of my stick in the snow.

This ridge like a true watershed divides what I like to think of as my country; for in a way I own it, having come by it honestly, and nearly its oldest resident now. To the south of me, all the way down to the river, it is mostly dry hillside with birch and aspen. To the north, falling way into Redmond and Banner creeks, it is spruce country, mossy and wet. Years ago, when I first lived here, this ridge was heavily wooded; the trail wound through the timber, companionable and familiar, with small clearings and berry patches. Then, eight years ago, came a pipeline crew clearing the ridges and hillsides into Fairbanks. And later they built a powerline to run beside it, from Fairbanks to Delta. The cleared way is overgrown with grass, with alders and raspberries, and the pipe is buried in the ground; but the ridge is windy now, and the trail drifts badly in heavy snow. Because of this, few fur animals come here, and I have no traps on this ridge.

I see some much-trampled snow at the edge of the timber, and turn aside to look. Moose have been feeding here at night, and the tops of many of the smaller trees are pulled down, broken and bitten. I find a couple of hard-packed beds in the snow, and piles of black, frozen droppings. The moose must be close by, but they are out of sight, bedded down in the timber. I stand very still and listen, but hear nothing.

I cover a good mile of steady walking as the light grows and the snow brightens; the trail visible now some distance ahead of me where it follows the open ridge, paced by the power poles, dipping and curving with the slope of the hills. And then near the top of the last rise of hill the trail swings sharply north, and I go down into the woods again. The country changes swiftly, becomes dense and shaggy, the scrubby black spruce dominant, with alder and a few scattered birches. The trail is narrow, rutted, and uneven to walk. There is more snow here on a north slope, and I soon see marten sign, their characteristic tracks crossing my trail at intervals.

I have gone only a short distance when I find a marten dead in a trap. It is frozen, hanging head down at the end of the trap chain—a female, small, and with dull orange splashes over its neck and shoulders, a grizzled mask on its frost-pinched face. I release it from the trap and put the hard, stiff body in my pack. I cut a fresh piece of bait and reset the trap—where one marten has been caught, the chances are good for another.

Encouraged by my luck and in good spirits, I go on, following the trail through the woods, turning and climbing, past windfalls and old, rotted firestumps under the snow. A small covey of spruce hens startles me, flying up from the snow into the trees with a sudden flurry of wings. I hear an alarmed clucking, and see one of the big black and grey birds perched on a spruce bough, sitting very still but watching me with one bright eye.

On a point of hill where a stand of birches form an open grove, I stop for a short time to rest and reset a trap. The sun is up now, just clearing the hills to the south. There is light in the trees, a gold light laid on the blue and white of the snow, and luminous shadows. Frost-crystals glitter in the still air wherever a shaft of sunlight pierces the forest.

This hill is open to the north, and I can see, closer now, the rounded summit of Banner Dome, rose and gold in the low sunlight. The Salchaket hills rising beyond it stand out clearly in the late morning sunlight. I can just see part of the shoulder of hill that rises above the cabin I am going to, six miles yet by this trail. The valleys of Redmond and Glacier creeks lie below me, still in a deep, cold shadow. The sun will not reach there for another month.

I keep a cache on this hill, a fifty-gallon oil drum with a tight lid bolted to it. I brought it here on the sled a couple of years ago, on the last snow of the season. It stands upright between two birches, with its rusty grey paint a little out of place here in the woods, but to me familiar. Inside it I keep a few traps, a spare axe, and some cans of emergency rations in case I should need them. Whatever I leave there stays dry and is safe from bears.

I stand with my pack off for a moment, leaning on my stick. A little wind from somewhere stirs in the birches overhead. I have sometimes thought of building a small camp here, a shelter under these trees. There are places we are attracted to more than others, though I do not always know why. Here, it is the few strong birches, the airy openness of the woods, the view, and the blueberry shrubs under the trees where in good years we have come to pick them. If I were to begin again in some more distant part of the country, to build a home, this is one place I would consider. Perhaps because I know it so well, it is already part of what I think of as home.

I take up my pack and stick, ready to go on. I have put on my mittens, finally; my gloves have gotten damp and become icy and stiff on my hands. From here the trail descends the long north slope into Redmond, a wandering, downhill track through stubby open spruce and over much boggy ground, the longest hill I have to walk. As soon as I start down I am out of the sunlight and into shadow again. It feels at once colder, with a chill blue light in the snowy hummocks.

It is six years now since I cut this part of the trail, and it is worn deep in the moss from our summer walking. So little snow this winter, it makes hard foot and sled travel over the humps and holes. So I walk, going from one side of the trail to the other, springing from hummock to hummock, and balancing myself with my stick. I go at a good pace, anxious to cover the remaining ground before the day is over.

I am halfway down the hill when I find another marten in a trap set on the snow under a spruce. The marten is still alive, tugging at the end of the trap chain, angry and snarling. For a moment I stand and look at the animal. No larger than a house cat, but supple and snaky in body, it lunges at me as if it would bite me.

I take off my pack and approach the marten with my stick. I hit it a sharp blow across its nose, and it falls twitching in the snow. I quickly turn it on its back, lay my stick across its throat and hold it there with one foot, while I place my other foot on its narrow chest. I can feel the small heart beating through the sole of my moccasin.

As I stand bending over it, the marten partly revives and

attempts to free itself, kicking and squirming. But in a short time its heart stops and the slim body relaxes. I remove my foot and the stick, open the trap jaws, and lay the marten out in the snow. It is a large, dark male with thick fur.

It is better to find them dead and frozen, I do not like to kill them this way. Mostly they do not live long when caught in a trap in cold weather; another few hours, and this one too would have frozen.

I reset the trap at the bottom of the tree, placing it on two small dry sticks. I arrange the toggle stick so that the marten will have to step over it and into the trap. I cut a fresh piece of moose gut, and with my axehead I nail it to the tree a foot above the trap. To shield the bait from birds, I break off large twigs of spruce and stand them in the snow around the trap, but leave a small opening for the marten. Finally, I gather some fresh dry snow in the palm of my mitten and sprinkle it around the trap. Thinking that it will do, I put the dead marten into my basket, and go on my way, walking downhill into the cold bottom of Redmond.

The day passes, another hour, another mile. I walk, watching the snow, reading what is written there, the history of the tribes of mice and voles, of grouse and weasel, of redpoll and chickadee, hunter and prey. A scurry here, a trail ended there— something I do not understand, and stop to ponder. I find a trap sprung and nothing in it. I catch another marten, another male, so dark it is almost black. I am in luck today.

Already sunlight is fading from the hilltops. I look at my watch—it is past one, and I still have a good three miles to go. The air feels much colder here in this boggy creek bottom. I do not have a thermometer, but I judge it to be at least in the mid-thirties. There is some ice-fog in this valley, a thin haze in the air above the creek, and that is always a sign of cold and stagnant air.

The trail is slick in places where spring water has seeped up through the snow and frozen into a pale yellow ice. We call it "overflow" or "glaciering," and it is common here in winter. I watch carefully while crossing; the ice is firm, but where ice and snow meet, a little water sometimes steams in the cold air. I feel with my stick as I go, suspecting more water under the snow.

At times while traveling like this, absent in mind or misjudging the snow, I have broken through thin ice and plunged halfway to my knees in slushy water. I have always climbed out quickly, and with so many socks on my feet I have never been wet to my skin. All the same, there is some danger in it, and I do not want to walk the rest of a day with frozen socks and trousers and icy moccasins. Today I am careful, and only once, while crossing a short stretch of overflow, do I look behind me and see water seeping into my tracks from the thin snow.

Twilight comes on slowly across the hills and through the forest; there are no more shadows. I stop again in a stand of spruce above the crossing on Glacier Creek. I have been feeling hungry for some time, so I nibble a frozen cookie from my pack. I have no water to drink, but I remove one of my mittens, and with the warm, bare hand ball up some snow until it is ice, and suck it.

Five years ago we camped here in a tent while hunting moose. That was before we built the cabin, and before I had cut a trail across the creek. The four dogs were with us, tied here among the trees. It was late in the fall, and below zero much of the time, but the tent with its big canvas fly and sheet-iron stove was warm enough. The tent poles still stand here, ready for use, and our cache is still here, a rough platform built into the trees eight feet above me.

I put the three marten I have caught in a sack, tie it, and hang it from a spike high in the cache. I will pick them up on my way home.

I take my pack and go off downhill to the creek—there is no water on the ice, and I am across safely and dry. Then on through the woods and through the swamp, across a low saddle between two hills, tired now, and glad to be getting to the end of it. Fresh marten sign in the snow, and one more marten caught.

I am within half a mile of the cabin, when I find a lynx alive in a marten trap. It has not been caught long, the toes of one big forefoot barely held in the small steel jaws. The animal backs away from me, crouched and growling, its big tawny eyes fastened upon me, and its tufted ears laid back.

I take off my pack, approach carefully, and when I am close enough I hit the lynx hard on its head with my stick. Stunned, the animal sags in the snow. I turn the stick and hit it again with the heavier end, and strike it again, until the lynx sprawls and relaxes, and I am sure that it is dead. For so large an animal, they are easy to kill, but I wait to be certain—I do not want it coming alive in my hands.

Sure that it is dead, I release it from the trap. It is a big male, pale, and a choice fur. I hang the trap in a tree and shoulder my pack. Pleased with this unexpected catch, I drag the big lynx by one hind foot the rest of the way to the cabin, leaving a thread of blood behind me in the snow.

I I

The cabin is hidden in a dense stand of spruce on a bench overlooking a small, brushy creek. The creek has no name on the maps, but I have called it Cabin Creek for the sake of this camp. The ground is perhaps 1,700 feet in elevation, and from the cabin I can look up and see the clear slope of Banner Dome another thousand feet above.

With its shed roof sloping north, the cabin sits low and compact in the snow, a pair of moose antlers nailed above a window in the high south wall. There are four dog houses to the rear of it, each of them roofed with a pile of snow-covered hay. A meat rack stands to one side, built high between two stout spruces, and a ladder made of dry poles leans against a tree next to it. A hindquarter of moose hangs from the rack; it is frozen rock hard and well wrapped with canvas to keep it from birds. Just the same, I see that camp-robbers have pecked at it and torn a hole in the canvas. Nothing else can reach it there, seven feet above the ground.

Nothing has changed since I was last here, and there has been no new snow. Squirrel and marten tracks are all around the cabin, and some of them look fresh; I must set a trap somewhere in the yard.

I leave the dead lynx in the snow beside the cabin; I will skin it later. I lean my walking stick by the door and ease the pack from my shoulders—I am a little stiff from the long walk, and it feels good to straighten my back. A thermometer beside the door reads thirty below.

I open the door, go inside, and set my pack down by the bunk. The cabin is cold, as cold as the outdoors, but there is birch bark and kindling by the stove, and I soon have a fire going. The small sheet-iron stove gets hot in a hurry; I watch the pipe to see that it does not burn.

As the cabin warms up I take off my parka, shake the frost from it, and hang it from a hook near the ceiling. The last time I was here I left a pot of moose stew on the floor beside the stove. Now I lift the pot and set it on the edge of the stove to thaw.

I will need water. Much of the time here I scoop up buckets of clean snow to melt on the stove. There is not much water in a bucketful of dry snow, even when the snow is packed firm, and many buckets are needed to make a gallon or two of water. But this year the snow is shallow, and it is dirty from the wind, with dust and twigs and cones from the trees around the cabin.

And so while the light stays I take a bucket and an ice-chisel, and go down to a small pond below the cabin. Under the snow the ice is clear, and in a short time I chop enough of it to fill the bucket. There is water under the ice, but I know from past use of it that the ice itself is cleaner and has a fresher taste.

Before going back up to the cabin I stand for a moment and take in the cold landscape around me. The sun has long gone, light on the hills is deepening, the gold and rose gone to a deeper blue. The cold, still forest, the slim, black spruce, the willows and few gnarled birches are slowly absorbed in the darkness. I stand here in complete silence and solitude, as alone on the ice of this small pond as I would be on the icecap of Greenland. Only far above in the blue depth of the night I hear a little wind on the dome.

I stir myself and begin walking back up the hill to the cabin with my bucket of ice. Before it is dark completely I will want to get in more wood. There are still a few dry, standing poles on the slope behind the cabin, and they are easy to cut. There will be time for that.

Past three o'clock, and it is dark once more. I am done with my chores. Inside the cabin I light a kerosene lamp by the window, and hang my cap and mittens to dry above the stove. The ice has half-melted in the bucket, and the stew is hot and steaming. I have eaten little this day, and I am hungry. I put on the kettle for tea, set out a plate, and cut some bread. The stew is thick and rich; I eat it with the bread and cold, sweetened cranberries from a jar beneath the table.

Fed and feeling at ease, I sit here by the window, drinking tea, relaxing in the warmth of the cabin. The one lamp sends a soft glow over the yellow, peeled logs. When we built this cabin I set the windows low in the walls so that we could look out easily while sitting. That is the way of most old cabins in the woods, where windows must be small and we often sit for hours in the winter, watching the snow. Now I look out the double panes of glass; there is nothing to see out there but the warm light from the window falling to the snow. Beyond that light there is darkness.

I get up from my chair, to put another stick of wood in the stove and more water in the kettle. I am tired from the long walk, and sleepy with the warmth and food. I take off my moccasins and lie down on the bunk with a book, one of a half dozen I keep here. It is Virgil's *Aeneid,* in English. I open the book to the beginning of the poem and read the first few lines. Almost immediately I fall asleep. When I wake up, it is nearly six o'clock; the fire has burned down and the cabin is chilly.

I feel lazy and contented here with nothing urgent to do, but I get up anyway and feed more wood to the stove. On my feet again, moving around, I find that I am still hungry—all day out in the cold, one uses a lot of fuel. So I heat up what remains of the stew and finish it off. Tomorrow I will cut more meat from the quarter hanging outside, and make another pot. What I do not eat, I will leave here to freeze for another day.

Having eaten and rested, I feel a surge of energy. I go outside to bring in the lynx, intending to skin it; I don't want to carry that heavy carcass home. The lynx is already stiff, beginning to freeze. I carry it in and lay it on the floor near the stove to thaw, while I make myself another cup of tea. When I can move its legs easily, I pull one of the big hind feet into my lap and begin to cut with my pocket knife below the heel where the footpad begins. The skin is stiff and cold under thick fur as it comes slowly free from the sinew.

But soon in the warmth of the room I begin to see fleas, red fleas, crawling out of the fur. One of them, suddenly strong, jumps onto me, and then to the bunk. That is enough. I put down my knife and take the lynx back outdoors. I will leave it here to freeze, and when I come again the fleas will be dead. I am in no hurry about it, and I do not want fleas in my clothing and in my bunk. Already I begin to itch.

Outside, I leave the lynx in the snow once more, and for a brief time I stand in front of the cabin, to watch and listen. The cold air feels good on my bare skin. The stars are brilliant—Polaris and the Dipper overhead. Through a space in the trees to the south I can see part of the familiar winter figure of Orion, his belt and sword; in the north I see a single bright star I think is Vega. I hear an occasional wind-sigh from the dome, and now and then moving air pulls at the spruces around me.

What does a person do in a place like this, so far away and alone? For one thing, he watches the weather—the stars, the snow, and the fire. These are the books he reads most of all. And everything that he does, from bringing in firewood and buckets of snow, to carrying the waste water back outdoors, requires that he stand in the open, away from his walls, out of his man-written books and his dreaming head for a while. As I stand here, refreshed by the stillness and closeness of the night, I think it is a good way to live.

But now the snow is cold through my stocking feet, and I go back indoors. I wash the dishes and clean the small table, putting things away for the night. I hang up my trousers and wool shirts, and hang my socks on a line near the ceiling. There is still some hot water in the kettle; I pour it into a basin, cool it with a cup of cold water from the bucket, and wash my face and hands. Having dried myself and brushed my teeth, I am ready for bed.

Lying on the bunk once more, with the lamp by my left

shoulder, I pick up my book and try to read again. A page, and then another. My mind fills with images: a fire in the night, Aeneas, and the flight from Troy. I drowse, then wake again. I remember Fred Campbell lying on his cot in the Lake cabin that good fall many years ago, the Bible held overhead in his hand as he tried to read. And soon he was sleeping, the book fallen to his chest. The same page night after night. I was amused at him then, but older now I see the same thing happens to me. It is the plain life, the air, the cold, the hard work; and having eaten, the body rests and the mind turns to sleep.

I wake once more and put away my book. I get up from the bunk and bank the fire, laying some half-green sticks of birch on the coals, and close down the draft. Ice has melted in the bucket, there is plenty of water for the morning.

I blow out the lamp and settle down in the sleeping bag, pulling it around my shoulders. I look into the dark cabin, and to the starlight on the snow outside. At any time here, away from the river and the sound of traffic on the road, I may hear other sounds—a moose in the creek bottom, breaking brush, a coyote on a ridge a mile away, or an owl in the spruce branches above the cabin. Often it is the wind I hear, a whispering, rushy sound in the boughs. Only sometimes when the wind blows strongly from the south I hear a diesel on the road toward Fairbanks, changing gears in the canyon. And once, far away on a warm south wind, the sound of dogs barking at Richardson.

I spend another day at the cabin, taking my time. I loaf and read, cut more wood and chop some ice. I thaw and skin the one marten, and roll the fur in a sack to take with me; it will mean a pound or two less to carry, and more room in the basket. With the ladder and a block and tackle, I take down the moose quarter, unwrap it, and saw a piece of meat from the round. It was killed late, and is not fat meat, but having hung frozen for so long it is tender enough. The outside of the meat is darkened and dried and will need to be trimmed. I put the piece I have cut on a board near the stove to thaw.

In the afternoon I go up the creek to look at some snares I have set there. I find that nothing has come but one lynx, and he pushed a snare aside. It may have been the one I caught.

From the creek I climb a couple of miles up the ridge toward the dome. It is easy walking in the light snow, and here on higher ground there is bright sunlight and the air seems to be warmer. There is plenty of marten sign in the open spruce mixed with aspen, and I set two traps.

I mark the days on a calendar, drawing a circle around the dates. The calendar shows a ship, full-rigged in the old romantic style of the sea, hard-driven from Cape Horn, or following the trades homeward. This calendar comes from Canada, and bears the trade name of *John Leckie & Company, Ltd., Edmonton, Alberta. Marine Supplies and Hardware.* Three years ago I bought a whitefish net from them by mail, and now each year they send me a calendar. Since we have others at home, I bring them here. They look fine against the log walls, and brighten their place by the window.

I remember how we built this cabin, the many hours here, the long walks in the rain that turned into snow. I had the big wall tent pitched in the woods, near where the cabin is now, a cot to sleep on, and the small iron stove with its pipe stuck through a piece of sheet metal in the tent roof. I would come here from home in the afternoons, packing some food, lumber, and tools. I worked on the cabin until dark, and slept overnight in the tent. Again the next morning, from the first light, I worked hard, trimming and fitting the logs, then walked home in the afternoon over the wet hills.

I worked from early August until mid-October, a few hours or a day at a time. Fall came early that year, and toward the end of it I was scraping frozen bark from the roof poles, determined to make a clean job of it. There was no dry sod for the roof, so we went to the creek to cut big batts of half-frozen moss and carry them up the hill one at a time. And finally we had a roof on the cabin, the door hung and windows fitted, and a fire in the stove.

That fall I shot a moose from the front of the cabin just at dusk. It was a long shot down into the flat below the hill, the moose only a dark shape in the frozen grass. Then came the work that evening and part of the next day, cutting the meat into quarters and dragging them up the hill to the camp. We hung the meat high on the rack I built that morning behind the cabin. We had a long walk home that afternoon in wet snow, carrying with us a chunk of the ribs, the tongue, the heart, the kidneys and liver. It was a hard fall, in many ways the hardest and poorest year I have spent in the north.

But the time and work was worth it, for here is the cabin now, snug and warm. No matter how long it stands here, it will always seem like a new thing, strange to come upon far in these hills at the end of a long hike, and to know we have built it.

I look around me, at the floor, at the walls, at the ceiling, the logs and poles. When the cabin was first built we had only hay for a floor, a deep bed of it spread on the moss. There was nothing to sweep or to clean, and each fall I brought in a few armloads of new hay to freshen the floor. But as cheery and rustic as it was, there were things about that hay floor I never liked. Frost was deep in the ground beneath the hay, and because the cabin went unoccupied for many weeks in winter, it was cold and damp to live in until the fire had thawed it. Mice and squirrels tunneled through the moss and into the cabin, and made a mess in the bedding. And so one spring before the trail went soft, I brought sledloads of lumber here. In August of that year I came and worked three days, putting in a proper floor. Now it is dry and warm, and the mice stay out. I sweep it now and then.

There is only the one room, eight feet by twelve feet, but it is large enough for a camp in the woods. The door opens west, and the two windows face north and south. Overhead I have cut a round hole in one wall for a vent, and fitted it with a metal lid. The peeled poles of the ceiling are still clean and bright yellow; smoke has not darkened them and the roof has never leaked.

Here at the back of the room I have built two bunks, one above the other, with a small ladder at one end to reach the upper. The table I eat from and the work table across the room are both fashioned from two-inch wooden pegs driven into auger holes in the logs. Boards are laid across the pegs and nailed in place. The few shelves are made in the same way. It is a simple means of making the essential furniture, and there are no table legs to get in the way underfoot.

Here and there I have driven nails and spikes into the

walls; some odds and ends of clothing hung there, a few traps, a piece of rope. A .22 rifle is propped on a couple of spikes at the foot of the lower bunk. Behind the stove hang pots and washpans, and into one log by the door I have driven a twelve-inch spike from which I hang the dog harness to dry.

There have been other winters here, not easy ones. I have come after a heavy snowfall, with the dogs dead-tired and me walking behind or in front of the sled, breaking trail. We were five or six hours getting here, the traps buried, something caught but hard to find in the snow. And then would come the journey home the next day over a soft, half-broken trail with a load of meat and three dogs; me again walking behind, steering, holding the snubline while the dogs pulled ahead.

Fifty years ago in the twilight of the goldrush, wagon roads and freight trails were still in use here. Though they are badly overgrown now and deeply rutted, I can still walk parts of them for a short distance; they go up the creek, across the divide and down Shamrock, to the Salcha River and Birch Lake, many miles from here. It is strange to think of it then, the country still busy with people coming and going, the dogs and horses, freight and men.

No one comes here now but Jo and myself, the dogs and us, the moose and the marten. Only once, three years ago, two men came from Banner Creek with a Cat to prospect on Glacier Creek, two miles over the hill. They cleared a small piece of ground on the bench above the creek, but they found nothing there and did not come back. I am glad of that, I like having this country to myself.

I am living out a dream in these woods. Old dreams of the Far North, old stories read and absorbed: of snow and dogs, of moose and lynx, and of all that is still native to these unpeopled places. Nothing I have yet done in life pleases me as much as this. And yet it seems only half-deliberate, as if I had followed a scent on the wind and found myself in this place. Having come, I will have to stay, there's no way back.

The hunting and fishing, the wild fruit, the trapping, the wood that we burn and the food that we eat—it is all given to us by the country. The fur of this marten is lovely when held in the light, shaken so that the hair stands from the pelt. And meat of the moose is good to have; it keeps us fed and warm inside, and I pay no butcher for it. Yet I cannot trap and kill without thought or emotion, and it may be that the killing wounds me also in some small but deadly way. Life is here equally in sunlight and frost, in the thriving blood and sap of things, in their decay and sudden death.

It can be hard and cruel sometimes, as we are prepared to see it clearly. I put the beast to death for my own purposes, as the lynx kills the rabbit, the marten the squirrel, and the weasel the mouse. Life is filled with contradictions—confused and doubting in the heart of a man, or it is straight as an arrow and full of purpose.

I look at my hands and flex my fingers. They have handled much, done things I hardly dreamed of doing when I was younger. I have woven my nets with them and made my snares. I have pulled the trigger of my rifle many times and watched a bird fall or a moose crumple to the ground. And with these hands I have gone deep into the hot body of the animal, and torn from it the still-quivering tissue of lungs, heart, liver, and guts. There is blood under the nails, dirt and grease in the cracks of the finger joints.

I have learned to do these things, and do them well, as if I'd come into something for which I had a native gift. And a troubling thought will return sometimes: having done so much, would I kill a man? I do not know. I might if I had to, in anger, perhaps, passion of defense or revenge. But not, I think, in the cold, judging light of the law. I have seen a war, a dead man floating in the sea off a Pacific island, and I was there. By my presence alone, I took part in many deaths. I cannot pretend that I am free and guiltless. Justice evades us; the forest with all its ancient scarcity and peril is still within us, and it may be that we will never know a world not haunted in some way by a return to that night of the spirit where the hangman adjusts his noose and the executioner hones his axe to perfection.

I put these thoughts away, and look out the window to the sunlit snow on the hillside across the creek. In this wilderness life I have found a way to touch the world once more. One way.

To live the life that is here to be lived, as nearly as I can without that other—clock hands, hours and wages. I relive each day the ancient expectation of the hunt—the setting out, and the trail at dawn. What will we find today?

I leave some of my mankindness behind me for a while and become part tree, a creature of the snow. It is a long way back, and mostly in shadow. I see a little there, not much, but what I see will never be destroyed.

I may not always be here in these woods. The trails I have made will last a long time; this cabin will stand twenty years at least before it falls. I can imagine a greater silence, a deeper shadow where I am standing, but what I have loved will always be here.

Night, and the day passes. Evening, another pot of stew—rice and chunks of meat, dried vegetables, onions, a little fat, and spice for flavor. The weather holding steady, still twenty-nine below. I continue to hear some wind on the dome.

I rise early on the morning of the third day, make my breakfast by lamplight. Oats and bread, some meat in the fry-pan. Might as well feed up, it will be another long day. I take my time this morning, dressing slowly, putting things away. I bring in more wood and stack it by the stove. Outside in the clear frost I hang the frozen lynx high on the rack; nothing will bother it there. Dawn comes slowly over the hills, lighting the snowy dome.

I pack my gear—the small axe again, a few traps. One marten skin to carry, three marten to pick up on the way. My pack will be as heavy as before.

The fire slowly dies and the cabin grows cool again. I fill a shallow pan with the remaining water and place it on the stove. It will freeze, and I will have water quickly the next time here. I put away my saw and the big axe; there is bark and kindling at hand when I come again. I close the door and latch it. I look around with care, at the cabin and the yard—everything is in place. I will be back in a week or ten days.

It is minus twenty-four degrees this morning; some thin clouds are forming, it may snow by evening. I take my pack and, stick in hand, set off up the trail toward Glacier Creek.

III

It is evening again, and I have come home by the river from Banner Creek. I came by another trail today, over the long divide between Redmond and Banner, another part of the country. It was hard walking in places; much of it is steep sidehill scraped and gouged by a Cat trail made many years ago, with several small springs and water under the snow.

I met with some wind on a high and open ridge where I could look east into the rose-grey morning sunlight. I felt too warm from climbing, and stopped to take the lining out of my parka. The wind came only now and then, not cold, a little loose snow blowing across the open trail.

Few traps and no marten there, but plenty of moose sign in the willows going down into Banner. One big red fox caught somehow in a trap set for marten, caught by the toes only, and not for long. He watched me as I came near, stretched out on the short chain. his eyes enormous with alertness and fear. I thought of trying to knock him out with a blow from my stick, so that I could free him from the trap and let him go. But I finally killed him, breaking his neck as I have learned to do. I put him into my pack with the others, tying him down, and took the trap with me.

I was close to Banner Creek, walking slowly on a straight and open stretch of the trail, when I came upon a set of wolf tracks. They were soon joined by others, and I saw that two, possibly three wolves had come out of the dense, sloping spruce wood to the north, and finding my foot trail, had turned to follow it.

Thinking they might return in a few days, I set two heavy snares in that open place, a few yards apart from each other. I propped the nooses over my trail, supporting them with some brush cut from the woods close by and stuck down in the scant snow. I tried to make the sets appear as natural as I could, and looking at them afterwards from a distance, it seemed to me that they might work. Yet somehow I do not expect much from them; the wind may blow them down, or the wolves go around them.

I went on down Banner Creek, walking the old road between the spruce and the birch, the snow so light this winter it hardly fills the frozen ruts. A side path turning off into the woods brought me into a brushy flat where I keep an ancient and tilting cabin. I stopped there to build a fire in the stove and make some tea. My feet were sore from walking that hard trail in soft moccasins, and it felt good to take off the pack and rest for a while. The cabin is old and damp and does not heat well, but it is better than no camp at all.

Afterwards I searched the brushed-in trails near the cabin where I have set snares for lynx. But I have caught nothing there this winter. Today one snare was missing; something had made off with it—what? The snow told me nothing.

In late afternoon I walked the last mile home along the Tanana, through the woods on the steep hillside between the river and the highway. The sun was gone, and light on the river, on the ice, a steely grey. Clouds were building a heavy darkness in the west. Sounds came to me along the river: water running somewhere out on the ice, a dog barking at Richardson. A car went by on the road, going to Fairbanks, going to Delta. People.

I sit here now, the long day over and the pack gone from my shoulders at last. My heavy clothing removed, moccasins hung up to dry, gloves and mittens drying on the rack above the stove. Half-sleepy, warmed by the fire, while Jo makes supper, and we talk. What happened while I was gone? Yesterday, today, the day before. A moose on the hill, water and wood, and no one came. The world is still the same, it will be the same to-morrow.

I am happy deep inside. Not the mind-tiredness of too much thought, of thoughts that pursue each other endlessly in that forest of nerves, anxiety, and fear. But a stretching kind of tiredness, the ease and satisfaction of the time well spent, and of the deep self renewed.

Tomorrow, marten to skin and meat to cut. What else? It is two degrees below zero this evening. The wind is blowing.

JOHN McPHEE

The encircled river

" 'KAMIKAZE PILOTS. THAT'S WHAT WE'VE GOT UP HERE—
KAMIKAZE PILOTS FROM NEW JERSEY.' "

Fans of television's Northern Exposure *will recall that one of the central characters, Maggie O'Connell, played by Janine Turner, was a bush pilot. This wasn't just a dramatic ploy; the skies of Alaska, and a few graves, are filled with bush pilots.*

Alaska is so big—yes, bigger than Texas—and so wild that most of it is accessible only by air. And much of it is so rough and undeveloped that the only aircraft that can land are float-planes that can settle on a river.

Both visitors and residents alike are accustomed to seeing the landscape from the air. But herein lies a problem. Traveling in the bush by air is relatively expensive and certainly beyond the means of many Alaskan residents, and many Alaskans came there from elsewhere precisely to be close to the wilderness.

John McPhee investigates some of the lore about bush pilots in the following excerpt from Coming into the Country.

✳ IN THE MORNING — COOL IN THE FOR-
ties and the river calm — we strike the tents, pack the gear,
and move on down toward Kiana. Gradually, the village spreads
out in perspective. Its most prominent structure is the sheet-
metal high school on the edge of town. Dirt-and-gravel streets
climb the hill above the bluff. Houses are low, frame. Some are
made of logs. Behind the town, a navigational beacon flashes.
Drawing closer, we can see caribou antlers over doorways — tes-
timony of need and respect. There are basketball backboards.
We are closing a circuit, a hundred water miles from the upper
Salmon, where a helicopter took us, from Kiana, at the start.
Under the bluff, we touch the shore. Kiana is now high above
us, and mostly out of sight. The barge is here that brings up
supplies from Kotzebue. The river's edge for the moment is all
but unpopulated. Fish racks up and down the beach are covered with split drying salmon — ruddy and pink. We disassemble
the Kleppers, removing their prefabricated bones, folding their
skins, making them disappear into canvas bags. I go up the hill
for a carton, and return to the beach. Into envelopes of cardboard I tape the tines of the caribou antler that I have carried
from the mountains. Protecting the antler takes longer than the
dismantling and packing of the kayaks, but there is enough time
before the flight to Kotzebue at midday. In the sky, there has as
yet been no sound of the airplane — a Twin Otter, of Wien Air
Alaska, the plane that brought us here to meet the chopper.
Stell Newman has gone up the beach and found some people
at work around their fish racks. He now has with him a slab of
dried salmon, and we share it like candy.

Children were fishing when we were here before. They
yanked whitefish out of the river and then pelted one another
with the living fish as if they were snowballs. Women with tubs
were gutting salmon. It was a warmer day then. The sun was so
fierce you looked away; you looked north. Up at the airstrip
behind the town — a gravel strip, where we go now with our
gear — was the Grumman canoe. It had been flown in, and
cached there, long before. The helicopter, chartered by the government and coming in from who knows where, was a new five-
seat twin-engine Messerschmitt with a bubble front. On its
shining fuselage, yellow-and-black heraldry identified it as the

property of Petroleum Helicopters, Inc. The pilot removed a couple of fibre-glass cargo doors, took out a seat, and we shoved the canoe into an opening at the rear of the cabin. It went in halfway. The Grumman was too much for the Messer-schmitt. The canoe was cantilevered, protruding to the rear. We tied it in place. It was right side up, and we filled it with gear. Leaving the rest of us to wait for a second trip, Pourchot and the pilot took off for the Salmon River. With so much canoe coming out of its body, the helicopter, even in flight, seemed to be nearing the final moment of an amazing pregnancy. It went over the mountains northeast.

There was a wooden sign beside the airstrip: "WELCOME TO THE CITY OF KIANA. 2nd Class City. Population 300 . . . Establish 1902 . . . Main Sources: Bear, Caribou, Moose, Geese, Salmon, Shee, Whitefish, Trout." The burning sun was uncomfortable. I walked behind the sign. In its shadow, the air was chill. I dragged the helicopter seat out of the sun and into the shade of a storage hut, sat down, leaned back, and went to sleep. When I woke up, I was shivering. The temperature a few feet away, in the sunlight, was above seventy degrees.

What awakened me were the voices of children. Three small girls had followed us up from the Kobuk, where we had watched them fish. They had crossed the runway and picked blueberries, and now were offering them from their hands. The berries were intensely sweet, having grown in the long northern light. The little girls also held out pieces of hard candy. Wouldn't we like some? They asked for nothing. They were not shy. They were totally unself-conscious. I showed them an imi-tating game, wherein you clear your throat—hrrrum—and then draw with a stick a figure on the ground. "Here. Try to do that." They drew the figure but did not clear their throats. "No. That's not quite right. Hrrrum. Here now. Try it again." They tried twice more. They didn't get it. I sat down again on the chopper seat. Stell Newman let them take pictures with his camera. When they noticed my monocular, on a lanyard around my neck, they got down beside me, picked it off my chest, and spied on the town. They leaned over, one at a time, and put their noses down against mine, draping around my head their soft black hair. They stared into my eyes. Their eyes were dark and northern, in beautiful almond faces, aripple with smiles. Amy. Katherine. Rose Ann. Ages nine and eleven. Eskimo girls. They looked up. They had heard the helicopter, and before long it appeared.

I sat in the co-pilot's seat, others in the seat I had been napping on. We lifted off, and headed out to join Pourchot, who was waiting on a gravel bar in the upper Salmon. The rotor noise was above conversation, but the pilot handed me a pair of earphones and a microphone. He showed me on a panel between us the mechanics of communicating. I couldn't think of much to say. I was awed, I suppose, in the presence of a bush pilot (mustache akimbo) and in the presence of the bush itself—the land and the approaching mountains. I didn't want to distract him, or myself. He kept urging me to talk, though. He seemed to want the company. His name was Gene Parrish, and he was a big man who had eaten well. He smoked a cigar, and on the intercom was garrulous and friendly.

Before us now was the first ridgeline. Flying close to ground, close to the mountainside, we climbed rapidly toward the crest, and then—crossing over it—seemed to plunge into a void of air. The ground ahead, which had been so near, was suddenly far below. We soon reached another mountainside, and again we climbed closely above its slope, skimmed the outcropping rocks at the top, and jumped into a gulf of sky.

Parrish said, "Y'all ever seen these mountains before?"

Some of the others had, I said, but I had not.

"Me, neither," he said. "Aren't they fabulous? Alaska is amazing, isn't it? Wherever you go, everything is different. These mountains sure are fabulous."

Indeed they were something like it—engaging, upsweeping tundra fells. They were not sharp and knife-edged like the peaks of the central Brooks. They were less dramatic but more inviting. They looked negotiable. They were, as it happened, the last mountains of the range, the end of the line, the end of a cordillera. They were, after four thousand miles, the last statement of the Rocky Mountains before they disappeared into the Chukchi Sea.

Parrish went up the side of a still higher mountain and

skimmed the ridge, to reveal, suddenly, a drainage system far below.

"Is that the Salmon River?" I said.

"Oh, my, no," he said. "It's a ways yet. Where y'all from?"

"I'm from New Jersey. And you?"

"Louisiana."

He said he had come to Alaska on a kind of working vacation. At home, where his job was to fly back and forth between the Louisiana mainland and oil rigs in the Gulf of Mexico, he seldom flew over anything much higher than a wave. Because the Messerschmitt had two engines, he said, he would not have to autorotate down if one were to fail. In fact, he could even climb on one engine. So it was safe to fly this way, low and close—and more interesting.

We flew up the sides of mountain after mountain, raked the ridges, fluttered high over valleys. In each new valley was a stream, large or small. With distance, they looked much alike. Parrish checked his airspeed, the time, the heading; finally, he made a sharp southward turn and began to follow a stream course in the direction of its current, looking for a gravel bar, a man, a canoe. Confidently, he gave up altitude and searched the bending river. He found a great deal of gravel. For thirty, forty miles, he kept searching, until the hills around the river began to diminish in anticipation of—as we could see ahead—the wet-tundra Kobuk plain. If the river was the Salmon, Pourchot was not there. If Pourchot was on the Salmon, Parrish was somewhere else.

The Salmon had to be farther east, he guessed, shaking his head in surprise and wonder. We rollercoasted the sides of additional mountains and came upon another significant drainage. It appeared to Parrish to be the right one. This time, we flew north, low over the river, upstream, looking for the glint of the canoe. We had as much luck as before. The river narrowed as we went farther and farther, until it became a brook and then a rill, with steep-rising mountains to either side. "I don't believe it. I just *can't* believe it," Parrish said. There was nothing much below us now but the kind of streak a tear might make crossing a pilot's face. "This just isn't right," he said. "This is not working out. I was sure of the heading. I was sure this was the river. But nothing ever is guaranteed. Nothing—nothing—is guarandamnteed."

He turned one-eighty and headed downstream. Spread over his knees was a Nome Sectional Aeronautical Chart, and he puzzled over it for a while, then he handed it to me. Maybe I could help figure out where we were. The map was quite wonderful at drawing straight lines between distant airstrips, but its picture of the mountains looked like calves' brains over bone china, and the scale was such that the whole of the Salmon River was only six inches long. The chopper plowed on to the south. I held the map a little closer to my eyes, studying the blue veiny lines among the mountains. The ludicrousness of the situation washed over me. I looked back at Kauffmann and the others, who seemed somewhat confused. And small wonder. A map was being handed back and forth between a man from New Jersey and a pilot from Louisiana who were amiss in—of all places—the Brooks Range. In a sense—in the technical sense that we had next to no idea where we were—we were lost.

There are no geographical requirements for pilots in the United States. Anyone who is certified as a pilot can fly anywhere, and that, of course, includes anywhere in Alaska. New pilots arrive steadily from all over the Lower Forty-eight. Some are attracted by the romance of Alaska, some by the money around the pipeline. The Alyeska Pipeline Service Company, soon after it began its construction operations, set up its own standards for charter pilots who would fly its personnel—standards somewhat stiffer than those of the Federal Aviation Administration. Among other things, Alyeska insisted that applicants without flying experience in Alaska had to have fifty hours of documented training there, including a line check above the terrain they would be flying.

One effect of the pipeline charters has been to siphon off pilots from elsewhere in the Alaskan bush. These pilots are often replaced by pilots inexperienced in Alaska. Say a mail pilot quits and goes off to fly the pipeline. His replacement might be three days out of Teterboro. The mail must go through. Passengers in such planes (passengers ride with bush mail) sometimes intuit that they and the pilot are each seeing the landscape in a novel way. Once, for example, in the eastern-Alaska interior, I rode in a mail plane that took off from Fairbanks to fly a couple of hundred miles across mountains to Eagle, a village on the upper Yukon. It was a blustery, wet morning, and clouds were lower by far than summits. As rain whipped against the windshield, visibility forward was zero. Looking down to the side, the pilot watched the ground below—trying to identify various drainages and pick his way through the mountains. He frequently referred to a map. The plane was a single-engine Cessna 207 Skywagon, bumping hard on the wind. We went up a small tributary and over a pass, where we picked up another river and followed it downstream. After a time, the pilot turned around and went many miles back in the direction from which he had come. He explored another tributary. Then, abruptly, he turned again. The weather was not improving. Soon his confidence in his reading of the land seemed to run out altogether. He asked in what direction the stream below was flowing. He could not tell by the set of the rapids. He handed the map to a passenger who had apparently visited the region once or twice before. The passenger read the map for a while and then counselled the pilot to stay with the principal stream in sight. He indicated to the pilot which direction was downhill. At length, the Yukon came into view. I, who love rivers, have never felt such affection for a river. One would not have to be Marco Polo to figure out now which way to go. I had been chewing gum so vigorously that the hinges of my jaws would ache for two days. We flew up the Yukon to Eagle. When we landed, a young woman with a pickup was waiting to collect the mail. As the pilot stepped out, she came up to him and said, "Hello. You're new, aren't you? My name is Anna."

That was a scheduled flight on an American domestic airline. The company was Air North, which serves many bush communities, and its advertising slogan was "Experience Counts." Another Air North pilot told me once that he liked being a bush pilot in Alaska—he had arrived from New York several months before—but he was having a hard time living on his pay. He said there was better money to be made operating bulldozers on the pipeline than operating planes for Air

North. As a result, experienced, able pilots had not only been drawn away to fly pipeline charters; experienced, able pilots were also flying bulldozers on the tundra.

Some people I know in the National Park Service who were studying a region near the upper Yukon chartered a helicopter in an attempt to find the headwaters of a certain tributary stream. When they had been in flight for some time and had not seen anything remotely resembling the terrain they were looking for, they grew uneasy. When they looked ahead and saw the bright-white high-rising Wrangells, mountain peaks two hundred miles from where they were going, they realized they were lost. The pilot, new in Alaska, was from Alabama. "This is different, unique, tough country," a pilot from Sitka once told me. "A guy has to know what he's doing. Flying is a way of life up here, and you have to get used to it. You can't drive. You can't walk. You can't swim."

In Anchorage, John Kauffmann had introduced me to his friend Charlie Allen, a general free-lance bush pilot with a wide reputation for having no betters and few peers. From the Southeastern Archipelago to Arctic Alaska, Allen had been flying for twenty-five years. He was dismayed by the incompetence of some people in his profession, and was not at all shy to say so. "Alaska is the land of the bush pilot," he said. "You have to think highly of this bush pilot, because he's dirty, he has a ratty airplane, and he's alive. It's a myth, the bush-pilot thing. It's 'Smilin' Jack.' The myth affects pilots. Some of them, in this magic Eddie Rickenbacker fraternity, are more afraid of being embarrassed than they are of death. Suppose they're low on gas. They're so afraid of being embarrassed they keep going until they have no recourse but to crash. They drive their aircraft till they cough and quit. Kamikaze pilots. That's what we've got up here—kamikaze pilots from New Jersey. Do you think one of them would ever decide the weather's too tough? His champion-aviator's manhood would be impugned. Meanwhile, he's a hero if he gets through. A while ago, some guy ran out of gas at night on the ice pack. He had been chartered for a polar-bear hunt. He chopped off his fuel tanks with an axe and used the fuel tanks as boats. He and the hunters paddled out. He was then regarded as a hero. He was regarded as Eddie

Rickenbacker *and* Smilin' Jack. But he was guilty of outrageous technical behavior. He was the fool who got them into the situation in the first place.

"Aircraft-salvage operators have a backlog of planes waiting to be salvaged in Alaska. Helicopters go out for them. In the past year and a half, I have helped salvage six planes that have been wrecked by *one* pilot. Don't identify him. Just call him 'a government employee.' Why do passengers *go* with such pilots? Would they go to the moon with an astronaut who did not have round-trip fuel? If you were in San Francisco and the boat to Maui was leaking and the rats were leaving, even if you had a ticket you *would not go*. Safety in the air is where you find it. Proper navigation helps, but proper judgment takes care of all conditions. You say to yourself, 'I ain't going to go today. The situation is too much for me.' And you resist all pressure to the contrary."

Allen paused a moment. Then he said, "You don't have to run into a mountain. Only a pilot is needed to wreck an airplane."

Of reported accidents, there have lately been something like two hundred a year in Alaska. Upwards of twenty-five a year produce fatal injuries, killing various numbers of people. Another fifteen crashes or so produce injuries rated "serious." The figures seem to compliment the fliers in a state where a higher percentage of people fly—and fly more often—than they do anywhere else in the United States. Merrill Field, a light-plane airfield in Anchorage, handles fifty-four thousand more flights per year than Newark International. On the other hand, if you get into an airplane in Alaska your chances of not coming back are greater by far than they would be in any other part of the country. Only Texas and California, with their vastly larger populations, consistently exceed Alaska in aircraft accidents. Government employees in Alaska speak of colleagues who have been lost "in line of duty." In air accidents during the past two years, the Bureau of Land Management has lost four, Alaska Fish and Game has lost one, U.S. Fish and Wildlife has lost three, the U.S. Forest Service has lost five, and the National Park Service has lost seven (in a single crash). A gallery of thirteen of the great bush pilots in the history of Alaska was presented in an Alaska newspaper not long ago. Of the thirteen, ten—among them Carl Eielson, Russ Merrill, Haakon Christensen, Big Money Monsen—died flying. I dropped in at a bar one day, in a small Alaskan town, where a bush pilot had one end of a plastic swizzlestick clamped between his teeth and was attempting to stretch it by pulling the other end. He had apparently been there some time, and he was challenging all comers to see who could stretch a swizzlestick the farthest. Jay Hammond, governor of Alaska, was himself a bush pilot for twenty-eight years, and a conspicuously good one. In an interview with him, I mentioned the sorts of things that cause disgust in pilots like Charlie Allen, and Hammond said, "There is nothing you can do by statute to assure competence." I wondered if that was altogether true—if, at the very least, regulations such as Alyeska's regarding pilots who come in from outside could not be extended to the state at large.

All this applies, of course, only to bush pilots and not to the big jet-flying commercial carriers, whose accidents are extremely rare and are not outstanding in national statistics. As we flew from Fairbanks to Kotzebue to begin the trip to the Salmon River, we were in a Boeing 737 of Wien Air Alaska. One Captain Clayton came on the horn and said he would be pleased to play the harmonica for us as soon as he had finished a Fig Newton. A while later, he announced that his mouth was now solvent—and, above clouds, he began to play. He played beautifully. The speaker system in that particular aircraft seemed to have been wired especially to meet his talent. He played three selections, and he found Kotzebue.

"This is not right. This just is *not* right," Gene Parrish said again, giving up on still another river and moving (west this time) to try again. Apparently, one of the streams he had passed over was, in fact, the Salmon. "I do my best," he said. "I do my best. I had the right heading—I'm certain of that. I do my best, but there ain't no guarangoddamntee." Of the next river he looked over perhaps twenty miles, without success. Then he began to mention fuel. He thought we should go back to Kiana and tap a drum. So he continued west, and crossed another mountain. Now he flew above a stream with a tributary coming into it that had a pair of sharp right-angled bends that formed the shape of a staple. Pictured on the Nome Sectional Aeronautical Chart was a staple-shaped pair of bends in a tributary of the Salmon River. The stream on the map and the stream on the earth appeared to be the same, but there was no guarangoddamntee. Forgetting Kiana for the time being, Parrish headed up the river. Down near the spruce, swinging around the bends, we hunted the gravel bars, looking for the shine of metal. There was much gravel but no aluminum. He turned once more for Kiana. There had been a hill on our left, and according to the map there should have been another tributary coming in on the far side of the hill. If the smaller stream was there, this was surely—so it seemed—the Salmon. Parrish could not resist having a look. He turned again, and flew north of the hill, which sloped down to the right bank of a tributary stream. We went on up the river. "This *must* be the Salmon, but it sure don't look right," Parrish said, and in the same instant Pourchot and the Grumman came into view. The chopper set down so near Pourchot it almost blew him over. We pulled out our gear, and wished Parrish well in his continuing tour of Alaska. In a whirling dust storm, the Messerschmitt took off, spattering us with sand and flying bits of dry debris. The dust would take a lot longer to settle than the laws of physics would suggest. Now we were alone between fringes of spruce by a clear stream where tundra went up the sides of mountains. This was, in all likelihood, the most isolated wilderness I would ever see, and that is how we got there.

THE NORTH

JON KRAKAUER

Brooks Range, Gates of the Arctic, 1994

"COMPARING MY SIZE 9 BOOT TO A FRESH GRIZZLY PRINT, I
ESTIMATE THE BRUIN WOULD WEAR SIZE 20 NIKES."

*More people are struck by lightning than are killed by grizzly
bears, but if you're in the wrong place at the wrong time in bear
country, your chances of being attacked skyrocket.*

*There are several stories about bears in this book. They are
all, to put it mildly, cautionary. See, for example, James Ramsey's bear story in the selection after this one by Jon Krakauer.
Ramsey spent a winter alone in the Brooks Range, the same
country Krakauer describes in this article, first published in*
Smithsonian.

*It's true that the bears who come to gorge on salmon at
McNeil River Falls in southwestern Alaska seem to agree on a
kind of truce with the humans who, under very controlled circumstances, come to watch them. This phenomenon is vividly described in* Brown Bear Summer: Life Among Alaska's Giants *by
Thomas Bledsoe, published in 1987, and can be seen in an excellent* National Geographic *video documentary.*

*But bears are always dangerous. A neighbor of mine in New
York, who spends three or four months of each year in a trailer*

eighty miles north of Anchorage and within sight of Denali, wouldn't go more than fifty feet from his door without a gun. A big one.

And sometimes you have no way of even knowing that you're in the wrong place. In July 1995, in the Chugach Mountains only twenty miles from downtown Anchorage, three hikers—a teenage boy and his grandparents—were walking on a long-established and normally safe hiking trail. But it happened that a bear had recently killed a moose very near the trail, so without ever wandering from the ordinarily safe path, the hikers came very close to the bear's kill. This is not something a bear will tolerate, and it attacked the innocent hikers. The boy was able to climb a tree and escaped unharmed. His grandparents were both killed.

THE ROUTE CLIMBED TO A HIGH DIVIDE that was notched like a gunsight between bald granite cliffs. Humping a big load up the pass, I was preoccupied with the weight biting into my shoulders and the rocks shifting underfoot, so I didn't see the bear until it was less than 75 yards away. I paused to catch my breath, glanced up, and there he was: a 350-pound grizzly, loping across the talus that spilled down from the notch. Because the wind was at his back, he hadn't yet noticed me; a single path led over the divide, and I was on it.

Since this was happening high in the Brooks Range, well north of the Arctic Circle, there were no trees for me to climb. I didn't have a gun. Running, I knew, might invite attack. Too scared to breathe, I tried to remain calm but felt my mouth go dry.

The bear kept coming. At 30 yards, catching my scent, he stopped abruptly and reared onto his hind legs. His shaggy blond fur rippled in the breeze. The grizzly sniffed the air, stared at me, sniffed some more. And then he dropped to all fours and bolted in the opposite direction, sprinting across a jumble of tank-trap boulders at a speed that defied belief.

The date was July 2, 1974. Two decades later the memory

is still vivid. For a long time after the bear ran off, I sat on a rock and just listened to the pounding of my heart. It was an hour after midnight. Mosquitoes swarmed around my face. Far above the divide, a prow of jagged granite burned orange in the twilight, illuminated by a sun that never set. Ranks of nameless mountains marched into the distance as far as I could see.

Over the preceding weeks I'd become attuned to wolf song and the whistle of golden plovers, walked through a snorting tide of caribou and gorged on fat grayling pulled from crystalline streams. Now I'd stared into the eyes of *Ursus arctos horribilis,* only to discover that the star of my nightmares was even more discombobulated by the encounter than I was. I would see four more grizzlies before the month was out.

I'd climbed and fished in the emptiest reaches of the American West, but Alaska made the wilds of the lower 48 seem insipid and tame, a toothless simulacrum. In the Arctic, for the first time in my life I was surrounded by real wilderness. Even as a callow 20-year-old I understood that such an experience, in the late 20th century, was a rare and wondrous privilege.

Six years later Congress recognized the singularity of the Brooks Range and set aside 8.4 million acres of it as Gates of the Arctic National Park and Preserve. The size of Massachusetts and Connecticut combined, Gates of the Arctic is the second-largest unit in our national park system, yet few Americans have ever heard of it and fewer still have been there. It is visited by some two thousand people a year, compared with the more than nine million who visit Great Smoky Mountains National Park or the nearly four million who go to Yosemite.

This gaping disparity is largely a function of access. Yosemite lies four hours by automobile from San Francisco Bay and the region's six million residents; tourists can gawk at El Capitan and Yosemite Falls without ever stepping out of their cars. Although Gates of the Arctic has scenery that rivals Yosemite's, it's situated in remote northern Alaska. It's impossible to drive through because there are no roads. Within the park boundaries, moreover, there are no ranger stations, no motels, no snack bars, no souvenir shops, no maintained campgrounds, no facilities of any kind, and no footpaths.

The fact that Gates is a hard place to get to, and even

harder to get around in, is its saving grace. Park regulations have been formulated to keep development and visitation to a bare minimum, but not everyone is pleased with this. Critics carp that Gates is an "elitist" park. What's the point of setting aside such an immense tract of land, they ask, if it's effectively off-limits to all but a tiny handful of the public?

The answer, explains John M. Kauffmann, a now retired civil servant who was in charge of planning the park in the 1970s, is that the "northern environment is easy to damage and slow to heal." Some Arctic lichens grow less than a sixteenth of an inch annually. Heavy traffic from all-terrain vehicles (ATVs) is apt to scar the muskeg for decades. "If Gates of the Arctic were to be made as accessible as Yosemite," Kauffmann says, "the very things that make it worth preserving would be destroyed."

In his book *Alaska's Brooks Range,* Kauffmann writes that when pondering how much development should be permitted in Gates, he and the other planners decided that it would be best to do nothing: "Visitors would take the Brooks Range on *its* terms, not theirs. . . . We borrowed a karate term to call it a black-belt park. Not for neophytes, it would be at the ascetic end of a spectrum of national parks . . . with no one park needing to be all things to all people. . . . We remembered Aldo Leopold's comment. . . . 'I am glad I shall never be young without wild country to be young in. Of what avail are forty freedoms without a blank spot on the map?' "

Thanks to aerial cartography and satellite navigation, there are no more blank spots on any map, alas, not even in the Alaskan Arctic. Every year more people troop through Gates. The National Park Service has estimated that by 2010, the annual tally will swell to 18,000 visitors. Some advocates, Kauffmann among them, believe many of the most extraordinary attractions have already been irreparably damaged. Last summer, curious about how one of our last big chunks of raw wilderness was holding up, I returned to the same part of the Brooks Range I had visited two decades earlier.

I embark for the backcountry, like most people who go to Gates, from the metropolis of Bettles (pop. 45), about 25 miles outside the park's boundary. At the time of my first trip there was a single bush pilot in town; now there are two competing air-taxi services employing a half-dozen pilots. Accompanied by Alaskan friends Roman and Peggy Dial, I climb into a 1954 De Havilland Beaver moored on the Koyukuk River. Pilot Jay Jespersen opens the throttle, the airplane's aluminum floats lurch free of the roiling current, and we fly north by northwest under a lowering sky.

Two hours later we bank hard over a small lake. Jay scans for moose or other obstacles, brings the Beaver down, and we wade ashore in a light rain. As the airplane flies off, the roar of its engine quickly fades and is replaced by a monumental silence. I feel a long way from anywhere. In fact we're closer to Siberia than Anchorage. The nearest highway is the haul road for the trans-Alaska oil pipeline, 180 miles to the east.

The lake where we landed is the source of the Alatna, one of the major rivers draining the Brooks Range. For the initial leg of our three-week ramble, we intend to paddle 47 miles downriver, but the mighty Alatna begins as an ankle-deep trickle, so our inflatable rafts remain in our backpacks, and we walk until the river becomes deep enough to float them.

DOING THE TUSSOCK-MOUND HOP

The Alatna flows down a broad, U-shaped valley bounded by rubbly escarpments rising into the clouds. Clumps of caribou—200 here, 75 there—file slowly across the stark terrain. From the air the valley had looked as smooth as a golf course, but it turns out to be the typical swamp of tussock tundra. The valley bottom is covered with millions of spongy, cauliflower-shaped mounds of cotton grass that make for slow, frustrating travel. One must either high-step over each mound, which necessitates walking in the sucking bog from which the cotton grass grows, or stride uncertainly from crown to tippy tussock crown, inviting pratfalls.

To escape the tussocks we search out gravel bars along the river, wading back and forth across the stream to link them. Everywhere the damp sand is imprinted with the tracks of cari-

bou, moose, wolf—and bear. Comparing my size 9 boot to a
fresh grizzly print, I estimate the bruin would wear size 20
Nikes.

The Dials, especially Peggy, share my "bearanoia," as she
calls it. In 1986 Roman walked, skied, and paddled a thousand
miles from one end of the Brooks Range to the other, and
Peggy, pregnant with their first child, accompanied him for a
month of the journey. Near the headwaters of the Nahtuk River,
a tributary of the Alatna, they surprised a grizzly sow foraging
among the blueberry bushes. Unlike the bear I'd met, which
ran away, this one bluff-charged them repeatedly.

"Bears have poor eyesight, so they'll bluff-charge in order
to see how you react," says the peripatetic Roman, a professor
of biology at Alaska Pacific University. "If you act like prey and
run, they'll assume that's what you are." Somehow maintaining
their composure, Peggy and Roman edged away from the grizzly's turf, and after charging four times she left them alone.

On this trip I'm carrying a weapon to defend against bear
attack, the first time I've ever done so: an aerosol can of pepper
spray of the sort urbanites use to ward off muggers. Back in
Bettles, I had shown my pepper spray to a bush pilot named
Barry Yoseph. "Yeah," he said as soon as he stopped laughing,
"I reckon them bears will be mighty pleased to see you carrying
that stuff. Should add a little spice to their supper."

LETTING THE RIVER SHOW THE WAY

After we've covered several miles on foot, the Alatna becomes marginally deep enough to float our tiny rafts. We have
only two inflatable boats for the three of us, so Roman and
Peggy share one, and I take most of the gear in the other. It's a
pleasure to let the river do the work, but shortly after casting
off, the Dials rip a hole in the bottom of their overloaded craft,
forcing us to stop and make camp on a gravel bar where we can
dry the boat over a willow fire and patch the leak.

By morning the rain clouds are gone. It's early August, but
the air already has a sharp autumnal bite. Lazing around camp
until noon, we sip coffee in the muted sunlight and watch the
underwater antics of small, wrenlike birds called dippers. When

we get under way, feeder creeks rapidly bolster the Alatna's volume, transforming it into a flume of whitewater that carries us south at three times our walking speed.

Within an hour of breaking camp we reach the vanguard of the northern tree line, a single puny spruce resembling an overgrown pipe cleaner, and soon thereafter scrubby northern forest known as taiga (from a Russian term meaning "land of little sticks") crowds the shore. The Arctic sun scribes a low arc, never climbing much higher than the horizon, casting the denuded bluffs above the valley in a spectral glow. At day's end, we have drifted more than 40 miles.

Twenty years earlier, six friends and I spent 32 days in the Brooks Range without seeing another soul. In the morning I am thus taken aback to see a group of ten people camped across the river. Before the day is out, moreover, a yellow Cessna disgorges two additional planeloads of wilderness seekers onto a nearby lake.

The Alatna, like most big rivers in the Brooks Range, flows fast but has no terrifying rapids. If the absence of trails makes hiking through this country a labor-intensive grind, traveling by water is downright cushy. This is why the great majority of visitors flock to the half-dozen navigable rivers — and why, in a park with so much acreage and so few humans, those visitors are often dismayed to encounter other people.

I'm disappointed too, although I shouldn't be surprised. Before we'd left Bettles, Chief Ranger Glenn Sherrill warned, "You can hike through 99 percent of Gates and you won't see anyone. Park use is heavily concentrated along the Alatna, the Noatak, the John, and the North Fork of the Koyukuk. The only other place you're likely to run into a crowd is in the Arrigetch."

The Arrigetch Peaks, a cluster of sheer granite spires west of the Alatna Valley, form one of the loveliest places in Gates of the Arctic, if not the world. Although the "crowd" to which Sherrill referred numbers no more than 150 people annually in the entire 150-square-mile Arrigetch massif, it's a problem because in the High Arctic that many people, no matter how careful, are bound to leave an indelible mark. Not very many years ago the trudge up Arrigetch Creek demanded attentive route-finding and nasty bushwhacking through all-but-impenetrable alder thickets. Now the march of boots has trampled a muddy thoroughfare up most of the lower valley. At popular campsites, the tundra has been worn down to bare earth. Bears in the area have grown habituated to human rubbish, prompting rangers to place steel barrels at the busiest camps so that the bruins won't pilfer backpackers' garbage or food.

As Peggy, Roman, and I hike up the creek from its confluence with the Alatna, though, we encounter nobody. Halfway up the valley the makeshift trail we've been following peters out, and we see no further sign of human passage whatsoever.

The higher we ascend, the more the country resembles the phantasmal scenery of an epic Tolkien novel. Our route takes us across soft carpets of reindeer lichen, and beneath sinister black cliffs and hanging glaciers. The creek, opaque with glacial sediment, is never far away. Most of the time the stream is a thundering cascade, frothing from drop to drop over gargantuan blocks of stone; at other places it slows and spreads into placid cerulean pools in which reflections of the surrounding alps shimmer like hallucinations.

EXHILARATION ON AN AIRY SUMMIT

At the head of the creek we find ourselves in a natural cul-de-sac, nearly encircled by soaring walls. We continue the only way possible: by going up and over the top. It's a rigorous climb of 4,000 vertical feet that culminates on an airy summit as slender as a thorn. The whole expanse of the Arrigetch is visible from this vantage, a dazzling chaos of mile-high granite pickets. As we descend to the west, into a virginal cirque cradling a half-frozen lake, I'm reminded that it's the astonishing wildness of this place, even more than its splendor, that's responsible for the intense tingling in my chest.

A mere two-day walk (albeit a strenuous one) from the relative hubbub along the Alatna has transported us into a landscape as primeval as that which moved Bob Marshall so powerfully six decades ago. Describing the country east of the Alatna, the celebrated conservationist wrote, "Nothing I had ever seen, Yosemite or the Grand Canyon or Mount McKinley rising from the Susitna, had given me such a sense of immensity.... No sight or sound or smell or feeling even remotely hinted of men or their creations. It seemed as if time had dropped away a million years and we were back in a primordial world."

Marshall wasn't the first Caucasian to penetrate the Brooks Range. An earlier explorer, Navy Lt. George M. Stoney, noted the "rugged, weather-scarred peaks, lofty minarets [and] cathedral spires" of the Arrigetch while exploring the Alatna as early as 1886, but Marshall was the Arctic's most ardent champion. He is responsible for the name "Gates of the Arctic," which he bestowed upon a pair of stately mountains bracketing the North Fork of the Koyukuk. Park planner John Kauffmann observed that Marshall's appellation has "captured the imagination of all who have heard it. It did much to bring about national park status for the area."

For millennia before Marshall or Stoney ever set foot in Alaska, of course, Athapaskan (Indian) and Nunamiut (inland Eskimo) hunter-gatherers lived and traveled throughout the Brooks Range. According to an oral history passed down over the centuries, the Nunamiut people were created by a giant deity named Aiyagomahala. After giving them life, he taught the Nunamiut to live off the land and showed them how to survive the brutal cold and long nights of the Arctic winter.

So that he and his teachings would be remembered, Aiyagomahala set one of his Brobdingnagian gloves down beside the Alatna River and transformed it into the most spectacular cordillera in the Brooks Range—the peaks I now see rising around me. The Nunamiut christened them the "Arrigich," which means "fingers of the hand extended."

Prior to 1890, bands of Nunamiut roamed across much of what is now the park. Contact with white explorers and whalers at the turn of the century, however, introduced epidemics of measles and influenza for which the Native people had no immunity. During this same period the herds of caribou that provided the people with most of their food, clothing, and shelter went into cyclical decline. Ravaged by famine and disease, the Nunamiut migrated from the mountains, their traditional homeland, to settlements on the Arctic coast. Even before Marshall's first trip to the Arctic, in 1929, they had all but vanished from the central Brooks Range.

Today the Nunamiut are back in Gates of the Arctic. Most of those who live within the park reside in the village of Anaktuvuk Pass, a settlement of plywood or prefab houses huddled on a broad, windswept divide near the source of the John River. There are only a few flush toilets in this community of 250 (the permafrost makes plumbing problematic), but there is electricity, cable television, a handful of telephones, a fancy new school—and an astonishing number of cars, given that there is nowhere to drive beyond the few blocks of gravel streets that constitute downtown Anaktuvuk.

Village existence is an incongruous blend of the timeless and the modern. A wage-based economy has supplanted the subsistence life of old to a great degree, but hunting and trapping remain an extremely important component of Nunamiut culture. On occasion this has led to conflict with the Park Service mandates.

LEARNING TO LIVE AND LET LIVE

The Nunamiut have forced the agency to rethink some of its fundamental policies. Initially, Kauffmann explains, some officials were inclined to regard Gates as they regarded parks in the lower 48, "where the rules were clear and long established, hunting, even for subsistence, was out of the question, and Native people were usually artifacts of the past rather than a living part of the ecosystem." In Gates, however, park administrators are making concessions to Alaskan politics, Native traditions, and idiosyncrasies of the northern lifestyle. Ultimately, the Alaska National Interest Lands Conservation Act of 1980 (ANILCA) decreed that subsistence hunting and trapping by local residents, Natives and non-Natives alike, would be permitted in the park.

For some time, officials tolerated subsistence hunters' driving their ATVs in parklands adjacent to Anaktuvuk. As a result, miles of ruts made by eight-wheeled, amphibious machines known as Argos crisscross the Nunamiut private lands, and scars extend into valleys across the northeastern quadrant of Gates.

The final details of a controversial compromise were hammered out between the Nunamiut and the Park Service last summer. The agreement rearranges park wilderness boundaries, allowing ATVs into 158,000 acres of ancestral hunting grounds now within Gates, but it prohibits mechanized access even for subsistence beyond these mutually recognized areas.

In any case, ATV tracks are nowhere in evidence on the back side of the Arrigetch massif, where Peggy, Roman, and I are camped in the rain at the foot of a mountain that looks like an Arctic version of Yosemite's Half Dome. The terrain here, like most of the higher reaches of the Brooks Range, is much too rugged for Argos, and few hikers wander this far from the rivers. The only tracks we've seen belong to caribou, Dall sheep, and bears.

"For dinner tonight, how about potato flakes and macaroni?" Roman asks as raindrops drum on the tent fly. "They taste great together."

"That's what you said about the tuna and spaghetti," Peggy says. We settle on freeze-dried chili instead.

In the morning, Peggy finds a week-old grizzly kill just beyond camp—the half-eaten carcass of a young caribou. Wondering when the bear will return to eat the rest of it, we try to take our minds off the subject by investigating the glassy chunks of quartz that lie scattered across the tundra like pieces of petrified ice.

Striking camp and moving on, we struggle up a steep pass as a storm builds to a howling gale. Sleet sprays the cliffs that cap the divide, making the rock too slippery to attempt without climbing gear. Pulling coils of rope from our packs, we spend the next three hours negotiating a 500-foot precipice, while icy water fills our boots and dribbles down our upstretched arms.

Shivering uncontrollably and soaked to the skin, on the far side of the pass we escape the wind but remain in dense fog that restricts visibility to a few dozen yards. Navigating by compass and altimeter, we pick our way through a dreamscape of lush heaths and tortured stone. Waterfalls tumble over sprawl-ing, glacier-polished slabs streaked with orange lichens. Mas-sive boulders appear out of the mist, jutting from meadows of heather, moss, and tufted *Dryas*.

My feet hurt. My pack feels like it weighs 200 pounds. I'm bone-tired, dripping wet, and want very badly to crawl into my sleeping bag. In 48 hours, however, an airplane is scheduled to meet us at a distant lake; if we are to arrive on time, we have to keep moving. There is still one more high pass to climb be-fore we can rest.

People who have never ventured into the "back of beyond" might wonder why anyone would want to. As I trudge forward, the answer is everywhere I look. The Brooks Range is such a seductive place to visit, not in spite of the hardships but be-cause of them. The fact that admission to this Eden requires a toll paid in sweat, pain, and fear makes its beauty all the more intoxicating.

It's after midnight when we reach the base of the next pass. The slope is steep and the footing loose, but as we push stub-bornly upward the fog lifts, unveiling a panorama of ripsaw mountains in the fading light. Scraps of cloud wrap the sum-mits like gauze. The ghostly blue tongue of a glacier hangs from a nearby ridge. By and by we stand atop the pass, a shank of wind-scoured rock marking the Arctic Divide. Snowmelt bur-bling from the cliffs at my back is bound for the Arctic Ocean; ahead, in the valley at my feet, we will camp tonight beside a creek that flows into the Pacific.

I'll be happy as hell to finally make camp. I look forward to a long, sybaritic soak, come tomorrow afternoon, in the hot spring that lies a half-day's walk down the valley. But the thought of leaving already saddens me. I'm not ready for the trip to be over.

As Bob Marshall wrote at the conclusion of an extended Brooks Range sojourn, "In a day I should be in Fairbanks, . . . in a week in Seattle and the great, thumping, modern world. I should be living once more among the accumulated accom-plishments of man. The world with its present population needs these accomplishments. It cannot live on wilderness, except incidentally and sporadically. Nevertheless, to four human beings, just back from the source streams of the Koyukuk, no comfort, no security, no invention, no brilliant thought which the modern world had to offer could provide half the elation of the days spent in the little-explored, uninhabited world of the arctic wilderness."

JAMES RAMSEY

Winter alone in the Brooks Range

"THE GRIZZLY TOOK A STEP TOWARD THE WINDOW AND ALMOST
CASUALLY, IT SEEMED, SMASHED THE WINDOW WITH ONE BRIEF
SWIPE OF HIS RIGHT FRONT PAW. THEN . . . HE PUT BOTH PAWS
ON THE SILL AND WITH PIECES OF BROKEN GLASS STILL
CLATTERING TO THE FLOOR, STUCK HIS ENORMOUS HEAD
THROUGH THE SHATTERED WINDOW."

*In the summers, James Ramsey is a guide in Denali National
Park. During the rest of the year, he looks for something different and has made extended winter stays in the Sonora Desert,
the Himalayas, and the South Pacific. He spent the winter of
1983 in the Schwatka Mountains in the Brooks Range of northwest Alaska. The mountains are named for the nineteenth-
century explorer Frederick Schwatka, who appears himself
elsewhere in this book.*

*"Northwest Alaska is wild and desolate," Ramsey writes in
his 1989 book,* Winter Watch. *"There are no roads, and very
few people. South of the Schwatkas are a few scattered Eskimo
villages, usually at the mouths of rivers that break free from the
mountains, flow across the flat Arctic tundra, and end their brief
but spectacular lives where they join the Kobuk River. Deep in
the mountains, near the rivers, are a few log cabins and sod igloos built more than a decade ago when the land was opened by
the State to anyone who had the courage and tenacity to go up
there and prove out a five-acre parcel of land."*

Ramsey spent 266 days, from September 15 to June 6, in one of these cabins, "forty miles from the nearest Eskimo village, and a lot farther than that, by any measurement, from the chaos and confusion of modern urban life."

But not very far at all, as it turned out, from the bears.

Two especially interesting and illuminating features of his book are his list of tools and supplies—I myself would have needed a lot more hot salsa and coffee—and the list of ninety-eight books he read in the cabin.

Day 37, October 21   (Low −15, High 0, sunny)

NOTHING. TODAY I DID NOTHING. I SAW nothing, felt nothing. I hardly left the cabin. I need a project. I have a project. It's personified by that little black case sitting over in the corner. It contains a machine for writing. I'm avoiding it. The winter I spent at Carlo Creek in the Alaska Range, I stared at that little black case until mid-January, when I finally opened it and began rewriting the Nepal story, *Getting High in the Himalayas.* This year I *will* begin writing *something* by November first, or consign the damn machine to the river and quit playing these mind games.

Errant thought with regard to typewriters and a few other items such as Ping-Pong paddles. I must be an audiophile, because I can't type with anything but a manual typewriter. (The only thing possible here.) But in more civilized climes, electric typewriters, not to mention word processors, just don't sound right to me, and for the life of me I can't use 'em. Same for Ping-Pong paddles. I'm a pretty good journeyman player with sandpaper-covered paddles, but can't do diddly with those effete soft rubber paddles. They just don't *sound* right.

Last night I toyed with the idea of making a major commitment to join the battle of saving the wolf. I don't at this point know what I could or would do, but it seems like a project I could sink my teeth into, no pun intended. Maybe a book. I'll let the idea simmer.

Day 38, October 22   (Low −15, High 0, sunny)

I'm not certain I can describe accurately what happened earlier today, but I will try. It is now about four hours after the incident.

In midafternoon, since it was sunny and windless I decided to go out to the tree I had found earlier and do a little sawing. The temperature was right at zero. I did not take my rifle. This was the same tree I had been sawing on previously during the red fox encounter. It's located about a half-mile north of the cabin. I had been there only a few minutes, clearing snow away from the tree, and was looking down at the place where I intended to start my cut, when something at the farthest extent of my peripheral vision attracted my attention. It's a little difficult to describe. I was looking down near my feet but what I saw was movement several hundred yards upstream and across the river. (This is something I have apparently learned since becoming a wilderness tour guide—"seeing" the big picture while focusing on a much more narrow field of view.) Once I looked in that direction I knew, without even a shade of doubt, and without thinking, it was a grizzly. It was still a long way off, and on the other side of an ice-choked, fast-flowing river, but it was coming in my direction. I didn't hesitate. I left the bucksaw and shovel right where they were, picked up the Hudson's Bay ax and sled, and began walking toward the cabin. The bear neither saw nor smelled me, but it kept on coming.

As I walked, I periodically checked the bear's progress. Each time I looked he was still four or five hundred yards away, still on the other side of the river, and still unaware of my presence. When I reached the trees near my cabin—I had been on an open river bar, as was the bear—I ran to the cabin, grabbed my .30-30 rifle, and ran back out to the viewpoint in front of the cabin.

The bear was still approaching, much nearer now. As he drew closer he began pausing and sniffing the air. I don't think he could smell me, but probably could smell the smoke from the fire in the cabin. I was hoping the bear, like the red fox, would continue down *his* side of the river, and that would be that: My first grizzly sighting in the Arctic. That wasn't to be.

When the bear was still about one hundred yards upstream he turned and headed purposefully for the river. I have watched too many grizzlies at Denali National Park not to know the bear was about to come over to my side of the river. In retrospect I think I should have fired a warning shot then. The noise of the rifle plus whatever small difficulty the icy river represented might have dissuaded him, but I didn't. The bear walked out on the icy shelf, hesitated a moment, then plunged into the torrent of ice and water.

He was across in seconds. Water and ice flew in all directions as he shook himself, and at that moment I put a bullet into the snow a few feet in front of him. The sound was tremendous, echoing off the water and back from the trees and nearby hills. The grizzly raised up as if to stand on his hind legs, went back down on all fours, moved his head from side to side, and began walking—not directly toward me and the cabin, because he was faced with an abrupt little cliff in that direction. He was heading toward the low spot I had used moments ago in coming back from the tree. I put two more bullets in front of him, and then showed myself for the first time, yelling and waving, knowing that the normal reaction of most grizzlies to human encounters is to avoid them. Not this one. He stopped momentarily after each shot, looked in my direction when I yelled, but kept coming. At that point he was about seventy-five yards upstream and about thirty feet below me.

Things now became rather surrealistic. (This has happened to me before, most notably when I made my first parachute jump. There were two of me, the person performing the action and a second person, a sort of disassociated spectator.) I had a strong feeling of inevitability. I *knew* the bear was heading for my cabin even though I had now lost sight of him; he was hidden by a jutting little promontory and the spruce trees surrounding the cabin. I can't say why—he could have followed the trail to Mike's cabin, or turned and gone upriver—but I was certain he was heading my way. I sprinted for the cabin, only fifty feet away.

I ran into the storm porch, closed and bolted the door, and wedged a good-sized spruce pole against the middle of the door. The latter was something I had learned in New York City, of all places. (The only way a door like that can be opened is to knock it off its hinges or shatter it, which I later decided a grizzly could probably do quite easily.) I did the same thing to the inner door. I was sure I didn't have much time, so I replaced the three shells I had fired, and looked around for something to make noise with. I grabbed a large metal pot and a hatchet, hoping I could scare the bear away with noise. Then I waited.

This all took place in only a minute or two, when suddenly the front window was completely filled with the image of a huge grizzly bear. There were no windows facing north, the direction from which the bear was coming, so its appearance was both instantaneous and appalling. This is a small cabin, partially sunk in the ground, and the windows are not very high above ground level. By piling snow on the lower walls I had in effect put the windows at ground level. Now, an adult grizzly bear and I were face to face, about five feet apart, separated by a few thin panes of glass.

I began banging the hatchet against the pot. From inside the cabin the noise was horrendous but, I later decided, probably not outside. The grizzly took a step toward the window and almost casually, it seemed, smashed the window with one brief swipe of his right front paw. Then, in retrospect it was in slow motion, he put both paws on the sill and with pieces of broken glass still clattering to the floor, stuck his enormous head through the shattered window. I had already dropped the hatchet and pot. I picked up my rifle, which was loaded and cocked, aimed between the eyes, which was no big deal since the end of the rifle barrel was a scant two feet from his head, and fired.

The bear was knocked back out of the window by the bullet's impact. He fell on his side and without the slightest twitch or spasm was still. Blood began flowing from his nostrils and mouth. I stuck the barrel of the rifle out the broken window and fired another shot behind the ear.

Then I leaned the rifle against the bed and began talking to the grizzly. I do not have particularly outstanding reflexes, either mental or physical. I was well aware of that when I came up here, so I had to decide in advance what I would do if I encountered a bear. What I decided was to avoid any encounter away from the cabin if at all possible. This mostly just requires a little common sense and alertness. But, what about *at* the cabin? I had decided that a bear prowling in the vicinity of the cabin had, of course, to be watched carefully, but that only if it attempted to break in would it have to be shot.

For the first few minutes after the killing the one overpowering thought in my mind was not about fixing the window, even though in the subzero temperature the cabin was already getting cold. Nor was it the removal of the carcass. It was somehow to communicate to the bear, and receive some sort of exculpation from the bear. I suppose I was more than a little hysterical at that point, but to the other observer, the other me, it seemed perfectly natural to explain this to the grizzly.

I do not now feel proud about its death. There is no sense of macho accomplishment. I eventually went outside and bled it, and moved it a little way from the door. It was too heavy to move far, and I could not dismember it so soon. Maybe tomorrow, if the wolves, or another bear—God forbid—don't get it tonight. Another bear would sit on and eat it for several days, and I would probably be forced to kill it too, just so I could get outside to get wood and water.

Day 39, October 23   (Low −5, High 5, cloudy)

I have re-read what I wrote last night, and it does seem a little hysterical, but it conveys in a general way how I was feeling. In self-defense I should mention that post-hysteria is better than pre-; the latter can get you into trouble.

I slept little last night. I kept getting up and shining a flashlight on the bear, hoping, I guess, that it would somehow just vanish. I had cut its throat about a half-hour after I'd shot it. Before I had done that I had repaired the window with clear plastic, which in retrospect seems like an odd choice of priorities.

I think it will be some time before I can confront exactly what this incident means. I do have the feeling that this was in some way predestined, and that in this encounter I in some way failed my responsibility. What would have happened if I had not fired that final shot when I did? It was the purposefulness displayed by the bear from the very beginning, how he reacted to my warning shots on the riverbed and, ultimately, how he responded to my pounding on the kettle that contributed to the feeling of inevitability I referred to earlier.

On the other hand, the grizzly was not acting in what would normally be considered an aggressive manner. He was not growling; no false charges; in fact, no aggressive displays at all, except for his determination to check out the cabin.

The bear did break the window, but almost casually as I have noted. This cabin is quite soundproof, and what sounded to me like an Arctic version of Times Square at midnight on New Year's Eve may have been loud enough outside only to arouse the bear's curiosity. I will never know, and not knowing, will always wonder whether the bear was preparing to charge or retreat at the moment I fired.

There is some small evidence for the latter. It now appears that although I aimed between the eyes, the bullet apparently entered through the mouth or throat and probably lodged in the brain. The bear is more likely to have raised his head if he intended to back out, but I suppose that is debatable. What is not arguable is that if the grizzly was going to charge into the cabin and I had not fired, I would not be writing this. (Today I strung two quarter-inch steel cables across the window in question, which won't stop a bear, but will slow him down.)

A question I do not like to ask is, what if I had not gone to get wood and had not seen the bear when he was still a long way off? I could have been bathing, washing dishes, etcetera, and the rifle could have been hanging in its usual place on the wall near the bed. Or, what if I had been out at the woodpile when the bear showed up, cut off from the cabin and my rifle?

I spent most of the daylight hours today skinning and butchering the bear. I didn't do a very good job, but I did get it finished. I stored the pelt, head, fore and hind legs up in the food cache. I rolled the remainder, still very heavy, onto a sled and dragged it several hundred feet away from the cabin. After wrapping it in two large plastic garbage bags and pouring water on it in an attempt to seal it in ice, I covered it with a large mound of snow, and then covered that with small logs and tree branches. With a little more snow and continued cold it should be safe from other animals. I have no desire for the meat, but Mike may be able to use it for feeding his sled dogs. If not, at least it's no longer right in front of the cabin door.

Day 40, October 24   (Low −15, High 0, some sun)

Delayed reaction to the bear incident. It has really colored my feeling about this place. If it wasn't a forty-five-mile hike out, I would probably have left today, the way I was feeling. Maybe it will go away.

Also, having had a chance to think a little more clearly about this whole incident, and the grizzly itself, I've come to the conclusion that there is really no logical reason for a bear to be out roaming around this late in the season. It's been very cold for some time, and the snow covers any vegetation the bear might normally eat, although it may have had a chance for a late kill of moose or caribou. Still, I think it is just too late in the year, especially here in the Arctic, for bears to be out of their dens. Maybe the bear failed to get the proper signals telling it when to prepare its den; maybe the den collapsed; maybe the bear was diseased. Something was out of whack.

Day 41, October 25   (Low −15, High −2, sunny)

Less than eight hours a day of sunlight beginning tomorrow and counting down.

As with the pilot who crashes a plane and lives, it's important to fly again soon or it may not happen at all. That is sort of what I had to do today. I had to bite the metaphorical bullet and return to the wood tree from where I had first seen the bear. I had avoided this trip two days ago with the rationalization that I had to skin and butcher the remains. Yesterday I had no such excuse, but I didn't go even though I had planned to. Why? Well, because I had this terrible advance feeling of *déjà vu*—that I would spot another bear, try unsuccessfully to frighten it off, and end up killing yet another grizzly.

I felt so strongly that this would happen that I very nearly did not go again today. But even worse was this feeling of paralysis I've been going through. Psychologically, this cabin and this area are no longer my turf. I couldn't enjoy it without peering behind each tree, and looking over my shoulder as I moved around, even inside the cabin with the door bolted.

So I said to hell with it, grabbed my rifle and sled, and went out to get some wood. Nothing happened, needless to say, but I spent far more time looking around than I did sawing— no doubt a wise precaution, but I felt it to be a negative personal reaction. It boils down to this: If I must go around trailing trepidation as I have the past couple of days, this true wilderness experience is being corrupted, either by me or by circumstance. The results are the same. If this feeling continues I have two choices, it seems to me. I must leave or I must put the gun away and deal with the grizzly on some other level. I don't want to die, but I don't want to kill another bear, either. Which probably means, if this were a rational world, I will leave. We'll see.

Day 42, October 26   (Low −15, High −2, partly cloudy)

I broke into my two-week (estimated) wood reserve today, which means the river had better freeze over soon or I'm going to begin ranging far afield for fuel. There is still about one day's wood at the site where I have been cutting most recently, but that's it for the known wood supply. (I'm referring, of course, only to dead and down, or standing, dead spruce trees.) The river could freeze any day, but I think it would take forty below or more for a couple of days to do it. The channels have narrowed by more than half as the edges freeze and the volume of water decreases.

Two apparently military jets flew over very high today, coincidentally while I was listening on the shortwave radio to news of the Lebanon massacre and the U.S. invasion of Grenada. We are very close to the USSR here, and since these are the first military planes I have seen, I suspect there is a connection.

Speaking of connections, at the top of this page in the original journal is the word "retribalizing." I obviously put it there to remind myself of something I wanted to write about. I wish to hell I knew what it was!

Day 43, October 27   (Low −10, High 0, cloudy)

Baked my first Arctic apple pie today using freeze-dried apples. I haven't sampled it yet, but it looks pretty good. It took twice as long as normal to bake it, but that was because of wet wood. A curious phenomenon: With temperatures below zero for the past two weeks or so, all the wood I have stockpiled appears to be bone-dry when I split it and it splits just like cedar. But as soon as it gets inside the cabin, it's wet. Either there is moisture there to begin with, but being frozen it *feels* dry, or the wood attracts moisture from the cabin just as a magnet does metal filings. In any case, it's been difficult keeping a good, hot fire going lately.

I haven't had any headaches for quite awhile, which tells me that ventilating the cabin was the correct solution to that problem.

There is a can of foul-smelling kerosene out back. Mike said it was jet fuel left behind by a now-defunct mining outfit which had a chopper. The kerosene was "rescued" some time ago for what was then an unknown future use. A use, I now believe, whose time has come. The odor is very strong; so strong, in fact, that if used in a kerosene lantern, which I tried, it will run you right out of the cabin. So I poured a little of it along each outside windowsill and around the snow-covered bear carcass, in case another bear shows up. I figured it wouldn't smell too appetizing, and might even cover up other smells that would. I know a bear has an incredible sense of smell, but I don't know how discriminatory it is. This is a test of sorts.

Day 44, October 28   (Low −5, High 10, cloudy)

The temperature went up to ten above today and it actually felt warm!

I was downriver about half a mile cutting wood when I suddenly saw what I took at first to be a dozen or so caribou running in a line. It turned out to be a team of fourteen sled dogs with Mike riding on the rear of the sled. Mike had come up to get a bigger sled so he could ferry some cargo from the village to his cabin. He wants me to return with him to his fish camp for a Halloween celebration at the Igloo. I'll probably go—especially after he showed me where there was a good supply of dry wood downriver about a mile. It sounds like an easy decision, but the thought of being around a half-dozen people all of a sudden after the past month and a half is somewhat disquieting.

Day 45, October 29   (*Low* −5, *High* 10, *partly cloudy*)

I got some wood today and baked cookies to take downriver tomorrow for the Halloween party. Participants will be Doug, Christy, Susan, Mike and me, and, the reason for the party, Doug and Christy's daughter, Anna.

The river "bridged" over with ice yesterday in two places near the cabin, but I don't think it will be safe to cross for a few days yet. It began overflowing yesterday, and the river bars where I have been cutting wood for the past several weeks will soon be covered with ice. Overflow is a curious phenomenon, neither ice nor water, but something in between, a viscous, partly frozen mush that seeks its own level and spreads out, eventually covering the river from bank to bank. Mike says this has already happened throughout the lower segment of the river up to within two miles of here. We'll be taking the dogs (or rather, they will be taking us) down an inside trail tomorrow for the first six miles and then follow the river for the next nine miles.

With regard to the bear, Mike was suitably impressed as evidenced by his carrying his rifle between his cabin and mine, something he does not ordinarily do this time of the year. Mike said he would have shot to kill at the time I was firing warning shots. I do not know whether this makes me feel good or just stupid.

Day 46, October 30   (*Low* 5, *High* 10, *light snow*)

South in the taiga (spruce forest) by dog power. I am always amazed how these relatively small animals can work so long and hard, and so together. The word "dog team" is no misnomer. The trip down was beautiful, the first six miles through snow-covered spruce along a winding trail Mike had pioneered, cutting a right-of-way where the trees were too thick to penetrate. And then nine miles on some of the strangest river terrain I have ever seen. Big blocks of ice of startling blue, upthrust in odd conjunctions by the force of the river, hidden now below the layer of ice. The river was frozen over but still active with overflow, which we had to skirt. Small, statuelike projections called niggerheads (surely they will never be called black heads) also had to be avoided. Frozen slush covered with snow, softening the sharp angles, visually, but not in fact; dangerous to dogs because it can cut their paws, and dangerous to us because the uneven surface can flip over a sled. It happened to us, but only once. Unlike the Nenana River, which along the stretch where I had spent another winter simply froze over with some odd contours where summer rapids lurk, this one becomes an obstacle course to be negotiated with care.

We reached Doug and Christy's in midafternoon. They live in a sod igloo. (Build a frame and roof with wood; stack sod outside about a foot thick, and frame in windows and door; usually built into the side of a hill, as is Doug and Christy's. "Igloo" is the Eskimo word for "house," including the one made from snow we all grew up learning about, but also including a variety of other structures.)

We picked up Annathea, six-year-old daughter of Doug and Christy, and took her with us to Mike's fish camp where the three of us spent the night. We all slept in sleeping bags on caribou hides in Mike's wall tent. Wall tents are strange. As long as a fire is going in the stove it is warm and very comfortable, even with temperatures of twenty or thirty below, but once the fire is allowed to die there is nothing to retain the heat, and the temperature very quickly matches that of outside—in this case, about twenty below zero. The dogs slept outside, chained to stakes, curled up in the snow, occasionally providing us with an Arctic lullaby.

Day 47, October 31   (Low −15, High 0, cloudy)

All Hallows Eve, less popularly known as James Ramsey's natal eve. Halloween in the Arctic! You will tip no outdoor toilets here. Slit trenches are apparently *de rigueur*. (At Mike's fish camp, we use half of a fifty-gallon drum and then burn it.)

We had dinner at Doug and Christy's—boo burgers, popcorn, pumpkin pie topped with Arctic ice cream (milk, oil, vanilla, and snow and add whatever flavor you want). Good oh! We topped off the evening by taking turns reading aloud stories by Edgar Allan Poe. The celebrants were Doug, Christy, Anna, Susan, Mike, and me. Anna had made me a birthday present, a little hand-crocheted chain made from red yarn.

I spent much of last night helping Anna with her first-grade correspondence studies. She is very bright, and because she is being tutored at home by her parents, is probably a couple of years ahead of her urban peers. Mike and I slept on the floor of their new sod igloo, not yet completed. Plenty of caribou hides, but still cold. The night was clear and starry.

ANNE MORROW LINDBERGH

Barrow, 1931

"WE SAT DOWN TO A REAL THANKSGIVING DINNER. PROVISIONS
WERE SHORT BUT THEY HAD ALL POOLED THEIR SUPPLIES FOR A
FEAST."

The Lindberghs were not the first to fly these northern skies. The
U.S. Navy had begun aerial mapping of Alaska in 1926. In May
of that year, a transpolar flight from Spitzbergen, Norway, to
Nome, Alaska, was directed by Norwegian explorer Roald
Amundsen, American sportsman Lincoln Ellsworth, and Italian
airship designer Umberto Nobile. They made it, but storms in
the region of Point Barrow seriously delayed them. In April
1928, an American crew went in the opposite direction, leaving
Point Barrow and heading up and over the pole to Spitzbergen.
Their greatest difficulty was getting off the rough surface of the
ice at Point Barrow; each of the first two attempts shattered the
plane's metal skis.

 In the month or so just before the Lindberghs' trip, American aviation pioneer Wiley Post was flying around Alaska, but
he did not go as far as the northern coast. When he did venture
this far north, on August 15, 1935, and with humorist Will
Rogers as his passenger, the plane crashed fifteen miles from
Barrow, killing them both.

After a search, two Eskimos located the wreckage and the bodies. When invited by the authorities to name the reward they'd like, the Eskimos asked for bicycles.

Barrow, the northernmost point of Alaska, is three hundred miles north of the Arctic Circle. Today it has a population of about 3,000, most of them Inupiat Eskimo, making this the largest Inupiat community in the world. In 1988, people everywhere heard of Barrow when three gray whales became trapped, barred from the open waters of the Arctic Ocean by the ice cover, and their predicament was broadcast worldwide on television. It took two weeks and a million dollars to set them free.

In 1930, Barrow had a population of 330 people and boasted two stores, an Eskimo school, a Presbyterian mission church, and a hospital. Point Barrow is an Eskimo village twelve miles to the north of Barrow; in 1930 its population was 82. Anne Morrow Lindbergh has apparently confused Barrow with Point Barrow, using the names interchangeably. She is actually describing Barrow.

It was August, not Thanksgiving time, when the Lindberghs arrived in Barrow, but the local people, informed by radio of their flight plan, seized the opportunity to give a warm welcome to their heroic guests.

✳ "DIT-DARR-DARR, DARR-DIT-DIT-DARR, darr-dit-dit-dit." "WXB - - - WXB - - - WXB - - - de (from) - - - KHCAL." The blurred buzz of my own radio-sending rang in my ears. Through the cockpit cover I could see fog on the water ahead, motionless piles of light gray cotton wool with dark gray patches here and there. Out to sea the white wall of fog stood impassable and still as the ice packs from which it rose. Inland under floating islands of fog stretched the barren Arctic land. We were turning toward it as our only chance of reaching Point Barrow, the bleak northern tip of Alaska. Could we get through that night? If the weather ahead was not worse. I must get my message to the Barrow operator.

"WXB - - - WXB - - - WXB," I called to him.

"Dit-darr-dit!" A sharp clean note came through my

receiver. There he was! Right on the watch, though I had called him off schedule. Then there really was a man waiting for us, I thought with relief. There really was a Point Barrow. We weren't jumping off into space. Somewhere ahead in that white wilderness a man was listening for us, guiding us in.

Now, my message: "Flying - - - thru - - - fog - - - and - - - rain - - - going - - - inland - - - wea (weather) - - - pse (please)?"

His notes came back clearly. I wrote rapidly not to miss a word, "Low - - - fog - - - bank - - - rolling - - - off - - - ice - - - now - - - clear - - - over - - - fog - - - expected - - - soon - - - pass - - - ground - - - vis (visibility) - - - one - - - mile." I poked the pad forward to my husband in the front cockpit. He glanced at it and nodded. That meant "OK. That's what I wanted to know. We'll push on."

On for hours through the unreal shifting world of soft mist. Here a cloud and there a drizzle; here a wall and there, fast melting, a hole through which gleamed the hard metallic scales of the sea. That was no mirage. That rippling steel below us was real. If one flew into it blindly it might as well be steel. At times we seemed to be riding on its scaly back and then, with a roar, up we climbed into white blankness. No sight of land; no sight of sea or sky; only our instruments to show the position of the plane. Circling down again, my husband motioned me to reel in the antenna. We were flying too near the water. The ball-weight on the end might be snapped off. Perhaps we might even be forced to land unexpectedly on open sea and have both weight and wire torn off at the impact. His gesture was a danger signal for me and I waited, tense, for the nod and second gesture, "All right now—reel out again." At times we would come out of the fog, not into daylight but into the strange gray night. The Arctic sun just under the horizon still lit the sky with a light that did not belong to dawn or dusk. A cold gray light that seemed to grow off the ice pack.

We should be very near by now. Would we be able to get through or would we have to turn back? The fog was closing in behind us. It might be impossible to return to Aklavik. A note from the front cockpit—"Weather at Barrow?" We were flying under the fog again, too low to trail a long antenna. I reeled out a few feet of wire, which would not allow me to transmit messages but was sufficient for receiving. It all depended on the man at Barrow. If only he would go on sending in spite of our silence. We were powerless to let him know.

"Weather, weather, *weather*—send us weather," I pleaded mentally and put on my ear-phones. Silence. Wisps of fog scudded past us. No, there he was, "Darr-dit-darr, dit-dit-dit-dit," calling us. Twice, three times, four times—then silence again, waiting for us to answer. I held my breath, "Weather, weather." There he goes again. "Do - - - u (you) - - - hear - - - me?" came the message. Silence again. He was waiting for my call. "Yes, yes," I answered silently, "but I can't send—go ahead—*weather!*"

"Darr-dit-darr; dit-dit-dit-dit." There he was again. My pencil took down the letters, slowly spelling out the message, "Fog - - - lifting - - - fast (Good man! He did it!) - - - visibility - - - two - - - miles (He did it! Good for him!) don't - - - think - - - u - - - have - - - any - - - trouble - - - find - - - lagoon." There it was—just what we wanted. I poked my husband excitedly with the pad. That operator at Barrow—he did it—we'd get through all right now. "Fog lifting, visibility two miles." Oh, what a grand man!

We could see the gray flat coast line now and watched it closely for Barrow. That might be it—a stretch of whitish irregular blocks—houses? No, as we came nearer, they were the strange pushed-up blocks of the ice pack crushed against a little harbor. Well, *these* were houses. We had come on a small low spit of land squeezed between two seas of ice blocks. Yes, there were houses. We peered down at them eagerly, four tipsy weather-beaten shacks and a few tents, the color of the ice blocks. Can this be Barrow? I almost cried with disappointment looking at that deserted group. No sign of a person, no sign of smoke, no sign of life. It *can't* be Barrow. Childishly, my first thought ran on, "Why, that radio man said they'd have a regular Thanksgiving dinner for us. There couldn't be any dinner down there—no smoke." I felt very hungry. We circled again. "No!" I realized with relief. "No radio mast! It isn't Barrow." We followed the shore line until we found a larger and newer group of houses between the ice pack and an open lagoon. This was

Barrow, ten or twelve red roofs, numerous shacks and tents, a church steeple and—yes, there they were—the radio masts.

We were landing on the lagoon. I pulled off two bulky pairs of flying socks and put on a pair of rubber-soled shoes for walking. Although it was not freezing weather, my feet became numb before we reached the small crowd of people on shore. A strange group huddled together in the half-light of the Arctic night. I looked at them—pointed hoods, fur parkas, sealskin boots—and thought at first, "They're *all* Eskimos." No, that must be the radio man in the khaki mackinaw. I felt a glow of gratitude and waved at him. As we climbed up the bank the crowd of Eskimos drew back, an attitude of respect and wonder never seen in the usual crowd. As they moved a great cry arose—not a shout, but a slow deep cry of welcome. Something in it akin to the bleak land and the ice pack.

Then, after shaking of hands and a confusion of voices, I found myself running across the icy moss toward a lighted frame house. My hostess, the doctor's wife, was leading me. I stamped my numb feet on the wooden steps of her home as she pushed open the door. The warmth of a kitchen fire, the brightness of gas lamps, and a delicious smell of sweet potatoes and freshly baked muffins poured out around me and drew me in.

A long table spread for our "Thanksgiving dinner" filled the living room. White cloth, rims of plates, curves of spoons, caught the light from swinging lamps above. I looked around quickly and felt the flavor of an American home—chintz curtains drawn aside, pictures of "woodland scenes" on the walls, bright pillows on the sofa, and there, in the window, a box of climbing nasturtiums.

In the other south window I noticed a tomato plant bent under the weight of one green tomato. My hostess smiled, "That tomato won't ever ripen, you know—it hasn't enough sun—but the leaves grow and we can smell it. Even the smell of growing vegetables is good to us." I looked outside at the pale gray moss on the ground. "I didn't use the dirt around here," she went on to explain. "I tried to, at first, but it's really nothing but frozen sand. Nothing will grow in it except that moss. I carried this earth in a box all the way from Nome."

No vegetables! I tried to realize what she was explaining to me. All their provisions came in by boat once a year around the tip of Alaska from the little mining town, Nome. There was only a month or two in the summer when the icy waters were clear enough for a boat to reach Barrow, and even then the ice pack, jammed against the shore for weeks at a time, might make it impossible. This year their boat, the *Northland,* also carrying our fuel supply, was waiting a hundred miles down the coast for a change in wind to blow the ice pack offshore. "The school-teacher and his wife are waiting for their daughter. She is on that ship."

The settlement "family" began to crowd in, piling their parkas and sealskin boots at the door of the warm room. Every member had a vital part in the life of the settlement.

The doctor and minister, our host, was leader of the community. He had built the manse in which we were staying. His son, "outside," had helped him to plan it. The doctor himself, directing the Eskimos, had measured and fitted every board and nail. He had placed special insulation in the floor, for it was impossible to have a furnace in the cellar. If you started to thaw out the ground underneath, the house might sink. And a furnace would require too much fuel in a fuel-less country. The windows, triple storm ones, were all nailed down. They were for light and not for ventilation. Windows that open and shut are always draughty. The rooms were ventilated by pipes which let in air indirectly but kept out rain and snow. Heat from the kitchen went up through ventilators in the ceiling to the bedrooms above. There were big stoves in all the rooms. The doctor installed the water tank, connected it with pipes for running water downstairs, and heated it from the stove. Aside from his work as architect and carpenter, he preached every Sunday, had a Bible class Wednesday nights, was doctor, surgeon, and dentist, and was preparing his boy for college.

His wife and another trained nurse had supervision of the hospital. The winter before there had been an epidemic of diphtheria in the settlement. The little hospital was crowded past its capacity but they had managed all the work with only the help of a few untrained Eskimo girls.

The schoolteacher and his wife carried on their work in a

frame building heated only by a stove. One of the Eskimo girls, sent from the Point Barrow School to college at Sitka, had come back to teach this year. The radio operator kept the community in touch with the outside world. Radio was their only means of communication except for the yearly boat and a few dog-team mails during the winter. He was responsible, too, for keeping the world in touch with them, sending meteorologists daily reports of the important Arctic weather. His wife was bringing up, besides a girl of nine, a six-month-old baby named Barrow.

An old Scotch whaleman completed the circle as we sat at dinner. He had not been "outside" for forty years, had never seen telephones or automobiles, although radio had come to take a regular part in his life and airplanes had landed near his home several times. The Wilkins Polar Expedition had based at Barrow and a plane carrying serum had flown up the year before in the diphtheria epidemic. It was strange to realize that radio and aviation, which typify the latest advance in civilization, had vitally affected this outpost, while railroad, telephone, and telegraph had not touched it.

We sat down to a real Thanksgiving dinner. Provisions were short but they had all pooled their supplies for a feast. Reindeer meat came out of the community cellar, a huge cave dug down in the icy ground. The radio operator carved a wild goose that had been shot near by. Among their remaining cans of food they had found sweet potatoes, peas, and beets. There was even a salad of canned celery and fruit. Someone still had a few eggs (not fresh, of course; preserved ones), which were brought over for mayonnaise. Someone else had flour for the soda biscuits. Someone brought coffee. But the greatest treat of the evening, the most extravagant, generous touch, I did not properly appreciate. The trained nurse had grown a little parsley in the hospital window box. They had picked it to put around the platter of meat. I treated it as garniture.

On Sunday the whole Eskimo village came up the hill to the white frame church. Men in their fur jackets and big sealskin boots; women with babies on their backs under their loose fur-lined calico dresses; little children with bright slit eyes shining out of fur hoods—all padded up the hill out of their tents and shacks. Sunday service was a great occasion and they were all smiling and laughing. No one wanted to miss it. I looked for the Eskimo friends I had made in the last two or three days. "Lottie," who led us over the ice pack the day before. When she ran she heaved from one side to another like a bear. I could see her green calico dress swaying in the crowd. "Ned" and his wife, who made us a fur cap and mittens. "Bert," who kept the village store and supervised the killing of the reindeer for the winter stock. We met him the day of the round-up, sledging back carcasses, cleaned and tied up in cheesecloth. Here were the Eskimo girls who helped with the Thanksgiving dinner, shy and smiling, their black hair brushed down sleekly; and the Eskimo woman who gave us a miniature whaling spear carved out of walrus tusk. They all crowded in between the wooden benches of the church. During the service there was a general shuffling and crying of babies. Whenever a baby cried too much, the mother would get up reluctantly, hitch her bundle higher up on her back, and pad out clumsily. But nothing distracted the congregation. Men, women, and children leaned forward earnestly watching the minister. Many could not understand English. Even those who had learned it in school were bewildered by psalms sung by a shepherd on a sun-parched hillside.

" 'We have gone astray like sheep,' " began the reading. Sheep, what did that mean to them? I saw stony New England pastures and those gray backs moving among blueberry bushes and junipers.

"Like the reindeer," explained the minister, "who have scattered on the tundras." The listening heads moved. They understood reindeer.

" 'Your garners will be filled.' " Big red barns, I saw, and hay wagons rumbling uphill. But the Eskimos? "Your meat cellars," the minister answered my question, "will be full of reindeer meat."

" 'Your oxen will be strong,' " read the next verse. "Your dogs for your dog teams will pull hard," continued the minister. " 'The Power of God.' " How could he explain that abstract word Power?

"Sometimes when the men are whaling," he started, "the boats get caught in the ice. We have to take dynamite and break up the ice to let them get out. That is power—dynamite—'the dynamite of God.'"

"For Thine is the Kingdom, 'the dynamite,' and the Glory forever and ever. Amen," I said over to myself.

The congregation was standing up to sing. The schoolteacher's small boy, who was organist, sounded the chords. "Gloree for me— Gloree for me." A buoyant hymn generally, but sung by these people in a high singsong chant, it held a minor quality of endlessness, as though it might echo on and on over the gray tundras—"that would be gloree, gloree for me."

TIM CAHILL

Prudhoe Bay or bust!

"GARRY'S THEORY REGARDING GLARE ICE WAS THAT YOU
SHOULD DRIVE IT AS IF YOU HAVE NO BRAKES. 'BECAUSE,'
HE EXPLAINED, 'YOU DON'T.' "

Tim Cahill's lively brand of personal reportage has been collected in A Wolverine Is Eating My Leg and Jaguars Ripped
My Flesh. The following excerpt from Road Fever describes the
end of an auto journey through both South and North America.

The 416-mile ribbon of gravel called the Dalton Highway
begins about 75 miles north of Fairbanks and leads northward
only to Prudhoe Bay and the oil fields of Alaska's North Slope.

Oil was discovered beneath the North Slope in 1968, but,
because of the environmental controversy that arose along with
plans for the trans-Alaska pipeline, construction on the road,
needed to bring building supplies to Prudhoe Bay, did not begin
until 1974. Some old Alaska hands still call it by its original
non-name, the "haul road." It passes just east of Gates of the
Arctic National Park, described by Jon Krakauer elsewhere in
this book.

DAWSON CREEK IS ABOUT FOUR THOU-
sand miles from Dallas and about two thousand miles from
Prudhoe Bay. It is also "mile one" of the ALCAN or Alaska
Highway. During the Second World War, the Japanese attacked
Alaska and occupied two islands in the Aleutians, the archipel-
ago that stretches south and west of the mainland.

The ALCAN Highway, a military supply route to Alaska for
U.S. forces, was built to defend the mainland, and it was completed in November of 1942. The Canadian portion of the highway was turned over to Canada at the end of the war. The
Alaska-Canadian Military Highway was opened to the public in
1948.

Driving the road used to be a survival trip. These days, the
road is asphalt all the way to Fairbanks.

I took the wheel out of Fort Nelson and pushed the truck
through Stone Mountain Provincial Park. It was the kind of
mountain road automobile enthusiasts dream about: moder-
ately challenging, with nicely banked turns winding through
staggering scenery. It was, incidentally, entirely free of police. I
took the corners hard, listening to the tires scream on the asphalt, and thought that I had never enjoyed driving more.

The sun dropped low in the sky, gathered itself, thought
better of setting just yet, made a southward detour, and began
to roll along the horizon. A black bear sow and two cubs were
wrestling around in the stubbly grass on the shore of a lake. I
saw two other black bear on the drive. There was a moose in a
small pond, standing belly-deep in the water, grazing on aquatic
plants. The slanting light was golden.

It was dark and our shifts at the wheel now lasted only
three or four hours. I was driving and we were somewhere
north of Whitehorse, in the Yukon Territory. There was a dream
I wanted to have and it was waiting for me every time I closed
my eyes. I thought: you should close your eyes. Your eyes hurt
and they need rest.

When I blinked for more than a fraction of a second, the
dream was there, playing on the inside of my eyelids. I was in
an antiseptic room wearing a white coat. I was a doctor or perhaps a scientist.

The road ahead ran straight and there were no lights anywhere.

"Close your eyes. There's no traffic. It's safe now. Close your eyes. It's good to rest your eyes. Close your eyes and see what happens."

I shook my head and a dull ache became a sharp pain.

"Close your eyes and it won't hurt anymore. You'll drive better if your head doesn't hurt. Just close your eyes."

I noticed that I had pencils and pens in the pocket of my white coat. There was someone at the door of the antiseptic room and I didn't know who it was, but I knew for certain that something good was going to happen.

There was a sound that I knew was our engine and another sound that was the hum of our tires on the road. These sounds bothered me. I wanted to open my eyes.

"It's only a short blink. Don't worry. Things happen fast in dreams . . ."

I stopped hard in the middle of the empty road and woke Garry.

"I think I'm tired," I said.

The days and nights began to run together: the beating of a great black wing. At six-fifteen that morning we passed into Alaska at the Tok border station. A few hours later, the morning sky was a light robin's-egg blue, but the sun wasn't up yet. There were some puffy clouds in the east, and the sun, which was still somewhere below the curve of the horizon, lit these clouds from below. There was no red in the light at all. The clouds were a bright golden color, spiritual in aspect, as if they had been sanctified by the light. I studied the clouds for half an hour, and then the sun finally appeared in a sky that had been pale blue for over an hour. It hung on the horizon, in the manner of a harvest moon.

The sky turned a deeper blue but the sun's rays only touched the tops of the fir trees and the uppermost branches of bare aspens and birches. We drove down a shadowed corridor, between the trees, with the golden sunlight trapped in the branches above.

There was a thin cover of snow on the land. We were driving along the banks of the Tanana River, about fifty miles out of Fairbanks. The river was low, not yet completely frozen over, and there were places where great blocks of ice, driven by moving water, had humped up at some obstruction. These great hummocks caught the light of the sun, which was now higher in the sky, and the ice was so bright that looking at it hurt my eyes.

Where there was running water, it flowed in twisted braids through an immense valley. The water was warmer than the air so that a low, thick fog rose off its surface. These narrow banks of fog wound through the valley ahead and they, too, were golden. Everything seemed golden in what we thought would be the final sunrise of the drive.

By ten-thirty that morning, we were in Fairbanks, at a GM dealership called Aurora Motors. It had taken exactly half an hour less than three days to drive from Dallas to Fairbanks, even counting the four short press conferences we had done along the way. The GM dealer, Jim Messer, had promised to help us with one last document. We needed a permit to drive the old North Slope Haul Road to Prudhoe Bay.

The 416-mile road, now called the Dalton Highway, was built in 1974 to service the Alaska oil pipeline. The road is about thirty feet wide and took twenty-five million cubic yards of gravel to surface. The gravel insulates the permanently frozen ground. If the permafrost was allowed to melt, the road would deteriorate rapidly. In some spots, the gravel is six feet deep.

In 1978, the road was turned over to the state of Alaska and the first fifty-six miles was opened to the public. In 1981, after a bitter debate in the state legislature, public access was extended another 155 miles, to Disaster Creek.

Disaster Creek is still about 206 miles short of Prudhoe Bay, which is really an oil field, a conglomeration of drilling rigs and pumping stations. Men and women go there to work, to produce oil, and the haul road is Prudhoe's main supply line.

Permits to drive beyond the public portion of the road are issued by the Department of Transportation and are granted for commercial and industrial use only. The haul road is patrolled by a state trooper and the checkpoint, where permits must be shown, operates day and night.

So we needed a permit to complete the last few hours of the drive. The Department of Transportation, when Garry contacted them, had seen no reason to be helpful. There was no appeal.

That left us two choices. We could attempt to run the checkpoint, get arrested, never reach Prudhoe Bay, and watch the days tick by in a jail cell. This choice was unacceptable: I had gotten to the point where the clock inside my head would not stop, not until we completed the race.

The other way was to drive the road legally, on a bona fide commercial or industrial mission. This was not an insoluble problem for experienced *documenteros*.

Jim Messer, the GM dealer at Aurora Motors, bought our truck on the spot, loaned it back, and hired us to deliver a load of spare parts to a garage in Prudhoe Bay. It took an hour to fill out the proper papers, to remove our plates, and to put the temporary plates on the truck. Aurora Motors now owned the Sierra, and we had a valid permit to drive the Dalton Highway all the way to Prudhoe Bay.

It's about seventy-five miles from Fairbanks to the start of the Dalton Highway. The first half of that is paved, and the pavement was covered over in glare ice so slick that, when we stopped, it was literally impossible to walk on the road. I drove along at a maddening fifteen miles an hour. Near a mountain called Wickersham Dome, the pavement ended, but the gravel was packed over with snow, and a hard layer of ice covered that. I still couldn't take it any faster than fifteen miles an hour.

We were very conscious of the hours ticking by. It was now the twenty-third day and the twelfth hour of the drive. We had about 450 miles to go. At fifteen miles an hour, it would take another day and then some to reach the end of the road. We hadn't taken that long to drive from the tip of Texas to the Canadian border.

The Dalton Highway starts just past Livengood, and, after fifteen more miles and another hour, Garry took over. He drove the ice at nearly thirty-five, feathering off on the throttle rather than braking for curves or for oncoming traffic. Garry's theory regarding glare ice was that you should drive it as if you have no brakes.

"Because," he explained, "you don't."

The ice stretched on for a hundred miles out of Fairbanks, but then it gave way, reluctantly and by degrees, to packed snow. Garry cranked it up to forty-five, the legal limit. He experimented once or twice with the brakes, saw that we had some friction, and pushed the Sierra to sixty.

We came over a steep sanded hill, perhaps two thousand feet high, and found ourselves in a thin winter mist that hunkered over this low summit. The mist was freezing on the branches of stunted fir trees, some of them only six feet high. As we drove down off the summit and out of the cloud, the trees became somewhat more robust but their branches were covered in thick layers of ice. The sky was bright blue and these ice trees glittered in the mid-afternoon sun.

Garry caught sight of a truck in the side mirror. He pulled over and stopped. It was the etiquette of the haul road. The Dalton Highway belongs to the trucks, especially those that are fully loaded, headed north. They take the center of the road and drive with the throttle to the floor. A heavily loaded truck has a lot of purchase on snowpack, and this one blew by us at seventy-five miles an hour. There was a valley below and a steep pitch after that. The trucker was working up speed to attack the next hill.

The Yukon River flowed below steep banks, and it was not yet completely frozen over. Blocks of water-driven ice piled up on the sandbars and sparkled under the sun. There was a large hangar-sized building fronting a trailer-park hotel. Garry got diesel and I went into the hangar, which was a café, and ordered some food to go.

There was a radiophone on my table. A sign said it would cost $3 to call Fairbanks and $2 a minute after that. Another sign above the phone cautioned me not to bring any fox carcasses back from above the Arctic Circle due to a rabies scare. I picked up a newspaper, which was, I saw, published by and for Christian truck drivers. There was a picture of a bunch of Christian truck drivers dedicating an orphanage somewhere in Oklahoma.

My bill for two turkey sandwiches, four Pepsis, and a thermos full of coffee was $22. The waitress, I saw, was reading a book about missionaries in Bolivia. The book was in Spanish and entitled *Commandos for Christ.*

The bridge across the Yukon was a sturdy wooden affair, nearly half a mile long. It had been built in 1975. Before that, Hovercraft had been used to ferry goods across the river.

The road began to rise up along shallow slopes and drop into huge and entirely unpopulated valleys, filled with snow. The slopes were labeled for the truckers: Sand Hill, Roller Coaster, Gobblers Knob. Occasionally, we would pull over for another one of the highballing trucks. Some of them were doing eighty over the smooth hard-packed snow.

A hundred miles north of the Yukon, we crossed the Arctic Circle and felt that we had truly come up in the world. The trees were gnomish and twisted. The pipeline, a huge metal monstrosity balanced on six-foot-high metal sawhorse stilts, ran along the right side of the road. From the higher points, I could see it rolling over lower snowy ridges, headed north.

Then, perhaps forty miles later, we had our first views of the Brooks Range. The mountains were shrouded in swirling silver clouds and looked darkly ominous. This range is a northern extension of the Rockies, the last major mountains in the United States to be mapped and explored.

It was four-thirty, and we had been driving with our lights on all day, because that is the law, but now we needed them. The sun, which had not risen very high in the sky anyway, was rolling south along the horizon. In another month, this land north of the Arctic Circle would undergo several weeks of twilight, and then the sun would finally set and darkness would own the land.

A light snow began to fall. The mountains to our right were great stone monoliths, so steep that the snow did not cling to their sheer slopes. The road was white, the land was white, the falling snow was white. Everything was white except for the sheerest rock slopes, which seemed to hover over the road, as if rock could float.

"We are," Garry said, "about halfway to Prudhoe."

We thought about that. It had been a halfway trip. Lima is halfway through South America. Managua is halfway through the total drive. Edmonton is halfway from Dallas to Prudhoe Bay.

"Another hundred miles," Garry pointed out, "and we'll be halfway through this last half."

We passed Disaster Creek and there seemed to be no check station. We were driving through a forest of small, stunted spruce trees. The branches on these trees were short and stubby, so that they looked like bottle washers. And then the forest gave up and we passed the last tree, the most northerly spruce on the Dalton Highway.

It was five o'clock, but the sun was still hovering slightly above the horizon and sometimes I could see it through the lightly falling snow: a dim silvery ball balanced on a snowy ridgetop.

We were making good time, running between two ranges of mountains, and then the road began its long convoluted climb into the Brooks Range. The snowpack was heavily sanded and we didn't need four-wheel drive.

The never-ending twilight was an alabaster glow to the south. Snow, dry and powdery, had been falling for hours, but here, in the mountains, wind sent it howling across the road so that it seemed to be falling horizontally. The peaks above us were white and rolling and rounded: the polar version of desert sand dunes.

There was a danger of vertigo because it was difficult to distinguish the white snow-packed road from the falling snow or the alabaster sky; it was hard to distinguish the mountains above from the drop-offs below. We were closed in on all sides by variations in white. There was a bluish tinge to the snow-sculpted peaks, and a chalky, mother-of-pearl quality to the sky. The world was all a permutation of ice.

There was a check station at the summit of what seemed to be the continental divide. We stopped and a man checked the permit, listened to our story, and came out of the building to take a photograph of the filthy truck parked in the cold silver Arctic twilight.

And then we were plunging down the north slope of the Brooks Range, running slowly in first gear, past signs that read, unnecessarily I thought, ICY.

It was nearly seven and not completely dark. The great plain ahead sloped down toward the frozen sea. The snow was only a foot deep, so that tufts of brown grasses and hummocky red tussocks punctuated the plain. There were no trees at all.

The snowpack had given way to gravel and we could make good time. Even so, every once in a while, a kamikaze trucker blew by us, and the pebbles he threw off pitted our windshield with half a dozen stars.

The mountains formed a vast horseshoe around the plain. We followed the course of the Sagavanirktok River as it fell toward the Beaufort Sea. The road was not nearly so flat as it had looked from the mountains. The land rose and fell like ocean swells.

The snow had ceased to fall, the sky had cleared, but now a heavy wind out of the east sent a low ground blizzard swirling across the Dalton Highway. At seven-forty there was a final streak of light, far to the south, and then it was dark. Directly ahead, to the north, hanging above the highway, a star appeared. I looked up and there were stars all over the sky. They seemed to pulsate with a kind of swirling crystalline clarity that I imagined was unique to the Arctic.

But no, it was fatigue and eyestrain. Every object I looked at—the illuminated compass on the dashboard, the notepad on the sucker-board, everything—seemed to have a small haloed aura around it. In my eyes, the polar night was alive with van Gogh stars.

We were halfway through the last half of the drive, about one hundred miles from Prudhoe Bay. It was time for a coffee party. I poured us both a cup from the thermos full of Yukon River coffee, then doctored it with an appropriate amount of South American instant. Roto coffee.

"Oh man," Garry said. "The beginning and the end were spectacular."

"Those mountains out of Ushuaia."

"And now that pass over the Brooks Range," Garry said. "What's it called?"

"Atigun Pass."

"That's the most spectacular thing I ever saw in my life."

At 8:06 in the evening of our twenty-third night, a thin pillar of pale green light, like the beam of a colossal spotlight, shot up through the van Gogh stars. It faded, then two more rays fanned out from the north and east. The northern lights— the Inuit people call them Spirit Lights—moved across the sky like luminous smoke.

There was a faint ruby tinge at the periphery of the major displays. Ahead, there was another faint glow on the horizon: the lights of Prudhoe Bay, forty miles in the distance.

"This is nice," Garry said.

"More fun than that fog in southern Peru."

"More fun than a pit search."

We were going to come in, in under twenty-four days. In our minds, we were already there, and we found ourselves throwing out references, words, and names that wouldn't mean much to anyone else in the world at that moment. We owned these words, these images:

Zippy.

Pedro.

The Atacama.

Santiago and Luis.

The dune buggy from hell.

The Mountain of Death.

Igor and the Cyclops.

Atigun Pass.

Spirit Lights over the Arctic plain.

And they arched over us like a benediction, the Spirit Lights.

The first building we saw was a guard station that led into Standard's oil fields. It was a small building with windows on all sides because the road ran around it in two lanes. There were four security guards inside. They wore blue pants, blue jackets, light-blue shirts, and blue ties.

We parked off the road and I checked my watch and calendar. We had driven from Dallas to Prudhoe Bay in a little under eighty-five hours. Three and a half days. We jogged stiffly over to the shack. The night was bitterly cold and we were wearing the clothes we had put on for the press conference in Dallas. Over those we wore our filthy diesel-soaked jackets that were sick of talking with Korean tires.

Everything we wore needed to be burned. We probably did not look like good security risks. The guards regarded us with some suspicion until we asked them to, please, sign our logbook.

"Hey," one of the men asked, "are you the guys trying to set that record?"

We admitted that we were.

"There's a guy from *Popular Mechanics* looking for you," the man said. "He flew in yesterday with a photographer. There's a film crew here, too."

"Could you, uh, please sign the logbook?" Garry asked. "Please put the time and date in there. The, uh, the clock is still running."

The guards conferred among themselves and decided that it was precisely 10:13 on the night of October 22. All four signed our logbook.

And the clock stopped.

Factoring in the five-hour time change from our starting point in Ushuaia, it had taken us twenty-three days, twenty-two hours, and forty-three minutes to drive from the tip of South America to the edge of the frozen Beaufort Sea in Alaska.

Garry caught my eye. "Another victory," we said in ragged tandem, "for man and machine against time and the elements."

The men in the blue jackets seemed to be amused by our condition.

"So," one of the guards said, "you guys think you got this record?"

We said that we did.

"Where did you start?"

"Tierra del Fuego, at the tip of South America."

"How many countries did you go through?"

"Thirteen," I said.

"How many miles?"

We hadn't figured it out, but it was somewhere near fifteen thousand.

"And how long," one of the guards asked, "did all that take you?"

"It took," Garry replied (and I could tell that he just purely loved saying these numbers), "twenty-three days, twenty-two hours, and forty-three minutes."

The guard stared at us, as if amazed. "What'd you guys do," he asked, "walk?"

BARRY LOPEZ

Prudhoe Bay, Pump Station One

"NO TOIL, NO WILDNESS SHOWS. IT COULD NOT SEEM TO THE
CHAPERONED VISITOR MORE COMPOSED, INOFFENSIVE,
OR CIVILIZED."

*Barry Lopez won the John Burroughs Medal in 1979 for his
best-selling* Of Wolves and Men. Arctic Dreams, *from which
the following excerpt is taken, was published in 1986 and won
the American Book Award.*

Oil was discovered beneath Alaska's North Slope, which
stretches from the Brooks Range northward to the Arctic Ocean,
in February 1968. Not everybody was pleased. Certainly the oil
field, the largest in the United States, would be a boon to the nation, to make no mention of its value to the oil companies. But
the proposal to build a pipeline across hundreds of miles of untouched Alaskan wilderness alarmed many other people, who
loudly opposed construction of the pipeline. Years of controversy
and study of the project's impact on the environment and wildlife followed. But in the end, of course, as even its most vigorous
opponents must have known, the pipeline was built and went
into operation in 1977.

It begins at Prudhoe Bay and snakes southward eight hundred miles to the port town of Valdez on Prince William Sound,

the flow of oil controlled by a dozen pumping stations along its length.

In March 1989, one of the environmentalists' worst fears became reality. A huge tanker vessel, the Exxon Valdez, *which had just left the port with a full load, struck a reef and poured ten million gallons of crude oil into the waters of Prince William Sound.*

THREE OF US WERE DRIVING NORTH ON the trans-Alaska pipeline haul road, pulling a boat behind a pickup. For miles at a time we were the only vehicle, then a tractor-trailer truck—pugnacious and hell-bent—would shoulder past, flailing us with gravel. From Fairbanks to Prudhoe Bay the road parallels the elevated, gleaming pipeline. Both pathways in the corridor have a manicured, unnatural stillness about them, like white-board fences running over the hills of a summer pasture. One evening we passed a lone seed-and-fertilizing operation, spraying grass seed and nutrients on the slopes and berms of the road, to prevent erosion. There would be no unruly tundra here. These were the seeds of neat Kentucky grasses.

One day we had a flat tire. Two of us changed it while the third stood by with a loaded .308 and a close eye on a female grizzly and her yearling cub, rooting in a willow swale 30 yards away. We saw a single wolf—a few biologists in Fairbanks had asked us to watch for them. The truckers, they said, had shot most of the wolves along the road; perhaps a few were drifting back in, with the traffic so light now. Short-eared owls flew up as we drove along. Single caribou bulls trotted off in their light-footed way, like shy waterfowl. Moose standing along the Sagavanirktok River were nodding in the willow browse. And red foxes, with their long black legs, pranced down the road ahead of us, heads thrown back over their shoulders. That night I thought about the animals, and how the road had come up amidst them.

We arrived at the oil fields at Prudhoe Bay on an afternoon when light blazed on the tundra and swans were gliding serenely in rectangles of water between the road dikes. But this landscape was more austere than any I had ever seen in the Arctic. Small buildings, one or two together at a time, stood on the horizon. It reminded me of West Texas, land throttled for water and oil. Muscular equipment sitting idle like slouched fists in oil-stained yards. It was no business of mine. I was only here to stay overnight. In the morning we would put the boat in the water and head west to the Jones Islands.

The bungalow camp we stayed in was wretched with the hopes of cheap wealth, with the pallid, worn-out flesh and swollen bellies of supervisors in ball caps, and full of the desire of young men for women with impossible shapes; for a winning poker hand; a night with a bottle gone undetected. The older men, mumbling of their debts, picking through the sweepings of their despair alone in the cafeteria, might well not have lived through the misery, to hear the young men talk of wealth only a fool would miss out on.

We left in the morning, bound for another world entirely, the world of science, a gathering of data for calculations and consultations that would send these men to yet some other site, the deceit intact.

Months later, on a cold March morning, I came to Prudhoe Bay for an official visit. I was met at the airport by a young and courteous public relations officer, who shook hands earnestly and gave me the first of several badges to wear as we drove around the complex. The police at road checkpoints and at building entrances examined these credentials and then smiled without meaning to be cordial. Here was the familiar chill of one's dignity resting for a moment in the hand of an authority of artificial size, knowing it might be set aside like a small stone for further scrutiny if you revealed impatience or bemusement. Industrial spying, it was apologetically explained—disgruntled former employees; the possibility of drug traffic; or environmental saboteurs.

We drove out along the edge of the sea ice and examined a near-shore drill rig from a distance—too chilly to walk over, said my host, as though our distant view met the letter of his and my responsibilities.

We ate lunch in the cafeteria of the oil company's headquarters building, a sky-lit atrium of patrician silences, of slacks and perfume and well-mannered people, of plants in deferential attendance. The food was perfectly prepared. (I recalled the low-ceilinged cafeterias with their thread-bare, food-stained carpets, the cigarette-burned tables, the sluggish food and clatter of Melmac where the others ate.)

On the way to Gathering Station #1 we pull over, to be passed by the largest truckload of anything I have ever seen: a building on a trailer headed for the Kuparuk River. In the ditch by the road lies a freshly fallen crane, the wheels of the cab still turning in the sunshine. The man with me smiles. It is −28°F.

At Gathering Station #1 the oil from four well areas is cooled. Water is removed. Gas is separated off. Above ground for the first time, the primal fluid moves quickly through pipes at military angles and sits under pressure in tanks with gleaming, spartan dials. The painted concrete floors are spotless. There is no stray tool or wipe rag. Anything that threatens harm or only to fray clothing is padded, covered. The brightly lit pastel rooms carry heat from deep in the earth and lead to each other like a series of airlocks, or boiler rooms in the bowels of an enormous ship. I see no one. The human presence is in the logic of the machinery, the control of the unrefined oil, the wild liquid in the grid of pipes. There is nothing here for the oil but to follow instructions.

Tempered, it flows to Pump Station #1.

The pavilion outside the fence at the pump station is drifted in with snow. No one comes here, not in this season. I climb over the drifts and wipe wind-crusted snow from Plexiglas-covered panels that enumerate the local plants and animals. The sentences are pleasant, meant to offend no one. Everything—animals, oil, destiny—is made to seem to fit somewhat naturally together. People are not mentioned. I look up at Pump Station #1, past the cyclone fencing and barbed wire. The slogging pumps sequestered within insulated buildings on the tundra, the fields of pipe, the roughshod trucks, all the muscular engineering, the Viking bellows that draws and gathers and directs—that it all runs to the head of this seemingly innocent pipe, lined out like a stainless-steel thread toward the indifferent Brooks Range, that it is all reduced to the southward journey of this 48-inch pipe, seems impossible.

No toil, no wildness shows. It could not seem to the chaperoned visitor more composed, inoffensive, or civilized.

None of the proportions are familiar. I stand in the wind-blown pavilion looking at the near and distant buildings. I remember a similar view of the launch complexes at Cape Canaveral. It is not just the outsize equipment lumbering down the roads here but the exaggerated presence of threat, hidden enemies. My face is beginning to freeze. The man in the blue Chevrolet van with the heaters blasting is smiling. No guide could be more pleasant. It is time to eat again—I think that is what he is saying. I look back at the pipeline, this final polished extrusion of all the engineering. There are so few people here, I keep thinking. Deep in the holds of those impersonal buildings, the only biology is the dark Devonian fluid in the pipes.

On the way back to the cafeteria the man asks me what I think of the oil industry. He has tried not to seem prying, but this is the third time he has asked. I speak slowly. "I do not know anything about the oil industry. I am interested mostly in the landscape, why we come here and what we see. I am not a business analyst, an economist, a social planner. The engineering is astounding. The true cost, I think, must be unknown."

During dinner he tells me a story. A few years ago there were three birch trees in an atrium in the building's lobby. In September their leaves turned yellow and curled over. Then they just hung there, because the air in the enclosure was too still. No wind. Fall came when a man from building maintenance went in and shook the trees.

Before we drove the few miles over to Deadhorse, the Prudhoe Bay airport, my host said he wanted me to see the rest of the Base Operations Building. A movie theater with tiered rows of plush red velour seats. Electronic game rooms. Wide-screen television alcoves. Pool tables. Weight-lifting room. Swimming pool. Squash courts. Running track. More television alcoves. Whirlpool treatment and massage. The temperatures in the different rooms are different perfectly. Everything is cushioned, carpeted, padded. There are no unpleasant sounds. No blemishes. You do not have to pay for anything. He shows me his rooms.

Later we are standing at a railing, looking out through insulated glass at the blue evening on the tundra. I thank him for the tour. We have enjoyed each other. I marvel at the expense, at all the amenities that are offered. He is looking at the snow. "Golden handcuffs." That is all he says with his wry smile.

It is hard to travel in the Arctic and not encounter industrial development. Too many lines of logistic support, transportation, and communication pass through these sites. I passed through Prudhoe Bay four or five times in the course of several years, and visited both lead-zinc mines in the Canadian Archipelago, the Nanisivik Mine on Strathcona Sound on Baffin Island, and the Polaris Mine on Little Cornwallis Island. And one winter I toured Panarctic's facilities at Rae Point on Melville Island, and their drill rigs on the sea ice off Mackenzie King and Lougheed islands.

I was drawn to all these places for reasons I cannot fully articulate. For the most part, my feelings were what they had been at Prudhoe Bay—a mixture of fascination at the sophistication of the technology; sadness born out of the dismalness of life for many of the men employed here, which no amount of red velour, free arcade games, and open snack bars can erase; and misgiving at the sullen, dismissive attitude taken toward the land, the violent way in which it is addressed. At pretensions to a knowledge of the Arctic, drawn from the perusal of a public relations pamphlet and from the pages of pulp novels. A supervisor at an isolated drill rig smiled sardonically when I asked him if men ever walked away from the buildings on their off-hours. "You can count the people who care about what's out there on the fingers of one hand." The remark represents fairly the situation at most military and industrial sites in the Arctic.

BERTON ROUECHÉ

On the Bering Sea: In a walrus-skin boat

"'I WONDER WHERE WE ARE,' I SAID. FULLER SHRUGGED. 'I DON'T KNOW,' HE SAID. 'MY GUESS IS SOMEWHERE OFF CAPE WOOLLEY.' 'WHERE IS THAT?' I SAID. 'NOWHERE,' HE SAID. 'IT'S JUST A NAME ON THE MAP.'"

Berton Roueché was born in 1911 and worked as a reporter for several newspapers before joining the staff of The New Yorker *in 1944. His "Annals of Medicine" department in that magazine won him a large and lasting readership over many years. The most notable of his many books is his two-volume work,* The Medical Detectives.

The following piece on the Bering Sea and the King Island Eskimos was first published in 1966.

These Eskimos are the same group encountered by Anne Morrow Lindbergh on her 1931 visit to Nome.

John Muir visited King Island in 1881. "Some fifty stone huts," he wrote, "scarcely visible at a short distance, like those of the Arizona cliffdwellers, rise like heaps of stones among heaps of stones. There is no way of landing save amid a mass of great wave-beaten boulders."

In 1939, the Federal Writers' Project Guide to Alaska *by Merle Colby described King Island as "a melancholy granite rock less than a mile long . . . inhabited by 137 King Island*

Eskimos, the best sailors on the Bering Sea and skillful ivory carvers. Its climate is divided into two seasons—four months of fog and eight months of ice."

THE ESKIMOS WERE WAITING FOR US ON the beach just beyond the boulder breakwater on the eastern outskirts of Nome. It was six o'clock in the evening, but the June sun was still high in the sky and the air was almost warm. Offshore a mile or two, the ice that had moved out in the night was white and clear on the horizon. We said goodbye to the friend who had driven us out from town, and unloaded our gear—boxes of food, seabags, sleeping bags, a portable Coleman stove, some photographic equipment—and carried it across the road and down the embankment and onto the beach. The beach was steep and stony, with dirty snow in the hollows and a heavy crust of ice at the edge of the water. The *umiak* was moored to the ice. It was an open dory made of walrus hide stretched over a wooden frame, and it looked to be about thirty feet long. The Eskimos—three men, three women, and three teen-age boys—were loading the boat from a pile of boxes and bundles and gasoline tins and oil drums and oars and ice lances and boat hooks and rifles. I counted a dozen rifles in the pile, and there were others already stacked in the bow of the boat. The Eskimos were King Island Eskimos. Their native place was a little island in the Bering Sea about a hundred miles northwest of Nome. They had spent the winter in Nome, and now that the ice was breaking up they were going back to King Island to take supplies to their friends and relatives there, to hunt for seal and walrus, and to collect for sale on the mainland the walrus-ivory carvings that the islanders had made during the winter. My companions—John Fuller, a teacher in a school for Eskimo children run by the Bureau of Indian Affairs, and Joseph Rychetnik, an outdoor photographer and a former Alaska state trooper—and I had arranged to go with them. Their boat would be the first to visit King Island since the ice had closed in last fall.

The Eskimos watched us coming down the beach. Some of

them smiled, and one of the men waved. They all wore parkas with the hoods thrown back and dungarees, and most of them wore sealskin mukluk boots. The women wore flowered-cotton Mother Hubbards over their parkas. Two of the women, two of the boys, and one of the men wore glasses. The man who had waved came up to meet us. He was the boat captain, and his name was Vincent Kunnuk.

"No more to do," he said. "Everything is ready. We only wait for the old man."

Fuller nodded. He seemed to know what Kunnuk meant.

Kunnuk looked at me. "The old man has the experience," he said. "There is always an old man on a boat. He knows the weather and everything about the ice."

"I'm glad to hear it," Rychetnik said. "I made one patrol to King Island when I was on the police, and I got stuck there for over a week."

"I wonder if I know the old man," Fuller said.

"May be," Kunnuk said. "He is Pikonganna—Aloysius Pikonganna."

"Aloysius, eh?" Fuller said. "Good. Real good."

Kunnuk went back to the boat. We followed him down with our gear, and he showed us where to stow it. The boat was powered by two outboard motors—one at the stern and the other hung in a well a few feet forward. Two motors were no more than enough. They would have a lot of weight to move. The boat held nothing yet except gear, but it already sat low in the water. There wasn't much more than a foot of freeboard left.

A car stopped up on the road. The door opened and a little man on crutches got out. He had a rifle slung across his back. He called out something in Eskimo—a string of purrs and a sudden bark—and laughed and swung himself down the embankment.

"Now we go," Kunnuk said. "The old man is here. He goes on crutches all his life, but it makes no difference. He does everything a man can do."

The sea was a deep, translucent green and as flat as a village pond. We moved slowly away from the beach with only the stern motor working. Kunnuk sat at the helm. He kept the motor throttled down until we were clear of the shoals and shallows along the shore. Then he nodded to the man at the well, and the second motor coughed and stuttered and came alive, and the shore began to slide away. I watched the beach flatten out and the tumbledown houses across the road shrink down behind the embankment and the big brown mountainous hills rise up in the distance. Snow still lay on the tops of the hills and in their sheltered folds. The boat cut heavily away to the right, heading generally west, between the shore and the ice floes out to sea. I felt a breath of cooler air.

Aloysius Pikonganna sat in the bow on a plank laid across the gunwales. He had a pair of binoculars on a strap around his neck and a toothpick between his teeth. Below him, huddled in the shelter of a canvas windbreak, were the three women and the youngest boy. The boy wore a little pale-blue souvenir fedora, and on the front of the crown was a crayon scribble: "I want to hold your hand." The other boys were packed in the stern with Kunnuk and the other men. Fuller, Rychetnik, and I sat amidships with the jumble of gear. I had a few inches of thwart to sit on and the iron curve of a fifty-gallon oil drum to rest my back against. Fuller was perched on the corner of an open box of pots and pans, and Rychetnik was sunk among his photographic equipment. But we were thickly padded with clothes. Rychetnik and I had on Bean hunting boots and two pairs of socks and Air Force survival pants and Eddie Bauer down-lined jackets over two heavy shirts and thermal underwear. Fuller wore an Eskimo uniform—fur parka, fur pants, and mukluk boots. He shifted on his box, and looked at me.

"Comfortable?" he asked.

"I'm fine," I said.

"I hope so," he said. "We've got at least fourteen hours of this ahead of us, you know."

"How about you?" I said.

"I'm OK," he said. "Besides, I'm used to it. This is just the way these cats are. They've always got room for one more."

"Just relax and enjoy it," Rychetnik said. "Be like me."

Pikonganna looked over his shoulder and raised a warning hand. There were ice floes in the sea ahead. The boat slowed down. Kunnuk stood up in the stern with his hand on the tiller and watched the drifting ice. Some of the floes were eight or ten feet in diameter, and some were twenty or thirty or fifty or more. All of them were four or five feet thick, but their edges were deeply undercut and they all were raddled with pools and puddles. We picked our way among them. A file of big black-and-white eider ducks came over the horizon. I watched them beating slowly along just clear of the water—and a dark shape moved on a floe far off to the left. It could only be a seal. One of the Eskimos let out a yell and grabbed up a rifle. But the seal was already gone. The Eskimo laughed and pulled the trigger anyway. The bullet whined away across the ice.

We came out from among the drifting floes and into a stretch of green open water. The boat began to move again. But after about ten minutes Pikonganna held up his hand again. There was more ice ahead. Everything in front of us was ice. The sea was a plain of shifting floes for as far as I could see. Kunnuk cut the motors, and we drifted up to the flank of one of the big floes. One of the men took a lance and chipped away the treacherous overhang and then jumped out on the floe. Pikonganna tossed him a line, and he stuck his lance in the ice and knotted the line around it. Another Eskimo followed him and secured the stern of the boat with another line and lance. Kunnuk came forward.

"Now we wait," he said. "But the ice is moving. It will open up pretty soon." He stepped on the gunwale and onto the ice. "The women will make us some tea."

The women were already at work. They uncovered a Coleman stove and handed it out and set it up on the ice not far from the boat. While two of them got the stove started, the other woman got a teakettle and went off across the floe to a pool of melted ice. Rychetnik and Fuller and I stood on the ice, stamping the circulation back into our feet, and watched her fill the kettle from the pool.

"Do they make tea out of that?" I asked.

"Relax," Rychetnik said. "Saltwater ice isn't salty. The salt is expelled when salt water freezes. That's good water in that pool. I mean, it's fresh."

"It's potable," Fuller said. "Let's take a look at the ice. But be careful where you step. This rotten ice is full of potholes."

We walked down the floe. The ice was plainly moving. There was a lead of open water just ahead, and I could see that it was getting wider. The farther floe was pulling away in the grip of the tide. But the lead was still far from wide enough. I looked at my watch. It was twenty minutes past nine. Though the brightness had gone out of the sky, it was still full light. Everything was still fully visible—the hills and mountains on the mainland, a bread-loaf island in the distance, the drifting floes through which we had come. But the sun had moved down behind the mountains in the north, and it was only there that the sky had color. Overhead, it was dirty white, like a snowstorm sky, and the sky on the southern horizon was a cold, slaty blue. The mountains stood against a glory of pink and green and yellow.

When we got back to the boat, the Eskimos were gathered around a tarpaulin in front of the stove. The tarpaulin was spread with food—a box of pilot crackers, a tin of butter, and a big square of whale blubber. The blubber looked like a block of cheese—pale pink cheese with a thick black rind. We stopped at the boat and got a bag of sandwiches out of one of our boxes, and then joined the circle of Eskimos.

"It's moving, Vince," Fuller said. "It's opening up over there real fast."

"I know," Kunnuk said, and took a swallow of tea. "But we wait awhile. Have some tea." He spoke to the women in Eskimo, and picked up a fan-shaped knife with an ivory grip and cut off a slice of blubber. "Have some *muktuk?*"

Rychetnik smiled and shook his head.

"No, thanks, Vince," Fuller said. "Not right now."

Kunnuk laughed and looked at me. "This is the best *muktuk*—from the bullhead whale. Black *muktuk*."

I took the slice of *muktuk*. I sat down on the ice, and one of the women passed me a plastic cup of dark, steaming tea. I looked at the *muktuk*. The blubber didn't look like fat. It had a softer, more gelatinous look. I took a bite of it. It was very tender and almost tasteless. The only flavor was a very faint sweetness. There was one more bite of *muktuk* left. I ate it and washed it down with a gulp of tea. Then I opened my sandwich.

It was almost eleven o'clock when we finally left the floe. The sky was still bright pink behind the mountains. We moved along a crooked lead of open water on one throttled-down motor. The floe on the left was piled with shattered slabs of pressure ice, sometimes to a height of four or five feet. Every now and then, the ice would give a kind of moan, and a big slab would slide into the water and the boat would lurch. Two of the Eskimos stood at the gunwales with lances and pushed the floating ice away. Pikonganna was standing at his lookout post. He looked at his watch, and turned and said something to one of the women. She reached under a pile of quilts and brought out a little plastic radio. It came alive with a thunder of Russian. Then a screech of static. Then a voice said, ". . . and partly cloudy tonight with widely scattered showers. Cloudy tomorrow. The present temperature in Nome is forty-two degrees." There was a moment of whistling silence, and then came the sound of guitars and a sob of Hawaiian music. The woman turned the radio off.

The lead began to broaden, and we were back in open water. The only big expanse of ice in sight was a shelf of anchored ice that stretched between the mainland and the distant bread-loaf island. Kunnuk came forward across the gear. He stepped over us and over the women and joined Pikonganna at the bow. They talked softly together for a couple of minutes. Then Kunnuk laughed and started back. He stopped where we sat, and balanced himself on the gunwale.

"The old man says we go around Sledge Island," he said. That was the bread-loaf island in the distance. "But after that— no sweat. No more ice."

I came out of a dull, uncomfortable doze. I was hunched against the flank of the oil drum, and I was stiff and cramped and cold. I sat up—and there was Sledge Island. It loomed hugely up no more than three hundred yards off the bow. There was a fringe of ice, a field of soggy snow, a rubble of boulders, and a brown grassy slope rising steeply to a brown grassy summit. My watch said five minutes to two. The sun was up from behind the mountains, but the sky was gray with cloud. We seemed to be making directly for the island. I looked at Fuller.

Rychetnik was asleep face down between a seabag and a metal camera case, but Fuller was awake. He was sitting under the spread of his big parka hood, smoking a pipe.

"It looks like we're going to land," I said.

Fuller took the pipe out of his mouth. "Boat trouble," he said. "Vince says there's something wrong with one of the motors. He wants to stop and take a look at it."

Rychetnik sat up as we scraped alongside the shelf of anchored ice. "Hey," he said. "Where are we?"

"Sledge Island," I said.

"Sledge Island?" he said. "We're only at Sledge Island?"

"Relax," I said. "Relax and enjoy it."

When the boat was made fast, Kunnuk and one of the other men lifted the motor out of the well and began to take it apart. The trouble seemed to be in the feed line. I watched them for a minute. Then I followed the others through the field of snow to a ledge among the boulders, where the women had set up their stove. I sat down on a rock and gazed at them. They were boiling down snow for tea. I felt more than tired. I felt disoriented. The midnight daylight was confusing. After my sleep, it should have been morning. It gave me a very strange feeling.

Rychetnik touched me on the arm.

"Let's take our tea down the line a ways," he said. "Jack and I think it's time for a little depressant."

The idea of a drink at half past two in the morning was no stranger than anything else. I got up, and we sloshed through the snow to the sheltering lee of a boulder. Rychetnik handed each of us a little two-ounce bottle of Scotch, and we emptied them into our tea.

"It's better not to drink in front of the Eskimos," Rychetnik said. "It doesn't seem right unless you're going to pass the bottle around. And this is no place to do that."

"Good God, no," Fuller said. "I've lived and worked with Eskimos for quite a few years. As a matter of fact, I'm a first sergeant in the Eskimo Scouts. I know them and I love them. I really love them. Those cats have to have something to survive in this environment, and they've got it. They've got every virtue. They're honest—they're completely honest—and they're loyal and they're generous and they're brave and they're always in good spirits. Nothing bothers them. But they can't drink. When they do, they get drunk. And when they get drunk, they go wild—they go absolutely wild."

We left Sledge Island with both motors working. I settled back in my oil-drum seat and listened to their steady, synchronized growl. The sea beyond the island was all open water. The only ice was off to the north, along the mainland shore. But the weather had also changed. The overcast was heavier now, and the breeze had sharpened, and the sea had faded from green to gray. I felt a drop of rain.

One of the women turned and caught my eye and smiled. She pointed toward the shore, and held up four fingers.

"Four years ago, we stay there one week," she said. "Bad weather. Then we stay three days at Sledge Island. More bad weather." She smiled again. "Was very bad trip."

"It sounds bad," I said.

She pointed again toward the shore. "Is called Pinguk," she said, and turned away.

I felt more drops of rain. There was a raincoat with a hood in my seabag. I felt around and found it and put it on and tied the hood under my chin. In the pocket was a pair of wool-lined rubber gloves, and I put them on, too. The rain burst into a spitting shower and then sank down to a long, cold drizzle. Rychetnik was asleep and snoring among his photographic gear, and Fuller sat humped on his box. Pikonganna stood on watch at the bow in a shiny translucent raincoat made of walrus intestines. I pulled up my legs and turned on my side and tried to fit myself against the curve of the oil drum. It wasn't very comfortable, but I was out of the wind and warm and dry. The last thing I remember was the rattle of the rain on my raincoat hood.

The boat was reeling and rolling, and it lurched me wide awake. It was almost six o'clock. I sat up and hung on to the thwart. We were rolling in a heavy chop. Rychetnik was also sitting up. He sat with one hand on the gunwale, bracing himself. It was still raining, and everything looked strangely dark. But it wasn't the darkness of night. Then I realized—it was fog.

The boat gave a sickening roll. We were running broadside to the wind and wallowing in the trough of the waves. Rychetnik looked at me and smiled and shook his head.

"This is getting kind of hairy," he said.

"What's the matter?" I said.

"Aloysius says it's too rough to go on," he said. "Too rough and too foggy. We're turning around and heading in to shore."

Fuller leaned over my shoulder. "Too rough and too foggy and only one motor," he said. "That motor conked out again."

"I wonder where we are," I said.

Fuller shrugged. "I don't know," he said. "My guess is somewhere off Cape Woolley."

"Where is that?" I said.

"Nowhere," he said. "It's just a name on the map."

"I know Cape Woolley," Rychetnik said. "I was up along there on my first assignment as a trooper. It was right around this time of year, too. I flew up from Nome with a bush pilot. As a matter of fact, it was Gene Farland. Three Eskimos had got drunk in Nome and gone out fishing in a skin boat and never came back. My job was to try to find them. Somebody said they had headed up this coast, so we took off. We flew along just above the beach—and pretty soon there was the boat. It was hanging up there in the driftwood. Then, a little farther on, we found the bodies. They weren't ten feet apart."

"What happened?" I said.

"There was a storm and they were drunk and the boat capsized and they went into the water," he said. "This is the Bering Sea. When you go into the water up here, that's the end of the story. You've had it."

"I don't know whether you've noticed," Fuller said, "but there aren't any life preservers on this boat."

The boat began to come around. It rocked and slipped and lumbered into the wind. Now that we were out of the trough, the heavy rolling stopped, and the boat sat a little steadier, but the head wind held us down to a bumpy crawl. We bumped through the chop for about an hour. It was a queer, empty twilit hour. There was nothing to see but the boat and the blowing rain and a few hundred feet of wild gray water vanishing into fog. It gave me an uneasy feeling. It was frightening to think that only half an inch of walrus hide lay between us and the clutch of that glacial water. But I was too tired and cramped and cold to really think about it.

A sheet of white ice emerged from the fog. It was shore ice anchored to a point of land. We moved along the flank of the ice, and the fog began to thin. The wind was blowing in off-shore gusts, and it tore the thinning fog away in sudden streaks and patches. Land appeared beyond the ice. There was a narrow beach piled high with driftwood, a low embankment, and then a misty reach of tundra. A rhythmic whistling sounded overhead. I twisted my head and looked. It was a string of twenty or thirty big, dark-headed ducks swinging out to sea. Their size and the whistling made them goldeneyes. They dropped and braked and settled down on the water.

Kunnuk and Pikonganna exchanged a couple of shouts, and we edged closer in to shore. The shore ice shelf was deeply undercut, and its surface was ravaged with cracks and potholes. But apparently it would do—or would have to do. We came alongside, lifting and falling in the chop, and two of the men leaned out and hacked away the flimsy overhang. Another man and one of the boys jumped out on the ice and held the boat fast with lines. Kunnuk came forward. His eyes were red, and his face looked drawn.

"Everybody out," he said. "This ice is no good. The old man says is too rotten to hold the boat. So we unload quick and get the boat up on the beach."

The man and the boy continued to hold the boat. The rest of us worked on the gear. We hauled the boxes and the bags and the cases and the rifles and the tins and the drums and the motors well up from the edge of the ice and covered them with some strips of tarpaulin. Then we went back to the boat and got a handhold on the bowline and dug in our heels. One of the women let out a wailing heave-ho yell, and we heaved. The bow of the boat lifted and hung, and then slid up on the ice. We braced ourselves, and the woman yelled again: "Hooooo-huke!" We heaved again. One of the Eskimos stepped through a pothole up to his thigh, and I slipped and sat down hard on the ice, but the boat came up another five or six feet. Another heave brought all but the stern of it clear of the water, and after that it was easier. With some of us pulling and the rest pushing, the boat slid over the soggy ice like a sled. There was no need now for the women to help. They got their stove and some other supplies and then went on across the ice and up the beach to the tundra. By the time we got there with the boat, the women had collected a supply of driftwood branches and logs, and even trees, and had a big fire going. We careened the boat a few feet from the fire and propped it up on its side with the oars and boat hooks. It made an excellent windbreak and a kind of shelter from the rain.

We stood around the fire and warmed ourselves and caught our breath. The wind tore at the fire, and the flames leaped and twisted and darted in all directions, and my face was scorched but my feet stayed cold. It was a hot and furious fire. It took a lot of driftwood to keep it going, and the wood that the women had collected went fast. It was the deadest driftwood I had ever seen. Years of weathering on this desert beach had dried it to papery husks, and it burned almost like paper. When the wood-pile was down to a few sticks and branches, Rychetnik and I volunteered to bring in another supply. It was plentiful enough. There was driftwood heaped head high at the high-water mark along the beach as far as I could see. It must have been accumulating there forever. We made a dozen trips and brought back a dozen logs—big, barkless silver-gray logs that weighed practically nothing. As we dropped our last load, Fuller came struggling up from the ice with a box and a bag of perishables. The women had their stove set up, and they were making tea and boiling a pot of mush. Rychetnik looked at them and then at his watch.

"Hey," he said. "It's eight o'clock. What are *we* going to do about breakfast?"

"Whatever you say," Fuller said. "But I didn't get any sleep last night and I'm really not too hungry."

"Neither am I," I said.

"Besides," Fuller said, "I'm not real eager to break out the stove right now and do a lot of cooking and washing up and getting packed again. It wouldn't be worth the trouble. My guess is this weather is going to clear, and I know these cats. They'll be wanting to take right off."

"But what about breakfast?" Rychetnik said.

"I brought up the rest of the sandwiches," Fuller said. "And we've got some cans of chocolate milk."

Fuller was right about the weather. The rain had stopped by the time we finished breakfast, and the clouds were breaking up. There were patches of bright sky overhead, and the air was bright and clear. Even the wind had dropped. It looked like a beautiful day, but we wouldn't be leaving soon. The sea was still running high and white. Fuller dragged himself away from the fire and lay down in the shelter of the boat. Almost at once, he was snoring. I was tired, but the change in the weather made me restless. Rychetnik was engrossed in his cameras. I got up and walked around the boat and out onto the tundra.

The tundra stretched endlessly away to the north and south, and far to the east, a smoky gray on the blue horizon, were mountains. It was an enormous, empty plain. There were no trees, no bushes, no grass. There were only weedy hummocks and pockets of bog and trickling, ice-water brooks. Some of the hollows were still drifted over with snow. I skirted a bog and stepped over a brook, and a bird flew up from almost under my foot. It was followed by another. They were tawny, long-billed birds—snipe. A few minutes later, I flushed a phalarope. The tundra wasn't as empty as it looked. There were shrieks and whistles and drumming wings at almost every step I took. I flushed more snipe and phalaropes, and also sandpipers and plovers and ptarmigan. The ptarmigan had a shabby look. Their plumage was still a confusion of winter white and summer brown. Once, in the distance, I saw a flight of sandhill cranes, and there were many strings of ducks and geese. The geese were mostly snow geese, but there were also emperor geese and brant. The sun came suddenly out. It blazed down like tropical sun. I unfastened my padded jacket, and then took it off. It was actually hot. I sat down on a hummock and folded my jacket into a pillow and lay back. The hummock was matted with lingonberry vines and tiny creeping willow, and it made a soft and springy bed. I closed my eyes and enjoyed the feel of the sun on my face.

I woke up cold and shivering. The sun was gone and the

fog was back, and it took me a moment to remember where I was. I put on my jacket and started back to the camp. My head was still thick with sleep. I stopped at a brook and squatted down and splashed some water on my face. That finished waking me up. I went on, stepping and stretching and hopping from hummock to hummock. The fog made everything seem very still. The mountains had disappeared in the fog, but I could see the camp across the tundra. A small white tent now stood not far from the driftwood fire. Several men were gathered at the bow of the upturned boat. One of them was Rychetnik. I waved, and he came out to meet me. He was grinning.

"We'll never get off this beach," he said.

"Not with this fog," I said.

"I don't mean only the weather," he said.

"Now what?" I said.

"More boat trouble," he said. "One of the Eskimos was sacked out under the boat, and he happened to look up—and what do you think he saw?"

"What?" I said.

"Daylight," he said. "There was a hole in the bottom of the boat about the size of a dime. Vince and Sam Mogg are patching it up. They think it probably happened when we were dragging the boat up over the driftwood."

"What about that conked-out motor?" I said.

"I think they've finally got that fixed," he said. "But don't start getting any ideas. There's something wrong with the other motor now. It needs a shear pin on the propeller shaft. They're going to fix that this afternoon."

"Do you have any more of those little bottles you had last night?" I said.

Rychetnik laughed. "No," he said. "But I've got a big one."

I followed him around the boat and around the fire and around behind the Eskimo tent. Fuller was there, sitting on a log in front of our portable stove and searching through a box of groceries. He looked refreshed by his nap, and resigned to a stay on the beach. I filled a pan with water from the nearest snow-melt brook, and Fuller found some paper cups, and Rychetnik got out a fifth of Scotch. We sat around the stove and drank our drinks. The Scotch was good with the cold snow water, and it made the fog and the beach and the miles of tundra seem less bleak. Then Fuller cooked us a lunch of bacon and eggs. It was the first hot food I had eaten in almost twenty-four hours, and nothing ever tasted any better. We finished off with bread and butter and strawberry preserves and a pot of strong boiled coffee.

We spent the afternoon hauling driftwood for the fire. The Eskimo tent had been raised for the women, and we could hear them talking and laughing inside whenever we stopped at the fire to rest and warm ourselves. We also worked to the sound of shooting. The Eskimo boys roamed up and down the beach with .22 rifles, and they shot at anything that made a target— a driftwood stump, a raft of ducks far out to sea, a flight of mile-high geese. Kunnuk sat alone in the shelter of the up-turned boat with a cigarette in his mouth and filed and shaped a nail into a new shear pin. When he finished, he walked down and stood on the edge of the beach and looked at the water. The next time I came back to the fire, he was sitting there with the portable radio in his lap. I sat down beside him. We listened to a snatch of Siberian Russian and the end of a talk about getting back to the Bible. A hillbilly tenor sang "Does He Love You Like I Do?" Then a voice said: "This is radio station KICY, in Nome, Alaska. The time is six o'clock. Here is the weather forecast for Nome and vicinity: Fair and cold tonight. Fair and warmer tomorrow. The present temperature in Nome is thirty-three degrees."

Kunnuk turned off the radio. "Good weather coming," he said. "Maybe we leave soon. Maybe by midnight."

But the fog hung on. At nine o'clock, it looked thicker than ever. I doubted that we would be leaving by midnight, and I didn't care. I hardly cared if we ever left. Work and the weather and a drink of Scotch had given me a big appetite, and I had eaten a big dinner of reindeer steak, macaroni and cheese, canned peaches, cookies, and coffee. All I wanted to do was sleep. Someone would wake me before we left. If we left. I found a corner deep under the boat and took off my boots and my jacket and my heavy survival pants and unrolled my sleeping bag and crawled in. Something poked into the small of my back. There was a stick or something under my sleeping bag. I tried to squirm it away, and it moved an inch or two. That wasn't enough. I would have to climb out and move the bag. But instead I fell asleep.

I slept all night. I awoke to a crying and croaking and whistling of birds. It was half past five. There was frost on the ground, and the air was cold, but the sea looked calm, and the sun was shining in a wide blue sky. The fog was completely gone. I sat up. Kunnuk was propped on his elbow in a sleeping bag on my left.

"We make it today," he said. "Look!" He handed me a pair of binoculars and pointed out to sea. "You can see King Island."

I looked, but I couldn't see it.

"Maybe I know better where to look," he said. "I was born there."

I got into my clothes and rolled up my sleeping bag. Underneath it was the end of one of the boat lines. I stooped out from under the boat and into the bright sunlight. Most of the others were already up. The women were boiling another big pot of mush. I washed my face in the snow-melt brook. The water felt even colder than it had the day before. It was so cold it made my nose ache. I was starting back when Rychetnik came up to get some water for breakfast, and we walked back together. The stove was going, and Fuller, in a bright-red hunting shirt, was peeling bacon into a frying pan. Then, while Rychetnik got the coffee started and I got out some cups and plates and knives and forks and spoons, he stirred up a bowl of pancake batter. He fried the pancakes in the bacon pan, and we ate them with butter and strawberry preserves.

We finished breakfast at a little after six, and a few minutes later the Eskimos began to break camp. The women did the packing. Kunnuk called us over to help the men with the boat. We rolled it back on its keel and swung it around and dragged it down and across the ice and let it into the water. The glare of the sun on the frosty ice was dazzling. Two of the boys held the boat against the edge of the ice, and we went back and got our gear. The ground where the women's tent had been was littered with bones and cigarette butts. Aloysius Pikonganna directed the loading of the boat. The arrangement was somewhat different from that at Nome. It was planned for safe and easy shooting if we happened to get a shot at a seal. Rychetnik and Fuller and I shared the forward thwart again, but the gear was all piled amidships and the women and two of the boys were also settled there. The other boy and a man called Norbert took over the motors, with Norbert doing the steering. Kunnuk and Sam Mogg joined Pikonganna in the bow with the guns. We pushed away from the shore, and I looked over the side of the boat. The water was a yellowy green and so clear that I could see the bottom, five or six feet below. The bottom was stone — big slabs of granite worn smooth by grinding ice. It was as smooth and flat and bare as a pavement.

The motors started up, first the one at the stern and then the other, and the boat began to move. The women huddled closer together. They bowed their heads and made the sign of the cross, and their lips moved silently in prayer. Then they sat back, and two of them lighted cigarettes. We left the last of the shore ice and came out into open water and into an easy swell. Yesterday's chop had gone with the fog. An acre of rafting eider ducks exploded off to the right. I watched the big birds beating slowly in to shore. The shore looked just as it had when we saw it on Thursday morning. There was no sign that anyone had ever camped there. Kunnuk turned and looked back down the boat. He was smiling, with a cigarette in his mouth, and sparks of sunlight glinted on his glasses.

"Everybody sleep good?" he said.

The women nodded and the boys grinned and Norbert yelled something in Eskimo. Everybody laughed.

"Good," Kunnuk said. "Now we got good weather. Now we travel."

Sam Mogg caught my eye.

"We got Sears, Roebuck weather," he said.

"What?" I said.

"Sears, Roebuck weather," he said. "I ordered it."

The radio came suddenly on. A familiar voice said, ". . . seven o'clock, and the present temperature in Nome is forty-four degrees. The wind is northeast at fourteen. The forecast is for fair and warmer today, tonight, and tomorrow." In spite of the sun, it was cold on the water. I could feel the forecast wind.

I zipped up my jacket and put on my gloves and listened to an operatic tenor singing "I Love to Laugh." He sounded very far away. When he laughed ("Ha-ha, hee-hee"), he sounded even remoter.

King Island came faintly into sight at about eight-thirty. It was just a cloud on the western horizon. I got out a pair of binoculars and fixed them on the cloud. The cloud became a bigger and darker cloud, but it was still no more than a cloud. Then it began to grow. It darkened and broadened and lifted against the sky. By nine o'clock, the cloud was visibly an island. It continued to grow, and to change. Through the binoculars I watched it shift from a little gray lift of land to a rocky mountain rising steeply from the sea.

The woman who had spoken to me before leaned forward. She was an elderly woman with a big, square face framed in her parka hood.

"King Island," she said. "You see?"

I nodded. "It looks like a mountain," I said.

"Ukivok is Eskimo name," she said. "Not King Island. Eskimo call it Ukivok."

"Ukivok," I said. "What does that mean in Eskimo?"

"We go up on top Ukivok," she said. "We go high up and pick green flower. Many green flower grow on top Ukivok now."

"What is green flower?" I said.

"Is good," she said. "Is like salad."

Floating ice began to appear up ahead. A flight of murre swung low across our bow, and in the distance a kittiwake soared. King Island rose higher and higher. I watched it through the binoculars. It looked to be about two miles long, and it really was a mountain. Its sides were weathered into crags and pinnacles, and they rose abruptly from a beach of anchored ice to a saddle summit that was still partly covered with snow and at least a thousand feet high. It seemed impossible that anyone could live there.

I turned to the woman behind me. "Where do the people live on Ukivok?" I said. "Where is the village?"

"Ukivok is name of village," she said. "Island and village is same name."

"Where is Ukivok village?" I said.

She smiled and shook her head. "Not this side," she said. "Too much mountain. On other side."

Fuller gave me a nudge. "Walrus," he said, and pointed off to the left.

I put up the binoculars again. I saw them almost at once—a row of six or eight enormous creatures sitting erect on an isolated floe. They were reddish brown, with big sloping shoulders and little round heads and drooping two-foot tusks. They had a prehistoric look. They also looked strangely human.

"You see them, Vince?" Fuller said.

"I see them," Kunnuk said. "Good ivory, too. But we don't hunt walrus today. No room in the boat."

The shelf of anchored ice was wider than it had looked at first. We were still two or three miles from the island when we came in sight of its outer edge. But there were stretches of open water showing within it, and it seemed to be breaking up. Pikonganna stood balanced on his lookout plank surveying the ice. He said something to Kunnuk. Kunnuk nodded and looked back at Norbert and raised his hand in a signal. The boat cut away to the right. We moved northward along the edge of the shelf through a wash of broken floes. After ten or fifteen minutes, a break appeared in the anchored ice. We turned into a calm blue lead as broad as a boulevard.

We followed the lead for about a mile. It ran between two glittering shores of tossed and tumbled ice. Pikonganna held up his hand, and the motors slowed. There was a sudden bend just ahead. We moved slowly around the bend. Pikonganna raised his hand again, and the motors cut off. Fifty yards beyond the bend, the lead abruptly ended. We drifted up to the dead-end ice, and two of the boys jumped ashore and made the boat fast with lines and lances. Kunnuk stepped over the bow and stood and helped Pikonganna down, and Sam Mogg handed Pikonganna out his crutches. Kunnuk and Pikonganna moved off across the ice. I watched them climb to the top of a big ice ridge. They stood there studying the surrounding ice with binoculars for a moment, and then Kunnuk turned and waved.

Sam Mogg gave a grunt. "Time to eat," he said.

The women set up their stove at the foot of the ridge. They

filled the teakettle with melted ice from a hollow in the floe and got out a bag of dried seal ribs. Rychetnik and Fuller and I sat down on a ledge of ice nearby and made an easy lunch of bread and butter and bologna and Swiss cheese and canned grapefruit juice and chocolate bars. From where we sat, King Island looked hardly a mile away. The cliffs that formed its northern tip loomed steeper than ever. Some of them were stained yellow with lichen, and the air around them was alive with birds. Kunnuk came down from the ridge. He stopped where we sat on his way to join the other Eskimos.

"Don't worry," he said. "We make it OK. The old man and I see plenty other leads."

There was another blue lead about a hundred yards back down the lead we were on. It was narrow and twisting, but it led in the right direction. The King Island cliffs rose dead ahead. We went up the lead, and after another hundred yards or so it opened into a kind of lake with many islands of floating ice. The lake was a haven for murre. There were murre stringing overhead and murre perched on the ice and murre bobbing on the water. They were very tame, and I got a good look at them. They were pretty birds with vivid penguin plumage and long, sharp bills. Sitting erect on the ice, they even looked like penguins.

Pikonganna suddenly stiffened and then sank slowly down on his plank. It was an alerting movement. Everybody tensed.

"*Ooguruk,*" he said, and pointed.

About a hundred and fifty yards to the right, a big, silvery bearded seal lay basking on a floating floe. It hadn't seen or heard us yet. Norbert cut the motors and we drifted silently toward the ice. Nobody spoke. The most accessible rifle of adequate caliber was a Remington .30/06, and the man closest to it was Fuller. It was Rychetnik's rifle, and he motioned to Fuller to take it. Nobody moved. Fuller swung the gun to his shoulder, steadied himself, and fired. A flight of murre veered loudly away. The seal gave a start, and lay still.

The boat nudged up to the floe, and Kunnuk vaulted over the gunwale and onto the ice. He had a revolver in his hand. Sam Mogg and Fuller jumped ashore and trotted after Kunnuk. Rychetnik and I got out on the ice and watched them. Kunnuk was the first to reach the seal. Apparently, it was still alive. He squatted down and shot it in the head. He put the revolver away and took out a hunting knife and cut two belt-loop slits in the skin just above the eyes. Sam Mogg and Fuller came sliding up, and Mogg threw Kunnuk a length of rope. Kunnuk threaded the rope through the belt-loop slits and made it fast, and then he and Mogg and Fuller dragged the seal across the floe to the boat. The seal was a young female. It was about six feet long and it weighed at least four hundred pounds, and Kunnuk and Fuller and Mogg were sweating when they got it up to the boat. They were grinning, too. Everybody was grinning, and Mogg slapped Fuller on the back. When Kunnuk and Fuller and Mogg had caught their breath, they rolled the seal over on its back, and Kunnuk got out his knife again and gutted and cleaned it. Then they hoisted the carcass over the gunwale and into the bow. The fur looked suddenly different. The brilliant silver lustre had begun to fade. By the time we were ready to leave, it was a dingy, leaden gray.

We moved along the lakelike lead. The wind and the tide were shifting the ice, and the lead grew wider and more open. There was open water now all the way to the looming cliffs. I stood up. There was open water everywhere ahead. An open lagoon stretched for two or three hundred yards between the shelf of anchored ice and the foot of the cliffs, and it seemed to encircle the island. We moved across the open water and into the shadow of the cliffs. Then, at a signal from Kunnuk, Norbert swung the boat to the left. We headed down the eastern face of the island. I looked up at the towering crags and pinnacles. Every ledge was a rookery. The rocks were alive with perching murre and kittiwakes and gulls and auklets and cormorants and puffins and terns.

Kunnuk turned around. He had his revolver in his hand. "You like to see some birds?" he said, and pointed the revolver overhead. "Just watch—I show you something."

He fired two shots, and then a third. The revolver was only a .22, but against the sounding board of water and rock it sounded like a bomb. It sounded like a hundred bombs. The shots went echoing up and down the face of the island, and a

cloud of birds came screaming off the cliffs. They flew screaming over our heads and across the lagoon to the outer ice and
then veered around and came streaming back. They came off
the cliffs and over the water in waves—hundreds, thousands,
tens of thousands of birds. It was impossible to even guess at
the number.

The elderly woman leaned over my shoulder. "Ukivok is
good place for eggs," she said. "All kinds of eggs." She smiled
at me. "Very good to eat."

We sailed down the lagoon in a turbulence of birds. Many
of them were birds that had never seen a man or a boat or
heard a shot before, and it took them a long time to settle down
again. The lagoon was irregularly shaped. Because of the broken line of the shifting outer ice, it was sometimes as wide as a
lake and sometimes no more than a river. We followed it across
a lake and through a little river and into another lake. I heard
the motors cut off and felt the boat begin to drift. Pikonganna
and Kunnuk were standing together on the lookout plank, and
Sam Mogg and Rychetnik and Fuller were on their feet. Even
Norbert was standing. I stood up, too. The lake we were in was
the end of the lagoon.

Kunnuk came down off the plank. "OK," he said. "We go
back. We go round the other way."

We all sat down. The motors started up, and the boat
swung around, and we headed back up the lagoon. The boat
suddenly slowed. Kunnuk was back on the lookout plank with
Pikonganna, and Mogg was standing below them peering out
between their legs. I couldn't tell what they were looking at. I
didn't see anything unusual. We were approaching the upper
end of the lake, and it looked much like the other end. And
then I realized. The outer ice was moving in on some shift of
wind or tide, and the little riverlike passage through which we
had come had almost disappeared. The passage was about two
hundred feet long, and ten or fifteen minutes ago it had been a
good hundred feet wide. It now was hardly twenty.

The boat began to move again. Pikonganna and Kunnuk
had come to some decision. We made our way across the last
of the lake to the head of the passage. The passage had an ugly

look. There was a ten-foot embankment of glassy ice on the island side, and the outer ice was pitted with holes and piled with pressure ridges, and it was moving fast. I could see it closing in. Rychetnik gave a kind of grunt.

"I don't like this very much," he said. "I don't think I like it at all. You know what this boat is made out of. If we get caught between the ice in there . . ."

"I don't like it, either," I said. "But I guess there isn't much choice."

"These cats know what they're doing," Fuller said. "I've never seen them take a chance they didn't have to."

The boat edged into the passage. The water was thick with chips and chunks of floating ice. We moved carefully between the embankment of anchored ice and the moving floe on one throttled-down motor. Norbert kept the boat inching along just off the lip of the floe, away from the height and bulk of the ice embankment, but every time I looked, the ice seemed higher and closer. I could already feel the cold of its breath. Kunnuk reached out with an ice lance and jabbed at the edge of the floe. He jabbed again, hard, and a slab of ice came loose and slid slowly into the water. The boy at the stern with Norbert poked it safely past the boat with an oar. It was rotten ice. The whole rim of the floe was rotten ice.

Kunnuk said something in Eskimo, and stepped up on the gunwale and jumped out on the floe. Mogg and Fuller followed him over, and Rychetnik and the boy at the stern followed them. They all had lances or boat hooks, and they spread out along the floe and began hacking at the rim of rotten ice. They worked just ahead of the inching boat, and Pikonganna hung over the bow with an oar and guided the slabs of floating ice to the island side of the passage. I found another oar and kept the ice moving and clear of the boat. Some of the slabs were the size of boulders, and it took all my strength and weight hanging on the oar to push them off and away. But I kept them moving, and the boat was also moving, and finally I raised my head and looked out over Pikonganna's shoulder and there was the end of the passage and a blue expanse of open water. Norbert shouted, and the women gave a quavering wail. We were through.

We went back up the eastern face of the island and around the northern end and down the western side. Everybody was talking and laughing. There was no ice anywhere on the western side except along the shore, but the island was the same. There were the same gray cliffs, the same patches of yellow lichen, the same thousands of screaming birds. There was no sign of a village, and no place where a village might even conceivably be built. So the village was down at the southern end of the island. We still had some distance to go. I looked at my watch, and I could hardly believe it. It had been nine hours since we stopped for lunch. It was almost nine o'clock.

Rychetnik had been dozing in the evening sun. He sat up and shook himself. "I'm getting kind of hungry," he said. "As a matter of fact, I'm starved."

"I've been thinking about our dinner," Fuller said. "I thought the first night on King Island we ought to have something real special. Anybody got any suggestions?"

"I suggest we all go down to the Four Seasons," Rychetnik said.

"We've got a ham," Fuller said. "It's one of those Polish hams. I guess we'll have that, and maybe some spaghetti."

"And a drink," I said.

"Don't worry about that," Rychetnik said.

The village was well around on the southern tip of the island. It was built on the slope of a chute of landslidden rocks. It hung on the slope about three hundred feet above a beach of ice and tumbled boulders, and it consisted of eighteen or twenty houses. The houses were wooden shacks with tarpaper roofs, and they were stepped out from the slope on tall wooden stilts. Scaffolding walks and ladderlike steps connected the houses, and a long flight of steps led down to the boulder beach.

"It looks even hairier closer up," Rychetnik said. "But I guess it's safe enough. The house we're going to stay in is the schoolhouse—what used to be the schoolhouse. The teacher left about ten years ago. It's the house with all those windows up there at the head of the steps. That's where I stayed when I was here before. It isn't any Hilton, but it's got four walls and a roof and some chairs to sit on and a table. It won't be too bad."

The boat turned in toward the shore, and I watched the village coming clearer. It was hard to think of it as an Eskimo village. It looked remoter than that. It looked Tibetan. A man came out on the balcony of one of the upper houses. There was a green and red and purple patchwork quilt hung over the railing to air. The man watched us for a moment. Then he raised both hands high over his head and waved. Pikonganna waved back. He was grinning from ear to ear. He reached down and slapped Kunnuk on the back.

"Home sweet home, boy," he said. "There's no place like home."

Kunnuk smiled and nodded. "That's right," he said.

PERMISSIONS
ACKNOWLEDGMENTS

JEAN ASPEN   From *Arctic Daughter: A Wilderness Journey*. Copyright 1988 by Jean Aspen. Reprinted by permission of Menasha Ridge Press, 1-800-247-9437.

PIERRE BERTON   "River of Ghosts" ("On the Yukon River") by Pierre Berton in *Writing Away,* edited by Constance Rooke. Copyright 1994 by Pierre Berton. Reprinted by permission of Pierre Berton.

TIM CAHILL   From *Road Fever*. Copyright © 1991 by Tim Cahill. Reprinted by permission of Random House, Inc.

KRIS CAPPS   "Beneath Tons of Ice and Rock" ("Ice-caving Beneath the Castner Glacier, Alaska Range"). First appeared in *Alaska* magazine, September 1995. Copyright 1995 by Kris Capps. Reprinted by permission of the author.

RICHARD ADAMS CAREY   From *Raven's Children*. Copyright © 1992 by Richard Adams Carey. Reprinted by permission of Houghton Mifflin Company. All rights reserved.

JIM CHRISTY   From *Rough Road to the North*. Copyright © 1980 by Jim Christy. Used by permission of Doubleday, a division of Bantam Doubleday Dell Publishing Group, Inc.

JOHN HAINES   Originally appeared as "Three Days" ("Near Richardson, alone"). From *The Stars, the Snow, the Fire*.

JOHN MCPHEE   From *Coming into the Country*. Copyright © 1976, 1977 by John McPhee. Reprinted by permission of Farrar, Straus & Giroux, Inc., and Macfarlane Walter & Ross. Published in Canada by Macfarlane Walter & Ross.

DOROTHY LAWRENCE MINKLER   "Bicycling to the Yukon" ("Valdez to Fairbanks, by bicycle, 1941"). Originally appeared in *Alaska* magazine, July 1995. Copyright 1995 by Dorothy Lawrence Minkler. Reprinted by permission of the author.

MARGARET E. MURIE   From *Two in the Far North*. Copyright © 1957, 1962, and 1978 by Margaret E. Murie. Reprinted by permission of Alaska Northwest Books.

ERNIE PYLE   From *Ernie's America,* edited by David Nichols. Originally published by Random House, 1989. Reprinted with permission from the Scripps-Howard Foundation.

JAMES RAMSEY   From *Winter Watch*. Copyright © 1989 by James Ramsey. Reprinted by permission of Alaska Northwest Books.

LIBBY RIDDLES and TIM JONES   From *Race Across Alaska*. Copyright © 1988 by Libby Riddles and Tim Jones. Published by Stackpole Books, 1988. Reprinted by permission of Stackpole Books.

BERTON ROUECHÉ   First published in *The New Yorker* as "First Boat to King Island" ("On the Bering Sea: In a walrus-skin boat"). From *Sea to Shining Sea*. Copyright © 1966 by Berton Roueché. Copyright renewed 1994 by Katherine Roueché. Reprinted by permission of Harold Ober Associates Incorporated.

JONATHAN WATERMAN   From *In the Shadow of Denali*. Copyright © 1994 by Jonathan Waterman. Reprinted by permission of Dell Books, a division of Bantam Doubleday Dell Publishing Group, Inc.